Octavia E. Butler

McFarland Literary Companions

Octavia E. Butler

A Literary Companion

MARY ELLEN SNODGRASS

MCFARLAND LITERARY COMPANIONS, 21

McFarland & Company, Inc., Publishers
Jefferson, North Carolina

ALSO BY THE AUTHOR (AND SEE PAGE ii) AND FROM MCFARLAND

Asian Women Artists: A Biographical Dictionary, 2700 BCE to Today (2022); *Edwidge Danticat: A Companion to the Young Adult Literature* (2022); *Television's* Outlander: *A Companion, Seasons 1–5* (2021); *Marion Zimmer Bradley: A Companion to the Young Adult Literature* (2020); *Coins and Currency: An Historical Encyclopedia*, 2d ed. (2019); *Gary Paulsen: A Companion to the Young Adult Literature* (2018); *World Epidemics: A Cultural Chronology of Disease from Prehistory to the Era of Zika*, 2d ed. (2017); *Settlers of the American West: The Lives of 231 Notable Pioneers* (2015); *Who's Who in the Middle Ages* (2001; paperback 2013); *World Epidemics: A Cultural Chronology of Disease from Prehistory to the Era of SARS* (2003; paperback 2011); *Encyclopedia of World Scriptures* (2001; paperback 2011); *Coins and Currency: An Historical Encyclopedia* (2003; paperback 2007); *World Shores and Beaches: A Descriptive and Historical Guide to 50 Coastal Treasures* (2005)

LIBRARY OF CONGRESS CATALOGUING-IN-PUBLICATION DATA

Names: Snodgrass, Mary Ellen, author.
Title: Octavia E. Butler : a literary companion / Mary Ellen Snodgrass.
Description: Jefferson, North Carolina : McFarland & Company, Inc., Publishers, 2022 |
Series: McFarland literary companions ; 21 | Includes bibliographical references and index.
Identifiers: LCCN 2022037592 | ISBN 9781476688756 (paperback : acid free paper) ∞
ISBN 9781476647463 (ebook)
Subjects: LCSH: Butler, Octavia E.—Criticism and interpretation. |
BISAC: LITERARY CRITICISM / Reference
Classification: LCC PS3552.U827 Z867 2022 | DDC 813/.54—dc23/eng/20220826
LC record available at https://lccn.loc.gov/2022037592

BRITISH LIBRARY CATALOGUING DATA ARE AVAILABLE

ISBN (print) 978-1-4766-8875-6
ISBN (ebook) 978-1-4766-4746-3

On the cover: inset Octavia Estelle Butler at a book signing during a 2005 promotional tour; background Shutterstock/diversepixel

Printed in the United States of America

McFarland & Company, Inc., Publishers
Box 611, Jefferson, North Carolina 28640
www.mcfarlandpub.com

For Sarah and Steve Hunt

Her soul is scattered, like ashes from the urn,
among her characters. They stand watch.
They serve, in the end, as protection from loneliness
and a wise investment in immortality.

—Susan Salter Reynolds
March 3, 2006

Table of Contents

Acknowledgments

Abigail Tayse, archivist, and Zoe Packel,
Kenyon Special Collection and Archives,
Chalmers Library, Gambier, Ohio

Appalachian State University, Boone, North Carolina

Brian D. Laslie, Command Historian,
United States Air Force Academy, Colorado Springs, Colorado

Davis Library, University of North Carolina at Chapel Hill

Diana King, Special Collections, University of California at Los Angeles

Duke University Library, Durham, North Carolina

High Point Public Library, North Carolina

Huntsville-Madison County Public Library, Huntsville, Alabama

Jessica Epstein, reference librarian, Robert W. Woodruff Library,
Atlanta University, Georgia

May Memorial Library, Burlington, North Carolina

Mooresville Public Library, Mooresville, North Carolina

M.W. Bell Library, Guilford Technical Community College,
Jamestown, North Carolina

Palm Beach County Library System, West Palm Beach, Florida

Ruth C. Kindreich, special collections, U.S. Air Force Academy, Colorado

Walker Library, Middle Tennessee State University, Murfreesboro

Preface

A zenith among speculative, nonwhite, and female writers, Octavia Estelle Butler took a stand on the majority's rancor toward nonwhites and women. The first black female sci-fi writer, she originated stories and themes that also resonate against current hostilities toward nonwhite refugees and the unemployed and disabled. Her allegories revisited villainy in its myriad forms—kidnap, oppression, sexual bondage, persecution, repudiation. Carefully dispensing black history in small bites, she educated readers on squalor and commercialized human flesh, a foundation of American capitalism.

The text of *Octavia E. Butler: A Literary Companion* bolsters student and book club reading and classroom lessons on sci-fi, racism, and pollution. With the neo-slave narrative *Kindred,* the author extended genre and style of historical fiction with an eyewitness view of barbaric cruelties. For social studies on ethnic oppression, *Wild Seed* depicts enemies and the female leader who guides one faction out of range. The essay "Positive Obsession" advances the writer's views on her private and published works. For older teens and adult reading, the Parable series examines emerging threats to American freedoms, particularly inadequate water supplies and armed gangs. The author's most dramatic model of voicing and character development, *The Parable of the Sower* follows Lauren Oya Olamina's religious development into a visionary. Entries rich in author and expert citations and journalists from educational institutions and media sources specify the location of critical thought from the *New York Times, USA Today, Los Angeles Sentinel, Le Monde, Marion Zimmer Bradley's Fantasy Magazine, Ms., O The Oprah Magazine, Chicago Tribune,* Readercon, *Philadelphia Tribune,* San Francisco *Chronicle,* National Public Radio, CNN, Oxford University, Nazareth College, *Callaloo, Seattle Times, Atlanta Journal-Constitution, Essence, Salon,* Purdue, Rutgers, *Minneapolis Star Tribune, Black Scholar,* and Pasadena and City College. Opinions from London, Paris, Toronto, Ottawa, Montreal, Vancouver, Alberta, Oxford, Turkey, Brazil, Colombia, Germany, Belgium, India, Malaysia, and the United Arab Emirates testify to Octavia's global influence.

The reader can engage a range of themes in *Unexpected Stories,* containing "Childfinder" and "A Necessary Being," an extension of the novel *Survivor.* Varied genres introduce humor and fear in *Bloodchild and Other Stories,* notably, the dialogue with God in "The Book of Martha," violence erupting from an epidemic in "Speech Sounds," and a coming-of-age episode set during a pandemic in "The

Evening and the Morning and the Night." In *Mind of My Mind,* a study of clairvoyants in the Patternist series, follows the rise of Mary Larkin against Doro, her tyrannic father/lover. *Clay's Ark* introduces the notion of catastrophic illness introduced by a spaceship crash in the American southwest. The last novel, *Fledgling,* broaches issues of Romanian folklore in a deconstruction of Dracula legends. In place of terror, Octavia inserted a racial clash that provokes fire bombing and arson against the first black female vampire.

Octavia E. Butler: A Literary Companion opens on a preface and introduction guiding the reader to titles ("Why Is Science Fiction So White?," "Amnesty," *Dawn*), historical entries (diaspora, slavery, miscegenation, capitalism), science (hybridizing, space, disease, reproduction), metaphysics (xenogenesis, exotic species, time travel), linguistics (diction, names, language), psychology (exploitation, dominance, survivors, adaptation), writing ("Furor Scribendi," Afrofuturism, allegory, grotesque, transition, details, tone), and religion (Earthseed, scripture). Genealogies from fictional lineages include the child prodigy Akin and slave cook Sarah and mute daughter Carrie. Gendered entries (motherhood, feminism, couples) present insight into the traits of major protagonists Lilith, An-yanwu, Dana Franklin, and Lauren Oya Olamina, all examples of Octavia's wonder women. Among males, the entries on villainy, Doro, and Rufus Weylin consider sources and results of wickedness and ego. Commentary on Gan and Larkin Bankole's coming of age adds nuance to family situations and briefly reviews character names and titles. A comprehensive biography of Octavia Estelle Butler isolates development that impacts her canon. A family tree identifies real characters from her autobiographical essays and speeches.

Following the A-to-Z entries, the companion presents 58 aphorisms from Butler's work that encapsulate experience and foresight. A glossary supplies a simple definition or translation of 418 terms that encompass Portuguese, Japanese, Dutch, German, Latin, Spanish, Ibo/Igbo, and Bantu. As an aid to lesson planning, the companion includes a Guide to Writing, Art, and Research Topics, which introduces 68 literary terms and themes, details, and character relationships for further research, discussion, comparative reading, or analysis. The text concludes with an extensive bibliography featuring works by authors such as Butler experts Gregory Jerome Hampton, Rebecca Holden, Martin Japtok, Jerry Rafiki Jenkins, Urvashi Kuhad, Habiba Ibrahim, Douglas Vakoch, Maxine Montgomery, Samuel Delany, Kendra Parker, Tananarive Due, Algie Williams, Nisi Shawl, Lynell George, Gerry Canavan, Consuela Francis, Aparajita Nanda, Shelby Crosby, and Jayna Brown. Primary and secondary indexing covers title ("Near of Kin," "Devil Girl from Mars," "Black to the Future"), subject (*sankofa*, Mormon, Acorn), and topic (shapeshifting, metamorphosis, Apocalypse). Overall, the introduction alerts the reader to the depth of Octavia Estelle Butler's works and determines why her name appears on school and college required reading lists.

Introduction

A sage, self-taught reader and writer, Octavia Estelle Butler learned in childhood to savor hard questions and research enough background material to satisfy intellectual curiosity. Difficult home conditions predisposed her to tackle unlikely goals, especially the literary stardom of an impoverished, fatherless black girl. A so-so student handicapped by shyness and dyslexia, she attached herself to a pink notebook and wrote out answers in plain English. Candor personalized advice on prioritizing actions toward a career in literature. For background, she followed print and television news and gathered topics to incorporate in her personal brand of speculative fiction.

Scenarios, adages, and characters bear the philosophies of Octavia's mother and grandmother, the female powerhouses who shaped a no-nonsense womanhood. The author favored hard daily work organized by a rigid dawn schedule that cost her sleep and leisure. The hoard of wire-bound notepads, receipts, utility bills, and oddments jotted on scraps of paper accounts day by day for the writer's evolution. Alongside budgeted shopping lists and travel schedules, she posted mottos that spurred her to ignore obstacles and keep on writing. During the thinnest of pay periods, she applied for day labor to relieve gaps in her wallet and introduce her to an underclass that distinguished fictional casts.

The delight of the unremunerated author, the Los Angeles Public Library proved Benjamin Franklin correct in 1731 that free access to information was a citizen's treasure. Her regular visits for reference look-ups and specialty books on anatomy, disease, firearms, jungle edibles, myth, and star treks supplied scholarly foundations for sci-fi projects as far-flung as acute myeloblastic leukemia and the location of Alpha Centauri. Upon witnessing the burned-out stacks after arson claimed more than a million books on April 29, 1986, she experienced grief for a loved one, the city touchstone for self-education. Home shelves organized world language dictionaries that suggested character names. Ragtag books scrounged from trash became serendipities.

As fame and prosperity altered Octavia's home conditions, success conferred pride on a daughter who cared for her only parent and who traveled north of Glendale to a welcoming milieu outside Seattle. A non-driver, she continued following urban bus routes and casting a critical eye on socioeconomic lapses in American ghettoes. She managed a steady round of sci-fi conferences, reviews for the *Washington Post,* and autographing that drew readers to bookstores and college auditoriums.

3

University lectures debated the value of "Bloodchild," a tale of male pregnancy. Public addresses aired her fears for a world sogged in too many wars and too many refugees.

Throughout Butler's writing, her mind debated the Baptist upbringing that stored biblical wisdom for later use. She chose Noah, Abraham, Ruth, Naomi, and Jesus as model doers and philosophers and distilled their wisdom into titles and plot lines. A wide-ranging interest in human nature paralleled period defects and crimes with the errors in judgment of scriptural icons Job and Jonah. Her basic belief that earthlings are terminally flawed fleshed out theme and direction in the Patternist, Xenogenesis, and Parable series. When a third Parable novel dried up, she turned to fun with *Fledgling,* a scan of vampire lore and its arrival in the twenty-first century as migration literature.

The unforeseen fall that ended Octavia's fifty-eight years in February 2006 left a trove of notes, beginnings, outlines, and stories still teasing scholars. At the Huntington Library archive, the learned questioner and the fan continue to piece together a solitary existence governed by an uncommon mind. Alongside the literature expert and feminist, psychologists and educators choose her methods and journals as studies of dyslexia. Their conclusions about coping methods derive from her self-direction to heed composition and editing fundamentals.

Writers admire Octavia's reverence for essentials: action verbs, precise diction, and sense impressions. Serious students of racial disharmony find direct address of skin prejudice dating from the ancient Nubians to slave era Nigerians and twenty-first-century American minorities. Whether leading readers through a Maryland plantation or following cargo masters onto the holds of slave ships, she grasped that soul-killing bigotry fed on rumor, animosity, and scriptural authority that legitimized perverse outrages punishing skin color. For allegory, her works replaced New World auction blocks with aliens breeding multi-species beings. The eugenics of lab experiments elicited from analysts surveys of long-discarded notions of human origins. In their place, she implemented the visionary's claim on interstellar travel and the possibility that more species await universal pathfinders.

Slow to rise in the literary world, Octavia reached acclaim and book awards that cultivated musings on earth's future. A maven of speculative fiction that hovers between tocsin and prophecy, she survives in print stories, essays, and novels that energize school and college discussions on individualism and compromise. From dramatic confrontations between dreamers and didacts, readers progress from simplistic little green men plots to serious probes of otherness, a miscellany of physical attributes, beliefs, and drive. With her guidance, narrow-mindedness becomes passé and bigots and fanatics obsolete. In their place, she posits a sphere open to change.

Butler Biography

An empathetic griot in the competitive realm of science fiction, Octavia Butler liberated herself from macho hero tales and achieved international prominence by re-patterning standard genres. In writing a subtle woman's consciousness of family, injustice, and hurt, she charged contemporaries with moral turpitude. For her probity, Kendra R. Parker, on staff at Hope College in Holland, Michigan, proclaimed her "the foundational figure in the development of black women's speculative fiction" (Parker, 2018). Her startling originality achieved two Hugos from fans and a Nebula award for momentum, gravitas, and range, which included twelve novels and a raft of brisk short fiction, pensive essays and verse, speeches, and book reviews. Her outlook focused less on technology gone sour than on capitalist class privilege, elitist scorn of non-whites, and bigotry, especially toward black females. Through "radio imagination," an auditory feed to the brain, from early childhood, she framed cinematic glimpses of future worlds changed by symbiosis. Gerry Canavan, a professor of English at Marquette University in Milwaukee, affirmed, "She showed that the genre was capable of better, and of more" (Canavan, 2016, 2).

1914

The eldest daughter and granddaughter of day-laboring women, Octavia's mother, Octavia Margaret Guy, was born to Estella Edna Haywood Guy on a Louisiana sugar plantation, where women chopped cane as did their slave ancestors. In addition to her nine children, Grandma Guy took in a homeless boy because it was the right thing to do. Shirlee Smith, a columnist for the *Pasadena Star-News*, reported, "When she wasn't chopping she was washing and cleaning for white folks" (Smith, 1994, A14). Octavia remembered her as dying young from overwork—"Made a success of it and it killed her" (Bogstad, 1978–1979, 32). No public school existed to educate the family. Critics have noted that Octavia Butler's verisimilitude tends to rely on the emotional stability and comfort of households like Grandma Guy's that weathered tragedy, fear, and uprooting. She disclosed to activist Frances M. "Fran" Beal a reverence for her matrilineage: "My grandmother on back had suffered a lot from oppression. They endured experiences that would kill me" (Beal, 1986, 15).

1924

The writer expressed pity for what Octavia Guy endured: "My mother had very little to fall back on" (*ibid*.). At age ten, she had to leave elementary school and work as a housemaid, sometimes seven days a week. Octavia commented, "She was the one that was kind of sacrificed" rather than her older brother George (Rowell, 1997, 50). The absence of learning made her feel stupid and inferior.

May 17, 1931

At age seventeen, Octavia Guy married Laurice James Butler in Louisiana. In "Persistence," an interview for *Locus,* the author admired her mother's response to challenges: "I could see *her* struggling to live according to the religion she believed in" (Butler, 2000, 6).

1932

The privations of the Great Depression influenced the author indirectly because of her mother's memories of hunger. Grandmother Estella Guy moved her clan to Pasadena, California, opened a tearoom, and invested in real estate in California, Louisiana, Michigan, and New York. Octavia Butler commemorated the cross-country trek in *Wild Seed,* in which An-yanwu, the supernatural homemaker, departs the pre–Civil War South to live on the Pacific coast. She altered her Nigerian name to Emma, meaning universal or whole.

April 2, 1943

During World War II, Octavia Guy's estranged husband left jobs as errand boy and messenger to join the military.

June 22, 1947

Native to Valley Street near Central Park in the northwest light industrial area of Pasadena, the future author was born, named Octavia Estelle Butler for her mother and grandmother. She later mused on life in the badlands: "I was born in the desert, raised in the desert, didn't know anything but the desert of Southern California" (Hampton, 2014, 146). In a ghetto ricocheting with gunfire, she came from humble origins—a domestic mother and shoeshiner father. The elder Octavia dreamed that her daughter would become a secretary, a sit-down job, but the younger Octavia viewed fealty to a boss as another humiliating form of bondage. She regretted that employers called her mother "the girl" even though she was a grown woman.

Lonely play embroiled the author in fantasy. She reflected on her mother's difficulty during parturition and the loss of four sons before Octavia's birth, a grievous family loss she incorporated in the story "Near of Kin." Because the boy who survived longest went to his grave un-photographed, the mother had him exhumed for a picture. The four infant deaths made her mother over-protective and revealed that she valued sons more than she cherished the only female child. Octavia concluded, "Anything that happens in your life that is important, if it didn't happen you would be someone different" (Sanders, 2004). The dictum proved true in her mother's choice of accordion lessons and bedtime stories, beginning with fairy tales before advancing to sci-fi. The genre suited the future writer because she lived the alienation found in sci-fi works.

Known as Junie for her birth month, Octavia described herself as an unsmiling outsider and introvert: "I'm comfortably asocial—a hermit in the middle of a large city, a pessimist if I'm not careful, a feminist, a Black, a former Baptist, an oil-and-water combination of ambition, laziness, insecurity, certainty, and drive" (Stewart, 2006, B10). Because of shyness, she looked at the ground so much that she joked in "Positive Obsession" that she might have "become a geologist" (Butler, 2005, 126). Her self-consciousness emanated from six-foot-half-inch height, deep voice, ironed hair, and crooked teeth that made her conceal her mouth when she laughed. Like Lewis Carroll's wanderer in *Alice in Wonderland*, Octavia stated, "I wanted to disappear" (*ibid.*, 128). In adulthood, she took public speaking courses to ease speeches before an audience and clipped an advertisement for a Dale Carnegie course. She declared in a letter to a publisher that her photo would not sell books.

1950

Preschool years shaped Octavia's views on racism and unremunerative labors, which denied joy to the women in her family. Because her mother and grandmother taught her to read, she observed, "I got my conscience installed early…. As a good Baptist kid, I read the bible … stories of conflict, betrayal, torture, murder, exile, and incest" (Butler, 2005, 83). In "Persistence," an interview for *Locus,* she extolled religion for "[keeping] some of my relatives alive, because it was all they had…. It's those people who have so little, and who suffer so much, who need at least for religion to comfort them. Nothing else is" (Butler, "Persistence," 2000, 6). The early wrestlings with fundamentalist doctrine foreshadowed one of fiction's stalwart superwomen, Lauren Oya Olamina, a minister's daughter who envisions a more pragmatic religion based on change. The grueling Earthseed credo in *The Parable of the Sower* took "twenty-five or thirty lumpy incoherent rewrites" before reaching the conclusion that the supreme deity is malleable and open to alterations (Butler, 1993, 24). A more liberal view of scripture in *Fledgling* depicted Shori, an Ina vampire, reviewing "metaphors and mythologized history" and the need to "make up your mind" about religious truth arising from oral tradition (Butler, 2005, 194).

The writer accompanied her mother to maid's work in Pasadena's white section of La Cañada and on Colorado Boulevard along the Rose Bowl Parade route. She recalled, "I was embarrassed and kind of angry that my mother was a maid," but she later included her mother's work in talks to school students whose parents had servile jobs (Carr, 1992, 36). While her mother cleaned toilets, she sat alone in the car and contemplated the insults and inequities of segregation and classism.

Analyst Karen Joy Fowler, a *New York Times* bestselling writer, declared that Octavia learned in time "that endurance and sacrifice are, in fact, the characteristics of the hero" (Fowler, 2006). The ideal recurs in *The Parable of the Talents* with day labor—painting, trash hauling, woodchopping, carpentry, fencing, yard and garden work—by which Lauren Oya Olamina supports a search for daughter Larkin Bankole.

1951

The rudiments of fantasy emerged in Octavia's fourth year, when she lived for a few months near her cousins. The family owned a radio, from which she heard on 93 KHJ "Boss Radio" *Superman, The Shadow, The Whistler, Johnny Dollar, I Led Three Lives,* and *My True Story.* Perhaps because of concern for ponies kicked by abusive children at a carnival, she began concocting horse lore on the front porch, where her mother sequestered her for ruining good shoes. She echoed the joy of horse stories in *Fledgling.* Her favorite wild horse books ranked from Walter Farley's classic *The Black Stallion* to Newbery Medal winners *King of the Wind* by Marguerite Henry and Will James's *Smoky the Cowhorse,* source of three period films. After she heard that horses lack intellect, she created a magic horse and dreamed she "could fly like Superman, communicate with animals, control people's minds," a motif of the Patternist series (Canavan, 2016, 3).

February 16, 1951

Circumstances altered with Laurice Butler's death, when the family began taking in boarders and limiting meals to beans and potatoes. The author incorporated the repercussions of fatherlessness into *Kindred,* in which protagonist Dana Franklin remarks that she didn't get to know her father. Northeast of L.A., for three years, Octavia occupied a stringent fundamentalist environment: a chicken farm between Barstow and Victorville, California, ruled by her Baptist mother Octavia and maternal grandmother Estelle Guy. In an essay for *Village Voice,* author Dorothy Allison observed that "Echoes of Butler's grandmother turn up in all her books" (Allison, 1989, 67).

In a home built by Octavia's uncles, the trio lived simply among farm animals with trucked-in water. To interviewer Janice Bogstad, the author recalled "men [who] tended to work themselves to death at fairly early ages, and the women wound up taking care of lots of children as best they could" (Bogstad, 1978–1979, 32). The family lacked electricity, TV, and phone but received a regular delivery of the Pacific coast's first agriculture journal, the biweekly *California Farmer,* a commentary on agrarian life from 1854. The use of kerosene lanterns led to an indoor blaze too isolated from a fire department to receive help. A memorable experience, she lived adjacent to a family who beat their children, a domestic abomination that she featured in the experience of telepaths Mary Larkin and Ada Dragon in *Mind of My Mind.*

The matriarchs insisted on Bible reading. Octavia admired the King James translation for "stories and verses that I still remember" (Govan, 2005–2006, 28). She revisited scriptural conundrums in the story "The Book of Martha," which demonstrated that she didn't accept descriptions of God or Satan as real. For her, religion was a "mental cage" (Butler, 2005, 209). She recalled, "The stories got me…. I read them avidly … and when I began writing, I explored these themes" (*ibid.*, 85). She stated in the preface to *Bloodchild and Other Stories* that mastering the structure of brief narratives "taught me much more about frustration and despair than I ever wanted to know" (*ibid.*, vii). The anthology flourished in Portuguese as *Filhos de Sangue e Outras Historias* (Children of Blood and Other Stories).

Octavia's mother fell prey to "the idea that comic books and science fiction could rot your brains" (Butler, 1998). To discourage bad behavior and the influence of Marvel and DC comic books and Spider-Man in *Amazing Adult Fantasy*, she ruled out cussing and tore *Superman* in half. Octavia developed appreciation of her mother's Baptist morals and the courage to clean houses for elitist whites just to support her daughter. Rather than think of working-class blacks as losers, she revered them as heroes on a par with Spider-Man and Superman: "They were fighting, they just weren't fighting with fists" (Sanders, 2004).

1952

In kindergarten, the author made up for the lack of a school library by joining her class on walks to Pasadena's Central Library on North Garfield Avenue to hear story hour in the Peter Pan room. To her distaste, science fiction described active boys: "Girls in those stories didn't do much" (Crisp, 1996, H3). In a critique of young adult mysteries, she complained, "Nancy Drew always seemed like a middle-aged woman" (Holden & Shawl, 2013, 129).

1953

Dyslexia inhibited Octavia's school performance at the unimaginative Dick and Jane level, causing her to feel like the "outkid" who thrived on depression ("Science Fiction," 2008, A8). Relying on sound rather than sight, she muffed spelling and arithmetic and failed at baseball and charged herself with laziness and lack of self-discipline. The more adept pupils teased and called her stupid, socially inept, graceless, and unattractive. She escaped bullies by treasuring Ray Bradbury and Robert A. Heinlein's works "for a nickel or a dime" from secondhand stores, checkouts obtained via a Pasadena library card, and the tattered storybooks and *Mad Magazines* retrieved from her mother's employers (Potts, 1996, 334).

Of her recycling method, Octavia described crates and used bookcases filled with challenging reading: "Some were years too advanced for me when I got them, but I grew into them" (Butler, 2005, 129). She complained of the dominant white milieu of young adult reading, "Heck, I wasn't in any of this stuff I read. The only black people you found were occasional characters or characters who were so feeble-witted that they couldn't manage anything, anyway. I wrote myself in, since I'm me and I'm here and I'm writing" (Fox, 2006, C16).

April 22, 1953

After Octavia's mother began dating a potential stepfather, he took Octavia to movies. The green, tentacled aliens who inhabit human bodies in the color film *Invasion from Mars* gave her nightmares.

Spring, 1953

From one of the family's roomers, in 1953, Octavia gained her first adult pulp sci-fi magazine, *Tops in Science Fiction,* a 25¢ publication of Fiction House in New York City that lasted only two issues. She sampled folklore and animal tales in the library stacks, which she termed "the open universities of America" (Ha, 2019). Keeping track in a pink notebook, she added comic books and sci-fi fiction from magazines she bought in grocery stores for 35–50¢—*Magazine of Fantasy & Science Fiction, Fantastic, Amazing Stories,* and *Galaxy Science Fiction.* In addition to the classics—Isaac Asimov, Ray Bradbury, Robert A. Heinlein—she favored pop science, *Mad Magazine* satire, and the horror and imagination of *Pilgrimage* by Arizona alien specialist Zenna Chlarson Henderson, 1960s English author John Kilian Houston Brunner, speculative fiction creator Ursula Kroeber Le Guin, and Staten Island scenarist and fiction writer Theodore Sturgeon, who wrote *The Synthetic Man* and *More Than Human* and contributed scripts to *Star Trek,* the first TV series to show an interracial kiss. She also admired John Wyndham for his *Day of the Triffids* and *The Chrysalids* and John Brunner's *Polymath, The Whole Man,* and *The Long Result.* One of her earliest purchases was a book about stars. She treated friends to copies of her favorites to elicit book discussions.

1957

Negative remarks bombarded Octavia for earning C's and D's. At Garfield Elementary School, teacher Isabel S. Gregg accused her of slowness, low achievement, and poor self-discipline and concentration. Her mother replied that she didn't feel competent to help her at home. A beloved aunt, nurse Hazel Guy Walker, informed Octavia that blacks can't be writers and suggested nursing as more practical. The future writer realized that criticisms were common from people having low self-image: They "will reach out from their own jealousy, their own hard tough nasty hurting nothing-hood and try to pull you back" (George, 2004).

The child chose to escape poverty's boredom by designing better worlds, a fact she reported in the essay "Positive Obsession." With savings of $5.00, she bought a book on horse breeds and a second reference work on "stars and planets, asteroids, moons and comets" (Butler, 2005, 126). A fan of Walter Farley and Austro-Hungarian author Felix Salten's animal books, especially *Bambi* and *Bambi's Children,* she began composing wild horse stories, a fun and liberating project.

The ten-year-old took writing classes from an elderly woman who specialized in children's fiction. On a secondhand Remington portable typewriter—a birthday present—set atop an antique wood desk, Octavia began shaping fantasy in her first five novels. In the essay "The Monophobic Response," issued in *Dark Matter: A Century of Speculative Fiction from the African Diaspora,* she accounted for her career: "Writing has been my way to journeying from incomprehension, confusion, and emotional upheaval to some sort of order" (Butler, 2000, 415). In a lyric salute to her subject matter, she wrote, "Science fiction is a handful of earth, and a handful of sky and everything around and between" (George, 2020).

While avoiding the standard aesthetics and techniques of science fiction, the author selected afrocentric subjects and themes. They featured the ethics of dominance and misapplication of power, elements of control missing from her life and the lives of most minorities. In the overview of Adwoa Afful, an affiliate of York University in Toronto, Octavia "re-connects and re-members, brings together black women dislocated by time and space" (Adwoa, 2016, 98). The early fiction sent to *Amazing* and *Fantastic* foretokened her life's work because of the flexibility of sci-fi settings, characters, and themes. She explained, "Science fiction has no walls…. It gives me the freedom to do whatever I want," a boon to marginalized black females (Crisp, 1996, H3).

December 23, 1957

On television, Octavia watched Nick Adams play the loner Johnny Yuma in *The Rebel* and the 9:00 p.m. weeknight production *Channel 9 Movie Theater,* which featured "The Boy with Green Hair." The parable stressed orphaning during World War II caused by the London Blitz and the trope of individual differences.

1958

After viewing the deception, mind control, and sabotage plot in *Devil Girls from Mars,* Octavia resolved to write better Martians-in-flying-saucers scenarios than the 1954 TV film from the prolific Edward and Harry Lee Danziger. The movie later earned a listing among the 100 Most Amusingly Bad Movies Ever Made. She began surveying background material from *Discover, Natural History, Scientific American,* and *Smithsonian,* a form of self-education that aids visionary Lauren Oya Olamina in the Parable series.

In medical texts, Octavia researched cancer, burn treatment, and brain damage. She later stocked home shelves with specialized encyclopedias on jazz, black history, anthropology, animals, world religions, and inventions. To circumvent dyslexia, she bought ecological and self-help audio tapes for her Walkman. She confided, "I love self-help tapes, good ones that boost your confidence and encourage you" (Govan, 2005–2006, 29). To replace the missing romance in her life, she wrote about male-female chemistry in the impromptu attraction between Valerie Rye and Obsidian in "Speech Sounds."

1959

At Washington STEAM Multilingual Academy, a junior high school, the author read no Langston Hughes, no Gwendolyn Brooks, no Zora Neale Houston: "The only blacks I came across were slaves.... Booker T. Washington and George Washington Carver" (Potts, 1996, 334). Abandoning the "Estelle" persona, she wrote contracts with "Octavia" to attain high professional goals. A science teacher, Mr. Pfaff, corrected spelling and typed Octavia's first story to send to a sci-fi magazine. Even though a faux literary agent bilked her of a $61.50 reading fee, she congratulated herself for starting young: "You're sure then that your stories are wonderful" (Crisp, 1996, H3). In high school, she claimed English author John Brunner one of her mentors for his quality storytelling in *The World Swappers* and *Slavers of Space*.

1960

The author's incomplete story "Hope" imagined a Nazi death camp where a girl must barter for the lives of her family with sex. In response to the era, she told interviewer Tananarive Due of *Essence* that new concepts of shapeshifting and telepathy derived "during the sixties, when you were supposed to be so terribly relevant" (Due, 2019, 75).

1961

From daydreams, the fourteen-year-old cast herself as "Silver Star," the spunky captive of Flash, the cavalier flier of a UFO who transports her over the heavens. One episode wedded Silver Star to Flash in a Martian ritual consisting of branding with a blade. She disclosed scavenging pornography from the garbage and applying adult scenarios to her notions of marital bondage to a sadomasochist. Her supermarket reading included *Amazing, Fantastic, Galaxy,* and *Worlds of If*, winner of Hugo honoraria for best professional magazine from 1966 to 1968.

After release from the Peter Pan room to adult library shelves, Octavia began plotting the Patternmaster works, which flourished in Dutch, French, and German. The set reflected poorly on black America with its cast of alien personae lurking in plain sight. The story emerged before her abilities to frame nuances of evolution, coital propagation, and mind control. In adolescence, while pondering suicide, she trusted her juvenilia as an escape from "major tragedies in life.... The story, you see will get you through" (Stewart, 2006, B10).

January 20, 1961

The inauguration of John Kennedy and the Cuban missile crisis piqued Octavia's immersion in news. After imagining a necklace monitor for criminals similar to ankle alarms, she admitted,

> Every now and then, something will happen that catches up with me …
> I thought, "Oh, hell" … But we have to pay attention to what's going on.
> If it's something that we're writing about, the best thing to do is to go ahead and integrate it [Weeks and Schwartz, 2000, A9].

Confusion denoted the extent of her dyslexia, which inhibited her ability to interpret presidential speeches, to spell, and to drive a car. Writing every morning from two to five a.m., she chose an organic autodidactic method to make up for past lapses in public school, where war drills made little sense. An early romance writer, she reported to American sci-fi specialist Steven Harper, "I was desperate to get published. I've been sending stuff out since I was thirteen, and they've been coming back since I was thirteen" (Harper, 2019).

1962

At age fifteen, Octavia plotted *Mind of My Mind,* later translated into Italian, French, and German. She chose sci-fi because "there is no issue you can't examine" (Mabe, 1999, D1). Of the decade's New Wave science fiction, critic Fred Pfeil, a teacher at Oregon State University and Stanford University, labeled it postmodern for recycling sci-fi's subcultural ghetto … "trashier," "pulpier," and "far more sophisticated, even more liberatory" than previous works (Holden & Shawl, 2013, 140). Because Octavia reconstructed earlier conventions, she introduced irony and social criticism to standard themes of time travel and alien contact.

The author's original scenarios reflected the gynocentric views of second wave feminism. Intrigued by a copy of *The Writer* abandoned on a bus, she began mulling over the commercial end of publication and perusing writer's magazines in the adult department of the Pasadena Library. Daily, therapeutic sunrise walks four miles along the San Gabriel Valley to Altadena gave her time to pass Vroman's bookstore on East Colorado Boulevard and to listen to audio books. She jotted down observations of the San Gabriels in 3×5 notebooks and on recycled envelopes, backs of used sheets, and blow-in cards. She regretted in "The Book of Martha" that city "lights and the smog obscured all but the brightest few stars" (Butler, 2005, 189).

November 22, 1963

For comfort after the slaying of President John F. Kennedy, Octavia wrote diary entries in her notebook, which she could conceal in code or Spanish. Of the era's violence some five years later, she described as "very strange … assassinations for midterm and finals," her reference to the subsequent shooting deaths of American Baptist minister Martin Luther King, Jr., a civil rights activist through nonviolent civil disobedience, and U.S. Senator from New York and 1968 presidential hopeful Robert F. "Bobby" Kennedy, an advocate of anti-poverty programs and gun control and an opponent of racial segregation, bombing in Vietnam, nuclear proliferation, and South African apartheid (Rowell, 1997, 60).

1964

Octavia's published works included the poem "The Deer" and classwork on the dictionary, one of her favorite reference works. She dreamed of saving enough cash to have her teeth straightened and electrolytic removal of facial hair to correct misidentification as a male. Confusing characteristics caused people to surmise incorrectly that she was lesbian or bisexual.

1965

At John Muir High School on Lincoln Avenue in Pasadena, Octavia read James Weldon Johnson's *The Creation,* took archery and a self-hypnosis class, and acquired a knowledge of Spanish. In Los Angeles, she gained an insider's knowledge of streets and bus routes, which her character Mary Larkin follows on her wedding day in *Mind of My Mind.* The author spoke through her protagonist the freedom of choosing public transportation: "When I rode the bus, I went when I wanted, where I wanted" (Butler, 1977, 227). To save on weekly expenses, she limited meat purchases to hamburger, fish sticks, and hot dogs. In a pinch, she pawned typewriter, television, and tape recorder for $15 each to pay utilities.

At the Open Door Workshop of the Screenwriters' Guild of America, West, the writer studied under Harlan Ellison and enrolled at Pasadena City College in night classes, which introduced her to a full panoply of black literature. Throughout her education, she declared, "I had all these ideas that had been rattling around in my heart … so I wrote bits and pieces" (Young, 2004, 30). One creative writing teacher surprised her with a dictum against putting black characters in stories unless necessary.

While earning an A.A. in history, the author chose the pseudonym Karen Adams to enter a college contest with the story "To the Victor," which won a first prize of fifteen dollars. The story dramatized mutants dueling by means of ESP. She haunted the Los Angeles Library on West Fifth Street and toyed with the fictional setting that became *Kindred,* a masterpiece of first-person slave memoir and the Ghanaian term *sankofa,* the Akan-Twi principle of retrieving what is left behind. At the suggestion she call her novel "Dana," she ruled out a title "attracting the ladies' romance readers" (Yerman, 2020, 268).

Octavia's first promising rejection slip contained one handwritten word, "Almost" (Harper, 2019). More rejection notes from John W. Campbell, editor of *Analog Science Fiction and Fact*, and Terry Carr, editor of Ace Books, increased her prospects. During this formative stage, she claimed Frank Herbert's *Dune* and Ursula Le Guin's *The Dispossessed* as her favorite works.

January 8–14, 1966

When Octavia was eighteen, U.S. news of the Vietnam War reported the strategy of B-52 bombers to crush the Vietcong tunnels of Cu Chi, which she later involved in the ambushes of Clayarks in *Patternmaster.* She incorporated what Dorothy Allison, essayist for *Village Voice,* depicted as "the concept of nigger, the need for a victim, and the desire to profit by the abuse or misuse of others" (Allison, 1989, 67). She wrote a *Star Trek* fan fiction and began plotting *Survivor,* based on research on the ancient Peruvians in explorer Victor Wolfgang Von Hagen's 1957 treatise *Realm of the Incas.* The novel envisioned human space travelers conceiving children with extraterrestrials in *terra incognita.*

In later works, the author avoided assumptions about compatible genitals and biological differences. Embarrassed by her previous naiveté and demeaning stereotypes of aliens, she banned the republication in English of *Survivor,* her weakest novel, which is still available in French, German, and Italian. Nonetheless, according to Canadian reviewer Deirdre Kelly of the Toronto *Globe and Mail,* Octavia began "pioneering territory with a lot of space for women's voices and visions to grow and be heard" (Kelly, 2013, A17). In the purview of English essayist Teri Ann Doerksen, a literary expert at the University of Manchester, the author positioned her works amid feminist, colorist fiction: "There is still a very good chance that if a reader finds a science fiction novel with a complex, interesting, multifaceted woman of color as a protagonist, the novel is by Butler" (Doerksen, 1997, 22).

Religion surfaced in the fictional reflection on the author's rebellion against fundamentalist intransigence by viewing the film *Bambi,* her first Disney movie. She spoke to a group of high school students on a socially repressive upbringing: "I belonged to a very strict Baptist sect. Dancing was a sin, going to the movies was a sin, wearing makeup was a sin, wearing your dresses too short was a sin—and 'too short' was definitely a matter of opinion with the ladies of the church" (Fry, 1997, 68).

1967

For an in-house competition judged by editor Robert Gottlieb, *Writer's Digest* gave fifth place to an unpublished story, "Loss." She enhanced her earlier porn with erotic fantasies of sadistic and masochistic bondage and pedophilia.

March 1967

At Pasadena City College, Octavia took the institution's first black literature class, wrote a term paper on Australia's Arnhem Land Aborigines, and took the dual post of treasurer and secretary to the Afro-American Club. Her journals "[overflowed] with the things that affect you ... what you feel and what's important to you" (Rowell, 1997, 48, 49). She cited aims to write a bestseller, own a house, provide her family with health care, and aid poor blacks to get a college education.

1968

Before graduating from college after three years with an A.A. degree in history, Octavia wrote on black nationalism and joined the black student union. She gained an idea from a member of the Black Nationalism and Black Power Movement about the purpose of slave servility to preserve life by avoiding bloodshed. While imitating the short fiction common to the era, she worked at the Pasadena Mall and a Broadway department store at undemanding telemarketing, mail advertising, factory assembly, warehouse shelving, dishwashing, potato chip inspector, hospital laundry, and typing. She credited her height and strength with hirings at warehouses and factories. The mindlessness of blue-collar jobs like the factory soldering she outlined for Jane in "Crossover" was disheartening because her "shoulders wanted to desert to another body" (Fry, 1997, 61). She pondered whether to have more freedom between 3:30 and 5:15 a.m. with a part-time job rather than full-time work and no writing opportunities. At least, she and the other "nonpeople" didn't have to smile while they were "rented for a few hours, a few days, a few weeks" (Butler, 1979, 53).

The author's work mode relied on daily effort and persistence in learning the craft of composition. She stated eagerness for more direction: "If somebody said, 'writing course' and 'free' in the same sentence, I was probably there" (Rowell, 1997, 58). She abandoned entry into California State University and took social science, humanities, and extension writing classes at UCLA, a strategy she called "a great way to rent an audience," a quip she repeated in the essay "Furor Scribendi" (Sanders, 2004). Poor performance in an academic setting forced her to give up the dream of a doctorate and toss out accumulated rejection slips. From author Theodore Sturgeon, she learned that writing demanded self-education.

June 22, 1969

At age twenty-two, Octavia acknowledged a lifetime of wishing to die out of feelings of shame, self-contempt, and worthlessness.

July 16, 1969

A fan of NASA's Mercury, Gemini, and Apollo lunar missions, Octavia continued viewing on television Apollo 11, an attempt to land a space crew on the moon, which succeeded on July 20. In "Brave New Worlds," an essay for *Essence*, she mused, "I believed I was watching humanity leave home" (Butler, "Brave," 2000, 166). An interview for *Locus* disclosed her view of the accomplishment, "We're not going to do that for any logical reason. It's not going to happen because it's profitable—it may not be. The going certainly won't be…. Unfortunately for us, we did" (Butler, 2000, 6).

Because additional space ventures took longer than Octavia predicted, she ruled wishful thinking as an obstacle to progress. She later observed that humankind should give up prophesying and instead "give warning when we see ourselves drifting in dangerous directions…. Best to try to shape it into something good" (*ibid.*, 164). Conservative politics caused her to condemn "short-term thinkers [as] opportunists" and to decry sell-offs of space stations (Butler, 1998, 322). The preparations and proposals for world betterment influenced her writing of the Acorn farmers' first flight in *The Parable of the Talents* aboard the ill-named starship *Christopher Columbus*.

Summer, 1970

To attend Clarion Science Fiction Writers Workshop in Clarion, Pennsylvania, Octavia borrowed money and left her tiny one-bedroom "worm hole" in the San Gabriel Valley for the first time except for ventures to Mexicali in Baja (Carr, 1992, 36). With a $100 scholarship from sci-fi writer Samuel Delany, she accepted the remaining $600 from her mother, who was saving the cash to pay for dental work. Terrified of joining a mostly white group for six weeks of "writer's boot camp," she worried that there would be no black attendees (Holden and Shawl, 2013, 263).

Female teachers, Joanna Russ and Kate Wilhelm, insisted on honesty—no stories cloaked by pseudonyms or initials. After writing a letter home, Octavia began composing "Crossover," featuring a sole, frightened woman. The Portuguese version took the title "Atalho" (Shortcut). The experience inspired a speech, "From Woe to Wonder," which she delivered in Kentucky at the February 24, 1995, literature and culture conference at the University of Louisville. After twenty-three years of rejections, she became a commercial success and a regular speaker and coach of new writers, much as Samuel Delany, Wilhelm, and Russ trained her. With the proceeds, she banked the cash and limited herself to a regular salary.

Joining Doris Lessing, Toni Cade Bambara, and Marge Piercy in applying sci-fi conventions to feminist themes, the author sold the story "Childfinder" to workshop leader Harlan Jay Ellison, an American fiction writer and scenarist for *Twilight Zone, Outer Limits,* and *Star Trek.* The story depicts Barbara as a locator and groomer of psychic powers in black children. Ellison chose her story for book three of the collection *The Last Dangerous Visions,* which remained unpublished. He urged her to try selling fiction to Clarion. Another, "Crossover," a story of destructive despair and alcoholism, she contracted to sci-fi editor Robin Scott Wilson for a Clarion anthology. The story derived from watching a low-paid factory worker slowly implode from mindless labor and the stress of caring for a sick mother.

Ruining Octavia's hopes for success were five years of rejected fiction. On return to California, she moved southwest to a Los Angeles duplex on West Boulevard and indulged fantasies of herself as "Shaar" and "Mishaari," a later version of Silver Star. With some fifteen others, she attended the Phlange sci-fi convention in Pittsburgh. She also wrote a term paper on Sophocles's *Antigone* and reviewed black authors for the *Washington Post.*

1971

At age twenty-four, Octavia published her first story, "Crossover," in *Clarion: An Anthology of Speculative Fiction and Criticism from the Clarion Writers' Workshop.* Fifteen years later, she joked, "I went into it as a completely anonymous person doing business by mail" (Crisp, 1996, H3). Among her attempts were stories in 1972 for *Confession* magazine, one step up from pulp fiction. She asserted, "I don't read much speculative fiction and don't plan to start" (Kearse, 2021, 13).

September 11, 1972

While scheduling writing from 2:00 to 5:30 a.m. before going to a full-time job, the author admitted relying on No Doz and trying to stretch her budget to cover necessary dental work. Within a year, her ailments and lethargy extended to urinary infection and fibroid tumors.

December 23, 1974

The shock of losing a telemarketing job and having to live on unemployment compensation forced Octavia to admit, "This is it. Either I'm going to make it, or

I'm not" (Williams, 1986, 72). She began outlining *Patternmaster.* On the subject of utopianism, she told *Black Scholar* interviewer Frances Beal, "I don't write utopian science fiction because I don't believe that imperfect humans can form a perfect society" (Beal, 1986, 14).

1975

The loss of a briefcase at Bullocks, a Los Angeles department store, cost Octavia half a novel. She surmised, "Some derelict picked it up, opened it—No money: paper, books, garbage—dumped it in the trash, and kept the briefcase" (Bogstad, 1978–1979, 31). The event forced her to secure extra copies of her writing kept in separate locations. She stocked up on carbon, 300-sheet packs of paper, and typewriter ribbons for 34¢ each.

December 1975

The author had no difficulty accepting Doubleday's terms for publishing *Patternmaster.* With her usual wry humor, she acceded, "It's always been easy for me to revise when someone was waving money" (Williams, 1986, 72).

1976

During a stint in Maryland near the Mason-Dixon line, Octavia derived details from slave narratives and journals of the wives of Southern planters, which she found in the Los Angeles Public Library, Baltimore's Enoch Pratt Free Library, and the Maryland Historical Society. She accessed the latter around the corner from The Hotel Sleazy, her name for the accommodation suggested by Travelers Aid. Lacking money for a camera, she took notes. On the profits of publishing *Survivor,* she centered an eastern shore tour of cabins and tools at Easton in Talbot County and the Grayline bus route to Mount Vernon and Washington, D.C. She focused on runaways Harriet Tubman, Frederick Douglass, and the three hundred seventeen slaves who operated George and Martha Custis Washington's estate, Mount Vernon, Virginia.

July 1976

At a point of desperation, Octavia entered the sci-fi market with the five-part Patternist collection, beginning with *Patternmaster,* issued by Doubleday. She based the maturity tale on a society hampered by false assumptions about gender and race. The plot turns on a standard hierarchy of beings—a telepathic master and his league of dominators, silent slaves, and bestial Clayarks, the quadruped troublemakers mutated by a disease imported from outer space. Teray, a dynastic son based on her adolescent crush on Flash, attempts to replace his father, Master Rayal.

The author took her first vacation in Seattle, Washington, where she traveled on a $199 Greyhound Ameripass to enjoy the climate. She chose New York for her next trip, where she ascended the 102-floor Empire State Building in midtown Manhattan. She shifted destinations to national parks and viewed the Grand Canyon in Arizona. Her main regret was being out of shape and relying on peppermint candy for energy and silver earrings for self-esteem.

1977

A prequel to *Patternmaster,* Octavia issued *Mind of My Mind,* an eerie novel fraught with parasitism and cannibalism. She set the action in a version of Pasadena, the twentieth-century town of Forsyth, a surname meaning "man of peace." The plot features daughter Mary and African father/lover Doro in a plausible power struggle over a generation of psionic children. With his exemplary daughter, Doro hopes to breed a race of clairvoyants.

Kirkus Reviews credited the narrative for "spare, vivid prose," opening on a dramatic revelation of child abuse and a mother's dissolute life entertaining a drunken knife-fighter (Fry, 1997, 58). The author polishes off the initial shock with the vampiric shapeshifter devouring his attacker in "an easy if not especially satisfying meal" (Butler, 1977, 3). A time leap features Mary, a veteran shoplifter at age nineteen who shares Octavia's love of books. Mary confides, "If I didn't have anything to read, I'd really go crazy" (*ibid.,* 13).

The author reframed *Kindred* as *The Guardian,* a reference to Dana Franklin's role in the life of white ancestor Rufus Weylin. The time traveler's terror journey viewed the plantation South, where "the everyday horrors of slavery are no metaphors" (Allison, 1989, 67). The version pictured Dana Franklin in an incestuous relationship with her great grandfather. Critic Gabriella Friedman compared the sentimental elements to two neo-slave narratives—Alex Haley's *Roots* and Toni Morrison's *Beloved.*

July 6, 1977

In a journal entry, the author awaited payment of three thousand dollars. To scrape through a shortfall, she pondered what to pawn and borrowed money for utilities and groceries. Her food shopping lists pared expenses to the penny.

1978

After Doubleday published *Survivor,* the author gave up temporary jobs and became a full-time writer. At Readercon, July 12–14, 2002, in Burlington, Massachusetts, she later joked about remaining single: "One of the reasons I don't have kids is that my first kid was writing. And if I had more, I'm not sure they could survive the sibling rivalry" (Devney, 2002, 9). The focus, escape from the rigidity of fundamentalist Christianity and Patternism, resulted in her least satisfying fiction, but literary historians valued the narrative for shedding light on ethnic belonging.

Octavia set the story during transracial adoption issues of the 1970s, "when domestic adoption was at an all time high in the United States" (Troy, 2010, 1123). To spare their Afro-Asian foster daughter Alanna from scorn, missionary parents Jules and Neila Verrick promote deception—a pose of accommodation—rather than force her to ally with fanatic Christianity. Critic Maria Holmgren Troy compared Alanna's service to differing cultures to "White Indians," the go-betweens who ease animosities between first peoples and European settlers (*ibid.*).

December 26, 1978

For *Kindred,* Octavia wrote and rewrote three trial versions. To the publisher's suggestions of titles, she jettisoned *Dana* and *Birthright.* Her plans for the novel anticipated the young adult market as well as sales in Italian, Portuguese, and Germany translations. In a buyer's market, she encountered turndowns and advice to revamp the novel into historical romance. She stopped petitioning sci-fi editors and sought placement in mainstream fiction. Eventually, she received a $5,000 advance and applied her earnings to hiring a college pal to compile a press packet. The author photo informed readers of Octavia's ethnicity and increased black readership.

August 4, 1979

Octavia's well researched masterwork, *Kindred,* focuses on choices and reverence for life. The conflict derives from the protagonist's awareness that a white slaveowner must survive to sire her great-grandmother. As a gesture to America's bicentennial, she pictured a black time traveler entering a time slip to 1824 Maryland to "try to fix a horribly broken past" (Due, 2019, 73). According to critic Tananarive Due, a writer for *Essence,* Afrofuturist fiction

> is Black artists' proclamation of "I am, I was and I WILL BE," straddling genres and styles to create Black art that imagines a world not quite our own … a thriving future for Black people, or any future [*ibid.*].

Kindred summarized the slave era's conflict in an era when a "whole society is literally arrayed against you and arrayed to really keep you in your place" (Sanders, 2004). Out of fear of black vengeance, planters chose to kill individuals who rebelled. The book sold a quarter million copies to readers interested in sci-fi, women's history, and black studies. Critics at the *New York Times, O the Oprah Magazine, PEN, New Yorker, Essence,* and *Washington Post Book World* endorsed the haunting qualities and rich character interaction.

For *Chrysalis 4,* the author wrote of family secrets in "Near of Kin," a coming-of-age narrative popular in German and Portuguese. The "sympathetic story of incest" sets the ethnic experimenters in the role of Lot's daughter's sexual adventuring (Boyd, 1995, L8). The author's intuitive dramas of black degradation derived from seeing her mother, Octavia Guy Butler, enter domestic jobs by the back door. In her honor, the author featured endurance as the backbone of black power.

1980

The year that Octavia congratulated herself for completing *Kindred,* Doubleday issued *Wild Seed,* an Afrofuturist, anti-colonial novel in the Patternist series. Translated into German and Italian, it retraces the black diaspora from Nigeria via Atlantic triangular trade to colonial North America. The author chose a new aspect of speculation by gleaning aspects of Ibo myth, "a different culture that really exists" (Bogstad, 1978–1979, 31). She reflected that the novel "was the most fun to write … my reward for writing *Kindred*" (Devney, 2002, 9).

The antagonist, the shapeshifter Doro, is a Nubian immortal endowed with telepathic powers. The author based the incest motif on the biblical menage of Lot and his daughters in Genesis 19:1–28. The story gained energy and direction from the power rivalry of a vampire and his shapeshifting wife. She based characterization on an Ibo myth of Atagbusi, a protective female shapeshifter revered at the Nigerian city of Onitsha east of the Niger River. Her ingenious resetting won a creative arts citation from the Los Angeles YWCA. Feminist sci-fi writers made her guest of honor at WisCon 4, an annual feminist science fiction convention in Madison, Wisconsin.

March 1980

As a participant in *Future Life* magazine's "Future Forum," Octavia presented her views on how confronting aliens would change humanity: "No science or philosophy, no racial, religious, national, or international interest would be unaffected" (Butler, 1980, 55). Because of advanced technology from another solar system, "Chances are they would have more control over our effect on them than we would over their effect on us" (*ibid.*). For contrast she cited the training of apes and chimpanzees in American Sign Language and established that humans "have already had contact with intelligent, nonhuman species" (*ibid.*). Octavia stated a personal maxim: "We humans are terribly clever, but we've never been clever enough to control ourselves" (Carr, 1992, 37). She demeaned humanity for its greed, savagery, and stupidity and skewered the faults of her own time: "We are our own standards of perfection, and we prove it regularly" (Butler, 1980, 56).

Summer 1980

Octavia submitted to *Transmission* "Lost Races of Science Fiction," an essay questioning the stereotyping of blacks as disruptive or out of fashion. She compared the false premise to the replacement of women with all males and gave actor Yaphet Kotto as an example of successful casting as technician Dennis Parker in the 1979 film *Alien.* Octavia and Martin Greenberg tried to compile a collection of black sci-fi, but failed to sell the idea because blacks weren't interested in the genre. Octavia charged black writers with self-limiting their narratives.

September 3, 1982

In a book review for the *Washington* Post, the author criticized Jean Marie Auel's novel *The Valley of the Horses* for poor characterization of its central figures, Ayla and Jondalar. With other writers, she toured Finland, Moscow, Leningrad, and Kiev in the Ukraine.

January 10, 1983

An entry in Octavia's notebook schedule reminded her to arise at 4:30 a.m. for an hour's review.

May 22, 1983

For the *Washington Post,* Octavia critiqued Claudia Tate's compendium *Black Women Writers at Work,* an anthology of works by Afro-Americans Nikki Giovanni, Margaret Walker, Gayl Jones, Maya Angelou, Toni Cade Bambara, and Toni Morrison.

October 17, 1983

For the *Washington Post* article "Black Feminism: Searching the Past," the author reviewed Alice Walker's *In Search of Our Mother's Gardens,* which exalted "the black black woman" (Butler, 1983, B2). Reverence for being "our essential mother," the black female African forebear, like the fictional oracle and healer An-yanwu in *Wild Seed,* drew on the sanctity of Yemonja, a Yoruban river deity, earth mother, and creator. Octavia identified the book of womanist prose as writing by "a black feminist or feminist of color" (*ibid.*). She admired Walker's survey of black female lives from 1966 to 1982, when womanism characterized "outrageous, audacious courage or willful behavior" (*ibid.*). Her book review cited Nigerian author Buchi Emecheta, who extolled maternity as a mark of distinction: "Having a child is easily the equivalent of being a man" (*ibid.*). Octavia also honored poet Langston Hughes, anthropologist Zora Neale Hurston, and critic W.E.B. Du Bois for "celebrating the blackness in themselves as well as in their work" (*ibid.*).

November 11–13, 1983

The author represented professional sci-fi writers at Portland State University, Oregon, at the annual OryCon V convention, which presents the yearly Endeavour Award to a Pacific Northwest author of sci-fi or fantasy.

mid–December 1983

The author wrote the beginnings of an autobiography and published "Speech Sounds" in *Isaac Asimov's Science Fiction Magazine.* Translators adapted the story of a "communication deficit" in the German version *Der süße Klang des Wortes* and the Portuguese "Sons de Fala" (Butler, 1998).

1984

Simultaneous with the publication of *Clay's Ark,* set in the Mojave Desert after an astronaut introduces a dangerous microbe, came the French version, *Humains, plus qu'Humains* (Humans More Than Humans), and an Italian translation, *Incidente nel Deserto* (Incident in the Desert). Tone and action advanced from decorum to scenes of shackling, incest, pedophilia, emasculation, decapitation, and gang rape. She used evolving chapters as distractions for a friend dying of myeloma over a twelve-month period. On a bus trip to visit her friend, Octavia observed a senseless, juvenile fistfight, source of the opening line of "Speech Sounds." She later remarked on the value of people-watching while she stood in line or rode buses.

June 1984

Isaac Asimov's Science Fiction Magazine issued "Bloodchild" with cover art. Adaptations appeared in Croatian, Japanese, German, Italian, and Portuguese. She introduced the story with the intent to depart "the beaten track, off the narrow, narrow footpath of what 'everyone' is saying, doing, thinking—whoever 'everyone' happens to be this year" (Yancy, 1996, E13).

August 30–September 3, 1984

The short post-apocalyptic fiction story "Speech Sounds" earned a Hugo Award for the year's best short narrative from the World Science Fiction Convention in Anaheim, California. The narrative depicted the Mohave region deprived of literacy and impaired by hostility, random violence, outrage, and envy. For the first time, she envisioned technological advances of her own time—bullet-proof glass, cars that spray dye and a nauseating gas on thieves, and a physician's bag equipped with electronic prescription keypad and analysis capability for specimens of blood and flesh. Octavia completed the second draft of an unpublished novel, *Blindsight,* featuring a psychokinetic cult healer who studied people and things by touch. She gained more notoriety after compiler Patti Perret included her photo in *The Faces of Science Fiction.*

1985

A second Hugo lauded the novella *Bloodchild,* which also earned a Nebula citation from Fiction Writers of America, a Locus Award for best short novel, and top novella from *Science Fiction Chronicle.* Her acceptance speech for the Nebula remarked that she preferred writing over speaking "in order to avoid moments like this" (Fowler, 2006). The complex story pictured inter-species breeding of humans with insectoids similar to caterpillars. On a UCLA Education Abroad Program, she journeyed to Machu Picchu in the Andes and the Amazon rainforest to gather details for *Xenogenesis*, which morphed into a series. Central to her curiosity, she needed data on the burrowing botfly (*Diptera oestroidea*), cause of the conflict in "Bloodchild." For background, she read anatomy manuals and molecular biology texts to discover "The [larvae] eat and they eat and they get bigger and bigger, and then there's a big knot that comes up under your skin, and as they get closer to the bone, it hurts and … well, I simply knew I'd have to do something about my botfly concerns or I couldn't go" ("Alternative," 1985).

July 1985

More challenges followed with ascending Huayna Picchu in Peru, where Octavia researched the Xenogenesis series. She gained insight into the *Imago* characters Jesusa and Tomás and their ability to scale sheer rock faces. The strain of climbing reminded her of rough patches in writing: "There comes a time when you want to either burn it or flush it" (Sanders, 2004).

From introduction to the botfly in the Peruvian rainforest, Octavia began researching tropical biota for *Xenogenesis* and the idea of insect eggs maturing under human skin into maggots, which she reduced to "something without a backbone." She stated, "When I have to deal with something that disturbs me as much as the botfly did, I write about it" (Butler, 2005, 310). By composing "Bloodchild," her "pregnant man" fable, she assessed dominance of sickly alien parasites who force male slaves to incubate the next generation of eggs (Williams, 1986, 70). The story reduced to interesting research the horror of larvae burrowing into flesh (Butler, 2005, 30).

1986

Following Octavia's interview with activist Frances M. Beal for *Black Scholar,* in an unpublished personal essay, the author reflected on "Why Did I Write *Kindred*?" At the time, she was composing *The Training Boar,* an unpublished reflection on Holocaust survivors whom humanoids kidnap. She named intelligence and hierarchy as the riskiest of human characteristics: "If you're going to have somebody sending people off to war for egotistical or economic reasons, both hierarchal sorts of reasons, you end up with a lot more dead people" (Sanders, 2004). To interviewer Sandra Y. Govan, she posed opposing possibilities of contact: "If we go to them, woe to them. If they come to us, woe to us" (Govan, 2005–2006, 31).

April 28, 1986

To Octavia's dismay, arson in the Los Angeles Central Library destroyed her research sources in the nation's largest book repository disaster. Flames, which broke out in the stacks and reached 2,500 degrees, required the efforts of more than 350 firefighters. The facility lost artifacts and some 2,100,000 books valued at over $50 million. She recalled that she wept "on the corner of Fifth Street and Grand in downtown Los Angeles and watched black smoke pour from the windows" (Butler, 1993,

4). She recalled arson like the slaughter of a "friend, teacher, lover, home" (*ibid.*). Her motivation for being there was personal: "The trip I made to the L.A. Library on the day of the fire was part of my effort to pay back a little of what I felt I owed to libraries in general" (*ibid.*). By volunteering to box charred works for freeze-drying, she helped rescue beloved books.

1987

The core novel *Dawn* launched the Xenogenesis trilogy with words from President Ronald Reagan on limited nuclear war. Drawing on the headlines of the Reagan-Margaret Thatcher-George Bush era, she developed the themes of hierarchical self-destruction and human reproduction by an alien third gender who suggests ways that earthlings can correct their faults. An unsigned review in *Fantasy Book Reviews* charged Octavia with "[engaging] in revolutionary guerrilla warfare upon our perceptions" ("Review," undated). The tenuous choice of the great-hearted Lilith Iyapo as hero dramatized Octavia's views on the fragility of freedom, particularly during U.S. clashes with the Soviets during the Cold War.

The narrative, rewritten at least three times with meticulous characterization of an isolated widow, intrigued audiences in Bulgarian, Portuguese, German, and Spanish. Octavia later relayed to Susan Palwick, an interviewer for *Isle,* "the general tendency of human beings … to simply tear things down without concern for what might come after" (Palwick, 1999, 150). Instead, people wait until disaster looms before taking action. Simultaneously, "Politicians … are interested in preserving the status quo," an easy method of courting votes (*ibid.*)

As a case in point, the protagonist Lilith Iyapo and the condescending Oankali in the Xenogenesis trilogy manipulate genetics through cloning, gene mapping, and interspecies breeding to spawn a new race for earth via exterminating humankind. The concepts came from Ronald Reagan's naive supposition that "nuclear war was winnable" and that people could cower underground until the danger passed (Sanders, 2004). The author stated to interviewer Faye Ringel, "That's how Ronald Reagan helped me write three novels" (Devney, 2002, 8). She summarized the competitive element of egotism: "We've one-upped ourselves to death" (*ibid.*). For the characters, she created the Oankali, a hybrid species able to survive nuclear disaster through hybridizing, a futuristic take on eugenic miscegenation.

May 1987

Omni magazine published Octavia's "The Evening and the Morning and the Night," later translated into French, German, and Portuguese. The pensive narrative earned a nomination for the Nebula award for depiction of a disease similar to Huntington's that causes victims to long for death. From intense research, she added aspects of Phenylketonuria (PKU), a mental disorder that requires a special diet from birth on produce, cereal, pasta, and bread, and Lesch-Nyhan, a metabolic anomaly causing neurological disability, head banging, gout, and biting the fingers and mouth.

June 1988

Octavia completed *Adulthood Rites,* part two of Xenogenesis, with a captivity narrative, which translators adapted in Portuguese, German, Bulgarian and Italian. The Italian title altered the original to *Ritorno all Terra* (Return to the Land). The post-apocalyptic plot enlarges on human interbreeding with aliens and migration to an exclusive settlement on Mars. She won a Locus best sci-fi novel award for *Dawn,* the previous volume of *Lilith's Brood.* Her novella "The Evening and the Morning and the Night" achieved her second *Science Fiction Chronicle* honorarium for examining genetic mental malfunction. She earned nominations for a second Locus honor, Nebula citation, and the Theodore Sturgeon Award from the University of Kansas. In notebooks, she pledged to support poor black students at Clarion College and its workshops and to promote broad aims that included college training.

July 1–3, 1988

Octavia accepted an invitation as guest of honor to InConJunction VIII, a regional convention held annually in Indianapolis. Her travels also took her to the Bahamas.

July 17, 1988

In a review for the *Washington Post* of Lois Gould's Renaissance yarn *Subject to Change,* Octavia reflected on a former teacher who declared that fiction writers should begin with short stories before attempting longer fiction.

1989

For *Writer's Digest,* the author disclosed in "How I Built Novels out of Writer's Blocks" that she began composing the Parable series in 1989. After downing her first coffee of the morning, listening to NPR, and reading the *Los Angeles Times,* she had "never before written so slowly" (Butler, 1999, 13). To correct the problem, she rid the manuscript of power seeking, an element unsuited to the protagonist, teen idealist Lauren Oya Olamina. Octavia began reading current news and, rather than prophesy, "observed what was happening around her, and then she extrapolated from what she knew" ("Sci-Fi," 2021). In Lauren's voice, she wrote a verse scripture in the style of the *Tao Te Ching,* Lao Tzu's compendium composed in the sixth century BCE.

February 1–4, 1989

The annual Life, the Universe, & Everything (LTUE) symposium on sci-fi and fantasy at Brigham Young University in Provo, Utah, featured Octavia as a guest of honor. Before experts involved in writing, film, music, stage, art, gaming, and speculative fiction, she impressed forum participants with short, incisive commentary on "Realism in Fantasy," "Putting the Science in SF," "Gaia: The Living Earth," and "Romance and SF."

March 30–April 2, 1989

A guest of honor invitation to AggieCon XX, the oldest student-operated multi genre convention, at Texas A&M University, College Station, continued Octavia's personal introduction to fans.

May 1989

Imago ended the *Lilith's Brood* trilogy, which appeared in Germany and in an omnibus collection as *Xenogenesis*. The story dramatizes the search for partners of shapeshifters. *Essence* published "Birth of a Writer," a personal essay later called "Positive Obsession," discussing her six-foot height and unbecoming timidity. She later reprised discomfort with her body in the memories of Larkin Bankole, an "oversized kid" in *The Parable of the Talents* who tried to "hide, vanish, make myself invisible" (Butler, 1998, 239).

Octavia viewed herself as a dancing bear. At the *Essence* conference for black women authors, she posed with a broad smile, suggesting that she felt less insecure among non-white females. Analyst Gerry Canavan posited that she "saw not race but men—masculinity ... on the level of biology—as the real problem to be solved" (Canavan, 2016). In *Imago*, she derided men with the observation, "Human-born males were still considered experimental and potentially dangerous" (Butler, 2000, 536). A repeat of her charge labels the entire gender "suspicious, hostile, dangerous" (*ibid.*, 555).

June 25–August 5, 1989

After holding discussions of *Imago* at the Aquarian Bookstore in Los Angeles on June 11, Octavia traveled by bus to Lansing, Michigan, to teach a three-hour session for the 22nd Clarion Workshop in Science Fiction and Fantasy, which had become a neophyte's rite of passage in the sci-fi field. During a six-week period, she considered writing on Chingis Khan and furthered her goal of helping seventeen young writers from Canada, the U.S., and Great Britain, who pay $2,000 for a Monday-Sunday program. From the U.S. Air Force Academy, she accepted a special achievement award. Of her future, she declared herself "a 42-year-old writer who can remember being a 10-year-old writer and who expects someday to be an 80-year-old writer" (Cellini, 1989, C1).

1990

During an interview with Larry McCaffery for *Across the Wounded Galaxies*, Octavia summarized earth's quandaries as a model of adolescent psychology. She believed that humankind floundered in sophomoric solutions: "The best thing we can do for the species is to go out into space" (McCaffery, 1990, 69). She typified the job of consensual space travel as a temporary aim until earthlings grew up.

April 18, 1990

Octavia was featured speaker at the Pasadena Public Library author series and began writing a television screenplay for WGBH in Boston.

June 7, 1991

After appearing in Claremont, California, at the Wild Iris Bookstore in late April, for WGBH in Boston, Octavia wrote a radio series titled "Biospheres." She began a decade-long effort to write *The Parable of the Trickster,* in which God is mentor, healer, and strategist of change. The antagonist Imara, a journalist, attempts to expose fraud in Lauren Olamina's philosophy. The author began her third parable book with Newt Gingrich as the villain, then switched to George W. Bush and "a nasty world ... not violent, just nasty and dull and awful" (Canavan, 2014, 75).

In an interview for *Locus,* the writer characterized achievers in space—the "people who go, who do fulfill that destiny and go to this other world" (Butler, 2000, 6). In a summary of Earthseed, Lauren Oya Olamina's faith in the Parable series, the writer explained, "If you look at any religion that lasts, it changes greatly" (Palwick, 1999, 158). She joked about her efforts, "Trees died as I went through reams and reams of paper!" (Govan, 2005–2006, 22). Among alternatives, she considered writing *The Parable of the Mustard Seed,* based on Mark 4:30–32.

December 26, 1991

After years of following Cold War news, Octavia brightened at Communism's collapse in the essay "Brave New World," she rejoiced: "The threat of nuclear war is gone, at least for the present, because to our surprise our main rival, the Soviet Union, dissolved itself" (Butler, "Brave" 2000, 164).

1993

Octavia introduced the *tour de force* Earthseed series with the first segment, *The Parable of the Sower.* She developed a fundamental aphorism: "All that you touch/You Change./All that you Change/Changes you" (Butler, 1993, 1). Basing the millennial road novel on Matthew 13:8, she stocked it with intercalary verse and rewrote it four times. English analyst Teri Ann Doerksen, a teacher at the University of Manchester, linked the allegory to diaspora—"the breakdown of the United States infrastructure, the loosening of federal regulations..., and the desperate journey of thousands of impoverished California refugees to the closed borders of Oregon" (Doerksen, 1997, 22). It is, according to Jacques Baudou, a journalist for Paris *Le Monde,* "sans aucun doute son oeuvre majeure (without any doubt her major work)" (Baudou, 2006, 29).

The writer began outlining *The Parable of the Talents*, a cautionary tale focused on a populace that has lost its faith in the future. For the sake of debate, she juxtaposes the writings of Lauren Oya Olamina and her skeptic daughter, Larkin Bankole. According to critic Nisi Shawl, the novel predicted "a parade of Reagan-like populists and zealots," which the U.S. realized in Donald Trump (Butler, 2014, 9). The author's notes portrayed President Jarret as a Hitlerian Reagan "young, vigorous, and utterly unencumbered by conscience" (Canavan, 2016, 246). She identified omens of inhumanity—throw-away laborers, pension scams, drug-addicted infants, and corporate prisons. In an interview with *Democracy Now,* she warned, "If we keep misbehaving ourselves, ignoring what we've been ignoring, doing what we've been doing to the environment, for instance, here's what we're liable to wind up with" (Butler, 2005).

Literary critic Gerry Canavan characterized the first parable as a marriage of "utopian thinking with the bleak near-term prospects" for nature, capitalism, and cities (Canavan, 2021, 263). She turned her gutsy grandmother, Estelle Guy, into a protagonist and shaped fictional right-winger president Andrew Steele Jarret into a preview of Donald Trump. She chose American war correspondent William L. Shirer's *The Rise and Fall of the Third Reich* as a major source on fascism. Carolyn Alessio, writing for the *Philadelphia Inquirer*, justified the reference: "As research for her latest science-fiction novel … the nefarious characters of history are a good reflection of the grim 21st century as prophesied by Butler" (Alessio, 1999, Q2).

Integral to modern social breakdown, the writer blamed slavery, gangs, and religion-turned-political. She credited its sources to "my being a news-junkie" (Butler, 1998). A bestseller at 100,000 copies per year and recipient of a third Nebula award, the final Parable novel appeared in French, German, Italian, Romanian, and Portuguese. The dystopia has sunk into contemporary trends of drugs, gated communities, sentry duty, spectacle, spiritual bondage, and self-destruction. Through an outlook in verse form, she characterizes democracy's lapse into fascism as the result of social injustice espoused in gentrification, militarism, terrorism, and racism. She claimed as lucky a fiction chronicle about something that mattered, particularly fifteen-year-old protagonist Lauren Oya Olamina's integrity in learning to work within the system and her formulation of a Darwinian religion she called Earthseed. The all-or-nothing prospectus reminds her, "Belief initiates and guides action—Or it does nothing" (Butler, 1993, 46).

Using words "as powerful, as simple, and as direct as I feel them," the author intended the Parable series to influence New Agers (*ibid.,* 78). She encapsulated the Reagan presidency as a flirtation with nuclear war. She gave as motivation from the Clinton era the declaration, "I was trying to give warning" (Sanders, 2004). At a pivotal moment in *The Parable of the Talents,* Lauren, the visionary, denounces war as a pointless cause of death, maiming, poverty, disease, starvation, and more strife. Of the ensuing space race to Mars, she viewed Cold War technical advancement in the U.S. and U.S.S.R. as "having a nuclear war without having one" (Sanders, 2004). Her text urged an optimistic view of the future beyond earth: "Destiny of Earthseed is to take root among the stars" (Butler, 1993, 77).

March 5–7, 1993

At the first Con-Dor assembly, held at the Town and Country Resort and Convention Center in San Diego, California, the author appeared as guest of honor.

August 1993

Omni issued Octavia's essay "Free Libraries: Are They Becoming Extinct?," which endorsed education for rescuing the poor from slums and for preparing the work force for jobs.

October 8–10, 1993

At the Cedar Bluff Holiday Inn in Knoxville, Tennessee, Octavia appeared as official guest at Concat 5.

February 15, 1994

Columnist Shirlee Smith honored the author in the Sunday *Pasadena Star-News* with a profile. Among her traits, Smith applauded "an unrelenting capacity to care for others in our community" (Smith, 1994, A14).

April 22–23, 1994

Octavia spoke on her published works at Vroman's, her neighborhood book store. At the Contemporary American Author Lecture Series, she accepted an invitation as writer-in-residence for Detroit's Marygrove College, where she offered free public speeches.

July 10, 1994

At the 25th annual Science Fiction Research Association National Conference in Arlington Heights, Illinois, Octavia opened the session with her essay "The Monophobic Response" and recapped the writing of the Parable series.

December 4, 1994

The *New York Times* chose *The Parable of the Sower* as a Notable Book of the Year.

1995

At age forty-eight, Octavia published an anthology, *Bloodchild and Other Stories,* winner of a *New York Times* Notable Book listing. The contents included "Amnesty," "Positive Obsession," and "The Book of Martha," which she characterized as cautionary tales. She based "Amnesty" on the persecution and imprisonment of the Taiwanese-American scientist Wen Ho Lee for spying for Communist China. The author set records for sci-fi by earning a nomination for another Nebula Award for Best Novel. She achieved a MacArthur Foundation genius grant and a $295,000 purse over five years for synthesizing mythology, spirituality, and mysticism with science fiction. She groused, "I hate the 'genius' garbage…. It doesn't say genius anywhere" (Mabe, 1999, D1).

The prize winner used the cash to buy a computer and a house in Altadena for herself and her mother. Living intentionally obscure, she dressed in jeans and sweatshirt and enjoyed an upright piano and *Star Trek* in private. She gave up worrying about finding jobs. For an office at her L.A. house, she withdrew to a manual typewriter in the dining room for a 3–4 o'clock drink of hot apple juice with lemon. She turned on NPR news and began writing self-help mantras in a notebook as a warm-up. For reference, she filled walls with maps and character lists and stockpiled back issues of *National Geographic*. By 7:00 a.m., she was ready for a four-mile walk accompanied by audio tapes.

May 26–28, 1995

Three months after an appearance at the Oxford Bookstore in Atlanta, Georgia, Octavia was special guest at ConQuesT 26, a regional sci-fi convention in Kansas City, Missouri. A lengthy itinerary took her to Folktales African American Bookstore in Austin, Texas, on June 9.

October 1995

The author's speech "Journeys" to the PEN/Faulkner Awards ceremony at Quill & Brush, Rockville, Maryland, appeared in the October 1995 edition of *Journeys*. In mid-month, she moved on to Santa Monica, California, to give a reading from *Bloodchild and Other Stories* at the Midnight Special bookstore. The year's invitations took her to Spelman College, the University of Pennsylvania, and UCLA. She chuckled, "I enjoy people—as long as I don't have to be around them too often" (Crisp, 1996, H3).

February 18–19, 1996

In celebration of black history month, Octavia signed autographs at Borders Book Shop in Lancaster, Pennsylvania, and delivered the Hazel I. Jackson lecture the next day at Millersville University. The festival allied her works with the films *Star Trek, Voyager, Classic Trek*, and *Deep Space Nine*.

November 18, 1996

In retirement, Octavia's mother turned the garden into a second child. She nursed her mother through terminal illness, which ended at age eighty-two with stroke, the same disease that killed the author. She buried Octavia Margaret Guy Butler in Altadena.

December 31, 1996

At the turning of the year's calendar, the *Los Angeles Times* recommended *The Parable of the Sower* among the top three novels of 1996.

Whitsun, 1997

From March 28–31, Octavia's convention appearances took her to the Adelphi Hotel for the British national science fiction convention in Liverpool, England, for an Eastercon book talk on the topic "Intervention." Fans lined up in the hotel lounge for her autograph.

March–April 1997

To Charles H. Rowell, an interviewer from *Callaloo,* the writer recommended that beginners learn and practice their craft and accept criticism as a correction of bad habits. To interviewer Joan Fry of *Poets & Writers,* the author shucked off the labels of speculative fiction/sci-fi/fantasy and claimed, "I'm a storyteller" (Fry, 1997, 58). Lynell George, a journalist for the *Los Angeles Times,* defined the narratives as "a way to break down old walls of perception, a tool to push readers beyond societal limits and expand their imaginations" (George, 2004). The novella *Imago* joined works by innovators Marilynne Robinson, Toni Morrison, Joyce Carol Oates, and Leslie Marmon Silko in W.W. Norton's *Postmodern American Fiction,* a college textbook.

April 10–12, 1997

Octavia joined the 28th annual gathering of black fantasy, horror, and sci-fi authors at Clark Atlanta University's Auburn Avenue Research Library. In a retrospect on the Harlem Renaissance, the black speculative fiction writers panel discussed "The African American Fantastic Imagination" and the concept "We are not alone."

May 12, 1997

The author surveyed in her journal the mounting socio-economic problems facing the twenty-first century. She anticipated "throwaway labor, the rich-poor gap" and other dilemmas derived from global warming (Brown, 2021). She predicted "food-price driven inflation," weather extremes, rising seas, decreasing plant and animal diversity, and Southwestern water wars (*ibid.*). Her diatribe forewarned of heat stroke and food poisoning from poorly refrigerated supplies.

May 18, 1997

At the 169th spring commencement ceremony, Kenyon College in Gambier, Ohio, conferred on Octavia an honorary doctorate.

February 19, 1998

In the speech "Devil Girl from Mars: Why I Write Science Fiction," a segment of MIT's *Media in Transition* program, Octavia endorsed Robert A. Heinlein's three sci-fi categories: What-If, If-Only, and If-This-Goes-On. According to Marlene D. Allen in an essay for *Callaloo,* the author "advocates for the enlightenment and insight that science fiction can provide as a prophetic tool for change" (Allen, 2009, 1255). The author described how, at age thirteen, she rebelled against idiot sci-fi movies and got "busy submitting terrible pieces of fiction to innocent magazines" (Butler, 1998). She acknowledged writing "consciously, deliberately, about people who were afraid and who functioned in spite of their fear" ("Devil," 1998). The description fits her "wonder women," who battle the impossible, such as Keira "Kerry" Maslin, the leukemia victim who outlives the disease in *Clay's Ark* and becomes a breeder of a new earthly species.

The author called 1960s Cold War mindset paranoia, a useful basis for such speculative fiction as *Star Trek* and *Twilight Zone.* Her humor extended to the sudden post–Sputnik funding of science education "because the Russians were coming. And we had to do something about it" (*ibid.*). In reference to gossip about President Bill Clinton's philandering with Monica Lewinsky, the author reflected on the state of human communication "as kind of media GIGO, garbage in, garbage out," which she summarized as a "point of diminishing returns" (*ibid.*). In the essay "Brave New Worlds: A Few Rules for Predicting the Future," she satirized "air-raid drills when I was in [Lincoln] elementary school, how we knelt, heads down against corridor walls with our bare hands supposedly protecting our bare necks" (Butler, "Brave," 2000, 164).

March 1998

The New York Science Fiction Society invited Octavia as guest at Lunacon 41, an annual sci-fi and fantasy convention at the Rye Town Hilton in Rye Brook, New York.

March 16, 1998

While readers in Hampton, Virginia, savored *Kindred* as the annual community read, Octavia spoke at Hampton University. In her office, she labored over a memoir, a nonfiction work, and the novel *Eyes,* all of which she abandoned.

June 22, 1998

The writer celebrated a 51st birthday in Washington, D.C., at Sisterspace bookstore and addressed the Smithsonian Associates literary forum. She followed a taxing schedule with a reading in New York at the Manhattan Theatre Club.

November 1998

At her ranch-style home in San Gabriel Valley northeast of Los Angeles, Octavia appreciated a career with no walls. She completed the Earthseed duo with *The Parable of the Talents,* set from 2032 to 2035, five years after the founding of the Acorn enclave in Mendocino. She dedicated the novel to her mother, Octavia Margaret Guy Butler, and maternal aunts Hazel Walker and Irma Harris. In opposition to extremist Christian America, the book and citations from Lauren Oya Olamina's "The First Book of the Living" earned kudos form the *Washington Post, New York Times Book Review, Los Angeles Times, Publishers Weekly, Wall Street Journal, Village Voice, United Press International,* and *Library Journal.*

The text, available in French and Portuguese, presents events from the perspective of Lauren and her daughter, Larkin Bankole. It prophesies the presidency of Andrew Steele Jarret, a hidebound demagogue urging "Make America Great Again." It bears a foretaste of Donald Trump's fascist jingoism that the *Die Welt* book review from Berlin called precognizant (Warner, 2018, 10). Reviewer Paul Di Filippo, in a critique for the *San Francisco Examiner,* compared the post-apocalyptic vehemence to a Falwellian theocracy.

In a retrospect for the *New York Times Book Review,* Stephen Kearse ranked the second parable far above the didacticism of the first for the rejuvenation of Lauren's voice. Similar in themes and atmosphere to Margaret Atwood's *The Handmaid's Tale,* the book imagined authoritarian religious fanaticism. She delayed the publisher while she rewrote the initial text, which did not please her. *Publishers Weekly* declared it a best book of 1998. It also won a James Tiptree, Jr., of Otherwise Award honor listing for quality fantasy and sci-fi. In the same week that she gave readings at Santa Monica's Midnight Special Bookstore and her neighborhood Vroman's in Pasadena, she began an unpublished memoir, "I Should Have Said."

December 12, 1998

Octavia's journal pondered the purpose of biomedicine and the adaptability of humans who venture to other worlds. If they change remarkably in adapting to an extraterrestrial environment, "Those who are visibly different will suffer most" while the most normal "will be the upper crust" (Brown, 2021, 96).

January 1999

Octavia's picture graced the first edition of *Black Issues Book Review* under the caption "Bestselling Futuristic Storyteller."

January 4, 1999

Octavia joined other authors for an interview with Pasadena radio KPCC-FM and a book signing at Borders.

February 2, 1999

In an interview for *Isle,* Octavia maintained hope for humanity, even though activism tends to wait until the brink of destruction before intervening. Using climate change, dying redwoods, and clearcutting as examples, she predicted that last minute corrections are "just going to make for an enormous amount of misery and death…. We almost have to be frightened into it" (Palwick, 1999, 151). She blamed profit motives for "our ignoring reality" (*ibid.*).

March 25, 1999

At the launching of the Nightjohn book club to recognize the legendary African itinerant who taught literacy to slaves, the author addressed an audience at the California African American Museum in Los Angeles's Exposition Park on the Parable series.

April 2–4, 1999

Another guest appearance took the writer to Minneapolis for Minion 34, where she served as speaker at the opening ceremonies and the author's roundtable. As reader at Directors Row, she interviewed with Janice Bogstad on "Power Relations" and led a discussion on "The Cold Equations" and "What's Depressing, What's Cautionary, What's Uplifting."

May 1, 1999

Kudos for *The Parable of the Talents* included a *Los Angeles Times* bestseller and a 1999 Nebula citation for best science novel, presented at the Marriott City Center Hotel in Pittsburgh. She specified to an interviewer from *Essence* that her sci-fi "[extrapolates] from what we are right now as human beings and how we are likely to deal with becoming something different, with dramatic change" (McHenry, 1999, 80). The magazine rewarded her for prose generating a "sharp and lucid … prophetic odyssey" ("Octavia," 1999, A9). Cal Flyn, a book reviewer for the London *Guardian,* declared, "Speculative fiction has never felt so prescient" (Flyn, 2021, 26).

June 1999

Octavia quipped about the dry season for writers with the essay "How I Built Novels Out of Writer's Blocks" in *Writer's Digest.* She urged fellow authors to abandon fear and "use everything that touches us…. It's all ore to be refined into story" (Butler, 1999, 12).

June 11–13, 1999

At the Best Western in suburban Tukwila south of Seattle, Octavia appeared as guest of honor at the debut of Foolscap I, a conference of sci-fi and fantasy readers, authors, composers, and visual artists. Author Nisi Shawl commemorated Octavia's advancement to sci-fi doyenne in the brochure essay "Daughter of Necessity." It credited the author with "a cosmological imperative: potential stories longing to be told" (Butler, 2014, 7).

June 13–July 24, 1999

At Michigan State University in East Lansing, the author repeated summer teaching at the Clarion West Writers Workshop, which hosted eighteen apprentices from fourteen states.

October 5, 1999

Octavia progressed to headliner of Novello, an annual book festival at the South County Regional Library in Charlotte, North Carolina, where she reminisced about her family's Louisiana background in the Jim Crow era. A panel discussed her "Alternate Realities" along with those of Anne McCaffrey and Orson Scott Card. Fans celebrated her sci-fi on October 6 at the West Boulevard Branch Library.

November 1999

To be near Mount Rainier, Octavia moved herself and 354 boxes from Los Angeles to a one-story house in Lake Forest Park on Lake Washington north of Seattle. Parisian reviewer Jacques Baudou wrote in *Le Monde* that she "se consacre à l'écriture et en viva longtemps chichement" (she dedicated herself to writing and lived a long time sparingly, Baudou, 2006, 29). Of the effects of a move north to Washington, she reflected on fictional migrations: "My characters have moved to Alpha Centauri, or whatever. (That was not literal.) But they suffer and learn about the situation there a little bit because of what I learn about from my move to Seattle" (Butler, 2000, 6).

The writer exercised on a treadmill, wrote self-help mantras on walls and doors, and stocked her great room shelves with sci-fi, anthropology, black history, books-on-tape, an Oxford English Dictionary (OED), verse, and murder mysteries, many by English maven Agatha Christie. For news, she preferred BBC or NPR, but sometimes retreated from depressing bomb stories and starvation, genocide, and rape in Chad and Sudan because "My psyche can't take in that much horror" (Govan, 2005–2006, 34). Mimi Howard, a political writer at the University of Cambridge, extolled the author for "maintaining a devotional relationship to keeping a journal, but also included putting newspaper clippings and editors cartoons … above her writing desk" (Howard, 2021, 37).

Octavia confessed to enjoying dictionary reading, even the big OED that requires a magnifying glass. From a Yoruba source, she chose for *Imago* the character name Ayodele (joy comes home); from a Turkish compendium, she named another Yedik (we ate). The solitude of the Pacific Northwest accommodated a need for privacy and order, but did not stanch mounting writer's block and depression from fatigue and side effects of blood pressure medication. Shirlee Smith, in a sketch for the *Pasadena Star-News,* remarked that Octavia didn't quit: "'Keeping on' has been the hallmark of Butler's career" (Smith, 1994, A14).

Modernized from a 75-pound manual Adler typewriter to computer, the writer broke her mental block by battling technology. Basing her work on scriptural parables, she planned an earth diaspora in *The Parable of Chaos, The Parable of Clay, The Parable of the Teacher,* and *The Parable of the Trickste*r, but she gave up the six-part sequence of adaptations with the latter title.

November 2, 1999

As writer-in-residence at Newcomb College in New Orleans, Octavia delivered the address "Trickster, Teacher, Chaos, Clay" and revealed the significance of a tough grandmother as role model. Current events and unflinching political opinions influenced her fiction, from disease and hunger to depleted rainforests, the Afghan War, and 9/11. She stated, "You can support causes or shoot off your mouth but there really isn't a big difference you can make" (Holden and Shawl, 2013, 219).

November 6, 1999

After overcoming fear of embarrassing herself in public, Octavia gave a reading from *The Parable of the Talents* in the Texas senate chamber at Austin. A book reviewer for the *Los Angeles Sentinel* described the novel as "often brutal, relentless, raw in its ability to describe one man's (or woman's) inhumanity toward another. Her reality is also uncommonly kind and forgiving" ("Octavia," 1999, A9).

December 31, 1999

After writing end-of-the-world scenarios, Octavia refused to quail at the Y2K hysteria. She assured all, "The world's not going to come to an end in 2000" (Alessio, 1998, F3).

2000

TV producer Ava DuVernay hired writer Victoria Mahoney to turn *Dawn* into a television production. Its cast will include Oprah Winfrey as Mrs. Which. Editor Sheree R. Thomas incorporated Octavia's story "The Evening and the Morning and the Night" and reissued her October 1995 speech "Journeys" as "The Monophobic Response" in the collection *Dark Matter: A Century of Speculative Fiction from the African Diaspora.* Of the possibilities of "other children" in the universe, the author ridiculed human xenophobia: "How dare someone be different! We're really not very tolerant unless we make an effort to be," especially with foreign peoples (Govan, 2005–2006, 32). Of earthly intolerance, she concluded, "I can't imagine us treating them well" (*ibid.*).

Tananarive Due declared Octavia the leader of the black speculative fiction movement exploring the what-ifs of human identity and potential. An interviewer for *Essence* and teacher at Spelman College, Due discovered Octavia working to a Motown beat in her Seattle home. She explained a need for wall maps and posters reminding her of essential themes and tenets.

April 2000

Of the triad of race, gender, and caste, Octavia identified social class as the most marginalizing concept. She defied limitations on black females by dramatizing their self-actualization. To a *New York Times* journalist, she explained that she created hominids "but I don't make up the essential human character" (Fox, 2006, C16).

April 21–23, 2000

To support the Compton Crook literary award for best first novel, Octavia appeared as guest of honor before some two thousand attendees at Balticon, the 40th Baltimore Science Fiction Convention, held at the Omni Inner Harbor Hotel.

Sponsored by the Baltimore and Maryland Regional Science Fiction Society, Octavia addressed "The Use of Race, Caste and Culture in Science Fiction & Fantasy." Conventioneers visited a costume display inspired by her fiction and saw a taped interview about her parable series.

May 1, 2000

Essence issued "Brave New Worlds: A Few Rules for Predicting the Future," in which she warned that "Superstition, depression, and fear play major roles" in prophecy (Butler, 2000, 164). To a young fan's questions of solving global problems, she stated a reason for reading history: "The past, for example, is filled with repeating cycles of strength and weakness, wisdom and stupidity, empire and ashes. To study history is to study humanity. And to try to foretell the future without studying history is like trying to learn to read without bothering to learn the alphabet" (*ibid.,* 165).

May 19, 2000

Octavia's *The Parable of the Talents* earned one of six nominations for a Nebula award for best novel. Mark Harris, a book reviewer for the *Vancouver Sun*, endorsed the work for its high moral ground.

June 1, 2000

In a fifteen-minute TV appearance on *The Charlie Rose Show,* the author stressed the human variances of her characters. An interview in *Locus* Magazine congratulated the author on her beginning of *Kindred* in college and on the realism in the Parable books. She stated the source of the parables: "I used religion because it seems to me it's something we can never get away from" (Butler, 2000, 6).

July 2000

Warner issued the Xenogenesis trilogy as *Lilith's Brood.* The *New York Times Book Review* selected Octavia's speculative fiction on inter-species hybridity as prime summer reading.

September 21, 2000

When Octavia lectured in San Marino, California, at the Huntington Library on *Parable of the Talents,* she paid tribute to novelist Terry McMillan for applying a unique style to the civil rights era. Octavia ignored criticism of her sci-fi books by composing what she was good at—complex characters. She appeared in Orlando, Florida, as guest of honor at the 21st International Conference for the Fantastic in the Arts.

October 2000

To champion important advocates of free expression, emerging authors, and genre defiers, the PEN American Center in New York City presented Octavia a lifetime achievement award.

2001

Parable of the Talents achieved shortlisting for an Arthur C. Clarke Award, presented in London by the British Science Fiction Association. Octavia started two novels, *Spiritus,* which began in 1976 as a speech, and *Paraclete,* the tale of a female author empowered with truth. She stated a professional maxim: "It is a writer's duty to write about human differences, all human differences, and help make them acceptable" (*ibid.,* 46). In a 2001 article for *MELUS,* interviewers Marilyn Mehaffy and AnaLouise Keating deduced that the hybrid species in awe works are intended to "[revise] contemporary nationalist, racist, sexist, and homophobic attitudes" (Mehaffy and Keating, 2001, 45).

January 8, 2001

For National Public Radio (NPR) Weekend Edition, Octavia wrote the essay "A World without Racism" revealing the barbarism common to elementary school kids, who fail to "accept one another's differences" (Butler, 2001). She reminded herself that any racial progress could get snatched away. The essay concluded, "Tolerance, like any aspect of peace, is forever a work in progress, never completed, and if we're as intelligent as we think, never abandoned" (*ibid.*).

December 29, 2001

The author gave an interview to NPR host Susan Stamberg, which began with questions about 9/11. Octavia blamed humankind for neglecting the planets and poured her feelings into a short story. She clung to the positive images in Arthur C. Clarke's *2001: A Space Odyssey* and "was sort of rooting for what he had in mind, the good parts of it, anyway … a way to achieve a lot of technological efforts without necessarily hurting anybody" (Stamberg, 2001).

January 26, 2002

At UCLA, Octavia participated in a panel discussion on "Science Future, Science Fiction" that accurately projected explosive political disputes and the need for religion to reduce tension and enhance chances of survival. Her philosophy of endangerment from economic self-interest inspired the SolSeed Movement, which venerates the nurturing of life on earth and on living spaces throughout the universe. Members' reverence for Gaia, the Earth Mother, fosters wisdom, empathy, and passion.

March 15–17, 2002

In Denver, Colorado, the Cleo Parker Robinson Dance Ensemble presented "The Coming of Dawn," based on Octavia's dramatization of the mythic Lilith Iyapo.

April 11, 2002

The author lectured in Ohio at Cleveland State University on "Envisioning the Future: Utopia, Dystopia and Beyond."

April 19–21, 2002

At the Days Inn Riverview, Niagara Falls, New York, Octavia accepted a guest of honor invitation to EerieCon 4, a three-day science-fiction, fantasy, and horror convention that involved 150 fans in verse, masquerade, gaming, and an art show.

May 2002

Oprah magazine published Octavia's essay "Eye Witness: Butler's Aha! Moment."

July 12–14, 2002

As guest of honor, Octavia attended Readercon in Burlington, Massachusetts, gave an interview to Faye J. Ringel, a humanities professor at the United States Coast Guard Academy, and mingled with fans at kaffeeklatsches. Reviewer Amy West, a writer for SciFiNow, praised her for "[taking] many of our traditional science-fiction ideas and themes and [turning] them not just on their heads but inside out" (West, 2002, 1). The writer joked, "I've ruined society two or three times. In *Dawn,* I took it apart. And in *Clay's Ark,* I did it again" (Debney, 2002, 3). Of human failings, she later added, "We *are* our own predators!" (*ibid.*, 4).

The author focused on a damaged earth's future at the panel discussion "Ecological Disaster as Foreground and Background." She spoke the next two days on fictional religions at the discussion of "Is God Change?" and "Biological Hard SF," a survey of biotechnology. The grueling weekend continued with the author's comments on "The Aliens Among Us" and the roles of gender and race in alien suppression. The session "The Future of Extrapolation" featured her views on prophecy.

October 3, 2002

To freshmen reading *Kindred* in Claremont, California, the writer continued her feverish schedule with a speech at Pomona College on fantastic realism. The *Los Angeles Times Magazine* followed her canon from "the biologically bizarre to the socially profound" ("Science," 2002, B2).

January 22, 2003

Octavia issued "Amnesty," an electronic publication at sci-fi.com. The story later appeared in *Callaloo* (Summer, 2004) and *Bloodchild and Other Stories* (2005).

March 3, 2003

The author introduced *Kindred* in Rochester, New York, at Nazareth College. During a community read of the neo-slave narrative, she visited the City Museum & Science Center, Bausch & Lomb Public Library, and Monroe Community College Theatre and gave a speech at the Shults Center Forum. Her historical novel achieved popularity at the University of Rochester's course "Slavery and the 20th Century African American Novel." While speaking at Valley Manor Apartments retirement home, she reflected on her maternal grandmother, who sparked fear in the young writer. Orphaned at age twelve, the elderly matriarch exemplified female daring by rearing her family alone during the 1930s.

March 27–28, 2003

The author attended a Howard University conference, "A New Frontier: Blacks in Science Fiction," and delivered a keynote address. She declared diversity essential to the growth of sci-fi. With the addition of women and people of color, "It's more a literature of ideas and the people than it ever was before, and it's a good thing" (Hampton, 2014, 135).

May 2–4, 2003

The author accepted a guest of honor invitation to DemiCon 14, an annual sci-fi convention at the Hotel Fort Des Moines in Des Moines, Iowa, to discuss the theme

"Contemplating the Future." Activities involved fans in anime, music, gaming, and masquerade.

January 16–18, 2004

Before writers, publishers, costumers, and cinema and television scenarists, Octavia appeared as special guest at Rustycon 21, held at the SeaTac Radisson Airport Hotel in Bellevue, Washington. She addressed the theme of "Strong Women in Science Fiction and Fantasy."

January 22, 2004

The author discussed research on slavery for *Kindred* at a Martin Luther King convocation at Loyola College in New Orleans. The lecture initiated the novel's 25th anniversary edition and a national tour, which included Spelman College in Atlanta, Georgia, where Dr. King delivered the 1960 address "Keep Moving from This Mountain." She found it easy to talk about *Kindred* because "my motivation for writing it was very personal" (Govan, 2005–2006, 17). The joy in speaking to audiences echoed Lauren Oya Olamina's enthusiasm in *The Parable of the Talents* for sharing her philosophy with audiences in east and west. Like Lauren, Octavia felt grateful that people bought the book as well as "whatever else of mine is in print too" (*ibid.*). She maintained a simplified creed: "Don't bore people" (Holden and Shawl, 2013, 114).

March 14, 2004

To interviewer Joshunda Sanders, a writer for *O: Oprah Daily,* the author compared the labor of completing a manuscript with mountain climbing and the determination to reach the top. Her comment applied to two short works, "The Book of Martha" and "Amnesty," both of which thrived in Portuguese and in English as online reads.

May 2004

Octavia's doctor diagnosed her with pneumonia and the onset of congestive heart failure. Shortness of breath and weight gain as well as medicine for hypertension limited her work output and slowed her during walks through airports. She had admitted in May 2000, "I hate to take medicine" (Butler, 2000, 164).

May 16, 2004

Octavia brooded over the Abu Ghraib prison scandal and the abuse of power to humble inmates of a different race, language, and religion, one of the human rights issues in *Survivor.*

June 11–13, 2004

The multidisciplinary black science fiction festival of literature and film in the Seattle Science Fiction Museum and Hall of Fame offered what journalist Therese Littleton of the *Seattle Times* called the "mothership" of black Americans in sci-fi (Littleton, 2004, K1). Octavia, the first lady of nonwhite speculative novels, joined other authors and attendees from as far away as Holland in discussing the theme "Black to the Future." She urged the audience to keep telling their stories, keep preserving the black past. For the *Los Angeles Times,* reporter Lynell George described the "fresh canvas to contemplate a history burdened by slavery, racism, segregation and lynching or to experiment with social taboos" (Lynell, 2004).

June 29, 2004

Alongside "Moonblind," a werewolf story by Tanith Lee, Octavia's "The Book of Martha" appeared in the David G. Hartwell and Kathryn Cramer anthology *Year's Best Fantasy 4.*

March 16, 2005

In Cocoa, Florida, Octavia joined authors David Brin and Michael Crichton on an 8:00 p.m. talk show, *Closer to Truth.* Their topic defined differences between sci-fi and science.

May 26, 2005

A fainting spell in her kitchen warned Octavia that her health was declining.

April 2005

Still enamored of the *Paraclete* plot, Octavia returned often to the novel "because I love it and because I want so badly to make a novel of it…. I'm desperate to write it" (Canavan, 2016, 120).

October 22, 2005

According to agent Merrilee Heifetz of Writers House in New York City, in Octavia's last months fighting hypertension and congestive heart failure with heavy medication, she attempted to escape depressing subjects and writer's block, but could barely walk without gasping for breath. She gave the keynote address at the fifteenth annual Gwendolyn Brooks Conference on Black Literature and Creative Writing at Chicago State University, where fans lauded her as a mentor and beacon to black female artists.

For fun, the author issued *Fledgling,* a stand-alone comic-erotic narrative and new black vampire novel based on the Dracula legend. Settings draw on Seattle and inland towns of Darrington and Arlington, Washington, as well as a national park, Snohomish County, and the Stillaguamish River. Translated into French as *Novice,* the plot explored gender, mutation, and racial diversity through a vampire motif that she debunks metaphor by metaphor. Shori Matthews's amnesia derived from Octavia's struggles with dyslexia and brain fog, later worsened by prescription drugs for high blood pressure. The book took her on a promotional tour that included Chicago, Dubuque, Iowa, and Los Angeles, where she autographed her works on Halloween at Eso Won Books on Degnan Boulevard near Leimert Park.

October 26, 2005

At the Segal Theater on Fifth Avenue, Octavia spoke at the City University of New York on "Conversations with Black Authors."

November 11, 2005

Octavia received the Langston Hughes Medal from City College for commitment to social change and a lifetime achievement citation from PEN Center West. Her literary and physical height led critic Nisi Shawl, a journalist for *Ms.* Magazine and the *Seattle Times,* to compare her to Mount Rainier: "She towered over everything; she made her own weather" (Holden and Shawl, 2013, 2). She gained multiple honoraria—"mother of Afrofuturism," "grand dame of science fiction," and "mother of black speculative fiction." In the collection *Bloodchild: And Other Stories,* the postscript "Furor Scribendi" (also called "Birth of a Writer" and "Positive Obsession") characterized her mania for writing. A translation adapted the essay into Portuguese.

The author began "Furor Scribendi" with her standard advice—"Read," a means of learning from all types of literature. A second proposal suggested taking writing, grammar, and vocabulary classes to strengthen rhetorical basics. Octavia believed in muscle memory or habit strength conferred by daily writing, even journal keeping of ideas and observations. From stage one, advance to the second, refinement. By revising personal writing, the beginner-maintained standards essential to a career. The last stage required submissions, even if the results are repeated rejections. Overall, she stripped composition of pomposity and urged playful ideas. By persisting, the new author learned and gained confidence.

November 19–20, 2005

After a University of Toronto appearance at Innis Town Hall, Octavia journeyed to Florida to sign books at the Miami International Book Fair. The long treks defined a public outreach in her final months, when ill health threatened exhaustion.

November 27, 2005

The London *Guardian* named Octavia a leading figure in literature and popular culture and listed *Fledgling* as a best book of the year for its examination of addiction, sex, miscegenation, race, and dominance.

February 24, 2006

On the morning the author died, she intended to appear on the last day of the Potlatch convention in Seattle and dine with attendees at the Best Western Executive Inn. In Lake Forest Park near Seattle, Washington, two neighbor girls discovered Octavia's collapse at age fifty-eight caused by brain aneurysm and a head wound from a tumble on an icy cobbled path outside her home. The *Seattle Times, Seattle Post-Intelligencer, Los Angeles Times,* and *Pasadena Star-News* reported her burial in Altadena, California, at Mountain View Cemetery. At the Science Fiction Museum and Hall of Fame in the Seattle Center, mourners gathered to honor Octavia, a former board adviser.

A memorial service a week later took place at the Lincoln Avenue Baptist Church. Her family—two aged aunts and a clutch of cousins—issued a verbal tribute:

> Her spirit of generosity and compassion compelled her to support the disenfranchised. She sought to speak truth to power, challenge prevailing notions and stereotypes, and empower people striving for better lives. Although we miss her, we celebrate the rich life she led and its magnitude in meaning [Pirani, 2018].

She left a dozen novels available in ten languages. Her agent, Merrilee Heifetz, credited the author with more than a million sales. An epitaph on a headstone from the novel *Parable of the Sower* accredits her with changing all that she touched.

June 21, 2007

At Vision Festival XII in New York, commissioned by Chamber Music America with the generous support of the Doris Duke Charitable Trust, vocal composer Nicole Mitchell and the Black Earth Ensemble performed the "Xenogenesis Suite: A Tribute to Octavia Butler" on flute, sax, trumpet, reeds, cello, keyboard, bass, and percussion.

June 25–August 3, 2007

At the University of California, San Diego, the Clarion Science Fiction and Fantasy Writers' Workshop conferred on a nonwhite author its first Octavia E. Butler scholarship, financed by the Carl Brandon Society.

July 24, 2007

An omnibus edition, *Seed to Harvest,* collected four of Octavia's Patternmaster novels, featuring Amber, a heroine modeled on the teen self-mythos of Silver Star.

November 17–19, 2006

The Octavia Butler Memorial Scholarship, funded by Warner Books, Seven Stories Press, Beacon Press, and the Science Fiction Hall of Fame and Museum, supported minority attendees at the Clarion Science Fiction and Fantasy Writers' Workshop, beginning June 25, 2007. At the 28th annual OryCon convention at the Portland Marriott Waterfront in Oregon, she received a posthumous Endeavour finalist honor for *Fledgling*. Additional acclaim from Diversity in Fantasy and Science Fiction, Speculative Fiction by Women and People of Color, and the LGBTQ+ Speculative Fiction award increased demand for her books.

February 29–March 3, 2008

At the Hotel Deca in Seattle, the Potlatch 17 convention honored *The Parable of the Sower* for its intersection of religion, caste, race, and gender.

May 31, 2008

In Pasadena, California, the second annual Leimert Park Village Book Fair conferred a posthumous tribute on Octavia and her stories with the theme "Celebrating Our Literary Legacy: Our Heritage, Our Words, Our Stories."

October 2009

Octavia left instructions in her will for eighty boxes of personal papers to pass to California collections at San Marino's Huntington Library, Art Collection, and Botanical Gardens. Their provenance agent Merrilee Heifetz ascribed to a "pack rat" mentality (Butler, 2014, 95). The letters, photos, outlines, notes on writing, drawings, speeches, and manuscripts share space with the archives of Jack London's works.

Thanksgiving, November 2009

For the Los Angeles Regional Science Fiction Convention, West Indian-American fantasist David Anthony Durham expounded upon Octavia's essay "Why Is Science Fiction So White?"

May 26, 2010

The U.S. Navy's bald Octavia the Android, futuristic technology created by the Office of Naval Research, debuted on Pier 88 in New York City during Fleet Week. The hairless robot, named for the author, solves problems and enables human interactions.

June 26, 2010

At the Museum of Pop Culture in Seattle (MoPop), the Science Fiction and Fantasy Hall of Fame added Octavia to its winners. British-American guitarist Vernon Alphonsus Reid honored the author with the song "Mind of My Mind," which he described as the magic outcome of a single rehearsal.

2011

A doctoral candidate, Ayana A.H. Jamieson, a professor of ethnic studies at California State Polytechnic University Pomona, founded the Octavia E. Butler Legacy Network. The archive amasses research, legacy, and principles of the author's canon and features the racial and gender fluidity of characters.

August 2, 2011

The NPR Science Fiction and Fantasy Panel chose Octavia's *Kindred, The Parable of the Sower, Wild Seed,* and *Lilith's Brood* among the best in sci-fi reading.

March 21, 2012

At the International Conference of the Fantastic in the Arts, attendees focused on *Fledgling* and the dynamics of dominion and oppression. Conference papers compared protagonist Shori Matthews to Mary Shelley, author of *Frankenstein.*

May 17, 2012

Octavia won a posthumous Kate Wilhelm Solstice Award for her significance to fantasy and science fiction and influence on speculative fiction. At the Nebula Awards Weekend at the Hyatt Regency in Arlington, Virginia, her name appeared on the list alongside winners Carl Sagan and Joanna Russ.

October 2012

The author's cousin, Ernestine Walker, requested assistance from agent Merrilee Heifetz of Writers House in identifying pictures and letters in Octavia's family archives. The two collaborated with Sue Hodson and Natalie Russell, the literary curator and her assistant at the Huntington Library in San Marino, California. In the massive cataloging, Heifetz located the lost stories "Childfinder" and "A Necessary Being."

October 9, 2013

In a global overview of art, books, music, film, TV, and pop culture, *Flavorwire* online magazine listed Octavia's *Dawn* alongside *Dracula, The Amityville Horror,*

1984, The Haunting of Hill House, Lord of the Flies, and *The Handmaid's Tale* as one of the fifty scariest books of all time.

late 2013

At San Marino, the Huntington Library opened to scholars an archive of 8,000 items relating to Octavia's life and career.

April 30, 2014

The author's short fiction "Childfinder," a tale of the mentoring of Valerie, a clairvoyant ten-year-old interested in the history of Harriet Tubman, and "A Necessary Being," a novella about the arrival of a rare youth to *Survivor's* closed society, appeared in the anthology *Unexpected Stories.* In the Foreword, novelist Walter Moseley applauded Octavia for creating characters that "stay on after the reading is finished" and for fitting "untried territories with the challenges, the tragedies, the imperatives of being alive and of becoming more" (Butler, 2014, 2). Critic Nisi Shawl declared "A Necessary Being" a "yes story" and marveled at the writer's skill at "inescapable *rightness*" (*ibid.,* 7, 8). She viewed Octavia's canon as "alternatives to the awfulness we face every day" (*ibid.*).

January 7–18, 2015

The Public Theater's Under the Radar Festival in New York City featured an operatic adaptation of *The Parable of the Sower,* reprised on January 4–15, 2018.

October 9, 2015

Contents of Ann and Jeff VanderMeer's *Sisters of the Revolution: A Feminist Speculative Fiction Anthology* celebrated diversity with short works by Ursula Le Guin, Angela Carter, and Octavia Butler, a trio that *Kirkus Reviews* identified as sci-fi superstars. Octavia's "The Evening and the Morning and the Night" appeared alongside Carter's "The Fall River Axe Murders" and Ursula Le Guin's "Sur."

November 12, 2015

At Saratoga Springs, New York, the World Fantasy Convention ended a forty-year honorarium of bigoted author H.P. Lovecraft by replacing his image on the award trophy with Octavia's picture. The gesture recognized writers of color by including them in a formerly whites-only genre.

2016

A review by Quebec studies specialist Amy J. Ransom of *Strange Matings: Science Fiction, Feminism, African American Voices, and Octavia E. Butler* declared the author "the most frequently analyzed sf writer in single-author studies" (Ransom, 2016, 235).

February 27, 2016

Los Angeles's Clockshop, an arts nonprofit, reclaimed Octavia's legacy through film, webinars, taped interviews, readings, tours, and panel discussions of complex issues: human frailty, religious dogma, and ambiguous gender identity and roles. Fans lauded her focus on sexuality, values, power, and ethnic politics and their impact on the salvation of humankind from its inhuman impulses.

March 11–13, 2016

Fans at FogCon 6 at Walnut Creek, California, declared Octavia the "ghost of honor" for her influence on other authors, an asset to the theme "Transformations."

October 7, 2016–January 7, 2017

Radio Imagination, Octavia's description of her creative thoughts, began a three-month research effort in the Butler archives at the Huntington Library. The topics opened on her views of Los Angeles and activism and included friendships with artists, concepts of radical reproduction, and personal legacy.

January 10, 2017

The release of the graphic adaptation of Octavia's *Kindred* by publisher Harry N. Abrams introduced the perspectives of editor John Jennings and cartoonist Damian Duffy on a #1 *New York Times* bestseller. A wealth of positive reviews at the Third Annual Black Comic Arts Festival at the Schomburg Center for Research in Black Culture at the New York City public library on January 25 revived fan enthusiasm, especially among young adult readers.

April 8–August 7, 2017

The guided tour of a California exhibit, "Octavia Butler: Telling My Stories," at the Huntington Library in San Marino coordinated one hundred items—personal notes on disease, community sketches, greeting cards, email copies, and lists of character traits. An in-house conference on June 23 offered a though-provoking study of "Convergence of an Expanding Field."

May 4, 2017

The graphic version of *Kindred* won an ICA Reads citation from the Institute of Contemporary Art, Boston.

June 3–5, 2017

The Shaping Change: Remembering Octavia E. Butler Through Archives, Art, and Worldmaking Conference at the University of California, San Diego, gathered one hundred artists, educators, and activists. Under the aegis of the Arthur C. Clarke Center for Human Imagination, a diverse group studied the significance of her philosophy of future earth problems. Her work impacted black feminist and activist Adrienne Maree Brown's concept of emergent strategy, a source of social reorganization.

June 28–September 9, 2017

As advertised in *The Straits Times,* the Singapore International Festival of the Arts featured American singer-actor Toshi Reagon's folk opera *The Parable of the Sower,* a post-apocalyptic study of dystopia in America. The suite interspersed spirituals with folk, soul, and rock music.

November 9–11, 2017

In the United Arab Emirates, American dramatist Toshi Reagon presented her operatic adaptation of *The Parable of the Sower* at the Abu Dhabi Red Theater. A week later, the sold-out debut of folk musician and storyteller Reagon's opera at Memorial Hall on the campus of the University of North Carolina at Chapel Hill featured the music of Reagon's mother, folk scholar Bernice Johnson Reagon, as well as Millicent Johnnie's choreography and the instrumental backup of strings, piano, and percussion.

2018

NASA and the International Astronomical Union named a landmark on Charon, Pluto's largest moon, the Butler Mons (mountain).

February 23–25, 2018

In Atlanta, Spelman College coordinated an Octavia E. Butler Conference by combining sponsorship from the Butler Literary Society, Spelman College art museum, honors program, college arts program, and Mellon programs. Discussions included "Postcritical Butler," "Thinking Beyond the Box," "Remapping Octavia Butler," "Unassuming Heroines," and "Mother Knows Best."

March 5, 2018

At StokerCon in Providence, Rhode Island, cartoonist Damian Duffy and artist John Jennings's graphic adaptation of *Kindred* for Harry N. Abrams Books won the 2017 Bram Stoker Award for Superior Achievement in a Graphic Novel and the 2018

Eisner Comics Award for Best Adaptation from Another Medium. At a time when a half million copies of Octavia's novel existed in print, critics praised the compelling story, impact of the graphic version, and historical complexity three decades before the Civil War. The duo continued mining Octavia's fiction for the graphic novel *The Parable of the Sower,* issued in 2020.

June 22, 2018

Two days after the opera adaptation of *The Parable of the Sower* opened in Amsterdam at the Holland Festival, Google selected Octavia's seventy-first birthday for a daily doodle of an outer space illustration.

October 9, 2018

In a prospectus on the U.S. justice system for *Ms.* magazine, attorney Dena Robinson, a promoter of reproductive rights, hoped the Supreme Court members would quote Octavia's contention that change is unavoidable. Robinson concluded, "In order to progress as a society, we must accept the truth that we are constantly changing, which could even apply to the way the Constitution is read" (Robinson, 2018).

November 2, 2018

An in-depth multidisciplinary introduction to Octavia's canon, "Take Root Among the Stars: Visionary Fiction and the Legacy of Octavia Butler," opened at the School of the Art Institute of Chicago featuring Nigerian Afrofuturist sculptor Denenge Duyst-Akpem.

December 12, 2018–January 26, 2019

The LeRoy Nieman Center in Chicago mounted a library display of maps, art, and inventions from Octavia's *The Parable of the Sower* entitled "Take Root among the Stars: The Legacy of Octavia Butler, Surviving the 21st Century & Beyond."

March 2019

Pasadena City College established an Octavia E. Butler scholarship for students seeking a four-year degree.

March 27, 2019

Amazon Prime began developing a TV series based on Octavia's speculative fiction about psionics or telepathy. Actor Viola Davis developed *Wild Seed* for Amazon Prime written by Nigerian Nnedi Okorafor and produced by Kenyan film director Wanuri Kahiu, an Afrofuturist narrative that empowers an undefined reality. According to Elizabeth Wellington, a journalist for the *Philadelphia Enquirer,*

Afrofuturism honors the past with black performers relating limitless black songs, crafts, and stories of the African diaspora. The author enlarged on the mass abduction of many peoples from Africa. Also in the works are FX/Hulu's streaming version of *Kindred* and director Ava DuVernay and actor Victoria Mahoney's TV version of *Dawn*, which sells 100,000 copies annually.

April 26, 2019

For a media adaptation, folk-gospel-rock creator Toshi Reagon and composer Bernice Johnson Reagon of Sweet Honey in the Rock turned *The Parable of the Sower* and *The Parable of the Talents* into musical theater. The project began in 1997 with a semester course at Princeton for Toni Morrison and a 2008 workshop for New York City Opera. The operatic version opened at the O'Shaughnessy in St. Paul, Minnesota, with Eric Ting directing.

May 30, 2019

Cartoonist Damian Duffy and artist John Jennings's graphic adaptation of *Kindred* in the Spanish edition *Parentesco* for Anaya Multimedia in Madrid found welcome in thirty global libraries. Visual contrasts between California and Maryland depicted "esclavos antes de la guerra de Secesión" (slaves before the Civil War) (Butler, 2019).

June 2019

To assist entrepreneurs and inventors with their creations, the Los Angeles Public Library offered photo preservation, 3-D printers, laser cutter, recording equipment, Adobe Cloud, MakerBot, Silhouette, SewArt, embroidery and serging machines, Green screen, CNC mill, and a do-it-yourself audiovisual studio in the 3,000 square foot Octavia Lab.

August 27, 2019

According to the Minor Planet Center, asteroid 7052, measuring 9.082 kilometers (5.644 miles) in diameter, received a renaming, Octaviabutler.

September 12, 2019

The French version of *Kindred* from Presque Lune, *Liens de Sang,* translated by Ariane Bataille, reached fans. The prologue opened on the hospitalization of Dana Franklin as she revealed how she "m'a coûté un bras" (cut my arm) (Butler, 2019, 5).

October 29, 2019

The boxed set of Parable novels from Seven Stories Press contained prefaces by activist Gloria Steinem and composer Toshi Reagon, the adapter of Octavia's series for stage musical.

December 14, 2019

The *Wall Street Journal* listed *The Parable of the Sower* among the year's twelve best books. An eerie parallel of the times, the novel blames racism, greed, and ignorance in Robledo, California, for setting teen reformer Lauren Oya Olamina on a crusade for a realistic faith.

January 2020

At UCLA, a program on "Octavia E. Butler's Parables: A Music Talk with Toshi Reagon" increased awareness of an adaptation of the Parable series to music. In the same month, artists John Jennings and Damian Duffy issued a graphic adaptation of *The Parable of the Sower,* the second of their editions based on cartooning.

February 8, 2020

USA Today suggested celebrating black history month with ten titles, one of them *The Parable of the Sower.* In Octavia's imaginative writing, reviewer Barbara VanDenburgh found elements of Margaret Atwood's *The Handmaid's Tale* and the supernatural in the 2010–2022 TV series *The Walking Dead.*

February 17, 2020

In celebration of a 125th anniversary, the New York Public Library listed 125 works that staff and readers loved. Among them, staff chose Octavia's *The Parable of the Sower.*

March 2020

John Jennings and Damian Duffy teamed with UCLA's president's series to discuss the graphic adaptation of *The Parable of the Sower.* At the suggestion of the Black Caucus of the American Library Association, the version appeared on Black Lives Matter Reading Lists.

May 2020

In early May at the Chicago Museum of Contemporary Art, Nicole Mitchel and the Black Earth Ensemble, a nine-member instrumental group, performed "Xenogenesis II: Intergalactic Beings," an homage to Octavia.

June 25, 2020

The University of California at Riverside featured John Jennings in a discussion of black speculative fiction in his graphic adaptation of *The Parable of the Sower.* Joining the colloquy, Nalo Hopkinson, author of the version's introduction, stressed the African focus on fantasy derived from folklore. Jennings envisioned comforting and motivating people through Afrofuturist art and dream symbolism that reflects reality.

August 9, 2020

Streaming versions in process from Amazon include *Dawn,* written by Ava Duvernay and directed by Victoria Mahoney, and *Wild Seed,* the Patternmaster classic co-authored for Viola Davis's JuVee productions by Nnedi Okorafor and Wanuri Kahiu. Fans of Octavia's fiction anticipated additional television adaptations of *The Parable of the Sower* and *Kindred,* directed by Janicza Bravo and written by Branden Jacob-Jenkins. Critic Rich Knight of *CinemaBlend* proposed actors Lupita Nyong'o and Clarke Peters in the parts of Lauren Oya Olamina and her lover Taylor Bankole, Kerry Washington as companion Zahra Moss, and Chiwetel Umeadi Ejiofor as the Reverend Olamina.

August 26, 2020

For its centennial promotion of the arts, the Huntington Library offered a twelve-month fellowship to study Octavia's works, which form required readings in four hundred college courses in twelve translations. The grant supports a scholar delving into her literary archive and personal reflections on the disenfranchised.

September 3, 2020

Fourteen years after Octavia's death, *The Parable of the Sower* scored #14 on the *New York Times* bestseller list and #13 on the NYT Paperback list for anticipating a collective destiny for earthlings. The triumphs continued in December with a #4 rating on Amazon's Black Fiction list and a #4 and #14 on the African American Science Fiction list for *Dawn* and *The Parable of the Sower.*

November 2020

In a live-streaming discussion, critic Lynell George surveyed Octavia's canon in a retrospect, *A Handful of Earth, a Handful of Sky: The World of Octavia E. Butler.*

December 29, 2020

The Minneapolis *World* named the two-hour opera *The Parable of the Sower,* starring Shayna Small as Lauren, as a source of comfort during the troubling Covid pandemic. The song "Looked in the Mirror" featured strings and percussion. The unidentified essayist claimed that, "Despite all the post–American madness depicted in the book, the protagonist still manages to embody hope and plant seeds for a divine future" ("Pop," 2020).

2021

The National Women's Hall of Fame in Seneca Falls, New York, inducted Octavia into membership in the same year that the Library of America issued a volume of her speculative fiction. Literary critic Emanuella Grinberg classified the omnibus edition for CNN as an esthetic mix of sci-fi, fantasy, and horror. In a reflection on the author's purpose, Stephen Kearse, a book writer for the *New York Times Book Review,* commended her career for "turning speculative fiction into a home for Black expression" (Kearse, 2021, 12). The chief takeaways of her "controlled and precise" scenarios, he explains, are "always insights, always futures" (*ibid.*). The graphic adaptation of *Kindred* won a Winter Read selection from the Community Library in Ketchum, Idaho, for its fresh form and careful visual abstracts.

February 17–20, 2021

A Boston *Globe* art season winner, the congregational opera *The Parable of the Sower* featured 30 black anthems from two centuries of American music. On March 19, Shanta Thake, a director of New York's Public Theater, acclaimed American songwriter Toshi Reagon's theatrical musical for promoting unity during changing times.

March 5, 2021

On Mars's 750-mile Isidis Planitia (Plain of Isis) region, fifteen years after the author's death, the Perseverance project team named the Jezero crater the Octavia E. Butler Landing. The naming acknowledges her childhood near the NASA Jet Propulsion Laboratory (JPL) at 4800 Oak Grove Drive, La Cañada, Flintridge, California. Scientists and engineers esteemed her for seeking a bold, just future for humankind and for creating resolute, inventive characters suited to a planet rover named Perseverance.

July 6, 2021

Through Harry N. Abrams publishing, 2018 Eisner-winning editor John Jennings, a media specialist at the University of California at Riverside, and artist Damian Duffy, holder of a Ph.D. in library science from the University of Illinois at Urbana-Champaign, issued the graphic speculative fiction novel *The Parable of the Sower.* Critics found the moral and environmental themes relevant to the corruption and bleakness of the Donald Trump presidency.

July 26, 2021

A24 Films bought rights to *The Parable of the Sower,* which 2020 Sundance festival winner Garrett Bradley will direct into a feature cinema. Produced by Paul Mezey, the adaptation contributes to an Octavia Butler renaissance.

July 29, 2021

For the drama series *Lovecraft Country,* HBO Max began adapting *Fledgling* for a ten-part streaming series written by Issa Rae and J.J. Abrams and produced for WarnerMedia by Jonathan I. Kidd and Sonya Winton-Odamtten.

August 16, 2021

In a selection of "best books about the post-human earth" by the London *Guardian,* the election of *The Parable of the Sower* posed cli-fi (climate fiction) as a subgenre of speculative fiction based on environmental anxieties.

September 16, 2021

To increase curriculum diversity, British students studying English literature received a new reading list of fiction. For visionary sci-fi, *The Parable of the Sower* contributed to book choices about social inequality, capitalist greed, and eco-crisis.

Sources

Afful, Adwoa. "Wild Seed: Africa and Its Many Diasporas," *Critical Arts* 30:4 (August 2016): 93–104

Alessio, Carolyn. "Review: The Parable of the Talents," *Chicago Tribune* (20 December 1998): F3.

_____. "Talking with Octavia E. Butler," *Philadelphia Inquirer* (10 January 1999): Q2.

Allen, Marlene D. "Octavia Butler's 'Parable' Novels and the 'Boomerang' of African American History," *Callaloo* 32:4 (Winter, 2009): 1353–1365.

Allison, Dorothy. "The Future of Female," *Village Voice* (19 December 1989): 67–68.

"Alternative Universe," *Los Angeles Times* (18 October 1985).

Baudou, Jacques. "Octavia Butler," *Le Monde* (2 March 2006): 29.

Beal, Frances. "Interview," *Black Scholar* 17:2 (March/April 1986): 14–18.

Bogstad, Janice. "Interview," 14:4 *Janus* (Winter, 1978–1979): 28–32.

Boyd, Valerie. "Gauging the Price of Being Human," *Atlanta Journal-Constitution* (5 November 1995): L8.

Brown, Adrienne Maree. *Emergent Strategy: Shaping Change, Changing Worlds.* Chico, CA: AK Press, 2017.

Brown, Jayna. *Black Utopias: Speculative Life and the Music of Other Worlds.* Durham, NC: Duke University Press, 2021.

Butler, Octavia. "Black Feminism: Searching the Past," (review) *Washington Post* (17 October 1983): B2.

_____. *Bloodchild and Other Stories.* New York: Seven Stories Press, 2005.

_____. "The Book of Martha," *Bloodchild and Other Stories.* New York: Seven Stories Press, 2005, 189–214.

_____. "Brave New Worlds: A Few Rules for Predicting the Future," *Essence* 31:1 (1 May 2000): 164–166, 264.

_____. "Devil Girl from Mars: Why I Write Science Fiction," *Media in Transition,* MIT (19 February 1998).

_____. *Fledgling.* New York: Seven Stories Press, 2005.

_____. "Free Libraries: Are They Becoming Extinct?," *Omni* 15:10 (August 1993): 4.

_____. "Future Forum," *Starlog/Future Life* 22 (November 1980): 55–56.

_____. "How I Built Novels Out of Writer's Blocks," *Writer's Digest* (June 1999): 12–15.

_____. *Imago* in *Lilith's Brood.* New York: Warner, 2000, 518–746.

_____. *Kindred.* New York: Doubleday, 1979.

_____. *Kindred* (graphic novel), adapted by Damian Duffy and John Jennings. New York: Abrams Comicarts, 2017.

_____. *Liens de Sang* (graphic novel). Melesse, France: Presque Lune, 2019.

_____. *Parentesco* (graphic novel). Madrid: Anaya Multimedia, 2019.

_____. *Mind of My Mind.* New York: Doubleday, 1977.

_____. "The Monophobic Response," *Dark Matter: A Century of Speculative Fiction from the African Diaspora.* New York: Aspect/Warner Books, 2000, 415–416.

_____. "Near of Kin," *Bloodchild and Other Stories.* New York: Seven Stories Press, 2005, 73–85.

_____. *The Parable of the Sower.* New York: Four Walls, Eight Windows, 1993.

_____. "Persistence," *Locus* 44:6 (June 2000): 6.

_____. "Positive Obsession," *Bloodchild and Other Stories.* New York: Seven Stories Press, 2005, 123–136.

_____. "Science Fiction Writer Octavia Butler on Race, Global Warming and Religion," (video) *Democracy Now*, November 11, 2005.

_____. *Unexpected Stories*. New York: Open Road Media, 2014.

_____. "A World without Racism," NPR Weekend Edition (1 September 2001).

Canavan, Gerry. *Octavia E. Butler*. Urbana: University of Illinois, 2016.

_____. "Recovering Octavia E. Butler's Lost Parables," Los Angeles Review of Books (9 June 2014).

_____. "Science Fiction and Utopia in the Anthropocene," American Literature 93:2 (2021): 255–282.

Carr, Elston. "Jump-Start the Time Machine," *LA Weekly* (19 March 1992): 36–37.

Cellini, Lisa A. "Invasion of the Writers," *Lansing State Journal* (13 July 1989): C1.

Crisp, Marty. "Interview," (Lancaster, PA) *Sunday News* (11 February 1996): H3.

Devney, Bob. "Orbita Dicta," *The Devniad Book 82B*, www.devniad.com (July 2002).

Doerksen, Teri Ann. "Octavia E. Butler: Parables of Race and Difference" in *Into Darkness Peering*. Westport CT: Greenwood, 1997, 21–34.

Due, Tananarive. "Interview," *Essence* 50:4 (4 October 2019): 72–75.

Flyn, Cal. "The Best Books about the Post-Human Earth," the London *Guardian* (16 August 2021): 26.

Fowler, Karen Joy. "Remembering Octavia Butler," *Salon* (17 March 2006), www.salon.com/2006/03/17/butler_3/.

Fox, Margalit. "Obituary," *New York Times* (3 March 2006): C16.

Friedman, Gabriella. "Unsentimental Historicizing: The Neo-Slave Narrative Tradition and the Refusal of Feeling," *American Literature* 93:1 (2021): 115–143.

Fry, Joan. "Interview," *Poets & Writers* (March/April 1997): 58–69.

George, Lynell. "Black Writers Crossing the Final Frontier," *Los Angeles Times* (22 June 2004).

_____. *A Handful of Earth, a Handful of Sky*. Los Angeles, CA: Angel City Press, 2020.

Govan, Sandra Y. "Interview," *Obsidian III* 6:2/7:1 (2005–2006): 14–39.

Grinberg, Emanuella. "Celebrating Octavia Butler: A Visionary among Futurists," *CNN* (10 March 2016).

Ha, Vi. "On Persistence: Octavia E. Butler & Central Library," www.lapl.org/collections-resources/blogs/lapl/persistence-octavia-e-butler-central-library, 11 June 2019.

Hampton, Gregory Jerome. *Changing Bodies in the Fiction of Octavia Butler: Slaves, Aliens, and Vampires*. Lanham, MD: Lexington Books, 2014.

Harper, Steven. "Interview," curiousfictions.com/stories/2159-steven-harper-an-interview-with-octavia-e-butler, 27 May 2019.

Holden, Rebecca J., and Nisi Shawl, eds. *Strange Matings: Science Fiction, Feminism, African American Voices, and Octavia E. Butler*. Seattle, WA: Aqueduct, 2013.

Howard, Mimi. "New Sun: A Feminist Literary Festival," the London *Art Monthly* 445 (April 2021): 37.

Kaplan-Levenson, Laine. "Sci-Fi Writer Octavia Butler Offered Warnings and Hope in Her Work," *Morning Edition*. Washington, DC: NPR (24 February 2021).

Kearse, Stephen. "The Essential Octavia Butler," *New York Times* (15 January 2021): 12–13.

Kelly, Deirdre. "The Brave New World of Female Science Fiction," (Toronto) *Globe and Mail* (25 February 2013): A17.

Littleton, Therese. "'Black to the Future': Fest Is Mothership for African Americans in Science Fiction," *Seattle Times* (6 June 2004): K1.

Mabe, Chauncey. "Sci-fi Pioneer Took the Road Less Traveled," (Fort Lauderdale) *South Florida Sun Sentinel* (28 February 1999): D1, D5.

Magadanz, Stacy. "The Captivity Narrative in Octavia E. Butler's *Adulthood Rites*," *Extrapolation* 53:1 (2012): 47–59.

McCaffery, Larry, ed. *Across the Wounded Galaxies*. Urbana: University of Illinois Press, 1990.

McHenry, Susan. "Botherworldly Vision: Octavia Butler," *Essence* 29:10 (February 1999): 80.

Mehaffy, Marilyn, and AnaLouise Keating. "Radio Imagination: Octavia Butler on the Poetics of Narrative Embodiment," *MELUS* 26:1 (2001): 45–76.

Mixon, Veronica. "Future Woman: Octavia Butler," *Essence* 9 (April 1979): 12, 15.

"Octavia E. Butler at African American Museum Tonight," *Los Angeles Sentinel* (24 March 1999): A9.

Palwick, Susan. "Interview," *ISLE* 6:2 (Summer, 1999): 149–158.

Park, Ed. "Parable of the Butler," *Harper's Magazine* 342: 2049 (February 2021): 93–97.

Parker, Kendra R. *Gale Researcher Guide: Octavia Butler and Afrofuturism*. Boston: Cengage Learning, 2018.

Pirani, Fiza. "Who Is Octavia Butler?," *Atlanta Journal-Constitution* (22 June 2018).

"The Pop Culture That Got Us Through 2020," Minneapolis *World* (radio) (29 December 2020).

Potts, Stephen W. "We Keep Playing the Same Record," *Science Fiction Studies* 23:3 (1996): 331–338.

Ransom, Amy J. "Octavia's Legacy," *Extrapolation* 57:1/2 (2016): 235–239.

"Review: *Dawn*," *Fantasy Book Reviews*, www.fantasybookreview.co.uk/Octavia-Butler/Dawn.html.

Robinson, Dena. "Imagining a More Just Supreme Court," *Ms.* (9 October 2018).

Rowell, Charles H. "Interview," *Callaloo* 20:1 (1997): 47–66.

Sanders, Joshunda. "Interview," *Motion Magazine* (14 March 2004).

"Science Fiction Author Will Speak at College," *Los Angeles Times* (3 October 2002): B2.

"Science Fiction Writer Octavia E. Butler to Be Honored at Leimert Park Village Book Fair," *Los Angeles Sentinel* (15 May 2008): A8.

Smith, Alex. "Novelist 'Did a Great Job' Seeing Our Future," Minneapolis *Star Tribune* (25 April 2019): E1, E3.

Smith, Shirlee. "Octavia Butler: Writing Is Finding Out That You Can," *Pasadena Star-News* (13 February 1994): A14.

Spector, Nicole Audrey. "John Jennings and Damian Duffy Are Disturbing the Peace," *Publishers Weekly* (1 November 2019).

Stamberg, Susan. "Interview," *NPR Weekend Edition* (29 December 2001).

Stewart, Jocelyn Y. "Obituary," *Los Angeles Times* (28 February 2006): B10.

Tatum, Beverly Daniel. "Octavia E. Butler Celebration of Arts and Activism," www.youtube.com/watch?v=Xo96kTkAWyw, 29 May 2014.

Taylor-Guthrie, Danille. "Writing Because She Must," *Chicago Tribune* (31 March 1996): 5.

Troy, Maria Holmgren. "Negotiating Genre and Captivity: Octavia Butler's *Survivor*," *Callaloo* 33:4 (Fall, 2010): 1116–1131.

Warner, John. "Worried about Climate Change?: 2 Octavia Butler Books Written in the 1990s Seem Prescient Today," *Chicago Tribune* (21 October 2018): 10.

Weeks, Linton, and John Schwartz. "The Past Is Back as the Future Is Present," *Vancouver Sun* (23 May 2000): A9.

Wellington, Elizabeth. "A Mix of History, Magic," *Philadelphia Inquirer* (26 February 2020): C1-C2.

West, Amy. "Our Guests of Honor," *Readercon 14* (12–13 July 2002): 1–8.

Williams, Sherley Anne. "On Octavia E. Butler," *Ms.* 14:9 (March 1986): 70–73.

Yancy, George. "Black Woman Pioneers Science Fiction Writing," *Philadelphia Tribune* (16 January 1996): E13.

Yerman, Forrest Gray. "Finding the Superhero in Damian Duffy's and John Jennings Graphic Novel Adaptation of Octavia Butler's *Kindred*," *The Bloomsbury Handbook to Octavia E. Butler*. London: Bloomsbury, 2020, 259–273.

Young, Earni. "Return of Kindred Spirits," *Black Issues Book Review* 6:1 (January–February 2004): 30–33.

Butler Genealogy

A family tree endowed with strong female forebears, Octavia's lineage pre-figures the wonder women who populate her books and stories. Most significant, Estella Guy, the author's maternal grandmother, instilled values and beliefs that anchored the author's canon.

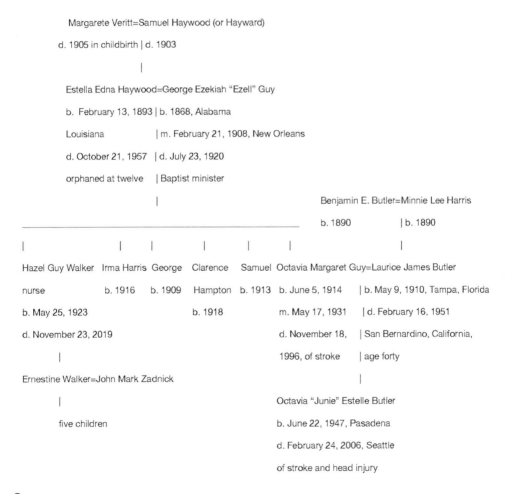

Margarete Veritt=Samuel Haywood (or Hayward)

d. 1905 in childbirth | d. 1903

          |

Estella Edna Haywood=George Ezekiah "Ezell" Guy

b. February 13, 1893 | b. 1868, Alabama

Louisiana | m. February 21, 1908, New Orleans

d. October 21, 1957 | d. July 23, 1920

orphaned at twelve | Baptist minister

          |

                                                   Benjamin E. Butler=Minnie Lee Harris

                                             b. 1890 | b. 1890

Hazel Guy Walker	Irma Harris	George	Clarence	Samuel	Octavia Margaret Guy=Laurice James Butler	
nurse	b. 1916	b. 1909	Hampton	b. 1913	b. June 5, 1914	b. May 9, 1910, Tampa, Florida
b. May 25, 1923			b. 1918		m. May 17, 1931	d. February 16, 1951
d. November 23, 2019					d. November 18,	San Bernardino, California,
					1996, of stroke	age forty
|					|	
Ernestine Walker=John Mark Zadnick					Octavia "Junie" Estelle Butler	
|					b. June 22, 1947, Pasadena	
five children					d. February 24, 2006, Seattle	
					of stroke and head injury	

Source

"Octavia Butler Genealogy," www.wikitree.com/wiki/Guy-1059.

The Companion

Adaptation

According to the advice of evangelist Laurel Oya Olamina's verse, Octavia viewed adjusting and evolving as the paramount antidotes to threat and tragedy, an underlying theme in *The Parable of the Talents, Adulthood Rites,* and *Imago.* Dorothy Allison, essayist for *Village Voice,* characterized the author's dystopias as "[addressing] the issues of survival and adaptation, in which resistance, defeat, and compromise are the vital elements" (Allison, 1989, 67). The lack of an heir motivates the female Hao Tahneh in "A Necessary Being" to suppress the urge to command and achieve detente with the male Hao Diut, a visiting outlander and rival for power. Likewise, flexibility is advantageous to the five active telepaths in *Mind of My Mind* whom Patternmaster Mary Larkin directs, but repugnant to human survivors in *Dawn,* who revile Lilith Iyapo's rapprochement with the alien Oankali. The author pictures both models of leadership as challenging, but essential to earth's revival and longevity.

As an example of tractability, Octavia cites Tate Marah, the first sleeper whom the pragmatic Lilith awakens from artificial hibernation to introduce to alien life. Continuing to enliven comatose women, Tate and Lilith initially appear capable of introducing human captives to a spaceship/planet before the survivors migrate to a renewed planet earth. Odious to conservative prisoners, the idea of coupling with extraterrestrials to produce a viable hybrid outrages human notions of propriety, the prime concern of *Adulthood Rites.* The author speculates that adaptability rewards beings like Lilith and her mutant son Akin, who harbor less prejudice toward gender and racial differences. The adapters are more likely to ease settlers' dissension on earth.

Octavia's Xenogenesis series implies that a more amenable human population might have saved itself from near extermination by fractious relationships and the mishandling of radioactive weapons. In the last nuclear family in *Clay's Ark,* the dispersal of an alien microorganism "changed, adapted, and chemically encouraged its host to adapt" (Butler, 1984, 47). Contagion requires extreme modifications of community, beginning with casual encounters and including the siring of a generation of feline offspring. To heighten the danger of desert survival amid a pandemic, the author turns adjustment into situational irony by selecting a dying sixteen-year-old as the lodestar of courage and spunk. Because the space bug rids Keira "Kelly"

Maslin of leukemia, she endures as a prospective mother despite knowing that her fetus is more nonhuman than human. In addition to accommodating an unforeseen loss of normal traits, she turns her biracial DNA into the basis of feline Clayarks, the author's term for a new post-epidemic race. Key to her proposal of hybridity lie basic Darwinian principles of evolution and survival of the fittest that the English naturalist recorded in 1859 in *On the Origin of Species.*

Early Modifications

A survey of the author's growth as an advocate of adaptation began with "Crossover," her first short story. She introduced the doom of the intractable Jane, the protagonist, beset by low self-worth, loneliness, and alcoholism, a trio of adversaries that swamp her. In contrast to her capitulation to squalor and escapism, a second 1971 story, "Childfinder," spotlighted the innovator Barbara's optimism in a hostile environment. While a coterie of "psychic brawlers" stalks and menaces a child recovery scheme, she maintains efforts at a long shot—supplying the future with black psionic citizens (Butler, 2014, 79). Success requires early detection of clairvoyance in children and rescue from Eve's nefarious organization. In comparison with "Crossover," "Childfinder" embraces adaptation to a harsh reality and the diversionary tactics that protect vulnerable black telepaths like Valerie and Jordan from stalkers and that encourage them to thrive in a menacing milieu.

In a survey of the author's life and works, literary specialist Gerry Canavan, an English professor at Marquette University in Milwaukee, elevated adaptation to an "animating and vitalizing endeavor [that] would drive our growth as a species and prevent us from exploiting, raping, killing, and otherwise immiserating each other" (Canavan, 2021, 6). On the basis of colonial pliancy rested the future of extraplanetary settlers fleeing vexing challenges, such as the distant Destiny of Earthseed among the stars in *The Parable of the Talents.* For the agrarian Tehkohn pilgrimage to the north in *Survivor* to escape Garkohn enemies, the protagonist, Alanna Verrick, feels her human habits giving way to tribal work ethics. Simultaneously, Garkohn hunters experiment with her bow and arrow, a weaponry new to men who prefer throttling animals with their hands. Canavan lauded the fictional struggle to abandon earth and mold a distant ecosystem to human need, a new society free of ethnic hierarchy and injustices to marginal groups—women, minorities, homosexuals, and the poor. He prophesied that the task, like a *Star Trek* future, would "spur humanity's growth as a species" and circumvent extremes prefacing extinction (Canavan, 2021, 265).

Patterns of Survival

In 1980, Octavia's Patternist series dramatized in An-yanwu, an immortal Nigerian bisexual, the amenability of Isaac's wife in Wheatley, New York, and a lesbian husband to Denice at an edenic Louisiana plantation in Avoyelles Parish, a home of First Peoples at the confluence of the Red River with the Atchafalaya. Unfamiliar with New World customs, dress, religion, and diet, she begins on day one learning

American ways and menus and reading the bible. Under control of the autocratic manipulator Doro, she agrees to a human marriage and accommodates Isaac, a mortal husband, by adjusting her appearance to normal aging. At a height of vigor, An-yanwu and Isaac fly together, a skill that brings them mutual joy. To keep him hale in his seventies from atherosclerosis caused by too much rich food, she cautions him about overwork, the kind of wifely alert delivered with love and a bit of concern. The text depicts a daring extreme—her creation of blood plaque-dissolving medicine that nearly kills her, a venture to the rim of extinction on his behalf.

For the dominant figure in the Xenogenesis series, accommodating future change sparks the will to survive. Through compromise, Lilith Iyapo, the healer and revitalizing Eve figure in *Dawn*, elects to persevere at all costs as an example to her son Jodahs, a maturing ooloi in *Imago*. For him, learning to heal requires trial and error. To comfort the neophyte, Nikanj promises that the beginner is normal: "You just need time to find out more about yourself" (Butler, 2000, 571). His wisdom, like that of Iosif Petrescu in *Fledgling*, captures the core of coming of age, a time of transformation from child to adult.

BUILDING ACORN

The same adjustment to growth infuses thirteen-year-old Keith Olamina and his sister, fifteen-year-old Lauren Oya Olamina, the protagonist of the Parable series. Keith creates a secure niche for himself among illiterate thugs because he can read and write, skills unavailable to the street poor. With disdain for his elders, he rationalizes killing an aged migrant for cash and firearms. By recasting adjustment to Keith's anarchy as a religious belief in change, Lauren draws refugees from Robledo's chaos to join a trek north to Cape Mendocino in northwestern California. The key to assimilation of strangers, acceptance of differences motivates the teenage leader to welcome Hispanic, Caucasian, and Asian pilgrims along with a single parent father and his daughter, prostitute sisters, and a black physician, who becomes her lover. Although the wanderers find evidence of carnage and arson, they build the barren land into a commune called Acorn. Like Geoffrey Chaucer's journeyers to Canterbury, the group escalates a spirit of *e pluribus unum* (one from many).

For the second volume, *The Parable of the Talents,* evangelist Lauren Oya Olamina recognizes a cycle of change in Earthseed as followers accept the inevitable need to collaborate: "Our new worlds will remake us as we remake them" (Butler, 1998, 321). In 1993, the author stocked the allegory with a final word on transformation strategies:

> All successful life is
> Adaptable …
> Understand this.
> Use it [Butler, 1993, 124–125].

Lauren's party acclimates to a nighttime threat—armed raiders. With survival in the balance, her pilgrims alternate sentry duty and share the use of a pistol. Hardening to apocalypse requires experience with firearms, night patrols, and the willingness to shoot roaming thugs or wild dogs. Lauren's habituation to the Acorn enclave begins with her seed stock and the planting of edibles and trees along with the burial of unidentified bones, representatives of each refugee's past losses. The multi-racial prodigals form new families composed of reclaimed orphans and the rejects from agro-business. By settling on the ashes of a burned residence, inhabitants reaffirm the Egyptian of the *bennu*, a solar bird, or the Mycenaean φοῖνιξ *(pho-inīx)*, the eighth-century BCE Greek poet Hesiod's trope of regeneration via extreme refitting of mortals.

AUTHORING CHANGE

Octavia, in the analysis of Meredith Minister, on staff at Shenandoah University in Winchester, Virginia, "reaches into the past through the use of overt and covert biblical and theological references" (Minister, 2020, 285). Her depiction of Lauren's selflessness draws on the Suffering Servant of Isaiah 53:10–12, the messianic bearer of earth's transgressions. For the short story "Amnesty," translator Noah Cannon copes from age eleven among alien invaders and hostile earthlings. She willingly accepts responsibility for understanding and salvation: "I want to vote for peace between your people and mine by telling the truth" (Butler, 2005, 155). British theologian Margaret Daphne Hampson, a professor at the University of St. Andrews, Scotland, rebuked Noah's accusers for disregarding the integrity and worth of aliens as "contrary to what I could count a true spirituality" (Hampson, 2012, 259). Because of Noah's pragmatism and pliability, she dedicates her translation of a nonhuman language to training other language specialists. Together, they upgrade communication between races, a source of mutual accord among humans and hybrid species.

In a 2003 review of women's experiences compiled in *Voices from the Gap*, the author placed herself in Lauren and Noah's position as adapters:

> Every story I write adds to me a little, changes me a little, forces me to re-examine an attitude or belief, causes me to research and learn, helps me to understand people and grow.... Every story I create creates me. I write to create myself [Butler, 2003].

Self-effacement reveals in Octavia the will of the autodidact to incorporate wisdom and compassion in the self, both as individual and writer.

See also Coming of Age; Couples; Earthseed.

Sources

Allison, Dorothy. "The Future of Female," *Village Voice* (19 December 1989): 67–68.
Brown, Jayna. *Black Utopias: Speculative Life and the Music of Other Worlds.* Durham, NC: Duke University Press, 2021.
Butler, Octavia. "Amnesty" in *Bloodchild and Other Stories.* New York: Seven Stories Press, 2005, 147–186.
———. "Childfinder," *Unexpected Stories.* New York: Open Road Media, 2014.
———. *Clay's Ark.* New York: St. Martin's Press, 1984.
———. *Imago* in *Lilith's Brood.* New York: Warner, 2000, 518–746.
———. *The Parable of the Sower.* New York: Four Walls, Eight Windows, 1993.
———. *The Parable of the Talents.* New York: Seven Stories Press, 1998.
———. *Survivor.* New York: Doubleday, 1978.
Canavan, Gerry. *Octavia E. Butler.* Urbana: University of Illinois, 2016.
———. "Science Fiction and Utopia in the Anthropocene," *American Literature* 93:2 (2021): 255–282.
Hampson, Daphne. *After Christianity.* London: SCM Press, 2012.

Minister, Meredith. "How to Live at the End of the World" in *Who Knows What We'd Make of It, If We Ever Got Our Hands on It?* Piscataway, NJ: Gorgias Press, 2020, 285–306.
"Octavia Butler," *Voices from the Gap*, http://voices.cal.umn.edu/ (23 April 2003).

Adulthood Rites

Octavia extended the captivity plot of *Dawn* in 1988 with *Adulthood Rites,* a bi-species tale of alien-controlled reproduction and resistance to change by the hybrid Akin. He bears the Yoruban name for "hero," a glimpse at his salvific destiny. For ideas, she read references on invertebrates, revolving creatures that writhe or roll rather than walk, a description that fits the creeping maggots she viewed in the Peruvian Andes in 1976 and of the Tlics in "Bloodchild." With a similar significance to the title *Kindred,* the protagonist Akin Iyapo Shing Kaalnikanjlo bears a reminder of his parentage by two species, human and Oankali, a triadic reproduction that Australian philosopher Val Plumwood labels "posthuman" (Plumwood, 1993, 20). The name also implies the menace of the Turkish word for "raid," a reference to the implanting of a child in Lilith Iyapo with sperm from Joe, her deceased mate, under secret facilitation by Nikanj, the un-gendered ooloi gene mixer. The decision to inseminate Lilith establishes alien dominance over future ethnicity in acts resembling rape.

Lilith and Joe's son Akin delights in his gift for sampling a jungle milieu. The pre-birth stimuli that influence him express the author's interest in fetal sense impressions that begin with physical contact and sight, an orderly coming-to-knowledge assessed in British anthropologist Ashley Montagu's classic text *Touching: The Human Significance of the Skin.* Curious from the first "body to body understanding," the infant ponders sound while his mother appraises his human traits, which outweigh his alien characteristics (Butler, "Adulthood," 2000, 255). In the future lies his destiny as a "solitary wanderer," a seclusion haunted by mother hunger for Lilith (*ibid.,* 160).

Joiners and Resisters

In the forest at the compound of Lo, the author capitalizes on contrast between Lilith, the earth mother, and resister Augustino "Tino" Leal, a human hold-out from Phoenix village armed with bow and arrow. He launches a flurry of questions about earth's reclamation from nuclear ruin. Duke University professor Marianna Torgovnick characterized the earthy elements scrounged from a recycling pit as "the sign and symbol of desires the West has sought to repress," in particular, gun and ammo manufacture (Torgovnick, 1998, 80). Through casual conversation, Octavia indicates a complex network of answers to earth's propensity for violence: "There's no magic bullet. Instead there are thousands of answers—at least. You can be one of them if you choose to be" (Butler, "Brave," 2000, 164). Appropriately, the surname "Leal" (loyal) recurs in *The Parable of the Sower* with the martyrdom of astronaut Alicia Catalina Godinez Leal, a name vibrant with the nobility and patriotism of explorers of the unknown.

Through Lilith's enlightenment of Tino, Octavia expounds on the barbaric nature of hybridization between earthlings and the Oankali and adds an inducement to doubters that all mixed breed children have some human traits. With verbal uplift, she emphasizes reciprocal benefits: "They change us and we change them" (Butler, "Adulthood," *ibid.*, 282). In Tino's close-minded opinion, miscegenation destroys purity: mixed beings form a "menagerie," his reduction of hybrids to beasts (*ibid.*, 285). The narrative defies Tino's abasement of Akin by situating Lilith in an archetypal maternal pose of the *virgo lactans*, the Virgin Mary breast-feeding the Child Jesus pioneered by European painters Joos van Cleve, Orazio Gentileschi, Leonardo da Vinci, Raphael, and El Greco. Nourished on hope, Akin later suggests the unlikelihood that humankind will override the penchant for hierarchy: "Perhaps this time their intelligence will stop them from destroying themselves" (*ibid.*, 470). The initial "perhaps" weakens Octavia's proposition that humankind is amenable to self-revision.

The author places the reader in context through unfamiliar concepts that bombard Tino. Central to human schooling lies the Oankali model of a thatch-roofed house grown from living plants similar in vigor and malleability to the verdant spaceship/planet they departed on return to earth. Antagonist Wray Ordway, bearing a Scandinavian name meaning "cornered spear-wielder," disputes the loss of independence to alien technology: "No one has the right to demand anything from you that you don't want to give" (*ibid.*, 287). From Nikanj, Tino hears a rebuttal—the Oankali notion of *quid pro quo*: "We have something you need. You have something we need," a reference to escape from a sterile world (*ibid.*, 289). Like the white kidnap victims in frontier captivity lore, human-Oankali babies offer comfort to infertile families who have lost children to violence or disease. In the foreword to *Unexpected Stories*, critic Nisi Shawl, a journalist for *Ms.* Magazine and the *Seattle Times*, referred to Octavia's alternative breeding as "imaginable, thinkable, workable, doable," a summation of the Oankali's tolerant, cooperative nature (Butler, 2014, 8).

Old-Style Violence

At the raid that brings the novel to a climax, Octavia revisits her probe of human violence against their own kind, the cause of African bondage in *Wild Seed* and *Kindred* and Noah Cannon's crisis in "Amnesty." The drunken, nomadic raiders—

Damek—Slavic for "red earth"
Galt—Anglo-Saxon for "wild boar"
Iriarte—Basque for "middle ground"
Kaliq—Arabic for "inventive"
Tilden—English for "fertile"

—become traders who plan to snatch and sell the "mongrel baby" (Butler, 2000, 321). They demonstrate bestiality that the author contrasts to Nikanj's serene delivery of Ahajas's infant. During Gabe's pivotal lesson in Phoenix currency, Akin acknowledges the slim chance of human survival by referring to the coin's triumphant bird emblem as a false prediction of peaceful regeneration. At the flourishing village of Phoenix, for a year, Akin acclimates in part by wearing cloth trousers and listening to oral lore—fairy tales and ominous myths, such as the Roman rape of the Sabine women implied by the character name Sabina. In a forerunner to the Industrial Revolution, a frequent theme in sci-fi maven Marion Zimmer Bradley's Darkover novels, village workers recycle trash in the Andes Mountains. Both brutes and victims, they plan to make guns, which the author identifies through resister Tate Rinaldi as a source of easy, impersonal killings, a problem in Octavia's time that she later spotlighted in the Parable series.

Paper production and the recovery of scripture, memoirs, and scientific data revisit the concept of reclaimed knowledge in Ray Bradbury's *Fahrenheit 451,* an irony amid merciless gunmakers. The flesh trade furnishes villagers two biracial females to produce human-looking offspring. From Amma (Indian for "mother") and Shkaht (Arabic for "smash"), abductees from Kaal-Osei (Hindi for "era" and Ghanaian for "noble") passed to the care of Neci Roybal (Latin for "slaughter" and Galician for "red earth"), the author chose sinister names. The latter designation pinpoints the cold-bloodedness of Neci, who conspires to amputate the children's bi-species tentacles without anesthesia. The barbaric conspiracy to restore racial purity reduces Margit's seven fingers to five, a sign of "normality" to small-minded people like Neci.

Octavia builds the dystopia to a depressing anticlimax. Reunion of Lilith with her three-year-old precedes a gap of seventeen years. As Akin reaches manhood, he contemplates the Human Contradiction, the opposition of creative thought and social superiority, the source of warring caste systems and self-destruction. Tate, now aged and near death, proposes salvation via a new civilization built underground on the cold planet Mars. Thrust into metamorphosis, Akin vegetates until the cataclysmic end, when Neci and her cohorts burn Phoenix village, a mythic paradox that can never reclaim itself from the ashes. The author later stated in *The Parable of the Sower* that conflagration is the bird's expected fate. Stacy Magadanz, a reference librarian at California State University San Bernardino, justified the loss as a prelude to a new civilization on Mars: "The primitive must disappear ... as a consequence of its irrationality and violence" (Magadanz, 2012, 48).

Sources

Butler, Octavia. *Adulthood Rites* in *Lilith's Brood.* New York: Warner, 2000, 249–517.
_____. "Brave New Worlds: A Few Rules for Predicting the Future," *Essence* 31:1 (1 May 2000): 164–166, 264.
_____. *The Parable of the Talents.* Seven Stories Press, 1998.
_____. *Unexpected Stories.* New York: Open Road Media, 2014.
Magadanz, Stacy. "The Captivity Narrative in Octavia E. Butler's *Adulthood Rites,*" *Extrapolation* 53:1 (2012): 47–59.
Plumwood, Val. *Feminism and the Mastery of Nature.* London: Routledge, 1993.
Torgovnick, Marianna. *Primitive Passions: Men, Women, and the Quest for Ecstasy.* Chicago: University of Chicago Press, 1998.
Tucker, Jeffrey. "'The Human Contradiction': Identity and/as Essence in Octavia E. Butler's 'Xenogenesis' Trilogy," *Yearbook of English Studies* 27:2 (2007): 164–181.
Turner, Jenny. "Ready to Go Off," *London Review of Books* 43:4 (18 February 2021).

Afrofuturism

Octavia's fiction inspires blacks with fantastic or surreal elements based on authentic music, dance, masking, fashion, cinema, photography, graphics, cartooning, mural painting, myth, and worship. To re-conceptualize abduction and futurity, she pioneered the use of *sankofa,* the Akan principle from Ghana of retrieving the best from the past. Her works featured the religio-folk themes that recouped African esthetics from centuries of white supremacy, ridicule, and alienation. American filmmaker Cauleen Smith described the intervening racism as "cognitive estrangement," a rupture of black reality from African impulses, which Swiss psychologist Carl Jung called the instinctive prods of the collective unconscious (Womack, 2013, 138). John Akomfrah, producer of the cinema "The Last Angel of History," endorsed the black renaissance by declaring the African memory oblivious to time and intervening injustices.

Before developing radical strategies to rescue black people from destruction, the author composed a pair of short stories in 1971 foreshadowing Afrocentric ideals that re-envision the past. The first, "Crossover," bombards Jane, a laboring-class protagonist, with clichéd obstacles—a drunken family, violent ex-con boyfriend, dead-end factory employment, low self-esteem, and retreat through sleeping pills and alcohol. The vignette so freights the lone female that she deserts her lover and seeks escape through wine and random sex. The study set a pattern for later character vulnerability to pain, exclusion, and erasure. Through speculative fiction, the author explored a black renaissance—what writer Tananarive Due called "a world where magic exists, a world of the future, a world with technologies we don't currently possess, or an altered past" (Littleton, 2004, K1).

Foreseeing a New Era

Moving from one social landscape to another, Octavia began a climb from predictable plot lines to a career in Afrofuturist fiction, which critic Ytasha Womack depicted as black heritage set "in golden eras from time long gone" (Womack, 2013, 81). Stephen Kearse, a book critic for the *New York Times,* credited her with reframing speculative fiction "into a home for Black expression," a fitting description of Damian Duffy and John Jennings's graphic versions of *Kindred* and *The Parable of the Sower* and of Toshi Reagon and Bernice Johnson Reagon's operatic adaptation of *The Parable of the Sowers* with a medley of Afro-American musical tropes (Kearse, 2021, 12). By the second story, "Childfinder," the writer advanced a sci-fi solution to bigotry: isolate the most promising clairvoyants among black children and shield them from all-white tyranny. For heroics against the conniver Eve, the author created Barbara, the shepherd of promising black child visionaries bearing the Latin name meaning "foreign woman."

Barbara's story depicts the revenge motive in nonwhite characters who incur pain and persecution similar to the sufferings of African slaves. The rescue of telepaths Jordan and Valerie resets bias in speculative futurism, a supple narrative that muses on unexplored solutions to injustice. Bypassing academic approaches, Octavia reroutes disaffected children through superpowers and mysticism. Essential to the author's prose, according to writer Nnedi Okorafor, were her gendered views of "strange disturbing African characters," particularly the gifted, psi-active Valerie and the immortals Doro and An-yanwu in *Wild Seed* and Doro's promising offspring Karl and Mary Larkin in *Mind of My Mind* (Holden & Shawl, 2013, 219). The author proposed that "psi could put humans on the road to utopia" if color bias did not obstruct the way (Butler, 2014, Introduction).

A GRAND PLAN

Suggested in critical examinations of social injustice in the early themes of poet Charles Chesnutt and historian W.E.B. Du Bois, Octavia's imagery dramatized abuse in her own time. From a feminist stance, she projected Barbara, Alanna Verrick in *Survivor,* Amber in *Patternmaster,* Belen "Len" Ross in *The Parable of the Talents,* and Lynn Mortimer in "The Evening and the Morning and the Night," the types of nonwhite superwomen who endure and thrive. In epigrammatic verse, Octavia ruminated on black history in the Earthseed books. In chapter 21 of *The Parable of the Talents*, idealist Lauren Oya Olamina versified a melancholy outlook on African beginnings:

> To survive,
> Know the past.
> Let it touch you.
> Then let
> The past
> Go [Butler, 1998, 376].

British analyst Theri Pickens, an English literature specialist at Bates College in Lewiston, Maine, summarized the dominant theme in practical terms: "What constitutes responsible citizenship and how one chooses to expose and repudiate exclusionary rhetoric and practices" (Pickens, 2014, 48).

Exposure and renunciation became Octavia's salute to black experience and mettle, some based on historic artifacts and precedent set by rebels Nat Turner and Denmark Vesey, abolitionist orator Frederick Douglass, and runaway Harriet Tubman, leader of more than three hundred refugees over the Underground Railroad. With an emergency pack, Lauren readies herself for an earth-saving crusade through intuitive, non-academic learning about weapons, home building, child education, and planting. John Hall, an English teacher at Presentation Academy in Louisville, Kentucky, differentiated between ethnic styles of self-education: "White supremacy operates in education as a form of oppression that devalues non-white ways of thinking, assessment, or knowledge creation," which extend from fables and storytelling to folk experience (Hall, 2021). Like refugees from the plantation South, Lauren and her followers have no institutional classes to enlighten them, only a type of resistance that imagines a future. Through hands-on learning, she and her pilgrims build the Acorn compound African style and create a vibrant homeland that puts all hands to work.

ALTRUISM AND PROFESSIONALISM

Along the way northwest to Cape Mendocino, California, the serendipitous addition of physician Taylor Franklin Bankole increased survivability for accident and shooting victims, the exhausted and sick, and newborns. He extended effectiveness of one man via a physician's assistant training program similar in success to that of a German altruist, Dr. Albert Schweitzer, the Nobel Peace Prize healer. With the aid of Jewish nurse-anesthetist Helen Bresslau Schweitzer, the doctor treated two thousand black patients in spring 1913 at Lambaréné, Gabon. In-house internships, like those sponsored by Lauren and Bankole, included the mission healers' daughter, Rhena Schweitzer Miller, who supplied medical technology to patients in Gabon, Nigeria, Ethiopia, and Haiti. The Schweitzers' example set a precedent for European altruism to Africans.

Kendra R. Parker, on staff at Hope College in Holland, Michigan, simplified the term Afrofuturism to a means to "explore possible futures for black people from black cultural perspectives" on deity, ritual, and belief systems (Parker, 2018, 3). Amid standard fantasy, magical realism, and speculative and science fiction, an integral glimpse of Afrofuturist method locates Afrocentrism, such as historical fiction about black bondage in *Kindred* and *Wild Seed* and in non–Western perspectives on liberation in *Survivor, Dawn,* and the Parable novels. Octavia's stylistic details incorporate reproductive justice, emerging technology, and interdependence of posthuman species found in the Tlic in "Bloodchild," black vampire Shori Matthews in *Fledgling,* and the Oankali in *Lilith's Brood* and survival tactics and space migration to Alpha Centauri in *The Parable of the Talents.*

See also Feminism.

Sources

Al-Nuaimi, Sami Abdullah, Zainor Izat Zainal, Mohammad Ewan Awang, and Noritah Omar. "Afrofuturism and Transhumanism: New Insights into the African American Identity in Octavia Butler's *Dawn,*" *Pertanika Journal* 29:2 (2021): 977–992.

Butler, Octavia. *The Parable of the Talents.* New York: Seven Stories Press, 1998.

_____. *Unexpected Stories.* New York: Open Road Media, 2014.

Canavan, Gerry. "Science Fiction and Utopia in the Anthropocene," *American Literature* 93:2 (2021): 255–282.

Dery, Mark, ed. *Flame Wars: The Discourse of Cyberculture.* Durham, NC: Duke University Press, 1994.

Grinberg, Emanuella. "Celebrating Octavia Butler: A Visionary among Futurists," *CNN* (10 March 2016).

Hall, John. "Parable of the Sower: A Positive Afrofuturist Obsession," https://sites.middlebury.edu/bltnmag/2021/05/28/4749/ (28 May 2021).

Kearse, Stephen. "The Essential Octavia Butler," *New York Times* (15 January 2021): 12–13.

Olusegun, Elijah Adeoluwa. "Breaking Mythical Barriers Through a Feminist Engagement with Magical Realism" in *African Women Writing Diaspora.* Lanham, MD: Lexington Books, 2021, 103–137.

Parker, Kendra R. *Gale Researcher Guide: Octavia Butler and Afrofuturism.* Boston: Cengage Learning, 2018.

Pickens, Theri. "'You're Supposed to Be a Tall, Handsome, Fully Grown White Man': Theorizing Race, Gender, and Disability in Octavia Butler's *Fledgling,*" *Journal of Literary & Cultural Disability Studies* 8:1 (2014): 33–48, 126.

Turner, Jenny. "Ready to Go Off," *London Review of Books* 43:4 (18 February 2021).

Womack, Ytasha. *Afrofuturism: The World of Black Sci-Fi and Fantasy Culture.* Chicago: Lawrence Hill Books, 2013.

Allegory

Octavia composed stories, novels, and speeches that carry moral significance in prototype and symbol, as with a depiction of anarchy in the desert dust storm in *Clay's Ark* and the heavy monsoon in *Dawn,* the introduction to the Xenogenesis series. In both instances, chaos in nature precedes the manipulation and colonization of a few surviving humans. By retracing the forced diaspora of West African slaves from Nigeria in 1690, the symbolic novel *Wild Seed* exposes white superstitions and animosities toward Ibo/Igbo captives. Treating blacks as subhuman during the march to the sea and the boarding of Atlantic trading ships reduces buyers and sellers to the worst of capitalists. Historical essayist Greg Timmons characterized profits on human trafficking in the essay "How Slavery Became the Economic Engine of the South," which indicts the creation of millionaires in the Mississippi River Valley (Timmons, 2020). The allegory fits the second of novelist Robert A. Heinlein's three sci-fi categories: What-If, If-Only, and If-This-Goes-On, a regret of the historic flesh trade.

In the same vein as Timmons, Octavia vilifies white rationalization of abduction and dispersal of families at auction as immoral elements of New World commerce. Out of a need to justify human bondage, in *Wild Seed,* fictional agent Bernard Daly surmises that African captives are cannibals. Because Doro, the immortal Nubian, chooses people with supernatural talents, he reverses the common belief that black slaves are the least useful of arrivals to the Western Hemisphere. The allegory builds anticipation that newcomers will thrive at Wheatley, New York, a seed village bearing the surname of Phillis Wheatley, a Sene-Gambian poet abducted in 1760 at age seven and sold to a Boston colonist, tailor John Wheatley (Butler, 1980, 221).

Rediscovering Collectivism

The author introduces the concept of seeding the landscape with productive people in a separate Patternist novel, *Mind of My Mind.* After a grueling power struggle between the murderous undying Doro and his daughter/lover Mary Larkin, she bests him by applying the logic of community and cooperation, paired concepts missing during his four thousand years of jockeying human mutants. The final scene depicts her telepaths spreading across the globe like seeds of tolerance and good will, the antidotes to colonialism and human bondage. The trope influenced Octavia's Parable series, which sharpened the strategy of concealing a principle in allegory to a short moral or spiritual exegesis on a par with Christ's New Testament parables.

To frame the masterwork *Kindred,* the author created an example of long-term clan belonging. For black writer Adana "Dana" Franklin, the transcendent call of her white great great grandfather, Rufus Weylin, draws her through a timeslip to his aid. He views his rescuer once at age five while he flounders in a river, a symbol of time, and later at age nine after breaking his leg during tree climbing, an icon of lineage. For logical reasons, she must save him to further her branch of the family tree, a visualization of genealogy that links humankind to Adam and Eve. Out of altruism, she chooses to educate him in his teens and strip his character of father Tom Weylin's anti-black mentality. By grooming Rufus with literacy and refutations of chattel slavery's torments, she hopes to put twentieth-century multiculturalism to work salving the hurts of subjugation. During readings from Daniel Defoe's shipwreck novel *Robinson Crusoe,* she examines the text from a slave trader's perspective and from the fate of a castaway like herself.

Heroes and Martyrs

In a resetting of beach wreckage in space, Octavia's *Dawn,* the first volume of the *Lilith's Brood* trilogy, delineates humans like Rufus and Dana as proud and stubborn. No matter the ingenuity of alien Oankali, the few survivors of earth's nuclear war label their rescuers "oppressors" (Kiran, 2021, 4). The author compounds the tale of resettlement on Mars with the evangelism of Akin, a mutant Christ figure in volume two, *Adulthood Rites.* A wunderkind born with teeth and capable of speaking in whole sentences by age two months, he and his mother Lilith Iyapo create a madonna and child pose that impresses earthlings with his beauty and intelligence. After his lone wanderings in the Amazon Basin and capture by human resisters, he influences followers in Phoenix village. The setting enlarges the phoenix legend into the miracle child's posthuman story, which unites intelligence with space eugenics, the source of resisters' techno-stress. The intersection fits Octavia's philosophy of sci-fi traumas, technophobia, and dystopia.

Following a reunion with Lilith, at age twenty, Akin begins a painful metamorphosis into adulthood and a ministry that guides his flock toward a diaspora to Mars, a means of ridding *homo sapiens* of supremacy, greed, and violence, the sources of gang rampages in *The Parable of the Sower.* Lauren Oya Olamina sanctions the author's use of illustrative storytelling by recalling,

> My father loved parables—stories that taught, stories that presented ideas and morals in ways that made pictures in people's minds…. Because he believed stories were so important as teaching tools [Butler, 1998, 19].

The revival of greenery from ash recurs in the burning of Los Angeles and Alexandra's home at Cape Mendocino, California, where Lauren's pilgrims plant fruit, vegetables, and oak trees, mythic symbols of strength and justice. By choosing Acorn as a commune name, the author bases allegorical significance on the oak's reliability and longevity.

In June 2020, Esther L. Jones, faculty dean at Clark University in Worcester, Massachusetts, endorsed cartoon versions of Octavia's *Kindred* and Parable series for exemplifying young heroes confronting political and social injustice. Media expert John Jennings lauded the graphic adaptation the previous January of *The Parable of the Sower* for dramatizing black female leadership and Afrofuturist imagination, an alternative outlet for minority strivers. He reported that "The voice of the African diaspora has historically been either sublimated, disrupted, or erased, and Black speculative re-imagination explores what would happen if it wasn't" ("University," 2020). To combat black disenfranchisement, he chose Octavia's Parable series as a source of uplift and motivation to the underclass. His work amplifies art championing symbols, tropes, and dreams that reflect black reality.

Sources

Butler, Octavia. *Wild Seed.* New York: Doubleday, 1980.

Gowler, David B. "Selfish and Proud: The Good Samaritan, Octavia Butler, and Wearing a Mask" in *A Chorus of Voices: The Reception History of the Parables.* Oxford, UK: Newstex (3 July 2020).

Jones, Esther L. "More Than Just Escapism: Science Fiction Builds Mental Resiliency," *Hispanic Outlook in Higher Education* 30:9 (June/July 2020): 18–19.

Kiran, Ayesha. "Human Identity and Technophobic Posthumanism in Octavia Butler's *Dawn*," *Indiana Journal of Arts & Literature* 2:8 (2021): 1–15.
Timmons, Greg. "How Slavery Became the Economic Engine of the South," www.history.com/news/slavery-profitable-southern-economy (2 September 2020).
"University of California Riverside: Afrofuturist Comics and Writing 'in a Time of Great Calamity.'" Washington, DC: Targeted News (20 June 2020).

"Amnesty"

Unlike Octavia's print works, the story "Amnesty" appeared in 2003 through electronic publication. From the beginning, she set communication at the pinnacle of translator Noah Cannon's adaptation to stranger-society, an allegory of the disparate languages of Babel in Genesis 11:1–9 and of captive Africans during the Middle Passage. The protagonist's detention by aliens mocks the sanguine name of her hometown, Victorville, California, which recurs in *Clay Ark's* symbiont society. Kimberly Gilson at Dalhousie University, Nova Scotia, summarizes the animosity as "humanity's conflict between biophilia and xenophobia—a love of life and a fear of difference," the principal opposition in the Xenogenesis trilogy (Gilson, 2020, 1).

As Noah comes of age and learns a skill, the town becomes an anti-utopia and breeder of vexation among human squatters, job seekers, and bounty hunters. Out of envy and suspicion, they accuse Noah of collaborating with the enemy, a similar charge to Augustino "Tino" Leal's cultivation of an alien family in *Adulthood Rites* and Lilith Iyapo's partnership with Oankali in *Dawn*. In an article for the *New Yorker*, critic Julian Lucas described Noah as "neither a victim nor a turncoat but, much like her biblical namesake, the only one preparing to live in a world made new," a reclamation that dominates *Survivor, Fledgling,* "Speech Sounds," and *Wild Seed* (Lucas, 2021, 75).

Earthbound Dissension

In anticipation of the story's publication, at the July 12–14, 2002, Readercon in Burlington, Massachusetts, Octavia summarized the chief flaw in other worlds: "You strand people on another world, and throw difficulties at them. But the real difficulties turn out to be other humans," a conclusion that proves true in *Adulthood Rites* when human raiders wound Tino and in *Fledgling* with the murder of Theodora Harden, Shori's symbiont (Devney, 2002, 6). Because Noah is a suspect on both sides of the impasse, the white race treats her as barbarously as did the anthropoids. Vicious human scourges question, torture, isolate, sleep-deprive, x-ray and scan, poison, and drug her for twelve years to gain inside information that she doesn't have. The pummeling and intimidation press her to suicide, a scenario similar to author Isabel Allende's fictional scenes in *The House of the Spirits* of Blanca Trueba under the fascist Augusto Pinochet military junta in Chile from 1973 to 1990.

The author enhances satire by characterizing humanoids as compromisers and the Mojave shanty towns as dens of human worshippers of extraterrestrials, plotters of alien annihilation, or thieves coveting space technology. The tactile engagement of the translator with her employer compares with the enjoyment the species gains from watching human dances, ice skating, and gymnastics. Because extraterrestrials communicate by rapid light, "They moved far too quickly for her to even begin to learn the language" (Butler, 2005, 149). For others, "enfolding" by limbless, deaf bush-like creatures proves terrorizing enough to precipitate insanity (*ibid.*). In contrast, aliens receive comfort from human hugs, which ease their homesickness. Noah deduces that life on earth addicts the humanoids to humans. Rather than massacre earthlings for firing nuclear weapons on alien bubble cities, the invaders deactivate the bombs and missiles and return one half of the unexploded arsenal to their attackers, a gesture of selflessness and forgiveness.

Knowing the Self

The greatest struggle of the era derives from a killing blow to the *Homo sapiens* ego. The aliens' suspicions that their prisoners possess "uncertain ability, intellect, and perception" create a bit of humor at the depiction of human abductees as anything but superior (*ibid.*, 153). Under a system fraught with what Julian Lucas called a "learn-or-die urgency," aliens cage the former "centers of the universe" as lab rats, a jab at earth egotism (*ibid.*, 76; 157). Octavia repeated the gibe in the essay "The Monophobic Response" by characterizing planetary self-importance as "the all-important Us ... our consuming interest in ourselves" (Butler, 2000, 415).

Despite past misdeeds, Noah holds no grudge. She spreads peace with humanoids "by telling the truth": that the disparate species are "fated to be together" (Butler, 2005, 155, 179). Of her talent for tolerance and adaptation, Octavia wrote in her journal on July 6, 2000, "Those who go slow, help one another, always work together, who accommodate rather than fight or deny, who begin to understand the essential changes, they will live" (Brown, 2021, 97). As a model of non-adaptation, Noah's wariest, most hostile recruit, Thera Collier, refuses amity with the invaders and dubs them "weeds" because of their resemblance to bushes (*ibid.*, 164). Another skeptic, James Adio, abets the plot to exterminate anthropoid-human mutants by killing newborns. Noah replies that her parents chose her biblical birth name for a reason, a suggestion of a savior of humankind from planetary genocide by choosing to occupy a symbiotic habitat and produce unprecedented offspring.

Sources

Brown, Jayna. *Black Utopias: Speculative Life and the Music of Other Worlds.* Durham, NC: Duke University Press, 2021.

Butler, Octavia. "Amnesty," *Bloodchild and Other Stories.* New York: Seven Stories Press, 2005, 147–186.

_____. "The Monophobic Response," *Dark Matter: A Century of Speculative Fiction from the African Diaspora.* New York: Aspect/Warner Books, 2000, 415–416.

Devney, Bob. "Orbita Dicta," *The Devniad Book 82B:* www.devniad.com (July 2002).

Gilson, Kimberly. "Coercion in Octavia E. Butler's Xenogenesis," https://dalspace.library.dal.ca/handle/10222/77973 (March 2020).

Lucas, Julian. "Stranger Communities," *New Yorker* 97:4 (15 March 2021): 73–76.

"Amnesty" Genealogy

The family tree of Noah Cannon pictures a female capable of weathering sexual assault and stillbirths. Living with three old brothers sets her apart by gender and readies her for a challenging coming of age.

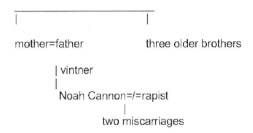

By linking her with an antediluvian patriarch in Genesis 6–9:1 and the Quran 17:3 and 37:75–79, the masculine name exemplifies a direct descendent of Adam and Eve. The ark builder, a sincere laborer and worshipper of Yahweh, attempts to save living creatures from a disastrous inundation. In a similar sorting out of different beings to prevent perpetual chaos, the translator tolerates alien peculiarities and enables them to ally with humankind. The origin of her surname from "wolf cub" suggests an aggressive personality suited to the fusing of two societies.

Sources

Butler, Octavia. "Amnesty," *Bloodchild and Other Stories*. New York: Seven Stories Press, 2005, 147–186.
Gilson, Kimberly. "Coercion in Octavia E. Butler's Xenogenesis," https://dalspace.library.dal.ca/handle/10222/77973 (March 2020).

An-yanwu

One of Octavia's fierce female survivors, the priestess An-yanwu lives alternately as male or female, husband of Isaac or wife of Denice, and resister of a coercive relationship with the Nubian immortal Doro. In Nigeria, she bears the colorless eyes and full set of teeth of a supernatural crone and the lactose intolerance common to Africans. She appears in 1690 in chapter one of *Wild Seed* after having slain seven stalkers, the parasites who capitalized on black bondage and breeding for profit. She later contends, "It was not her business to kill. She was a healer," a respected elder in Wheatley, New York (Butler, 1980, 383). In 1840 at her feminist utopia in Avoyelles Parish, Louisiana, she grooms for success freedmen, a few whites, and former slaves. By living peaceably and forging new clan bonds, she mirrors the Druid earth mother "gathering family ... her descendants ... like her children" (*ibid.*, 526).

The former Anasi, the African trickster spider, An-yanwu becomes a shapeshifter after an oracle cures her of sickness, Octavia's touch of magical realism. She occupies what Ghanaian-Canadian scholar Adwoa Afful of York University in Toronto termed "speculative temporal space," a timelessness devoid of earthly boundaries (Afful,

2016, 103). By devouring leopard, eagle, shark, and dolphin meat, she learns the physical codes of their flesh and comes to value the dolphin shape and buoyancy as escapes from stress and grief. Among the ignorant, her powers generate "envy, suspicion, fear, charges of witchcraft" (*ibid.*, 126). A part of the female holocaust of the seventeenth century, she patiently outfoxes the know-nothings who confuse herbalism with sorcery and poison her to curb her oracular and healing potential.

MEETING A NEMESIS

An-yanwu's chance encounter with the Nubian immortal Doro establishes their distant kinship after fourteenth-century Kushites in the Nile Valley bred with Nigerians, passing on Arab traits. He compliments her strength with an ironic twist: "You are a powerful woman. You could live in any place I chose," a revelation of his sovereignty over chosen seed people and his domination of women (Butler, 1980, 229). Through a cycle of lives, ten marriages, and forty-seven children, An-yanwu recalls being the eighth wife of a polygamist, a primitive androcentric marital style that Richard Moss reclaims in *The Parable of the Sower*. At age three hundred, she reflects on bondage and patriarchy, but prefers channeling a god's voice. Doro values her as a "carrier of a bloodline I believed was lost—and, I think, of another that I did not know existed," an unusual lapse in his 3,700 years of hybridizing humans (*ibid.*, 110).

Like An-yanwu's shapeshifting paternal clan and her mother's prophecy, storytelling, and healing, she becomes a eugenic marvel, the "wild seed of the best kind" (*ibid.*, 22). Delighting grandson Okoye by imitating a tortoise or monkey in animal fables, she foreshadows the homemaker and eternal mother of a Louisiana plantation (*ibid.*, 51). She possesses supernatural powers of leaping river gorges, but recoils from Doro's heartless search for psionic issue and his suggestion of engineering her sons and daughters as breeding stock. Distaste for his cavalier murders causes her to consider flight back to "her people, her compound, her home" in a simpler, less coercive environment (*ibid.*, 70). Frances Bonner, a women's studies expert at the University of Queensland, Australia, lauds her for "accepting the constraints of her world and trying to make something decent and productive out of the indecent situation in which she finds herself" (Bonner, 1990, 51).

MORALITY AND RESISTANCE

The narrative contrasts taboo concepts, beginning with An-yanwu's revulsion at drinking animal milk and shudder at the mortality of ordinary humans she loves and reveres, such as Stephen, Margaret Nneka, and Luisa. A sudden metamorphosis to leopard links her to the seventeenth-century Benin myth of the leopard people. The transmutation reveals her blood-thirst for a meal on Doro's son, Lale Sachs, a potential rapist. As the plot progresses to compulsory marriage to Doro's son Isaac, she rebels against incest, a "doglike disregard for kinship" (*ibid.*, 293). The question of morality leads Doro to the ultimate decree—in his land, people must obey. In confrontation with him, An-yanwu concludes that "what she wanted meant nothing," Octavia's reflection on the diminution of married women (*ibid.*, 300). Under stress, she converts to leopard, dog, eagle, or dolphin, her favorite ocean-based guise for relaxation, meditation, and challenge.

The author extends An-yanwu's weariness with life as though viewing the lethal exhaustion of a prisoner of war. After bearing Doro a son, she charges Doro with his usual sins of killing without compassion. She declares, "The human part of you is dying," a demise that his son Isaac predicted before marrying An-yanwu (*ibid.*, 64). At the crux of their power struggle, Doro ponders his fear of losing all humanity and retaining only the vampirish hunger for new human flesh. Like the quandary of Joseph, the legendary thirteenth-century Wandering Jew of Europe, Doro longs to die. At the end of his millennia of parasitism, he abandons attempts to turn An-yanwu into what Professor S.A. Smyth at University of California at Los Angeles terms an incubator of mutants and begins acclimating to the roles of husband and father. Octavia indicates that his adaptation derives from a lose-lose dilemma rather than a surge of love for An-yanwu.

Sources

Afful, Adwoa. "Wild Seed: Africa and Its Many Diasporas," *Critical Arts* 30:4 (August 2016): 93–104.

Bonner, Frances. "Difference and Desire, Slavery and Seduction: Octavia Butler's Xenogenesis," *Foundation* 48 (Spring, 1990): 50–61.

Butler, Octavia. *Wild Seed*. New York: Doubleday, 1980.

Pitts, Michael. *Alternative Masculinities in Feminist Speculative Fiction: A New Man*. Lanham, MD: Lexington Books, 2021.

Smythe, S.A. "Black Life, Trans Study: On Black Nonbinary Method, European Trans Studies, and the Will to Institutionalization," *Transgender Studies Quarterly* 8:2 (2021): 158–171.

An-yanwu's Genealogy

Octavia's summary of An-yanwu's family ties cites nebulous beginnings for a Nigerian immortal. The family tree traces the many husbands and liaisons that form

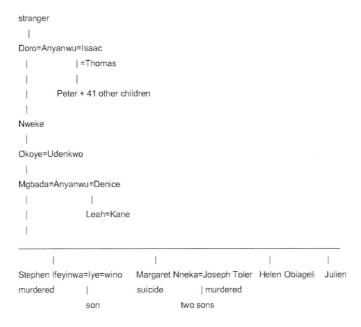

her genealogy, especially her decision to become the female lover of Denice, mother of Leah.

Constant disasters derive from an allegorical shapeshifting that violates nature. After brother-in-law Joseph Toler forces Stephen Ifeyinwa off a balcony, An-yanwu morphs into a leopard, her embodiment of vengeance, and rips out Joseph's throat. The suicide of Margaret Nneka by hanging leaves two orphaned sons among the many foundlings that their grandmother nurtures and teaches to read.

See also Wild Seed.

Sources

Afful, Adwoa. "Wild Seed: Africa and Its Many Diasporas," *Critical Arts* 30:4 (August 2016): 93–104.
Butler, Octavia. *Wild Seed.* New York: Doubleday, 1980.
Pitts, Michael. *Alternative Masculinities in Feminist Speculative Fiction: A New Man.* Lanham, MD: Lexington Books, 2021.

"Bloodchild"

In a foreshadowing of the Xenogenesis trilogy, the author's most anthologized short story perused the nature of libido and purpose of love. She was quick to outline "Bloodchild" by theme and conflict and focused on an imbalance of human rights and consent, pervasive topics in *Kindred,* the Patternmaster series, and *Dawn.* Told through an Asian narrator, the allegory is generous in insights about bondage, interspecies seduction and love, and forced parturition with grub-like alien beings in a protected preserve. Critic Glenn Grant's review for the Montreal *Gazette* noted a human-with-alien symbiosis that "brings fresh perspectives" to gendered, family, and ethnic issues (Grant, 1994, 13). In an essay for *Ms.,* Sherley Anne Williams, a Fulbright scholar and English department chair at the University of California at San Diego, extrapolated a pseudo-feminist theme: "The story explores the paradoxes of power and inequality and starkly portrays the experience of a class who [resemble] women, throughout most of history" (Williams, 1986, 70).

Octavia's reversal of gender fate aims a glaring exposé at female bondage, a topic that returns in agricultural debt slavery and forced prostitution in the Parable series and the control-mongering short story "Amnesty." Donna Haraway, a feminist professor at the University of California, Santa Cruz, summarized conflict arising from "forced reproduction, unequal power, the ownership of self by another, the sibling-ship of humans with aliens" (Haraway, 1989, 378). By subverting romanticized views of mothering, "Bloodchild" repositions males in an obligatory martyrdom to family patrons armed with claws and a stinging tail, a punitive representation of the phallus. Comparing the plight of males in the role of child-bearers and hosts for parasitic grubs who "parceled us out to the desperate and sold us to the right and powerful," Williams declared symbolic females peripheral and typecast "chiefly for their reproductive capacities," a parallel of plantation women in *Kindred* (*ibid.*).

Literary critic Jayna Brown, a professor at Pratt Institute in Brooklyn, New York, summarized Octavia's intent to survey "effects of indigenous microorganisms on humans," a threat she introduced with a mysterious disease in "Speech Sounds" and an extraterrestrial pathogen in *Clay's Ark* (Brown, 2021, 97). By overturning identities of tyrants and bondsmen, the plot elevates the Tlic to First Peoples and the reader to outlander in an isolated settlement on an inhabited planet. The bitter conflict—Gan's sibling seduction by semi-human godmother and owner T'Gatoi—supplants earthly morals with the creation of a hybrid third race that threatens to claim the human body for breeding fierce wormlets. Because Terrans live on a reservation, they ostensibly occupy a safe haven from the snatching and clawing of parasitic Tlic hordes that devour flesh. Amy West, a reviewer for *Readercon 14,* summarized the startling perspective of "Bloodchild" as its "placement of the alien not outside of us but within us," a suggestion that racist colonialism destabilizes the individual by weakening basic virtues (West, 2002, 1).

The bulk of the story simulates human birthing with a Gothic near-death experience of Bram Lomas. While bearing the eggs of Tlic parasite T'Khotgif Teh, he signals at a call box for help and comes under the knife of T'Gatoi, who excises small ravenous larvae filled with Bram's blood. In the estimation of critic Karen Joy Fowler, a journalist for *Salon,* the short story is a composite of crossbreeding with extraterrestrials and mutual dependence between victims and predators. The allegory "distilled [the plots] to a disturbing essence" similar to human bondage and potential cannibalism (Fowler, 2006). The grisly allegory replicates the capitalistic foundation of the antebellum South on propagating black children for plantation bondage or sale, an historical plight that protagonist Dana Franklin surveys in detail in *Kindred.*

See also Names.

Sources

Brown, Jayna. *Black Utopias: Speculative Life and the Music of Other Worlds.* Durham, NC: Duke University Press, 2021.

Butler, Octavia. *Bloodchild and Other Stories.* New York: Seven Stories Press, 2005.

Fowler, Karen Joy. "Remembering Octavia Butler," *Salon, www.salon.com/2006/03/17/butler_3/* (17 March 2006).

Grant, Glenn. "Black Woman Author Is Rarity in SF," (Montreal) *Gazette* (26 March 1994): I3.

Haraway, Donna. *Primate Visions: Gender, Race, and Nature in the World of Modern Science.* New York: Routledge, 1989.

Kearse, Stephen. "The Essential Octavia Butler," *New York Times* (15 January 2021): 12–13.

Parker, Kendra R. *Gale Researcher Guide: Octavia Butler and Afrofuturism.* Boston: Cengage Learning, 2018.

West, Amy. "Our Guests of Honor," *Readercon 14* (12–13 July 2002): 1–8.

Williams, Sherley Anne. "On Octavia E. Butler," *Ms.* 14:9 (March 1986): 70–73.

"Bloodchild" Genealogy

An allegory of species tyranny through pedophilia and gender oppression, the story reframes imperialism through mixed families in the closed society on a confining planet. The child-bearer, in this case male, falls victim to brainwashing: a home-centered ideal elevates procreation to the prime value of men. By sacrificing their blood to neonates, male moms replicate the human act of lactation at a potential loss of life for the sake of newborn larvae.

Telling the horrific tale of seduction by a velvety, libidinous Tlic, Gan, in his

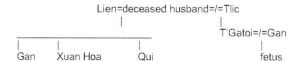

Lien=deceased husband=/=Tlic

T'Gatoi=/=Gan

Gan   Xuan Hoa   Qui   fetus

coming-of-age narrative, reflects on his Asian parents and siblings and protects sister Xuan Hoa from a horrific birth experience. He yields to the mutant dominator T'Gatoi, a velvety centipede who seeks him as a host/breeder.

Sources

Barrett, Michele. *Women's Oppression Today: The Marxist/Feminist Encounter.* London: Verso, 1988.
Butler, Octavia. *Bloodchild and Other Stories.* New York: Seven Stories Press, 2005.
Japtok, Martin. *Human Contradictions in Octavia E. Butler's Work.* Cham, Switzerland: Palgrave Macmillan, 2020.

"The Book of Martha"

In a complete detachment from space and time, a gently amusing dialogue between God and Martha Bes, a forty-three-year-old black woman, casts reassuring evidence of kindness in the afterlife. The author chose a symbolic Greek-French name meaning "fine lady of the house." The beatification of Martha for hosting Jesus in Luke 10:38–42 and John 1–12:1–8 contrasts the French legend of St. Martha of Tarasque, a monster tamer. Octavia hybridized traditional sci-fi by merging it with anecdote about a woman endowed with cosmic power, a concept she pursued in *Wild Seed* with the shapeshifter An-yanwu. At 5:00 a.m. in the kitchen, character witticisms set a light tone with Martha's viewing of the almighty. He appears as a twelve-foot-tall white man in the stereotyped long white robe and the guise of Michelangelo's 1513 statue of Moses, a droll depiction of white males as commanding, even in marble.

Aiding the theme of form and substance, God shapeshifts and alters settings with the pizzazz of Lewis Carroll's fantasy *Alice in Wonderland*, becoming a beardless black man, then a black woman. Reflecting the dissonance of the Trump presidency, Patricia Ventura of Spelman College and Edward K. Chan of Tokyo's Waseda University, editors of *Race and Utopian Desire in American Literature and Society*, stated a 21st-century need for Octavia's imaginary deity and anti-racist satire. The editor warned of rising fascism: "In a time when white supremacy is reasserting itself in the U.S. and around the world, there is a growing need to understand the vital relationship between race and utopia as a resource of resistance" (Ventura & Chan, 2019, 147).

An Immature World

Octavia's "save the world" storytelling involved precise, unvarnished criticisms of the early 2000s, a "greedy, murderous, wasteful adolescence" (Govan, 2005–2006, 25; Butler, 2005, 192). To an omniscient God, sacrifice is an essential adjunct to radical improvisation because earthlings are mere teens given to violence, waste, greed, and destruction. In the 1977 novel *Mind of My Mind,* Jesse Dana comments on an omnipotent creator: "He made us. He knows just how far wrong we can go" (Butler, 1977, 106). To reduce sorrows and suffering, God assigns Martha the rehabilitation of people who don't respect each other or nature. When the task ends, she has to return to a caste at the bottom of society. Speaking from the author's experience with hard times and poverty, Martha claims to have risen above homelessness and to have rescued her mother from need, two self-congratulatory facts lifted from Octavia's biography.

For verisimilitude, Octavia laces the two-way conversation with socio-economic problems—overpopulation, disease, handicap, disaster, war, and murder—and probes Martha's fear of fallibility while righting disorder, a common apprehension among elected officials. She breaches decorum by shouting at the supreme authority and by impugning his motives for passing control to a mortal. God returns the favor by reminding her to avoid shallow answers, like lowering the birthrate, and to picture impact in the future. Applying the metaphor of the dwarf star siphoning material from a giant, he expresses the importance of invention and competition, both human qualities, especially in the writer, who is skilled at dreaming up characters and scenarios.

An Answer for God

In a radical vision of change, the story, according to Elon University writer Emily Lange, puts Martha "in a maternal relationship with the whole of humanity, a caretaker role that places the burden of survival on her shoulders" (Lange, 2020, 30). The protagonist negotiates engineered dreams like private utopias—individualized heavens that satisfy more completely than reality. She posits that satisfaction would thwart aggression by making humans envision a mature form of justice. Rather than grasp too soon for a better tomorrow, she opts for two tuna salad sandwiches, for which she offers the reader a recipe, a droll side note that humanizes Martha's domestication. She shares her snack with God and adds sparkling cider, a standard non-alcoholic Baptist beverage.

Ultimately, Octavia's anecdote answers the question "Is utopia possible?" In a critique for *Utopian Studies,* Claire P. Curtis, a political science specialist at the University of Charleston, South Carolina, notes that "The Book of Martha" recognizes that "humans are primarily concerned with personal security," a self-centering that forces Martha to be realistic about ways to improve the human race (Curtis, 2008, 412). She realizes that it is not possible "to arrange a society so that everyone is content" (Butler, 2005, 202). Her writing career would be doomed if people sought pleasure and gave up reading, negating her creativity and forcing her into martyrdom. The subject of self-education echoes Octavia's warnings in "Brave New Worlds: A Few Rules for Predicting the Future," an essay for a May 2000 issue of *Essence.* She replied to a young fan's question about problem solving that reading history is a way "to study humanity" and "foretell the future" to avoid repeats of errors (Butler, 2000, 165).

See also Names.

Sources

Butler, Octavia. *The Book of Martha*, novella in *Bloodchild and Other Stories.* New York: Seven Stories Press, 2005.

_____. "Brave New Worlds: A Few Rules for Predicting the Future," *Essence* 31:1 (1 May 2000): 164–166, 264.

_____. *Mind of My Mind*. New York: Doubleday, 1977.

Curtis, Claire P. "Theorizing Fear: Octavia Butler and the Realist Utopia," *Utopian Studies* 19:3 (2008): 411–431.

Govan, Sandra Y. "Interview," *Obsidian III* 6:2/7:1 (2005–2006): 14–39.

Lange, Emily. "Creativity and Sacrifice in Two Short Stories from Octavia Butler and Maurice Broaddus," *Femspec* 20:2 (2020): 26–45.

Ventura, Patricia, and Edward K. Chan, eds. *Race and Utopian Desire in American Literature and Society.* Cham, Switzerland: Palgrave Macmillan, 2019.

Capitalism

After viewing an exhibition at Pasadena's Armory Center for the Arts, Octavia began exploring the faults of what Bryan Yazell, on staff at the University of Southern Denmark at Odense, condemned as "unfettered capitalism" (Yazell, 2020, 166). A pamphlet listed human bondage and ownership of ideas as two profiteering evils, the abstract villains in "Amnesty" and the implications in *Fledgling* of Raleigh Curtis, named for English explorer Sir Walter Raleigh, who searched the Orinoco for El Dorado. For *Adulthood Rites,* she revealed in the alien Oankali the need to develop controlled breeding of "nonsentient animals" and predictable offspring as commodities (Butler, 2000, 259). Neo-feudal companies in *The Parable of the Talents* indenture educated workers and trade them like liquid assets on a Monopoly board. She included in the Parable novels the U.S. sale to "a Euro-Japanese company" its space probes into extraterrestrial life (Butler, 1998, 81). The fictional study of profit applications debunked the old notion that spending money for earth's needy would prove more beneficial than "wasting time or money in space" (*ibid.*, 82).

In "Persistence," an interview with *Locus,* the novelist stated the dangers of socially apathetic conglomerates. She commented on the amorality of capitalism:

> I've been around people who don't have [a conscience], and they're damned scary. And I think a lot of them are out there running major corporations. How can you do some of the things these people do if you have a conscience? [Butler, 2000, 6]

She viewed embedded morality as essential to humanity, a necessary trait of homesteaders building a business in *The Parable of the Talents* on unstable ground. In the estimation of Ikea M. Johnson at Louisiana State University, earth is "a roving mad world destroyed by unhealthy and capitalistic pursuits" (Johnson, 2020, 95). Among traders at the Acorn commune, some sell or barter produce or reconditioned furniture and tools. Physicians, however, can avoid private practice and count on high incomes from "privatized or foreign-owned cities, towns, or huge farms" (Butler, 1998, 160). Physician Taylor Franklin Bankole models the Hippocratic style of medical care by delivering babies and attending accident and shooting victims without undue concern for payment, a parallel to Christ's healing of lepers and the blind.

In a corrupt world, the author saw no hope for ethical business. In *Dawn,* the first of the Xenogenesis trilogy, aliens interpret positive relationships between beings as a form of commerce, the barter system that enables the Oankali to hybridize their genetic makeup. The author's diatribes darken in *Clay's Ark,* in which she lists "corporate governor" as a lost cause alongside "human rights, the elderly, the ecology, throwaway children … the vast rich-poor gap and the shrinking middle class" (Butler, 1984, 58). Out of despair, protagonist Dr. Blake Jason Maslin works at a ghetto hospital, where his one-man effort, like that of Bankole, is "like trying to empty the Pacific with a spoon" (*ibid.*).

The opening paragraph of *Wild Seed* sets the tone of seventeenth-century New World exploitation in an Ibo/Igbo ghost village in 1690, when black bondage began replacing indenturing of whites in the British colonies with a centuries old form of biocapitalism. Following a raid by enslavers, stalkers, "their machetes ready, their intentions clear," kidnapped only a salable commodity, leaving the flesh of Nigerian rejects rotting (Butler, 1980, 1). The narrative considers the distance of Triangular Trade and the destiny of "a healthy, vigorous people," including tool, pottery, and vegetable trader An-yanwu, a Kushite-Igbo innovator who enjoys simple marketing (*ibid.*). The introduction of the oracular healer contrasts human trafficking with a healing service that brings patients to her village and income to her people, a reasonable *quid pro quo.* The nobility of herbalism silently rebukes exploiters for turning human bodies into trade items, the commodities of the Royal African Company on the Gambia River from 1660 to 1708. By 1840, An-yanwu's Louisiana plantation in Avoyelles Parish turns an agricultural profit from freedmen's labor by paying wages and purchasing candles, cloth, soap, and medicine that were previously slave-made. The idealistic business plan makes the most of human potential.

THE FLESH TRADE

The author exorcized the idea of bondage in "Amnesty," a more predictable sci-fi story. It projected a human population as hirelings of aliens who extract and refine profitable minerals. The rule of supply and demand forces the unemployed to cooperate with the invaders and their subcontractors, who offer salaried jobs. Noah Cannon, a valuable translator, instructs recruits on capitalistic values: "What's important to them is . . what use we can be to them. That's what they pay us for" (Butler, 2005, 180). In exchange, human workers indulge "enfolding" or hugs, the physical touch that eases alien homesickness. Thus, "We get to live, and so do they," a simple transaction on a par with An-yanwu's trading (*ibid.,* 181).

A less palatable exchange in "The Evening and the Morning and the Night" describes Hedeonco, a cancer cure underwritten by profits from oil, Big Pharma, and chemical labs that suggests "hedonism." Octavia regrets that "They had trusted God and the promises of modern medicine and had a child," Lynn Mortimer, the victim of double parental DNA. When the treatment predisposes people to the fictional Duryea-Gode Disease (DGD), a self-cannibalizing syndrome generating manic violence, the only resort is humane retreats. In a positive art-centered environment, staff alternate restraints with kindness. Self-expression relieves patients of the curse of investments in lethal substances from Hedeon Laboratories, the toxins that marine biologist Rachel Carson demonized in the treatise *Silent Spring.*

Corporate Bondage

For *Kindred,* the author examined human bondage as a model of investment, exonerated indirectly in Ephesians 6:5 by a command for servants to obey masters. She introduced a black female and white male working for minimum wage by inventorying an auto parts factory warehouse, the kind of "slave market" job that dominated Octavia's energies while she became a writer (Butler, 1979, 52). When Dana marries Kevin Franklin, the pair occupy the same castes—day workers, freelance writers, and middle-class Californians. The aspect that sets them apart from the ordinary day laborer, their sizable home library attests to imagination and learning that bode well for the future of intellectuals who reject an assembly line mindset.

To usher the assets of literacy into her family's antebellum past, on June 9, 1831—more than 32 years before the Emancipation Proclamation—Dana risks the torments of time travel to a Maryland plantation. She gradually introduces illiterates Nigel and Joe to reading, which could end their subservience to moneyed whites as ignorant as their owner. Under the insidious economic system supervised by money-grubbing planter Tom Weylin and overseers Evan Fowler and Jake Edwards, profiteering on black husbandry requires evaluation of breeding stock and selling the young like farm beasts. Punishments serve a capitalistic entity—lashings of the defiant and sale of slave-bred children for profit or spite, one of the most anti-family, anti-black aspects of Southern agrarianism. The biblical sins of the fathers visit Rufus after Tom Weylin's death and Margaret Weylin's abdication of power over the plantation. To retire agricultural debt, Rufus must sell thirty-eight slaves, a disruption of workers' families and a loss of breeding stock. The idea of split families and children without parents fueled Quaker and women's abolitionism, a freedom drive that grew about the time the novel takes place.

Profits Before Morals

The prescient author detailed other greed-stoking investments in *The Parable of the Sower,* where Keith Olamina turns literacy lessons into marketable talent. Critic Marlene D. Allen, an American literature teacher at the United Arab Emirates University in Al Ain, identified postmodern capitalism and the suppression of workers as a repeating cycle as culpable "as the antebellum system of slavery did in the historical past" (Allen, 2009, 1358). On the Pacific coast, Canadian border factories treat workers as expendable; an offshore cash source exploits rising terror of the Apocalypse. To make the most of panic, rich California residents lure whites to Olivar, an oceanfront suburb of Los Angeles that Lauren Oya Olamina terms "another fortress" (Butler, 1993, 126). The setting calls to mind Charles Dickens's boy hero Oliver Twist who sleeps under a counter among coffins and jogs a workhouse breakfast server in the 2020 film version by asking, "Please, sir, I want some more." Of the slim promise of survival under the duress of commercialized farming, Lauren predicts "There'll be other Olivars ... a source of cheap labor and cheap land," a jaundiced view of a world dominated by corporate wealth (*ibid.,* 129).

On a flight north from Robledo, Zahra Moss rejects a detour to Olivar to become "some kind of twenty-first century slave" (*ibid.,* 170). Ironically, as dealings in water increase corporate menace, the Pacific Ocean gnaws at the California coast under climate change. The company Kagimoto, Stamm, Frampton (KSF) profits from desalinization technology and plans for utilities and agribusiness. The company name, meaning "origin," "descent," and "enclosure," suggests the financial bind foreign money—Japanese, German, Canadian—places on credulous city boards "selling themselves to KSF" (*ibid.,* 120–121). The prospectus—a "company town" concept—creates debt slavery in a state where wages have stagnated. The insidious form of capitalism promised more misery for peasants like Latinos Doe and Grayson Mora and Afro-Japanese laborer Emery Tanaka Solis, who shields her daughter Tori from a gainful pursuit that sold her two brothers (*ibid.,* 128). Under Lauren's leadership, the migrants initiate a radical American populace that disengages citizens from imperialist capitalist moguls through education and self-empowerment.

See also "Crossover"; Slavery.

Sources

Allen, Marlene D. "Octavia Butler's 'Parable' Novels and the 'Boomerang' of African American History," *Callaloo* 32:4 (Winter, 2009): 1353–1365.
Butler, Octavia. *Adulthood Rites* in *Lilith's Brood.* New York: Warner, 2000, 249–517.
_____. "Amnesty," *Bloodchild and Other Stories.* New York: Seven Stories Press, 2005, 147–186.
_____. *Kindred.* New York: Doubleday, 1979.
_____. *Mind of My Mind.* New York: Doubleday, 1977.
_____. *The Parable of the Sower.* New York: Four Walls, Eight Windows, 1993.
_____. *The Parable of the Talents.* New York: Four Walls, Eight Windows, 1998.
_____. "Persistence," *Locus* 44:6 (June 2000): 6.
_____. *Wild Seed.* New York: Doubleday, 1980.
Johnson, Ikea M. "On Compassion and the Sublime Black Body: Octavia E. Butler's Parable of the Sower," *Journal of Comparative Literature and Aesthetics* 43:2 (Summer, 2020): 92–101.
Mizota, Sharon. "She Blazed Sci-Fi Trails," *Los Angeles Times* (31 October 2016): E4.
Yazell, Bryan. "A Sociology of Failure: Migration and Narrative Method in U.S. Climate Fiction," *Configurations* 28:2 (Spring 2020).

"Childfinder"

A tense face-off between a scrappy psionic society and an insidious anti-psi organization, Octavia's "Childfinder" anticipates the dream training of the next generation in the Pattern novels *Wild Seed* and *Mind of My Mind* and virtual corporate enslavement in the Parable series. Her delineation of the innovator and the obstructionist pictures a world in which the perceptive must guard their mental strategies from psionic snoops, the inheritors of what analyst Kristen Lillvis, an English researcher at Marshall University in Huntington, West Virginia, calls "post-human multiple consciousness" (Lillvis, 2017, 97). In the Foreword to *Unexpected Stories,* critic Nisi Shawl, a journalist for *Ms.* Magazine and the *Seattle Times,* described "Childfinder's" revelation of "an obliviousness to privilege and an ignorance of racial injustice" (Butler, 2014, 9). For redress, the black heroine applies "incredible superpowers … to systemic oppression," a crusade that Octavia assigns to her wonder women (*ibid.*).

In a journal entry for January 3, 1999, the author mentioned another aspect of social engineering—the importance of genetic diversity "lest some essential trait be lost" (Brown, 2021, 98). The author's backstory pictures the courage of Harriet Tubman, the historic "Moses" of the Underground Railroad, a prophecy for the child Valerie's future that recurs with Lilith Iyapo in *Dawn,* Lauren Oya Olamina in *The Parable of the Sower,* and Shori Matthews, the introductory black vampire in *Fledgling.* Pitted against Eve's unscrupulous organization, Barbara, the ironically childless finder, grooms the most promising black children as superior mentally empowered, a literary flight from slave territory to liberation in the north.

Octavia foresaw that human intelligence and restrictive hierarchies "don't work together" (Williams, 1986, 72). In the speech "Devil Girl from Mars: Why I Write Science Fiction," a segment of Massachusetts Institute of Technology's *Media in Transition* program on February 19, 1998, she summarized the pivotal conflict in "Childfinder." A two-sided confrontation pitted the anti-psionic stalkers against Barbara's refuge for young black mind readers as perceptive as Valerie and Jordan. In human terms: "They couldn't conceal their disagreements and animosities and contempt, and they were killing each other" (Butler, 1998, n.p.). The author predicted an explosive upheaval and eventual self-destruction along with a waste of talent.

The story, a link to *Mind of My Mind* and *Wild Seed,* unites the clairvoyant few against the mundane many. Like special forces, Jordan and his fellow psi-wielders encircle their mentor Barbara to shield her from thugs the author calls "psychic brawlers" (Butler, 2014, 79). Barbara anticipates success in her gifted teens to "endure unthinkable hardships in the name of children, in hopes that at least *some* future will exist" (*ibid.*) She exerts more subversive methods of crippling potential white rivals to secure Extra Sensory Perception for a black-only counterculture.

See also Afrofuturism.

Sources

Behrent, Megan. "The Personal Is Historical: Slavery, Black Power, and Resistance in Octavia Butler's *Kindred," College Literature* 46:4 (2019): 795–828.

Brown, Jayna. *Black Utopias: Speculative Life and the Music of Other Worlds.* Durham, NC: Duke University Press, 2021.

Butler, Octavia. "Childfinder," *Unexpected Stories.* New York: Open Road Media, 2014, 77–80.

_____. "Devil Girl from Mars: Why I Write Science Fiction," *Media in Transition,* MIT (19 February 1998).

_____. "Foreword" in *Unexpected Stories.* New York: Open Road Media, 2014.

Lillvis, Kristen. *Posthuman Blackness and the Black Female Imagination.* Athens: University of Georgia Press, 2017.

Williams, Sherley Anne. "On Octavia E. Butler," *Ms.* 14:9 (March 1986): 70–73.

Clay's Ark

A "Mad Max" post–World War III novel on a par with Cormac McCarthy's end-of-time thriller *The Road,* Octavia's *Clay's Ark,* the fifth and last of the Patternmaster series, focuses suspense on the downside of faster-than-light travel by starship. Discord echoes a familiar sci-fi fear of interstellar travel—the post–Ark program's return of a single diseased star voyager. A throwback to the raw meat-eating beast, the first Clayark or infected mutant represents the trope of the "last man" afflicted with symbiogenesis, "a prisoner within his own skull, cut off from conscious control of his body" (Butler, 1984, 31). In the estimation of Gerald Jonas, a reviewer for the *New York Times,* the concept reflects a standard means "to put human pride (and arrogance) to the test" by advancing a potential cannibal who eats Patternists (Jonas, 1996, 16). Chapter one thrusts the reader into the pathetic fallacy by orchestrating a Mohave dust storm and cloudburst outside Needles in southern California and near Twenty-Nine Palms, Palos Verdes, Barstow, and Victorville. For maximum comprehension, the inch-by-inch narrative broadens and deepens the psychological terrors of victims and the pernicious intent of desert goons, whom the innocent believe to be criminal road warriors.

Opening on a suspenseful dystopia, the confrontation of two authoritarian abductors—the astronaut Asia Elias "Eli" Doyle, one of Octavia's black heroes, and the biker Orel Ingraham—with Dr. Blake Jason Maslin and his sixteen-year-old twin daughters Keira and Rane pits the Maslins' carbine against handguns, an imbalance favoring the Maslins over carjackers. Yugoslav scholar Darko Suvin, a fellow of Canada's Royal Society, referred to the conflict as the "interaction of estrangement and cognition" (Suvin, 2016, 7). From a book about firearms, the author found useful data that also impacted the novel's hostage situation with a kitchen gunport and automatic rifles, grenades, and explosives, a series of details that she enlarged in the Parable series. Varied ordnance indicates the story's volatility and stress on a man-made disaster leading to women's suppression by a wasteland cult, the underlying thesis of Mary Shelley's *The Last Man,* Margaret Atwood's *The Handmaid's Tale,* and Michael Crichton's *Andromeda Strain.*

The Unforeseen

Within the apocalyptic narrative, elements imply a serendipitous end to racial divisions. Names identify Maslin, the benevolent internist, as "white counselor" and his biracial twins as the ethereal Keira (dark) or Kerry (dark-haired) and ethical, but audacious Rane (queenly). Additional implications derive from their black mother Jorah (spring rain) and an off-road seizure by biker Orel Ingraham (eagle, Saxon ram). His partner, geologist Asa Elias "Eli" Doyle (healer, the Lord God, black stranger), survive the starship *Clay's Ark* explosion after it crash-lands in the American Southwest. Infected at the outstation on Proxi Two, Eli feels responsible for bearing a harrowing disease, an independent microbe that endangers victims by altering their genetic code, one of the author's interests in hybridization and bi-species offspring. He concludes that physical alterations "had turned them all into breeding animals," causing fertile young women to produce agile felines capable of hypersensitive hearing, speed, and seeing in the dark, sense impressions that return in Akin in *Adulthood Rites,* An-yanwu in *Wild Seed,* and Shori Matthews in *Fledgling* (Butler, 1984, 37).

A prophetic model of plague literature, *Clay's Ark* settles on mass death, zealotry, and dominance as the controlling themes. Speeding from one hostage situation into total anarchy, the Maslin trio survives a second car gang that blindly shoots at attackers, a turbulent shift of setting and characters that raises questions about life sanctity. Until the Maslin grandparents in Flagstaff can arrange ransom, Blake and his daughters exhibit the viral extremes of hunger and raging libido, a flagrant lust that causes the physician to sexually abuse daughter Keira. Among the ranch house kidnappers, Eli's mates debate how to isolate the virus and how to rear their mutant children in an unprecedented environment overrun by armed car nomads, a question that dogs Haitian parents living in high crime ghettos in Edwidge Danticat's *Brother, I'm Dying*. At the height of transformation, while Rane rampages in a random shootout, Keira takes the greatest risk by allowing her failing body to accept the galactic virus and all its inevitabilities, which including healing her myeloblastic leukemia. The divergence dramatizes a Jekyll and Hyde dichotomy that seals the twins' fate.

A TENTATIVE OUTLOOK

Octavia leaves the world terminally ill with the space virus and dependent on mutant scions alone to populate the globe. Author Eileen Hunt Botting, a feminist political philosopher at the University of Notre Dame, interpreted the spreading pandemic as a trope for "theorizing the deeper political pathologies of human society," the bureaucratic corruptions and gang warfare found in the Parable series (Botting, 2021, 2). She classified Eli's control as a miniature of "top-down models of governance" devoid of female rhetoric, reproductive decision-making, and democratic leadership (*ibid.*). A rushed, open-ended resolution leaves Keira family-less and dependent on her lover, Stephen Kaneshiro, to care for her before the birth of a mutant child. In a paradoxical review, New York sci-fi author Carl R. Moore acknowledged the ambiguous good of the surviving nuclear family, "however strange and alien, however shocking and unlikely, and however offensive to others that kinship might be" (Moore, 2020).

As is common to the author's themes, the narrative probes community response to dysfunction and future collapse from an "organism ... built to survive" (Butler, 1984, 93). Stephen reports a Louisiana group "shooting anyone who seems a little odd to them. Mostly Asians, blacks, and browns" (*ibid.*, 212). To post-human examples of virulent gang forays, child abuse, female subordination, and genocide, the novel posits a new breed of earthling devoid of humanity, a fictional dystopia that Briana Whiteside, an English major at Southern Illinois University, dubs "an extraterrestrial zombie story" (Whiteside, 2013). In a tentative evaluation from the February 15, 1984, issue of *Kirkus Review,* the unnamed critic finds reason to admire the novel, but admits to the "basic triteness of its premise and its backdrop" of a spaceship crash ("Review," 1984). On a more positive note, Norman Sondak, a journalist with the *San Diego Union,* adds *Clay's Ark* to a list of the best of the macabre. Nudged by the author's time setting of 2021 "as the precise date for the man-made disasters," reader thoughts on the 2020–2021 Covid pandemic returned the author's themes and plots to urgent analysis (Botting, 2021, 5).

See also Race.

Sources

Botting, Eileen Hunt. "Predicting the Patriarchal Politics of Pandemics from Mary Shelley to Covid-19," *Frontiers in Sociology* 6 (24 March 2021): 1–8.

Butler, Octavia. *Clay's Ark*. New York: St. Martin's Press, 1984.

Jonas, Gerald. "Review: *Clay's Ark*," *New York Times* (29 December 1996): 16.

Moore, Carl R. "Review: *Clay's Ark*," *Deep Dark Night*, *https://carlrmoore.com/2020/09/21/573/*.

Prakash, M., and K. Lavanya. "Transformation of the Human Race in Octavia E. Butler's Clay's Ark," *European Journal of Molecular & Clinical Medicine* 7:11 (2020): 1729–1731.

"Review: *Clay's Ark*," *Kirkus Review* (15 February 1984).

Suvin, Darko. *Metamorphosis of Science Fiction*. Bern, Switzerland: Peter Lang, 2016.

Whiteside, Brianna. "Review: *Clay's Ark*," *Cultural Front*, www.culturalfront.org/2013/03/octavia-butlers-clays-ark.html.

Clay's Ark Genealogy

Octavia predicates her *ad hoc* desert survivalists on their need to breed with healthy humans to avoid contagion. The changing names of a seductive car-gamer from Petra (rock) to Smoke suggests an impalpability, a people soon to die out, leaving a post-human population of hybrids to inhabit the planet by adapting to symbiosis with an extraterrestrial microbe. The motif influenced the author's later descriptions of human breeding with caterpillars in "Bloodchild," Oankali and ooloi in *Lilith's Brood,* and vampires with symbionts in *Fledgling.*

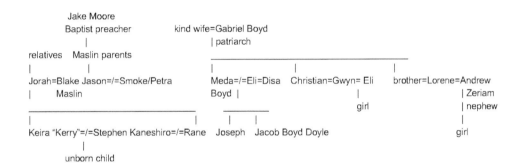

To heighten optimism, Octavia breached racial boundaries by creating a bi-racial family born to white and African parents. She paired Keira Maslin with Stephen Kaneshiro, a Japanese survivor whose given name reflects the fate of the first Christian martyr in Acts 7:57–60 and whose surname means "gold castle," an allusion to success.

Sources

Botting, Eileen Hunt. "Predicting the Patriarchal Politics of Pandemics from Mary Shelley to Covid-19," *Frontiers in Sociology* 6 (24 March 2021): 1–8.

Butler, Octavia. *Clay's Ark*. New York: St. Martin's Press, 1984.

Suvin, Darko. *Metamorphosis of Science Fiction*. Bern, Switzerland: Peter Lang, 2016.

Coming of Age

Perhaps because of a difficult girlhood spent with a no-nonsense maternal grandmother, Estella Haywood Guy, and mother, Octavia Guy Butler, the author seemed preoccupied with writing maturation and initiation scenarios about the frustrations and choices of young people. Her developing characters appear in varied situations, from Rufus Weylin's inheritance of Southern agrarian bondage in *Kindred* to Nikanj's acceptance of an inevitable late stage of life in *Adulthood Rites*, Doro's transformation from vampiric monster to loving husband in *Wild Seed*, and Shori Matthews's search for evidence of her past in *Fledgling*:

Name	Source	Description
Akin	*Adulthood Rites*	a mutant living apart from his mother while he grows up
Alan Chi	"The Evening and the Morning and the Night"	a future groom who forces himself to witness his mother's struggle with Duryea-Gode Disease (DGD)
Alanna Verrick	*Survivor*	a rescued outlander who mediates between conflicting factions
Carrie	*Kindred*	a mute slave girl who faces slurs and threats
Diut	"A Necessary Being"	a blue-toned mountain Hao (magistrate) and tribal authority
Doro	*Wild Seed*	an immortal child who rejects boundaries to murder and to manipulating his offspring
Gan	"Bloodchild"	a naive boy who learns about alien reproduction with humans
Iray	*Patternmaster*	a young wife easily seduced by a tyrannic brother-in-law
Jane	"Crossover"	a young factory worker who fails to establish self-esteem
Jodahs	*Imago*	an adolescent ooloi in *Imago*
Jordan	"Childfinder"	a protective leader of mind readers who protects their leader
Keira "Kelly" Maslin	*Clay's Ark*	survivor of blood cancer and expectant mother of a mutant
Keith Oyamina	*Parable of the Sower*	a belligerent son who rebels and steals to obtain freedom
Larkin Bankole	*Parable of the Talents*	a misguided kidnap victim who rejects her birth mother
Lauren Oya Olamina	*Parable of the Sower*	teen visionary who outlines the Earthseed religion
Lynn Mortimer	"The Evening and the Morning and the Night"	a future bride who must battle a terrifying inherited malady, Duryea-Gode Disease (DGD)
Mary Larkin	*Mind of My Mind*	a wayward teen who must overpower her father Doro's control
Marcus Olamina	*Parable of the Sower*	teen orator who develops a pulpit ministry
Noah Cannon	"Amnesty"	rape victim who becomes a translator of alien language
Paul Titus	*Dawn*	a survivor of nuclear war who must adapt to alien life

Name	Source	Description
Rane Malin	*Clay's Ark*	a victim of an extraterrestrial microbe
Rufus Weylin	*Kindred*	the inheritor of a plantation who must overcome his father Tom's brutal example of slave mismanagement
Shori Matthews	*Fledgling*	an amnesiac who has lost contact with her Ina beginnings
Teray	*Patternmaster*	jealous husband in early marriage who ends his first relationship
unnamed niece	"Near of Kin"	an insecure daughter questions the relationship of her mother Barbara with Barbara's brother Stephen
Valerie	"Childfinder"	mind reader who avoids adult guidance
Valerie Rye	"Speech Sounds"	an inexperienced history teacher who adopts two homeless children

Teray, the newly transitioned adult in *Patternmaster,* suffers jealousy and caution about his wife Iray's friendship with housemaster Joachim. To Teray's credit, the suspicions locate the lapse in his marriage and point him toward a true soulmate, Amber the healer.

With more potential than Teray, Diut comes under intense scrutiny in "A Necessary Being," particularly his response to miscegenation. At the court of the female Hao Tahneh, his liberal views of the mixed caste magistrate-hunter marriage of Jeh and Cheah suggests to the Rohkohn elite that Diut is still inexperienced at making tribal decisions that set a precedent for the young. He narrates his troubled rise to magistrate after an indulgent rearing by Hao relatives and adjudicators, not warriors. He demeans himself as "nothing more now than a judge colored blue," a pun on his imperious skin tone and emotions (Butler, 2014, 38).

More examples of characters-in-progress dramatize the dangers of mental drift. At odds with adult control, fifteen-year-old Lynn Mortimer hates diet hassles in "The Evening and the Morning and the Night." Of youth's haphazard choices, the first-person character questions a reason to enroll in college: "I had been going to school all my life and didn't know what else to do" (Butler, 2005, 37). In "Childfinder," Valerie, a teen telepath, also avoids the appearance of cooperating with adults and displays a snarky attitude and disinterest in reading a book about Harriet Tubman, a role model for black trailblazers. A more serious test of maturity awaits University of California at Los Angeles history professor Valerie Rye in "Speech Sounds," who witnesses three street killings and adopts two foundlings, and Gan, a sexually naive teen who learns "adult things" in "Bloodchild" (Butler, 2005, 25). The author summarizes Gan's challenge as "a boy who must absorb disturbing information" about surgical delivery of wormlets that will determine his adult reproductive life (*ibid.*, 30). After receiving an impromptu introduction to hybrid birthing, he cringes from the possibility of his own pregnancy with Tlic eggs, a flip of the standard female thinking about parturition, delivery, and motherhood.

To develop more views on mixed emotions, the author individualizes examples of coming-of-age memories. For *Fledgling,* Shori Matthews becomes the newly hatched bird amid the ruins of her Romanian family. Plagued by amnesia, she attempts to assemble the past by researching the Ina and learning the rituals and tenets of a vast European network of vampires. In "The Evening and the Morning and the Night," a tragic story of inherited disease, Alan Chi and his bride-to-be Lynn Mortimer force themselves to view Alan's mother and her rehabilitation from a disease that both Alan and Lynn will face. Octavia cites as another model of fearful baggage the seizure and rape of translator Noah Cannon in "Amnesty." Lauren Oya Olamina, the fifteen-year-old evangelist in the Parable series, struggles with approach-avoidance conflict—the love of her father, the Reverend Olamina, and her marked deviation from a fundamentalist Baptist doctrine to the Earthseed concept. In *The Parable of the Talents,* she attempts to reclaim her brother Marcus, the survivor of child prostitution, burns, and beatings. Her scriptural verse recognizes maturation as being "cast from paradise," an idealized childhood that preceded the destruction of a gated community (Butler, 1998, 101).

Mixed Species

The author reserves until the second Xenogenesis volume, *Adulthood Rites,* a description of the homeship as a growing sphere plated "like the shell of a turtle," a familiar refuge from universal turmoil and threat like the world turtle in Chinese, Lenape, and Hindu mythology (Butler, 2000, 262). In *Dawn,* an abductee of aliens, Paul Titus, was fourteen when the Oankali rescued him from earth's nuclear war and helped him adapt to the spaceship/planet. During lengthy captivity, he fails to escape boyhood and evolve sexual manhood. Retaining his sexual naivete for fifteen years proves frustrating enough to precipitate an assault on Lilith Iyapo, the first available female. She charges the alien captors with "[keeping] him fourteen for all those years," setting the stage for a teen tantrum at her disinterest in his wooing (*ibid.,* 97). The author implies that immature children like Paul need to socialize during their growing-up years and to trust family to "teach him to be a man" (*ibid.,* 101). She compares his acclimation to the jungle with young men living alone in deserts or forests to test their virility, a macho self-image explored in Edgar Rice Burroughs's Tarzan adventure lore.

The pattern of "subadult" indiscretions returns in *Adulthood Rites* in the maturing of Lillian Iyapo's son Akin, a crossbreed of human with ooloi. Gregory Jerome Hampton, a professor of black literature at Howard University in Washington, D.C., characterized him as "a child in sexual and gender limbo," neither male nor female, child or adult (Hampton, 2010, 51). Throughout puberty, he must learn how to fight aggressive boys, a common test-of-manhood battle reflecting his resistance to humanizing thoughts and inclinations. In the pattern that anthropologist Margaret Mead researched in the 1920s in *Coming of Age in Samoa,* he pleasures himself with casual sex, a stop-gap assertion of masculinity that relieves tensions.

Like a modern Holden Caulfield, Akin skulks about the Amazon Basin resenting his youth, debating discipline wielded by father Dichaan, and glaring at the shuttle that comes to pick him up. By forbidding communications, elders remind Akin that he must undergo metamorphosis: "So much had to wait until he was an adult" (Butler, 2000, 430). He burdens himself with right opinions about resisters yet finds

his thinking "being ignored because" his logic still fit the category of child thinking (*ibid.*). As growth changes begin, he nurses fears; his older sister Ayre becalms
him with the promise, "Your body will know how to respond," a prediction aided by
his intuition of rightness and the pheromones from his ooloi companion Dehkiaht
(*ibid.*, 436). The emergence of tentacles alters his perspective from forward-looking
eyes to multi-focal tentacles that creolize his viewpoint. In aging, he escapes ocu-
lar limitations for a panoramic view of humankind and its faults that enable him to
evaluate the causes of stagnation and planetary doom.

The Teen Complex

A kaleidoscope of emotions plagues characters in Octavia's speculative fiction.
To character transition from normal to telepath in *Wild Seed*, the hybridizer Doro,
an immortal Nubian, inadvertently summarizes the teen years: "Open to every
thought, every emotion, every pleasure, every pain," a description that fits gang
member Keith Olamina and his sister Lauren in *The Parable of the Sower* and Shori
Matthews, the prototype black vampire in *Fledgling* (Butler, 1980, 260). Another
model, the endurance training of humans in *Dawn*, introduces survivors of earth's
implosion to terrain and orienteering skills similar to the protocols taught to Boy
and Girl Scouts. As the ooloi Nikanj nears metamorphosis, he requires Lilith Iyapo's
companionship. On the cusp of change involving deep sleep, he explains his insecurity: "If you're there, I'll know and I'll be all right" (Butler, 2000, 83).

The search for support during a difficult transition recurs in *Mind of My Mind*
with the enlargement of teen intellect into full psionic mode, which exposes the
brain to external sufferings of other people. For Mary, a dazzling telepath, a panoply
of adversaries recognizes her command of full psionic powers. The story pairs her
with a husband, Karl Larkin, an experienced telepath for a decade, who, like Lilith
guarding Nikanj, enables her emergence into womanhood. A comparison of mind
readings ranks Mary's skills above Karl's abilities to delay danger and harm or kill
adversaries. To aid five additional telepaths in Mary Larkin's complex web, she offers
a similar service to transitioning beginners, who sometimes die in the process. To
her father/lover Doro, she states the standard goals of all pre-adults—"jobs, interests, goals" (Butler, 1977, 73). Through intuitive understanding of the young, Mary
accepts her own need "to be kicked out of the nest" (*ibid.*). Octavia endorses her
adaptation to a stunning destiny, which results in suppression of Doro, her father/
rival and a vampiric monster.

Cutting the Cord

Complex perspectives on parent-child relationships burden the plot of *Clay's
Ark*. Because a space-age pathogen infects Dr. Blake Jason Maslin and seizes control
of his libido, he molests his biracial daughter Keira, a sixteen-year-old wasting away
from leukemia. As his middle name suggests, the modern Jason must sail unknown
waters by assessing a rapidly deteriorating milieu of mobile muggers and kidnapping to an amoral cult. Out of love and admiration for her principled father, Keira

can forgive his unforeseen sexual assault and grieve his death during a flight from highway felons. In a morally compromised resolution, she discovers that the alien microbe destroys her cancer. With a renewed anticipation of normal life, she finds the courage to mate with Stephen Kaneshiro, a Japanese cultist, and to anticipate the birth of a mutant infant. The author accords Keira an unusually mature capacity for compromise in a chaotic world no longer recognizable.

In a similarly anarchic milieu, the author depicts Lauren Oya Olamina, the fifteen-year-old philosopher of *The Parable of the Sower,* as ready for the Apocalypse in Robledo, California. She caches emergency supplies in the gated compound where her household lives and joins the family in target practice with BB guns, pistols, and a submachine gun. Individual training becomes a rite of passage for stepmother Cory, Lauren, and her brothers. For background, she reads up on the Black Death and anticipates a huge reshuffling during the Pox. Simultaneously, Octavia poses the impulsive, illogical rebellion of Lauren's thirteen-year-old brother Keith, who chooses guns and gangs as a means of elevating his stature. The remainder of the dystopian novel depicts the collapse of Keith's world and its replacement by Lauren's Earthseed, an agrarian cooperative. In the sequel, *The Parable of the Talents,* the evangelist speaks the author's wish that the earth itself could outgrow its immaturity and seek a destiny in the stars, a location beyond worldliness and mundane dissension.

Sources

Butler, Octavia. *Adulthood Rites* in *Lilith's Brood.* New York: Warner, 2000, 249–517.
_____. *Bloodchild and Other Stories.* New York: Seven Stories Press, 2005.
_____. *Dawn* in *Lilith's Brood.* New York: Warner, 2000, 2–248.
_____. *Mind of My Mind.* New York: Doubleday, 1977.
_____. "A Necessary Being," *Unexpected Stories.* New York: Open Road Media, 2014, 11–76.
_____. *The Parable of the Sower.* New York: Four Walls, Eight Windows, 1993.
_____. *The Parable of the Talents.* New York: Four Walls, Eight Windows, 1998.
Hampton, Gregory Jerome. *Changing Bodies in the Fiction of Octavia Butler: Slaves, Aliens, and Vampires.* Lanham, MD: Lexington Books, 2010.
Turner, Jenny. "Ready to Go Off," *London Review of Books* 43:4 (18 February 2021).

Couples

The pairing of sexually active beings dominates much of Octavia's glimpse of species reproduction and intimacy. She cites as models the two Haos, Diut and Tahneh in "A Necessary Being," Lilith Iyapo's successful multiracial marriage to Joseph "Joe" Li-Chin Shing in *Adulthood Rites*, and Diut's judge-hunter couple Jeh and Cheah in *Survivor.* Deceptive mating offers short-term protection from bias, as with the implied sex slavery of Dana Franklin to Kevin, who poses as her owner and master in *Kindred*, and the bond in *The Parable of the Talents* between Zahra Moss and Lauren Oya Olamina, who cross-dress as a heterosexual pair to avoid assault. Lauren explains period couple logic of skin color: "Mixed couples catch hell whether they are gay or straight," a statement applicable to the Franklins, to Wright Hamlin and Shori Matthews in *Fledgling,* and to Rufus Weylin and Alice Greenwood in *Kindred* (Butler, 1998, 177).

For the Xenogenesis novel *Dawn,* the release of eighty earthlings from leafy pods after years of restorative sleep originates a frenzy of pairing male with female. For Chinese-Canadian husband Joseph "Joe" Li-Chin Shing, the introduction of a three-way coupling with Lilith Iyapo and the ooloi Nikanj arouses human revulsion and defense of macho monogamy. The pleasure of unprecedented coitus with an alien lures Joseph back to bed and to the admission that other options exist for satisfaction, Octavia's gesture to acceptance of divergent modes of copulation. At the hands of the axe murderer Curt Loehr, Joseph dies without knowing he has sired a daughter. The loss illustrates the dangers of inborn aggression in humans and any offense to their domestic contentment, a subject that Marion Zimmer Bradley examined in the Darkover series.

In refutation of eugenics and the primacy of racially pure blood, the writer speculated on interbreeding within bold populations and the possibilities of transhumanism, the redemption of *homo sapiens* via calculated change. In the estimation of Martin Japtok, an English expert at Palomar College in San Marcos, California, Octavia's fictional couples spotlight the "individuals and families who share oddities" (Japtok, 2020, 5). They exemplify voluntary interracial and interspecies relationships and the resulting offspring:

AR—*Adulthood Rites*   Kin—*Kindred*
AMN—"Amnesty"   LB—*Lilith's Brood*
BC—"Bloodchild"   MMM—*Mind of My Mind*
BOM—"The Book of Martha"   NB—"A Necessary Being"
CA—*Clay's Ark*   NK—"Near of Kin"
CF—"Childfinder"   PM—*Patternmaster*
Cross—"Crossover"   POS—*The Parable of the Sower*
Dawn—*Dawn*   POT—*The Parable of the Talents*
EMN—"The Evening and the Morning and   SS—"Speech Sounds"
   the Night"   Sur—*Survivor*
Fl—*Fledgling*   WS—*Wild Seed*
Im—*Imago*

Couple	Title	Relationship	Offspring
Ahajas & Nikanj	*Dawn*	loving alien couple allied with Dichaan	Tiikuchahk
Alan Chi & Lynn Mortimer	EMN	future man and wife fearful of DGD Disease	none
Alanna Verrick & Diut	Sur	a pair challenged by tribal struggles with speciesism	Tien
Alice Greenwood & Isaac Jackson	Kin	a close couple separated after Isaac's sale to Jackson, Mississippi	none
Alice Greenwood & Rufus	Kin	forced concubinage that results in Alice's suicide	Aaron, Joe, Miriam, Weylin Hagar
Allie & Mary Sullivan	POT	lesbian lovers betrayed during a testimonial	none
Amber & Teray	PM	strong relationship based on equity	unborn child
Andrew Zeriam & Lorene	CA	incest between cousins	girl
An-yanwu & Denice	WS	normal African household	Leah
An-yanwu & dolphin	WS	mystic union of immortal with animal	none

Couple	Title	Relationship	Offspring
An-yanwu & Doro	WS	shapeshifting Nigerian coerced by an immortal	many children
An-yanwu & Isaac	WS	shapeshifting Nigerian wed to a psionic human	Peter and forty-one others
An-yanwu & Thomas	WS	a healer who redeems a drunken hermit	none
Barbara & Stephen	NK	an incestuous brother/sister affair	daughter
Blake Jason Maslin & Jorah	CA	loving biracial parents who produce twins	Keira & Rane Maslin
Bram Lomas & T'Khotgif	BC	human-Tlic breeding couple	grisly birth
Cheah & Jeh	NB	miscegenated couple who quash pro-testers	children
	Sur	unusual pairing of a hunter with a judge	two children
Coransee & Iray	PM	an amoral brother who seduces his sister-in-law	none
Cory Doran & the Reverend Olamina	POS	doers of good deeds and trainers in shooting	Lauren, Keith, Marcus, Bennett, Greg
Curtis & Lauren Olamina	POS	devoted teen couple, sexually active	none
Dana & Kevin Franklin	Kin	successful biracial Californian couple	none
Doro & Mary	MMM	incestuous affair	none
Doro & Rina	MMM	amoral breeder of psionic children	Mary Larkin
Doro & suicidal wife	MMM	constant womanizing	Isaac & Lale Sachs
Diut & Kehyo	Sur	lapsed lovers	none
Eli Doyle & Gwyn	CA	polyamorous relationship	girl
Eli Doyle & Meda Boyd	CA	an essential mating to produce virus-free children	Jacob Boyd Doyle, Joseph
Eli Torrey & Rachel "Rae" Davidson	MMM	lovers with unequal healing talents	none
Francisco & Inez	Im	normal mates	nine children
Gabe & Tate	*Dawn*	a rocky partnership in the spaceship/planet	none
Gabriel Boyd & wife	CA	patriarchal family with two children	Christian & Meda
Gan & T'Gatoi	BC	a human's sexual relationship with a semi-human	unborn child
Harry Balter & Zahra Moss	POS	migrants who love and trust each other	Tabia, Russell
	POT	a marriage that thrives until Zahra's death	Tabia, Russell
Hugh & Lea Westley	MMM	foster parents	Vaughn
Iray & Teray	PM	a weak link between husband and wife	none
Iye & Stephen Ifeyinwa	WS	a successful marriage ruined by blood-shed	son
Jan & Karl Larkin	MMM	short-term lovers	Margaret
Jane & ex-con	Cross	a fractious affair interrupted by a prison term	none

Couple	Title	Relationship	Offspring
Jansee & Rayal	PM	a long dynastic marriage of siblings	Coransee, Teray
Javier & Paz	Im	mates	child died
Joe & Lilith Iyapo	Dawn	a contented mixed-race couple united by Nikanj	daughter
Joel & Shori	Fl	a new man in Shori's life	none
Joseph Toler & Margaret Nneka	WS	a faithful wife of a lazy wastrel and murderer	two sons
Jules & Niela Verrick	Sur	a missionary couple that fosters Alanna	Yahnoh
Karl & Mary Larkin	MMM	married managers of a telepathic household	Karl August Larkin
Karl Larkin & Vivian "Vee"	MMM	a parasitic lover at Karl's house	none
Keira Maslin & Stephen Kaneshiro	CA	survivors in a desert cult who form a nuclear family	unborn mutant
Lauren Oya Olamina &	POS	the unlikely mating of an older doctor with a teen	Larkin Bankole
Taylor Franklin Bankole	POT	visionary	
Leah & Wray Ordway	AR	humans living in a jungle village	twenty children
Lilith Iyapo & Sam	Dawn	loving parents of Ayre until a car accident kills him and his father	Ayre
Lilith Iyapo & Nikanj	Dawn	a three-way alliance with an alien and Joseph	daughter
Margaret & Tom Weylin	Kin	an off-balance Maryland couple who live apart	Rufus
Mateo & Pilar	LB	committed parents	Augustino Leal
Naomi Chi & Nigerian	EMN	marriage destroyed by DGD disease	Alan Chi
Natividad & Travis Douglas	POS	successful mixed-race couple	Domingo
Obsidian & Valerie Rye	SS	an afternoon's lovemaking preceded by murder	none
Okoye & Udenkwo	WS	Nigerian newlyweds	none
Renee/Shori & Wright Hamlin	Fl	rescuer and rescued who become lovers	none
Sarah & slave	Kin	plantation breeder who loses three children to sale	Carrie
Shori & Theodora Harden	Fl	a passionate relationship with a lonely librarian	none
Tehkorahs & Wray Ordway	AR	human husband and his ooloi mate	two daughters

Japtok observed that "Love is a functional term [that] plays an ambiguous role," notably clouding the racial and gender dynamics listed above (*ibid.*, 7).

Octavia sets romance against murderous and riotous scenarios such as the spur-of-the-moment coitus of police officer Obsidian and teacher Valerie Rye after the bus altercation in "Speech Sounds" and Lauren Oya Olamina's instant attraction in *The Parable of the Sower* to Dr. Taylor Franklin Bankole, a physician older than her father. The unions, whether marital, casual, or experimental, tend to accentuate the Greek concept of short-term Ἔρως (*Eros* or physical desire) over long-term ἀγάπη (*Agape* or unconditional love and affection). At the meeting of Mary with Karl Larkin in *Mind of My Mind*, he spurns Doro's order to wed daughter Mary because of

Karl's erotic relationship with his mistress Valerie. In *The Parable of the Talents,* the author acknowledged the flaw in such forced marriages: "To be led by a tyrant is to sell yourself and those you love into slavery" (Butler, 1998, 226). Only over time does the Larkin mating bear reciprocal affection and result in the birth of son Karl August Larkin, a trial-and-error marriage anticipating An-yanwu's civilizing effect on Doro in *Wild Seed.*

The author deliberately analyzed earth with "hard-nosed and unsentimental" fiction as cautions to improve the world and the self (Japtok, 2020, 2). In *Kindred,* Maryland plantation owners Margaret and Tom Weylin live apart, whether in-house or separated, and seek differing goals for their investment. The affection of their union dwells on Rufus, the only child, who learns little of conjugal tenderness from his parents' bullying and coddling. Octavia implies that a life of buying, disciplining, and selling slaves rots the soul, depriving Tom of the ability to feel affection, even for son Rufus. The absence of a paternal model limits Rufus's knowledge of selfless love for mistress Alice Greenwood and for his rescuer Dana Franklin. Because the boy has grown into a monster, the novel concludes on Rufus's attempted rape and stabbing, which sets Dana free of impromptu snatching to the past.

In contrast to the Weylins, Jansee and Patternmaster Rayal share a lasting sibling/spousal relationship in the Patternist series that produces sons Coransee and Teray. Despite an agreeable background, the antagonistic brothers violate the Greek concept of φιλία (*Philia* or brotherhood) through violence and conspiracy to replace their all-powerful father. Nonetheless, Teray displays devotion to Amber, the lover who replaces his unfaithful first wife Iray. Conversely, within a welter of passionate, traitorous, and coercive couplings in *Wild Seed,* the author dramatizes an unusually long-term connection between the immortal Anwanyu and Isaac, a psionic human, the sire of forty-two children. For Lilith Iyapo and Nikanj in *Dawn,* the author poses an off-kilter alliance between a human female and tentacled alien. The duo negotiates a tolerant espousal that produces a daughter. Other models of compromise ally a biracial couple, Blake Jason Maslin with Jorah in *Clay's Ark,* and two bi-species couples, Wright Hamlin and vampire Shori Matthews in *Fledgling* and Gan and the Tlic seducer T'Gatoi in "Bloodchild." The author endorses marital concessions as models for governments and nations.

See also Hybridization; Miscegenation.

Sources

Allison, Dorothy. "The Future of Female," *Village Voice* (19 December 1989): 67–68.

Butler, Octavia. *The Parable of the Talents.* New York: Seven Stories Press, 1998.

Holden, Rebecca J., and Nisi Shawl, eds. *Strange Matings: Science Fiction, Feminism, African American Voices, and Octavia E. Butler.* Seattle, WA: Aqueduct, 2013.

Japtok, Martin. *Human Contradictions in Octavia E. Butler's Work.* Cham, Switzerland: Palgrave Macmillan, 2020.

Kaplan, Tugba Akman. "The Importance of Surrounding Communities in Identity Formation within Afro-futuristic Context," *RumeliDE* 9: 261–275 (21 August 2021).

"Crossover"

Octavia's 1971 vignette of hurt, disappointment, anxiety, and bleak drudgery, published in *Clarion Journal,* reflects on the life of the single woman managing alone. She exonerated Jane for an emotional meltdown: "Those grindingly dull jobs … were capable of sending anyone up the wall" (Butler, 2005, 120). The author developed a distaste for mindless tasks in repeated castigations of capitalism, the root of human enslavement. She reprised the grimness of unfulfilling, poorly paid blue-collar labor in *The Parable of the Sower,* in which Emery Tananka Solis and daughter Tori flee agrarian bondage to flesh traders who sell Emery's two sons.

Jane's backstory tells of a scar-faced ex-con caught in an unavoidable knife fight. The plot enacts a reunion at the end of his jail term with his lover, who had warned him about the results of violence. The limited nutrition of a canned meal, distaste for drunks in a scuzzy neighborhood, headaches, and a longing for sleep imply that Jane suffers an unhealthy mental state worsened by alcoholic family, fear, and her lover's absence. The combination of ills impeach ghetto life for the poor health and reduced longevity of its residents.

Beyond factory misery, a sexless isolation, and drunkenness, Octavia's protagonist fends off suicidal thoughts with over-the-counter sleeping pills, an easily accessed solution. The three-month hiatus in her love life results from her lover's jail sentence for a knife fight that is forever carved into the left side of his cheek and into Jane's mind. Lack of narrative development defeats the reader's attempt to extend clues about Jane, why she hates her name, why she refuses help from a neighbor, why she "stored up viciousness," and why she "crosses over" (*ibid.*, 118). The smashed ashtray offers an ambiguous attitude toward her former amour, whom she deliberately misses with the projectile. A subtext suggests that, like crushed cigarettes, her affection for him is extinguished, but not her concern for his welfare.

The story's brevity in no way diminishes its power at the climax, her rhetorical question "What am I that I could need you anyway?" (*ibid.*). Octavia measures Jane's despair with return toward the squalid surroundings and the coaxing wino and explains her choice of drinking to mask gloom. Like a relentless phantom, the knifing victim trails after, deepening her hopelessness. The keen imagery and characterization suggest that the author had viewed a similar no-win situation among lone women in her own family who were "sucked down" by low self-image and addiction (*ibid.*, 119).

In "Positive Obsession," a self-castigating essay issued in the May 1989 issue of *Essence*, Octavia summarized her personal faults as "ugly and stupid, clumsy, and socially hopeless," an epiphany of the emotional effects of dyslexia, which impaired her reading and prohibited driving a car (*ibid.*, 128). The intensity of her style prophesied a future of more quite-short stories before she engineered her own crossover and became a stellar novelist capable of writing complex plots about winners and losers. In the Afterword and in *Kindred* and the Parable series, the author pictured other disaffected factory workers and their lapses into self-destruction and addiction to relieve the daily woe of mechanized labor, which grinds employees into dehumanized cogs in the wheels of industry. Alerted to the escapism that fails Jane, Octavia was glad to have writing as an outlet for frustration.

Sources

Butler, Octavia. "Crossover," *Bloodchild and Other Stories*. New York: Seven Stories Press, 2005, 111–122.
_____. "Positive Obsession," *Bloodchild and Other Stories*. New York: Seven Stories Press, 2005, 123–136.
George, Lynell. "Black Writers Crossing the Final Frontier," *Los Angeles Times* (22 June 2004).
Hampton, Gregory Jerome. *Changing Bodies in the Fiction of Octavia Butler: Slaves, Aliens, and Vampires.* Lanham, MD: Lexington Books, 2014.

Dawn

The first of *Lilith's Brood,* a trio of Xenogenesis speculative posthuman novels, *Dawn* adapts a popular colonial era genre, the captivity narrative, a source similar in conventions to the liberation efforts of slave narrative. The frontier hostage prototype, according to Linda Colley, an expert on imperial history at the Swedish Collegium in Uppsala, thrived on "the sometimes porous boundary between history and imaginative literature" (Colley, 2003, 200). Racist lore transformed Native Americans into demonic savages and reformatted cliffhangers into potential rape and torture scenarios, a narrative that Mark Twain chose not to finish in *Huck Finn and Tom Sawyer Among the Indians.* Octavia took a humorless stance toward irredeemable human faults, the genetic propensities that promote superiority, suspicion, exploitation, gun violence, and genocide.

In the essay "Future Forum" for *Starlog,* the author predicted that engaging with aliens "would turn the various human cultures upside down…. No science or philosophy, no racial, religious, national, or international interest would be unaffected" (Butler, 1980, 55). Her fictional version of earthlings in captivity issued a radical view of human sexuality, group dynamics, and "what it means to be other," the source of insidious notions of deficiency, ugliness, and intolerance (Allison, 1989, 67). In the estimation of Hoda M. Zaki, a political science expert at Hood College in Frederick, Maryland, the author charged earthfolk with "a pervasive human need to alienate from oneself those who appear to be different" (Zaki, 1990, 241). The controlling theme of Xenogenesis examines the reproduction of an organism that bears no resemblance to its parents, thus arriving "othered" into the nuclear family through forced concubinage of an alien with a human.

Inventing an "Other"

For action, Octavia opted for a standard sci-fi catastrophe preceding themes of gendered polarization and threats to earth's longevity by a Cold War mentality. Following nuclear cataclysm a quarter millennium in the past, earth dwellers find salvation from Oankali traders, tentacled nomads and self-transformers "who leave only deserts behind them" (White, 1985, 8). Although they rebuke humans for hierarchical behavior, the sixteen-fingered "daisy hands" with a "sea-slug appearance" have their own dominance issues to account for (Butler, 2000, 23, 25). The narrative depicts the curious mutation savvy of gene-mongers who propose exterminating *Homo sapiens* and replacing them with a hybrid race that can survive without violence.

In the description of Sarah Dillon, an English specialist at the University of

Cambridge, themes of "intimacy and separation" draw on the imagery of the palimpsest with its layered discourse (Dillon, 2007, 3). The alien sky wanderers divide themselves into male, female, and the flexible ooloi, multi-gendered restructurers of genetics who normalize multi-sex and same-sex relations. In the third volume of *Lilith's Brood*, Akin identifies ooloi as "themselves—a different sex altogether," a creolized identity more propitious to the universe (*ibid.*, 524). By re-engineering "DNA as naturally as we manipulate pencils and paintbrushes," the traders offer humans no choice in bartering with other beings for future genetic diversity or in raising a crop of people to repopulate "the waiting earth" (*ibid.*, 167). The dual-purpose leaves open to readers whether ooloi and their doctrine of rape and non-consensual reproduction are exploitive or a godsend to earth.

Post-Disaster Renewal

In a post-apocalyptic milieu, the Oankali's self-contained spaceship exemplifies a natural, holistic, living bioregion devoid of warring factions. According to Aparajita Nanda, a teacher of English and black studies at the University of California at Berkeley, the self-contained home and transport "[responds] to Oankali needs and vice versa, creating thereby a virtual symbiotic community" (Nanda, 2021, 217). The free breeders examine their hostage, Lilith Iyapo, a black twenty-six-year-old widow capable of mediating a complex interstellar predicament. She resists interrogation through cooperative bargaining with humanoids "from a number of other worlds," an indication of extensive cross-hybridizing across the universe (Butler, 2000, 12).

Communication between Lilith and a "powerfully acquisitive" alien introduces her to Jdahya, an Oankali named the Urdu word for "commander" (*ibid.*, 41). Octavia narrates through Jdahya an overview of the old world made fresh. Stripped of bad attitudes, marginalization, deadly microbes, and "radioactivity and history. You will become something other than you were" (*ibid.*, 34). She blames the downfall on an outdated tendency toward war and hierarchy, her chief indictments against human nature. The Oankali negotiate by offering the ability to heal and regrow limbs, to repopulate earth with "Medusa children," and to engage in future gene trades that keep the species in constant upgrade (*ibid.*, 42). A shadow of capitalistic zeal reduces Oankali likability to nil.

Essential to progress, Lilith conciliates opposites, a female talent that she shares with Noah Cannon in "Amnesty," Dana Franklin in *Kindred*, Shori Matthews in *Fledgling*, Mary Larkin in *Mind of My Mind*, and Alanna Verrick in *Survivor*. In a prime function on the spaceship/planet, Lilith reintroduces humankind to speaking English, cooperating, and living in a jungle zone on a renewed biosphere. The primal tutorial resembles the fundamental needs of the medieval social and agrarian forms in Marion Zimmer Bradley's Lythande stories and *Darkover* series. At the novel's core, Lilith takes charge of awakening eighty sleeping humans. She fears for their cohesion once they arise and realize that earth is forever changed and that they must adapt to a diaspora aimed at the Amazon Basin. Essential to the deal, the pacifist Oankali reject slaughtering animals for meat. They kill Curt Loehr, a bloodthirsty earthman who rebels against Lilith and murders with an axe her Chinese-Canadian mate Joseph "Joe" Li-Chin Shing, an example of biracial husband. The termination of a barbarian begins the extraterrestrial refinement of human traits.

Reproductive Adjustments

After pondering the possible titles *The Training Floor* and *Lilith,* Octavia chose an allegorical genre for *Dawn,* the debut of earth's rejuvenation under alien influence. Known for imagining variant reproductive methods, she described a sexual threesome—a male and female joined in the middle by Nikanj, a third-gender ooloi, a strong-tentacled parasite and expert seducer and gene manipulator. The species echoes the Eloi in H.G. Wells *The Time Machine,* a race named for the Hebrew term for "lesser gods." The punishment for refusing the *menage à trois* condemns any human holdout to sterilization. Although Joe avoids Nikanj's asexual stimulus, which demeans his manhood, he accepts the ooloi as maestro of Lilith's vast project. A British recap by *Fantasy Book Review* diminishes their relationship as "part manipulation, part friendship, and part fencing match [making] for some fascinating undercurrents" ("Review," undated). In *Adulthood Rites,* Nikanj admits being an accessory to alien coercion: "We control children in ways we should not" (Butler, 2000, 259).

Octavia augments the first of her trilogy into a bitter and murderous climax resolved by the rapid transport of fractious captives to earth and Curt Loehr's corpse to a freezer. She had warned in "Future Forum," an essay in the November 1980 issue of *Starlog/Future Life,* that "confrontation with the different—with humans who look, sound, or believe differently, with animals who are not quite what we thought they were, and most likely in the future, with any vulnerable aliens we discover—brings out the worst in us" (Butler, 1980, 56). The fervent human animosity at meeting ooloi causes Lilith, one of Octavia's super amazons, to work harder at the hopeless task of restoring peace amid irreconcilable differences.

At a surprising epiphany, Lilith learns a valuable bit of data—that her body's carcinogenic tendencies heal Nikanj of a lethal axe wound to a tentacle. Her reaction to the post-battle antipathies admits the value of compassion: "We're all a little bit co-opted" (Butler, 2000, 240). In the analysis of Sami Abdullah Al-Nuaimi, Zainor Izat Zainal, Mohammad Ewan Awang, and Noritah Omar, collaborators for Al-Buraimi University College in Oman and the Universiti Putra Malaysia in Selangor, Lilith achieves the power and influence "to prevent race minorities and rearticulate a new African American identity" (Al-Nuaimi, 2021, 979). The four critics endorsed the characterization of a black female who "can help African Americans to beat their biological and social limitations" (*ibid.,* 983). With no choice of homeland or a future for the human race, Lilith accepts her bi-species pregnancy with Joseph's and Nikanj's son. As the new race's mother, she remains isolated on the spaceship/planet, tethered emotionally and physically to the ooloi seducer. The rapid closure in a "dark forest" and the open-ended questions about humanity's reseeding on earth in *Adulthood Rites* and *Imago* foreshadow epic struggles (Butler, 2000, 248).

See also Adulthood Rites; Imago; Lilith Iyapo; Lilith's Genealogy; Reproduction.

Sources

Allison, Dorothy. "The Future of Female," *Village Voice* (19 December 1989): 67–68.

Al-Nuaimi, Sami Abdullah, Zainor Izat Zainal, Mohammad Ewan Awang, and Noritah Omar. "Afrofuturism and Transhumanism: New Insights into the African American Identity in Octavia Butler's *Dawn*," *Pertanika Journal* 29:2 (2021): 977–992.

Butler, Octavia. *Adulthood Rites* in *Lilith's Brood*. New York: Warner, 2000, 249–517.

_____. *Dawn* in *Lilith's Brood*. New York: Warner, 2000, 2–249.

_____. "Future Forum," *Starlog/Future Life* 22 (November 1980): 55–56.

Colley, Linda. "Perceiving Low Literature: The Captivity Narrative," *Essays in Criticism* 53:3 (2003): 199–218.

Dillon, Sarah. *The Palimpsest: Literature, Criticism and Theory*. London: Bloomsbury, 2007.

Kiran, Ayesha. "Human Identity and Technophobic Posthumanism in Octavia Butler's *Dawn*," *Indiana Journal of Arts & Literature* 2:8 (2021): 1–15.

Lennard, John. *Reading Octavia E. Butler: Xenogenesis/Lilith's Blood*. Penrith, CA: Humanities-Ebooks, 2012.

Magadanz, Stacy. "The Captivity Narrative in Octavia E. Butler's *Adulthood Rites*," *Extrapolation* 53:1 (2012): 47–59.

McCaffery, Larry, ed. *Across the Wounded Galaxies*. Urbana: University of Illinois Press, 1990.

Nanda, Aparajita "A Palimpsestuous Reading of Octavia Butler's *Lilith's Brood*" in *Palimpsests in Ethnic and Postcolonial Literature and Culture*. Cham, Switzerland: Palgrave Macmillan, 2021.

"Review: *Dawn*," *Fantasy Book Reviews*, www.fantasybookreview.co.uk/Octavia-Butler/Dawn.html.

White, Ted. "Love with the Proper Stranger," *Washington Post* (25 June 1989): 8.

Zaki, Hoda M. "Utopia, Dystopia, and Ideology in the Science Fiction of Octavia Butler," *Science Fiction Studies* 17 (1990): 239–251.

Details

The author's incorporation of telling objects and incidents inserted the slivers of meaning that elevated her to master writer. Examples span her canon: the stages of Meda Boyd's labor and delivery in *Clay's Ark* before she gives birth to the feline mutant Jacob Boyd Doyle, the gnawing of larvae on human flesh in "Bloodchild," Iosif Petrescu's large, dark-adapted eyes in *Fledgling,* and the burial of Bankole's younger sister Alexandra and her murdered family in *The Parable of the Sower* to prevent dog and cannibal scavengers. For the infant mutant Akin in *Adulthood Rites,* probing his habitat requires tasting leaves and bark with his gray, slug-like tongue, the evidence of bi-species sense organs. The tone of Octavia's stern marching orders to new writers brooked no excuses for failing to use sensory impressions. Perceptible details enlighten the reader to threats, as with the emotional flashes of yellow and gray in the skin tone of Chief Judge Ehreh in "A Necessary Being," the odor of gasoline during Silks raids in *Fledgling,* and the sounds of murderous stalkers in *The Parable of the Sower.*

To affirm human need for diversity in *Dawn*, Octavia contrasted color versus colorlessness. A monochromatic cell reduces Lilith Iyapo to solitary confinement before she exits imprisonment to become a nursery teacher. When she begins leading newly awakened earthlings, the Amazon Basin atmosphere activates fish that swim with piranhas, eels, turtles, and caimans under woven lianas. Pupils enjoy a self-sustaining training ground, an island beneath a sylvan canopy. Her first view of the universe satisfies a human need to see evening sky and stars, the symbols the author elevates to potential new worlds. Glimpses of Africa and Arabia delight her with familiar global shapes until "tears blinded her," an indication of how much a prisoner in solitary confinement misses the familiar (Butler, 2000, 116).

MENACING ATMOSPHERES

Octavia demonstrates the value of straightforward signs to characters who differentiate between hazard and reassurance. At the end of a Washington Boulevard bus riot in "Speech Sounds," University of California at Los Angeles history professor Valerie Rye recognizes a local policeman as harmless—a left-hander "less impaired, more reasonable and comprehending, less driven by frustration, confusion, and anger" than rampaging passengers (Butler, 2005, 92). For translator Noah Cannon in "Amnesty," the author alluded to Noah and the flood, an ancient story of the pious man of God who follows Yahweh's dictum to build a boat that will salvage pairs of earthly animals from drowning. In exposition of the Tehkohn in *Survivor,* Octavia integrated hidden doors and escape passages to enhance the macabre as characters fled invaders. Infrequent use of missionary handcarts ties the society to frontier Mormon Brigham Young, who eluded anti-sect violence by fleeing over the Emigrant Trail to Utah after vigilantes murdered Joseph Smith in his Carthage, Illinois, jail cell on June 27, 1844. Specifics clarify the diet of wild game, fruit, and tubers, which hominoid farmers plant in soil with a shovel-shaped device. At Diut's dinner with Alanna Verrick's missionary parents, the sharing of eye contact over a meal symbolizes an alliance preceding escape to the north.

Octavia incorporated color symbols as indicators of both evil and hope. To reveal the perplexity of time traveling writer Dana Franklin in *Kindred,* she gradually discloses essentials, beginning with the red-haired child Rufus Weylin, the future owner of a Maryland plantation manned by scarred slaves who jerk to the zing of the whip. Turkish critic Tugba Akman Kaplan, a social psychologist at Istanbul University, emphasized that "The white men in the antebellum South show perseverance when it comes to taking extreme measures towards African-Americans" (Kaplan, 2021, 44). Membership in Dana's family tree begins with freedwoman Alice Greenwood, a surname suggesting promise. The name takes on extra value to the women after Dana rebuffs a patroller from rape with the whack of a tree limb, a black-against-white crime punishable by death. Another portentous sign of chattel ownership, the youngest children imitate slave auctions and field work without understanding the significance of their reenactments, which predict a deracination of black family members for the sake of white profits.

DEHUMANIZING ELEMENTS

The author's canon proceeded toward reflections of racist history. In *Wild Seed,* the long-lived mutant Doro summarizes his exploitation of "seed" people to form a super race: "I bring them together in groups, I begin to build them into a strong new people" (Butler, 1980, 9). His choice of the Nigerian shapeshifter An-yanwu for her supernatural powers introduces him to a hut with thatched roof and clay couches, the natural elements of West African domesticity. An overview of table manners depicts the scooping of pounded yam with fingers and a dip in peppery soup prepared by a "wild seed woman" (*ibid.,* 10). The details undergird an Afrocentric novel that views bondage from an African perspective through the commonplaces that abductees will miss after they enter wood slave ships, the facilitators of Triangular Trade with the Americas.

To express Afrofuturism through self-liberation, the author permeates *The Parable of the Sower* with memorable aspects as chilling as a black arm suspended from a scrub oak, dogs consuming a living child, and Kayla Talcott's spontaneous singing of "We Shall Not Be Moved" as a eulogy to the Reverend Olamina. Octavia upends the new settlement at Acorn by overwhelming farmers with a 2032 version of crusaders, the Christian bullies who topped chain mail with tabards and flaunted period backstory with the iconic St. George's Cross that identified the Knights Templar in 1145 during the Second Crusade. Dangers extrapolated from the Underground Railroad jeopardize Lauren's pilgrimage up highway I-5 to Portland, Oregon, in *The Parable of the Talents* past guard dogs and a farm woman armed with a rifle. Similar in rapacity to campaigners against Islam, Christian America militiamen take on the aura of Hitler's SS in the control of concentration camps through the allotment of high-tech dog collars, demeaning markers as perilous as Jews' yellow stars and tattooed wrists.

See also Food.

Sources

Butler, Octavia. *Dawn* in *Lilith's Brood*. New York: Warner, 2000, 2–249.
_____. *The Parable of the Sower*. New York: Four Walls, Eight Windows, 1993.
_____. "Speech Sounds," *Bloodchild and Other Stories*. New York: Seven Stories Press, 2005, 87–110.
_____. *Wild Seed*. New York: Doubleday, 1980.
Kaplan, Tugba Akman. "Identity and Language Formation within an Afrofuturistic Scope in Octavia Butler's *Kindred*," *Biruni University 1st International Congress* (12 June 2021): 43–51.
Turner, Jenny. "Ready to Go Off," *London Review of Books* 43:4 (18 February 2021).

Diaspora

In Afrofuturistic views of the world's refugees, Octavia pictured the terrorized and disenfranchised during migration to bondage, escape, better climate, and new possibilities, a postmodern Underground Railroad. In harmony with the Akan-Twi notion of *sankofa*, retrieving the best of the past, her speculative fiction cited as examples models of race formation: hybrid vampiric humans from Romania in *Fledgling*, bi-species offspring in the desert cult in *Clay's Ark*, Tlic-human conceptions and births in "Bloodchild," and the human-Oankali mutant Akin in the Xenogenesis series. For a diseased milieu in "Speech Sounds," escape from crazed street scenes sends protagonist Valerie Rye, a mute University of California at Los Angeles history professor, toward two foundlings who bear no evidence of an infection that permanently silences humans. The rescuer, one of Octavia's superwomen, leads the youngsters toward a promising future after burying victims of an uncommunicative past. The positive ending suggests the need to revisit history and share with the younger generation the dangers of silencing.

As indicated by Valerie's loss of lover Obsidian, the writer refrains from turning diaspora into a *deus ex machina* triumph but rather a spirited epiphany of humanity and self-preservation. The travel motif in *Patternmaster* not only offers an out for the persecuted but also relieves the opening chapters of a tedious political colloquy. On the road, Teray, the hunted son of siblings Jansee and Patternmaker Rayal, delineates dominance as the center uniting citizens. By outfoxing his conniving brother Coransee, Teray thwarts the dominion grabber's intention to demote or kill his rival. Father Rayal reiterates to Jansee the worth of god-like control: "Sister-wife, that is power worth killing for," his justification of ridding the kingdom of infected Clayarks (Butler, 1976, 4).

The author invests the symbolic path with irenic elements. On horseback, Teray and Amber, an independent healer, gallop down the coast toward the ancestral homeland of Forsyth, a place name taken from the surname "man of peace." The expedition advances harmony in the couple's lives, but not without violence and savagery, a dichotomy that besets Valerie Rye and Alanna Verrick, protagonist of *Survivor*. For the missionaries who rescue Alanna, the departure north into the mountains by "miniature wagon train" takes on the gravity of the epic escape in Exodus 1–19 of Moses and the Israelites in 1260 BCE from peonage to the Egyptian Pharaoh Rameses II (Butler, 1978, 173). The open-ended trek leaves unanswered how Alanna's followers fare on their haphazard journey.

NONFICTION JOURNEYS

By setting *Wild Seed* among kidnappers and transporters in 1690, Octavia exchanged imaginary journeys like those of Teray, Amber, and Alanna for historical dispersals. From Bonny and New Calabar, distribution centers on Nigeria's Bight of Biafra, data on African flesh trafficking inform readers of details and locales of the black uprooting from their homeland. Ironically, the deracination generates oneness. Adwoa Affua, a Ghanaian-Canadian affiliate of York University in Toronto, noted the importance of tribal equality during transport, where "one is never privileged over the other" (Afful, 2016, 95). Unintentionally, the loading of ships for the Middle Passage introduced black captives to a form of democracy and source of unity and ethnicity that remains dynamic.

The author dramatized the need of African captives to identify their families by male names, the septs of Nigerian dynasties. Unfortunately for Udenkwo, a grieving mother of a five-year-old, descendants of the Kushite-Ibo/Igbo seer An-yanwu "are so numerous, so well scattered, and so far from them in their generations that they do not know me or each other" (Butler, 1980, 22). The lament from the American slave system echoed the despair of chattel, who lived among disparate tribe members and speakers of some of Africa's three thousand languages. As a stabilizer of migration, Octavia created the homemaker An-yanwu, the fictional originator of a liberating plantation that houses freedman, runaways, and auction purchases to work and live without coercion or color branding.

SEEKING AN EDEN

Octavia's chef d'oeuvre, the Parable series, achieved a more thorough study of diaspora. For eighteen-year-old Lauren Oya Olamina, flight from effects of the

California Apocalypse in *The Parable of the Sower* forces her to join throngs heading north on highway I-5 from Robledo, California, toward Portland, Oregon. The standard group trek resembles that of black Haitians in flight from the Dominican Republic in Edwidge Danticat's *The Farming of Bones* and Colonel Kit Carson's forcible displacement of the Navajo across the Southwest to Bosque Redondo, New Mexico, in Scott O'Dell's young adult novel *Sing Down the Moon*. In the same plight as Dominicans and Navajo, some of Lauren's followers lack pragmatic direction. They invest their hopes in the coastal corporate city of Olivar or dream of fleeing north to Canada or Alaska. Neither goal proves achievable.

Octavia enacted mixed outcomes of Lauren's pilgrimage. The arrival of her company at Cape Mendocino in northwest California provides the fundamentals of an agrarian commune, an Afrofuturist return to the land. The multi-racial group forms ad hoc couples and begins the long job of turning Acorn into an Earthseed community, a promising blend of farming and faith. In *The Parable of the Talents*, the diaspora takes on an international flair after the leader posts scriptural writings on the Internet and draws converts to her vision of a civilization in the stars. At age eighty-one, she agrees that her ashes should accompany them to enrich the soil, a symbolic spiritual guidance through her writings. The legacy of deracination and fragmented culture and lineage hardens her followers, preparing them for the hardships of star travel.

See also Earthseed; Lauren Oya Olamina; Time Travel.

Sources

Afful, Adwoa. "Wild Seed: Africa and Its Many Diasporas," *Critical Arts* 30:4 (August 2016): 93–104

Butler, Octavia. *The Parable of the Sower*. New York: Four Walls, Eight Windows, 1993.

_____. *The Parable of the Talents*. New York: Seven Stories Press, 1998.

_____. *Patternmaster*. New York: Doubleday, 1976.

_____. *Survivor*. New York: Doubleday, 1978.

_____. *Wild Seed*. New York: Doubleday, 1980.

Grecca, Gabriela Brischini. "'A Racist Challenge Might Force Us Apart': Divergence, Reliance and Empathy in *Parable of the Sower*," *Ilha do Desterro* 74:1 (January–April 2021): 347–362.

McKoy, Sheila Smith. "Yemonja/Yemoja/Yemaya Rising" in *Recovering the African Feminine Divine in Literature, the Arts, and Practice: Yemonja Awakening*. Lanham, MD: Lexington Books, 2020, 55–68.

Turner, Jenny. "Ready to Go Off," *London Review of Books* 43:4 (18 February 2021).

Diction

The author's titles illustrate a balance of academic Greco-Latin terms with Old English, Scandinavian, German, and French. She underscored the terms Xenogenesis, extinct, hypnotic, diaspora, lineage, adaptability, and amnesty, the focuses of her canon. To authenticate the novel *Wild Seed* and its African settings, she incorporated Ibo/Igbo terms such as Orumili for the Niger River, nneochie for grandmother, and nwadiani, a kin-specific reference to her daughter's son Okoye. For protagonist An-yanwu, the narrative identifies an earlier name "Anasi," similar to the trickster spider Anansi of Ghana's Akan folklore. An-yanwu's controller Doro, a long-lived Nubian, chooses when and how to exclude her from conversations by switching dialects, a language trick that works for the Oankali to baffle earthlings in *Dawn*.

With the cunning circumlocutions of the gleeman, bard, or scop, the author evoked tenth-century Scandic wordcraft for "Bloodchild," a figurative coupling that yields a concise, dynamic trope or coding for an exotic being. Kenning, an Old English noun compound, implies a fetus capable of suckling its host's blood before birth. The term "kenning" derives from the Old Norse gerund "knowing," a raw, intuitive introduction to the bloodchild that enlightens the virgin Gan on the realities of birthing a hybrid human-Tlic race. The use of two-part words recurs in witch-children in *Wild Seed*, whose mystic powers invest An-yanwu and Isaac. Such precise one-word riddling enhances folk, epic, and mythic writing with allusive imagery, such as the Anglo-Saxon battle-tree for warrior, bonehouse for body, brainbox for cranium, moonrise for dusk, valkyrie for chooser of the slain, and mindhoard for thoughts. The literary device specified sci-fi elements in the titles *Storyworks* and *Starlog* and enlivened Marion Zimmer Bradley's sci-fi with emphatic spondees scanning (/ /) and the Gothic implications of *Darkover, Stormqueen, Firebrand, and Witchlight*.

Octavia created similarly nuanced word pictures for *Patternmaster, Clay's Ark, Imago, Dawn, Kindred, Fledgling, Adulthood Rites, Wild Seed*, "Crossover," "Bloodchild," and "Childfinder." The method enriched her texts with explicit language:

bridewealth—(*Wild Seed*)—dowry or inheritance
Clayarks—(*Clay's Ark*)—attackers infected with an extraterrestrial microbe
elderfather/eldermother—(*Fledgling*)—a Scandinavian term for a guardian
homeship—(*Imago*)—a self-contained headquarters in space
homeworld—("Bloodchild," *Dawn*)—an origin before migration to another
    planet
housemaster—(*Patternmaster*)—residential authority
jailbait—(*Fledgling*)—a provocatively sensual underage girl
Kevinsick—(*Kindred*)—Dana's longing for a reunion with Kevin Franklin
muteherd—(*Patternmaster*)—a group of simpleminded humans treated like
    beasts
pseudotree—(*Adulthood Rites*)—an immense alien plant containing a
    residence
shipgrowing—(*Dawn*)—raising a living ship like a plant
werewolves—(*Fledgling*)—human males taking the form of wolves
witch-scare—(*Wild Seed*)—the eruption of witch searches for suspected
    sorcerers
youngerson—(*Fledgling*)—unmated offspring

She also considered using the grafted titles "Worldmaking," "DiaPause," "Darkside," "Xenograft," "Sidelights," "Lifesong," and "Breakthrough."

The Parable novels depend on more combined words or kenning than other of Octavia's works:

The Parable of the Sower

animalborne—spread by animals
borderworks—factories on the Canadian border

compu-conference—an electronic meeting aided by facial views on screen
earthlife—plants and animals
Godseed—a source of life
Godshaping—creating a divine image
sleepsack—a cheap, portable source of bedding
switchback—a winding road, trail, or railroad track
touchring—technology that communicates sensations

THE PARABLE OF THE TALENTS

Al-Can—Alaskan-Canadian
change-aunt—a woman with a special relationship to a child
dia-pause—hibernative sleep on space flights
dovetree—a vulnerable compound
dreamask—a source of virtual reality scenarios
housetruck—an armored vehicle
man-strong—fully grown

Sources vary from nature and topography to technology and religion. The ability to link simple segments to create exact meanings enables Lauren to flesh out her theological vision as Earthseed, a scriptural collection and an alternate name for the Parable series.

See also Language; Names.

Sources

Davis-Secord, Jonathan. *Joinings: Compound Words in Old English Literature.* Toronto: University of Toronto Press, 2016.
Granja, David Jacobo Viveros, María Catalina Caro Torres, and María Alejandra Velasco Velandia. *Living British Literature: From the Anglo-Saxon World to the Early Renaissance.* Bogota, Colombia: Universidad Pedagógica Nacional, 2021.
Livingstone, Josephine. "Old English," *New York Times Magazine* (6 January 2019): 24–25.

"Discovery, Creation, and Craft"

Already a rising sci-fi star after publishing *Kindred* and *Wild Seed* and beginning work on *Clay's Ark*, Octavia tackled the question of low status black women writers. In a May 22, 1983, she reviewed for the *Washington Post* of critic and Princeton black studies professor Claudia Tate's interviews with eleven females in *Black Women Writers at Work* and editors Amina and Amiri Baraka (LeRoi Jones)'s collection of fifty black women writers in *Confirmation: An Anthology of African American Women*. Octavia surveyed an era of emergence for classic female authors. She worded novelist Margaret Walker's exuberance in wanting "to write all the books I have in me," beginning with the 1978 poetry and ballad collection *For My People*. Walker followed with the 1966 historical fiction classic *Jubilee*, a marital dilemma retrieved from the post–Civil War (Butler, 1983, 1). From Tate, the author repeated warnings of conflicts in ethnicity and gender, a double whammy on black female artists, particularly Octavia, a competitor in the sci-fi field, monopolized by white males.

For focus, Octavia incorporated one of her prominent themes, the oppressive male disdain for women, as reported by Alexis DeVeaux, a women's studies scholar at the State University of New York at Buffalo. Of androcentric challenges, Octavia cited woman-centered themes that bypass macho sporting competitions and the myths of the he-man. From Toni Morrison, Nobelist author of *Beloved*, Octavia saluted the black female writer for an ability "to combine the nest and adventure" (*ibid.*, 1). The phrase aptly described Octavia's female heroics: Keira "Kerry" Maslin awaiting the birth of her hybrid infant in *Clay's Ark*, newly married time-traveling writer Dana Franklin's education of black readers in *Kindred*, and shapeshifting Nigerian healer An-yanwu's metamorphoses in *Wild Seed* from dolphin, leopard, shark, or eagle to the matriarch of an antebellum Louisiana plantation. Over three centuries of healing and protecting her people, the variances in An-yanwu's lifestyle illustrate a balance of womanly need with agency.

Essential to honest reportage, Octavia cited the works of Alabama-born poet and dramatist Sonia Sanchez in a recommendation of substantive writing devoid of artifice, a quality of her 1969 verse anthology *Home Coming* and the 1973 polemical *A Blues Book for a Blue Black Magic Woman*. Sanchez maintained that black experience equates with universal experience. Other models cited Gullah-speaking griot Vertamae Smart-Grosvenor, author of the 1970 culinary memoir *Vibration Cooking: or, The Travel Notes of a Geechee Girl*, and American Book Award winner Louise Meriwether, author of the 1970 autobiography *Daddy Was a Number Runner* and the 1973 black resistance history *Don't Ride the Bus on Monday: The Rosa Parks Story*. The reviewer's conclusion about black women writers' strengths quoted poet and novelist Maya Angelou, author of the 1969 classic autobiography *I Know Why the Caged Bird Sings*. For Angelou, command of composition, combined with improvements to self, resulted in "supremacy and success," the goals that Octavia had long pursued (*ibid.*, 6).

Source

Baraka, Amiri, and Amina Baraka, eds. *Confirmation: An Anthology of African American Women*. New York: Quill, 1983.
Butler, Octavia. "Discovery, Creation, and Craft," *Washington Post* 13:21 (22 May 1983): 1, 6.
Tate, Claudia, ed. *Black Women Writers at Work*. New York: Continuum, 1983.

Disease

Octavia's fascination with illness impacted her canon with unthinkable ailments and ordinary contagion—nutritive deficiencies forced on humans by alien experiments in "Amnesty," mutes and mentally challenged Clayarks in *Patternmaster*, and the silencing of urbanites by disease in "Speech Sounds." A mystical "microbial winnowing" begins strengthening of the Ina in *Fledgling*, a model of Darwin's theory of survival of the fittest (Butler, 2005, 195). The author created irony from jealousy of earthlings who spread conspiracy notions that the Ina have a secret form of longevity. Even dead and buried, the Ina heal underground, revive, and gain notoriety in Romania as "'the walking dead' or the 'undead'" (*ibid.*). The supernatural connotations created terror of the folkloric Dracula.

After the sores, cholera, and measles infecting the street poor in *The Parable of the Sower*, the sequel, *The Parable of the Talents*, features a cholera outbreak that incites arson in Los Angeles. Harry Balter incurs a concussion and Jorge Cho's mother dies of flu, as do workers in the Christian American concentration camp. After a bad scrape on a gate, Lauren Oya Olamina and her companion, Belen "Len" Ross, immunize themselves against tetanus. The failure of community efforts at clean water, sanitary sewers, and immunization revives whooping cough, venereal disease, and rabies among rats and dogs, a spread of pestilence that reduces human fate to that of hapless beasts.

The loss of communication among characters in "Speech Sounds" contributes to the suffering of University of California at Los Angeles history professor Valerie Rye. The stroke-like disease "stripped her, killing her children one by one, killing her husband, her sister, her parents" from "paralysis, intellectual impairment, death" (Butler, 2005, 95, 96). By creating the fictional Duryea-Gode Disease (DGD), a terminal genetic syndrome in "The Evening and the Morning and the Night," Octavia extended esteem for scholars. Unlike predators who "went bad," they "went good—spectacularly—and made scientific and medical history" (Butler, 2005, 37). Essential to biology student Lynn Mortimer, advances in genetics and rare diseases lessen the harm of cancer and the rampant urges that cause people to destroy themselves and others. In her future hovers possible evisceration, cannibalism, and dismemberment, a horrifying inherited ailment to which she is doubly susceptible from both parents.

While pondering marriage and motherhood, Lynn bears a surname laden with death. She refers to herself and her four roommates as "lepers twenty-four hours a day" (*ibid.*, 39). Like Lynn, her depressed lover, Alan Chi, anticipates "double DGD" because of the genetics of mother and father, an ill fate she risks for her own offspring by copulating with him (*ibid.*, 43). For the enlightenment of readers, the author compares a beneficial diet of "dog biscuits" to the treatment of diabetes with insulin (*ibid.*, 38). By incorporating characters' fear of producing blighted children, she commiserates with humans who bear any type of untreatable anomaly—Tay-Sachs, sickle cell anemia, Marfan syndrome, Huntington's chorea, cystic fibrosis, and phenylketonuria (PKU), the body's failure to digest protein. Even with the knowledge of future grief, she rejects sterilization, which "would be like killing part of yourself," the author's reversal of abortion issues (*ibid.*, 42).

Health Motifs

Abridged by analyst Karen Joy Fowler, a *New York Times* bestselling author, Octavia's canon "is all about the body—about disease, about reproduction, about the horrible realities of the food chain—depictions of fluid-spilling, flesh-eating, oozing, gooey physicality" (Fowler, 2006). Accounts of blood sucking, beheading, burning alive, and cannibalism in *Fledgling* made her "one of the field's scariest writers" (*ibid.*). For *Patternmaster*, she depicted race survival on a strong-minded minority fathered by "The Founder," whose "specialty had been living" until his daughter killed him and created Patterning (*ibid.*). The author contrived a space age infection spread by toxic saliva and brought to earth by Clay's Ark, "the only starship ever to leave Earth and then return" (Butler, 1976, 10). The disease the rocket carries combines with militarism and weapons-making to create a viable deterrent to a Patternist takeover. Of the healer's skill, Teray, Jansee and Patternmaster Rayal's son, claims to be an inept medic: "I miss symptoms unless they're really obvious. Pain, profuse bleeding" (Butler, 1976, 80). Fortunately, Octavia pairs him with Amber, a consummate healer.

The author's survey of cures for impairment incorporates the magical. In *Mind of My Mind*, faith healer Rachel "Rae" Davidson, like a psionic MRI, evaluates tissue, organ, and psychological problems on the inside before stimulating new tissue, retuning organs, and eliminating psychological faults. After leaving a New York congregation in the hands of the inept minister Eli Torrey, she acknowledges his lack of supernatural gifts. Sarcastic in the trickery of the gullible, Rachel admits, "No one will be healed, I know, but no doubt he'll entertain them," a quip at the expense of huckster preachers (Butler, 1977, 65). Unfortunately for Mary, Rachel's psionic controller, the therapist still has the strength to "give me a heart attack or a cerebral hemorrhage or any other deadly thing she wants to ... killing the very old, the very young, the weak, even the sick that she intended to heal" (*ibid.*, 67). With practice on a paring knife slice to the arm, Mary learns that she, too, can halt pain and restore healthy tissue, a self-license that enhances agency and authority.

Fearful Pestilence

To emphasize the terminal illness of Keira "Kerry" Maslin in Clay's Ark, Octavia gave her a healthy twin, Rane Maslin, a loving doppelgänger. In contrast to her assertive sister, Keira wears the pallor and death-like lethargy of acute myeloblastic leukemia, which causes too many white blood cells in the bone marrow and vascular system. Chemotherapy had ruined hair follicles and ravaged muscle tissue, leaving Keira nearly immobile. The earthly blood disorder contrasts an organism from Proxi Two, a microbe introduced from space by the starship *Clay's Ark* and its sole survivor, astronaut Asa Elias "Eli" Doyle. The author explored the paradox of the bipolar organism, one that can kill or benefit by suppressing other diseases, neutralizing toxins, and bolstering libido, speed, and sensory impressions through reinfection. For Gabriel Boyd, death from dehydration and exhaustion follow a stroke-like decline into incontinence and drooling. The narrative reflects that tiny microbes make "a damned efficient invader," as contrasted to humanity's fear of intrusive spaceships (Butler, 1984, 34).

In the neo-slave narrative *Kindred*, the lack of medical care for debilitated non-whites encourages spread of malaria and infection among plantation dwellers, especially those like Alice Greenwood, who had suffered a lashing. The mysterious cyclical fever that fells Rufus Weylin illustrates the absence of anatomical knowledge in the early 1800s when hit-or-miss purging and bleeding were the only remedies. Dana

Franklin, the time-traveling guardian, treats Rufus successfully with sleeping pills, aspirin, and Excedrin, her only choices of antidotes for what turns out to be dengue fever, a tropical malaise spread by mosquitoes. For impact on the present, Octavia chose a mosquito-borne disease that threatens half the world with pain, fever, nausea, rash, and joint ache that can worsen to internal bleeding, shock, and death.

From modern research, *Wild Seed* narrates the rapid demise of African American slaves from malaria, cholera, snakebite, yellow fever, typhus, and smallpox. As a salute to West African stamina, the writer contrasted the longevity of non-whites born lactose intolerant, yet resistant to the infections that "swallowed white men" (Butler, 1980, 92). An-yanwu, the immortal Nigerian protagonist, possesses an authoritative voice that impresses patients with the power to neutralize poison, control seasickness, heal leprosy and tumors, cure blindness, and exude a healing balm from saliva that stems infection. She summarizes her purpose on earth as "creator of medicines and poisons, binder of broken bones, comforter," a Christ-like mission based on maternal benevolence (*ibid.*, 284).

FUTURISTIC MIRACLES

Through extraterrestrial knowledge, in *Lilith's Brood*, the author envisioned immediate panaceas for such ailments as brain damage from a car accident that clouds Sam's recognition of wife Lilith Iyapo and his Nigerian parents. Octavia proposed a method of removing the threat of "new tissue gone obscenely wrong" via the insertion of correcting genes and the control of a carcinogenic diet (Butler, 1987, 551). In *Dawn*, the first of three volumes, Octavia endorsed the anatomical breakthroughs of alien technology after an ooloi surgeon excises Lilith's cancer. Her internal reprogramming continues with a brief puncture to the spine that alters the mind's perception of language, a hands-on edu-medical method of breaching the speech barrier between races.

The pattern of diagnoses and healing continues in volume two, *Adulthood Rituals*, in which Augustino "Tino" Leal suffers amnesia from a blow to the skull and from digestive ulcers and headaches, psychosomatic punishments for betraying humankind. Earth-based ghosts continue to batter Tino in memories of his previous life. By volume three, *Imago*, manipulation of tumor-forming abilities turns humans into treasure for the aliens, who value cancers as "regenerative abilities we had never been able to trade for before" (*ibid.*). By applying the growths to amputations, the Oankali sprout new limbs, the author's idealized use for cancer as a remedy.

In *Imago*, the text admits the down side of depending on the ooloi for therapy. With exceptional knowledge and skills, they can also plague humankind with damaged immunity, "neurological disorders, glandular problems ... diseases they don't have names for," such as neurofibromatosis, the cause of swellings that protrude under Aaor's arms and limit the vision, sight, appearance, and movement of siblings Tomás and Jesusa Serrano y Martín (Butler, 2000, 552). Tomás's narration of tribal history divulges that deformities existed before the nuclear war, a likely cause of additional anomalies similar to widespread terminal cancers in Japanese survivors of an explosion of the atomic bombs in August 1945, which journalist John Hersey cataloged in two editions of *Hiroshima*.

Octavia interrogated medical complexities in the Parable series through the journal writings of Dr. Taylor Franklin Bankole. From treating the poor, he "watched poverty, hunger, and disease become inevitable for more and more people" who lacked access to wellness (Butler, 1998, 8). For fifteen-year-old Lauren Oya Olamina in *The Parable of the Sower*, fetal brain damage begins at birth because of her mother's addiction to Paracetco, a treatment for Alzheimer's disease and an echo of the West German sleep-inducing sedative thalidomide that maimed fetuses in the 1950s. For added condemnation, the Big Pharma name suggests "parasite," much as Hedeonco in "The Evening and the Morning and the Night" implies "hedonism." The effect of a smart drug elicits a deluge of empathy for human pain, which Lauren's body ingests through "an organic delusional syndrome" (Butler, 1993, 10). While defending herself from "paints" and "pyros" on the long walk from Los Angeles northwest to Cape Mendocino, she expects to incur suffering from firing bullets on night raiders (*ibid.*, 159). Although she is a crack shot, her fellow migrants rescue her from gun battles and speed recovery from non-lethal wounds.

Sources

Butler, Octavia. *Adulthood Rites* in *Lilith's Brood*. New York: Warner, 2000, 249–517.
———. *Clay's Ark*. New York: St. Martin's Press, 1984.
———. *Dawn* in *Lilith's Brood*. New York: Warner, 2000, 1–248.
———. "The Evening and the Morning and the Night," *Bloodchild and Other Stories*. New York: Seven Stories Press, 2005, 33–70.
———. *Fledgling*. New York: Seven Stories Press, 2005.
———. *Imago* in *Lilith's Brood*. New York: Warner, 2000, 518–746.
———. *Mind of My Mind*. New York: Doubleday, 1977.
———. *Parable of the Sower*. New York: Four Walls, Eight Windows, 1993.
———. *Patternmaster*. New York: Doubleday, 1976.
———. "Speech Sounds," Bloodchild and Other Stories. New York: Seven Stories Press, 2005, 87–110.
———. *Wild Seed*. New York: Doubleday, 1980.
Fowler, Karen Joy. "Remembering Octavia Butler," *Salon* www.salon.com/2006/03/17/butler_3/ (17 March 2006).
Turner, Jenny. "Ready to Go Off," *London Review of Books* 43:4 (18 February 2021).

Dominance

Octavia characterized control as a human propensity based on birth, money, and authority. In her writings, despots clutch at superiority through predation, the issue for Garkohn enslavers in *Survivor*, or brutishness, the grotesque factor of male impregnation and aborted alien larvae in "Bloodchild." Unlike the mutual partnering in *Fledgling*, "Tales of dominated and dominating cultures," in the estimation of Stacy Magedanz, a reference librarian at California State University, San Bernardino, become the underlying incentive in *Clay's Ark* for desert raids. The theme recurs in "Speech Sounds" after a bus riot and a domestic knifing (Magedanz, 2012, 47). In *The Parable of the Sower* and its sequel, *The Parable of the Talents*, the urge to prevail motivates theft and terrorism among "power-drunk" scavengers like Keith Olamina and his gang, who frequently pay for overreaching with harrowing deaths (Butler, 1993, 241).

The author's biography dispelled the childhood misery of taunting and belittling with speeches and fiction that soothed the hurt and retrieved her from social death. She warned, "Simple peck-order bullying is only the beginning of the kind of hierarchical behavior that can lead to racism, sexism, ethnocentrism, classism and all the other 'isms' that cause so much suffering in the world" ("Science," 2008, A8). The concept explained in *The Parable of the Talents* the rise of preacher-turned-politician Andrew Steele Jarret, whose name identifies a macho, spear-wielding foundry worker, the forger of the Christian American demagoguery who "fixes things" through murder, arson, scapegoating, child abduction, and fear-mongering.

To the Victor, the Spoils

As a result of reading, hearing, and observing news in the *Los Angeles Times*, local radio, and National Public Radio, the author predicted doom for humankind, an overarching theme in the Xenogenesis series. Because of size and strength variances, women and children become likely victims, a truism demonstrated in the lopping of two extra fingers from a girl mutant. According to *Village Voice* journalist Dorothy Allison, "Her women are always in some form of bondage, captives of domineering male mutants or religious fanatics or aliens who want to impregnate them" (Allison, 1989, 67). More than her male characters, the females must more painfully "confront the difference between surrender and adjustment," the choice of Lillian Iyapo, captive of Oankali gene traders in *Dawn* (*ibid*.). In *Imago*, she characterized earthlings in a dog-eat-dog round of "dominating, often killing other life" in the finale by incinerating the Phoenix compound (Butler, 2000, 564). The impasse grips Tahneh, the barren Hao or head magistrate in *Survivor* and "A Necessary Being," who must relinquish sovereignty to her successor, an outsider who replaces the blood inheritor she can't conceive. Thus, female biology inhibits her authority and high status, bifurcating her identity into Rohkohn plenipotentiary and needy woman.

Writing about ecofeminism enabled Octavia to shape self-reliant women who escape the parasitism of the strong, the feat of Mary Larkin in *Mind of My Mind*, who overwhelms her vampirish father Doro in the Patternist series. To Marty Crisp, an interviewer for the Lancaster, Pennsylvania, *Sunday News*, she accounted for the creation of female protagonists endowed with grit and activism, qualities of protagonists Noah Cannon in "Amnesty" and Valerie Rye in "Childfinder." For Lauren, protagonist of *The Parable of the Sower*, leading thirteen survivors from chaos in Cape Mendocino, California, requires low-key persuasion of fellow vagabonds as well as shootouts with raiders. In an undated entry to a journal, she prized "people searching for order and stability in their own ways," a description of An-yanwu's Louisiana plantation in *Wild Seed*, Barbara's child cadre in "Childfinder," and Lynn Mortimer's re-evaluation of fearful disease in "The Evening and the Morning and the Night" (Brown, 2021, 101). Unlike male-dominated fiction, Octavia promoted the Greek concept of arete (ἀρετή, excellence), a fitting description of Beatrice Alcantera's compassionate nurse care. Crisp stated, "Who wins and who loses is less important than bringing out the best of each man and each woman" (Crisp, 1996, H3).

The essay "The Monophobic Response" lobbed caustic scorn at earth's "sibling rivalry" and greed for "territory, dominance, and exclusivity" (Butler, 2000, 415). In the estimation of *Salon* analyst Karen Joy Fowler, a *New York Times* bestselling author, Octavia "had a particular fascination with relationships of dominance and submission, master and slave, predator and prey" (Fowler, 2006). In the essay "Why Is Science Fiction So White?," the author censured science fiction publishers for promoting few female or nonwhite writers. The reason, the lack of authenticity, pointed to a false premise that "all the power was in male hands, and women stayed in their male-defined places" (Butler, 2018, 16). To reposition control, she created extraterrestrials and otherworldly settings to insert readers into shameful, fearful shoving matches to achieve preeminence.

For "Amnesty," the writer considered the imbalance of necessary intimidation versus the consent of the governed. She demonstrated human frailty by picturing the bush-shaped aliens who communicate through lightning. They subdue translator Noah Cannon by "enfolding" her in a tight wrestling hold that allows her no leeway. The invaders' conquest extends to caging, rape, torture, and murder of the early captives, who serve as lab rats. The nonhumans test their quarry in lethal laboratory experiments much as Hitler's death camp scientists at Dachau gauged viability in freezing water and survival of lethal doses of sulfanilamide and phosgene gas or malaria and hepatitis on inmates at Sachsenhausen in Oranienburg, Germany, and Natzweiler in Natzwiller, France. They sometimes tested mass sterilization on identical Jewish and Roma twins at Auschwitz in Oswiecim, Poland, and Ravensbrück in northern Germany.

FICTIONAL AUTHORITY

Octavia imagined grotesque sway over the vulnerable in speculative fiction. For the Patternist novel *Wild Seed*, she dramatized ethnic and racial warfare in central Africa, where black and white enslavers sell prisoners of war to the English owners of the Royal African Company, the monopoly launched in 1660 by British King James I. Struggle for commercial eminence in 1690 follows the immortal Nigerian An-yanwu and other newly captured blacks to the Hudson River through Dutch farmland to Wheatley, New York. At dinner, talk of the February 8 Schenectady massacre informs her of a coalition of papist French, Mohawk, and Algonquin and of whites and African apprehension. The Nubian Doro, An-yanwu's parasitic mate, confesses that he must leave her to regroup his "fragmented people," a hint at his intent to subjugate all underlings (Butler, 1980, 289).

Supremacy sets the action and atmosphere of the sequel *Mind of My Mind*, introducing Doro's first legitimate challenger. As nineteen-year-old Mary reaches full potential, she accepts the challenge of overcoming her father/lover Doro, a wicked immortal who experiments with psionic humans to engender the first master race. Octavia describes the emergence of morality and ethics in Mary as enabling her to generate a mass cartel of patterned telepaths who cooperate and appreciate each other's assets. While Doro contemplates his loss of primacy, she distributes over the world a positive network of altruists. Her big-hearted principles thwart Doro's faith in absolute control.

A disturbing example of opportunities ignored, Rufus Weylin in *Kindred* is a realistic, if narcissistic round character endowed with multifaceted traits and recurrent murder threats. A charming brat in early boyhood named for his red hair, he expresses frustrations by setting fire to the stables and bedroom drapes. To flee his hard-edged father, Tom Weylin, who afflicts him, Rufus turns to an affectionate mother, Martha Weylin. The gap in his principles derives from admiring Tom's mastery with the whip and disrespect for a soft, nurturing mom who distances herself from disciplining farm chattel. Cruel precedents mar Rufus's teens with the vicious undertone of the male planter's supervision of slaves. By callously satisfying his lust for mistress Alice Greenwood, he aggrandizes himself as heir to the complex. His death from double stabbings suits the solitary and terrified beginner who never learned skilled management.

See also Doro; Rufus Weylin.

Sources

Allison, Dorothy. "The Future of Female," *Village Voice* (19 December 1989): 67–68.

Brown, Jayna. *Black Utopias: Speculative Life and the Music of Other Worlds*. Durham, NC: Duke University Press, 2021.

Butler, Octavia. "Amnesty," *Bloodchild and Other Stories*. New York: Seven Stories Press, 2005, 147–186.

_____. *Imago* in *Lilith's Brood*. New York: Warner, 2000, 518–746.

_____. "The Monophobic Response" in *Dark Matter: A Century of Speculative Fiction from the African Diaspora*. New York: Aspect/Warner Books, 2000, 415–416.

_____. *The Parable of the Sower*. New York: Four Walls, Eight Windows, 1993.

_____. "Why Is Science Fiction So White?," *Transmission* (Summer, 1980): 16–18.

Crisp, Marty. "Interview," (Lancaster, PA) *Sunday News* (11 February 1996): H3.

Fowler, Karen Joy. "Remembering Octavia Butler," *Salon* www.salon.com/2006/03/17/butler_3/ (17 March 2006).

Magedanz, Stacy. "The Captivity Narrative in Octavia E. Butler's *Adulthood Rites*," *Extrapolation* 53:1 (2012): 47–59.

"Science Fiction Writer Octavia E. Butler to Be Honored at Leimert Park Village Book Fair," *Los Angeles Sentinel* (15 May 2008): A8.

Tüzün, Hatice Övgü. *Dystopias and Utopias on Earth and Beyond*. London: Routledge, 2021.

Zaki, Hoda M. "Utopia, Dystopia, and Ideology in the Science Fiction of Octavia Butler," *Science Fiction Studies* 17 (1990): 239–251.

Doro

A macabre body-snatcher, trickster, and mastermind of hit-or-miss eugenics, Doro is uniquely insufferable. Octavia described him as an Ibo/Igbo abungi or obunje, an evil Nigerian child spirit that kills the offspring of a persecuted woman. In the estimation of novelist Dorothy Allison, essayist for *Village Voice*, he bears the traits of "a 4000-year-old psychic vampire and patriarch," an ultra-human monster (Allison, 1989, 67). He avouches an acquisitive nature, simply: "I control powerful people…. My people," the best of whom reside in Wheatley, New York, and a Louisiana plantation (Butler, 1980, 188).

One key to Doro's narcissism is ambition. While identity-hopping through six millennia, his intent is to breed "others who won't die" into hyper-psychic mind readers (*ibid.*, 607). Already a wanderer at transition to psionics at age thirteen, in a ghost village, he kills and migrates to first his mother, then his father's body before slaying other residents who lapse into madness incited by enslavers. Greedy Egyptians imprison him for a half century before he emerges as an immortal parasite and breeder of mutants. Hybridizing yields his best experiments—Isaac and Anneke, who adore and obey him. To his dismay, extreme autocracy provokes loneliness until he finds a suitable mate, a comeuppance that Octavia designed solely for him.

In the estimation of Butler scholar Gerry Canavan, an English professor at Marquette University in Milwaukee, Doro parlays his intense glamour into "a borderline abusive gaslighter" who enables his son Isaac's mother to kill herself, selects An-yanwu's name, and attempts to dupe his daughter Mary Larkin, an unprecedented mind reader (Canavan, 2016). Part of his mythos involves an obsolete language "so old that no one living can read it" (Butler, 1980, 280). According to *Star Tribune* book reviewer Eric M. Heideman, the editor of *Tales of the Unanticipated*, the satanic villain exudes "a cobra like fascination, charming and intelligent, but with no trace of conscience," the mark of the psychopath (Heideman, 1995, 73). After surviving for 3,700 years, he aims to expand his timelessness into "a complete entity" of homo superior (Butler, 1977, 99). To do so, he grooms future generations of hybrids who, like him, bear Arab blood and an innate "arrogance and hostility" (Butler, 1980, 109).

FINDING A MATE

In a 1690 *Wild Seed* encounter with An-yanwu, an Ibo/Igbo oracular healer, Doro recognizes her ethnicity as a cross between 1000 BCE Kushites and Nigerians, an ancient African genealogy that discloses his longevity. He admits that he has worn out his current body, a tall, handsome black in his late twenties. Bereft of compassion, he casually annihilates failed human breeding stock like houseflies because he "wanted an empire" built on successful propagating techniques (Butler, 1977, 54). In a whimsical moment, he suggests that he and An-yanwu change genders for mutual sex, a perversion she rebukes as "a vile thing.... Surely an abomination" (*ibid.*, 242). He manipulates her as lover and breeder and considers disposing of her until he realizes how much an undying mate can rid him of emptiness.

In the estimation of Jayna Brown, a media specialist at the Pratt Institute in Brooklyn, New York, the author differs with Doro on the subject of eugenic improvement of the species on suspicion "of its ethical and political ramifications" (Brown, 2021, 98). Instead of manipulating humans, Octavia's journal entry for December 12, 1998, proposed that designers of the future "adapt to the new world and adapt the world to them" (*ibid.*). Reflecting on prehistoric African customs, Doro charges Europeans, especially missionaries, with the hypocrisy of pretending "to be acting for the benefit of our victims' souls" (Butler, 1980, 104). He compares black cannibalism to scriptural mythology about Christ's blood and flesh transubstantiating into Holy Communion, a nineteenth-century development that turned pagans into Christians. Late in *Wild Seed*, he touches An-yanwu's soul with his centuries of solitude and betrays her trust by absorbing her being into his greedy self, his most daring maneuver.

The arrogant, long-lived Nubian bursts into *Mind of My Mind* with a paternal objective—to determine the well-being of his unique daughter Mary, one of thirty-seven psionic offspring. The action swirls past a survey of welts and contusions on the three-year-old and a quick exchange of bodies with a knife wielder, one of Doro's cycle of metamorphoses. The rapidity of Doro's swapping his corpse for the attacker's form terrifies Mary's mother Rina, one of Doro's many mates, and reminds her of his immense clout and death-dealing ideology. The fierce father tidies up household business by promising to murder Rina if she batters Mary again. The threat suggests how deeply Doro has placed his hopes on Mary's uniqueness.

Experiment's End

Doro's son Karl Larkin calls thousands of years of research "human husbandry" and recognizes Doro's preposterous volition: "He had no more regard for traffic laws than he did for any other laws" (Butler, 1977, 32). According to Mary, her father/lover indulges a hobby that scatters "half-crazy latents" about the country, racial inferiors who exist a notch below the psychically adroit (*ibid.*, 54; Allison, 1989, 67). She registers surprise that he appears to care for her above his other experiments and wants her to succeed in enslaving five incompatible active psis. Out of habit, he bullies and strikes Mary before he forces her to wed Karl, whose surname means "manly" and "fierce." Doro silences Jesse Bernarr for threatening a coup against Mary's sovereignty and beats Jan Sholto for allowing their son Vaughn to die in a traffic accident. Mary acknowledges during Doro's attack on Jan "how bad Doro's beatings could be" (*ibid.*, 69). The buildup of bluster, mauling, and perversion tags Octavia's miscreant as her worst.

In a discussion of Doro's shifting bodies, he claims not to care about what race he takes because "I'm not human.... A mutation. A kind of parasite. A god. A devil" (*ibid.*, 55–56). His bizarre history carries him from birth to age thirteen, the standard age for character metamorphosis in fantasy and speculative fiction. After killing his parents during transition, he loses a half century during an Egyptian slave raid and awakens at age fifty in a prison feeling at first cursed, then blessed with dynamism. In 2730 BCE, he applies to humans his observations of animal breeding for food and begins building a gifted race. In an unforeseen complication, hybridizing threatens his management of the project. Mary, his most forceful active, views each member of the gargantuan Doro family as "just one more tool he was using" to achieve his empire (*ibid.*). Instead, she augments the possibilities of patterning by overthrowing Doro's self-aggrandizing algorithm.

Octavia alters the tone of a lengthy character dialogue with Doro's strategy for a biogenetic experiment to "grow into something impressive and worthwhile ... the founders and the leaders of a new race" (*ibid.*, 78). Because he recognizes Mary's joy in command, he causes her to examine reasons for draining dynamism from lesser telepaths. In secret, he recognizes an imbalance of father-daughter faculties and identifies in himself envy and suspicion of the town-sized community she governs. Unlike Mary, he must kill to survive and ponders exterminating his increasingly superhuman daughter to retain primacy to avoid self-destruction. The author creates a male-female balance of mastery by forcing Doro to accept a nurturing, loving mate, An-yanwu. Graciously, she words her egalitarian method: "I am not the vampire he is; I give in return for my taking" (*ibid.*, 205).

See also An-yanwu.

Sources

Allison, Dorothy. "The Future of Female," *Village Voice* (19 December 1989): 67–68.

Bogstad, Janice. "Interview," 14:4 *Janus* (Winter, 1978–1979): 28–32.

Brown, Jayna. *Black Utopias: Speculative Life and the Music of Other Worlds*. Durham, NC: Duke University Press, 2021.

Butler, Octavia. *Mind of My Mind*. New York: Doubleday, 1977.

_____. *Wild Seed*. New York: Doubleday, 1980.

Canavan, Gerry. *Octavia E. Butler*. Urbana: University of Illinois, 2016.

Crisp, Marty. "Interview," (Lancaster, PA) *Sunday News* (11 February 1996): H3.

Heideman, Eric M. "Review: *Mind of My Mind*," (Minneapolis, MN) *Star Tribune* (26 March 1995): 73.

Trafford, James, and Pete Wolfendale, eds. *Alien Vectors: Accelerationism, Xenofeminism, Inhumanism*. Abingdon, UK: Routledge, 2020.

Doro's Genealogy

Octavia tackles a massive nonmonogamous family tree in *Mind of My Mind* by coordinating Doro's thirty-seven children and his many liaisons, which produce John Woodley, captain of his sloop *Silver Star*. Similarly, the author interjects in the narrative Okoye, the Nigerian seer An-yanwu's grandson. Relationships between the pansexual manipulator and his wives/daughters Emma, Rina, Jan Sholto, and Mary precede Mary's assemblage of active telepaths—Rachel Davidson, Ada Dragan, Jesse Bernarr, Jan Sholto, and Seth Dana plus Seth's dependent brother Clay Dana, who

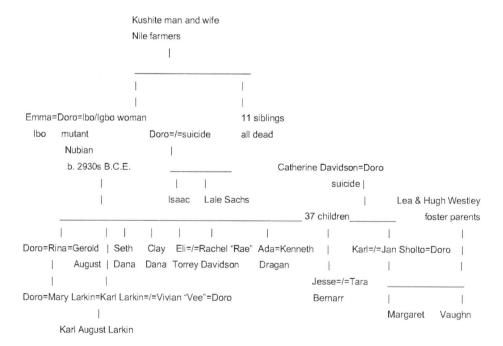

nears transition. The author delineates motives and attitudes in each, generating an album of Doro's experimental personalities and their control by "this pattern thing" (Butler, 1977, 54).

The naming of Mary and Karl Larkin's baby for his father includes the middle name "August," a Latin adjective meaning "majestic and noble." The choice suggests the accomplishments of Caesar Augustus, the nineteen-year-old heir of Julius Caesar in 44 BCE. By surviving sixteen years of civil war, on January 16, 27 BCE, he founded the Roman Empire and accepted the Senate's entitlement as the augustus (emperor). During fifteen years of widowhood, the title adapted to his wife Livia, the augusta (empress). By alluding to a grand reshaping of Roman ascendancy to an inherited crown, Octavia implied that Karl and Mary's son would accomplish great things. The surname "Larkin" foretokens Lauren Oya Olamina's lost daughter in the Parable series, in which a search for the toddler defines the evangelist's lengthy pilgrimage up I-5 to Portland, Oregon.

See also An-yanwu; *Mind of My Mind*; *Wild Seed*.

Sources

Butler, Octavia. *Mind of My Mind*. New York: Doubleday, 1977.
_____. *Wild Seed*. New York: Doubleday, 1980.
Trafford, James, and Pete Wolfendale, eds. *Alien Vectors: Accelerationism, Xenofeminism, Inhumanism.* Abingdon, UK: Routledge, 2020.

Earthseed

A new worldview that fifteen-year-old Lauren Oya Olamina evolves in the Parable series from a Baptist upbringing, Earthseed fuses ecology to spirituality. Paradoxically "an answer, as well as, in some cases, a problem," it skirts magic, myth, the supernatural, and utopianism as well as racism and gendering to affirm life's interconnection (Butler, 2005). Lauren concludes that "Earthseed prepares you to live in the world that is and try to shape the world that you want" (Butler, 1998, 246). Reared by an old-time fundamentalist preacher, she allows free thinking to move beyond scriptural inerrancy credited to a grandfatherly male divinity and bases her theology on "patterns of history, in science, philosophy, religion, or literature" (*ibid.*, 117). She becomes adept at assessing personal values and traits, especially her followers' loyalty, probity, and stout-heartedness. In *The Parable of the Talents,* she explains to her brother Marcos Duran the doctrine's positive nature: "Human beings are Earthseed. We have no devils" (*ibid.*). She proposes "a collection of truths" as a guide to believers (*ibid.*).

In the Akan-Twi spirit of *sankofa,* Octavia labored at a Ghanaian doctrine that preserved the best of the past. Aparajita Nanda, an English and black studies professor at the University of California at Berkeley, simplified the Earthseed doctrine as a blend of science with traditional faiths of Christians, Jews, Buddhists, and Hindus. The Hindu ethos legitimates chaos and cataclysm for prefacing change and rebirth, a necessity if earth is to survive. The key to regeneration, according to Nanda, lies in adaptation "to a mutually beneficial life with other species, embracing diversity as a form of sustenance" (Nanda, 2021, 216). Nanda lauds progressive audit of past errors and pitfalls, a consensus building that Donna Spalding Andreolle, a specialist in American studies at Stendhal University in Grenoble, France, calls a new Christianity.

CONTROLLERS OF DESTINY

The sexless deity receives full validation in chapter seven and in Lauren's explanation to traveler Travis Douglas how she formulated a theology based on action rather than dogma or *deus ex machina* (celestial intervention). Deborah Dundas, a reviewer for the *Toronto Star,* termed the concept a "post–Trump reality" for its empathy for refugees and survivors of civil anarchy (Dundas, 2018, E12). Pilgrim Harry Balter equates the axiom with the second law of thermodynamics: When energy is transferred or transformed, more goes to waste and degenerates to disorder, a description of the anarchy that turned Los Angeles into a hellhole. Lauren credits the Almighty—"Trickster, Teacher, Chaos, Clay"—with evil and good, a conundrum Octavia may have derived from Nubian and Asian lore (Butler, 1993, 221). Belief in diversity and sharing becomes the yoke that links sister prostitutes Allison and Jillian Gilchrist to Lauren's group and enables the journeyers to accept Hispanic, black, Asian, and mixed-race members.

German critic Gesa Mackenthun, an expert in North American studies at the University of Rostock, labeled Octavia's allegory a transition story that proposes "feasible ideas about how to orchestrate economic and social change" (Mackenthun, 2021). Lauren's theology strips religion of a personal loving divinity and equates God with diversity, "the one unavoidable, irresistible, ongoing reality of the universe" (Butler, 1993, 219). Before embarking on displacement from Robledo, California, she embraces a form of Deism that "prevails ... something that I think my dying, denying, backward-looking people need" (*ibid.,* 25). On February 17, 1998, Octavia gave the pilgrims something to anticipate. She proposed harnessing Earthseed to resettlement in the stars: "Some form of religious passion [to] cause us to take on in a serious way, the fantastically expensive difficult possibly multicentury effort to establish human settlements in extrasolar planets" (Brown, 2021, 104).

AN IDEALISTIC THEORY

The author trusted that faith would enable Lauren and her pilgrims to elude earth's historical cycles and create what Naomi Alderman, a book critic for the London *Guardian,* called "a society that tries hard not to leave people out ... to be vigilantly alert to the people we are leaving out, whoever they are" (Alderman, 2017, 2). Rather than worship an omnipotent god as did the Israelites in the bible, on the Acorn farm commune, climate refugees of the 2027 Apocalypse adapt to threats of raiders, arson, murder, abduction, and rape. Critic Gerry Canavan, on staff at Milwaukee's Marquette University, stressed that "Earthseed doesn't just reconcile science fiction and religion, it remakes science fiction as religion" (Canavan, 2016). After seventeen months of shackling in dog collars and escape from a Christian

America concentration camp, in March 2035, Lauren must admit, "No one knows better than I do how miserably I failed my people" (Butler, 1998, 323). She directs her flock to new destinations. The axiom becomes the source of human endurance and a prophetic future to live on the moon among the heavenly constellations.

In choosing Earthseed as a spiritual unifier, Octavia acknowledged the value of religion throughout world history and posited that the same belief system could achieve an age-old ideal—boosting Terrans to "galactic actors ... to take root among the stars" (Canavan, 2021, 264; Butler, 1993, 77). Laura Lievens, a Belgian English language specialist at the Université Catholique de Louvain, applauded the hypothesis as a "tool for collaboration in a time of collapse" (Lievens, 2020, intro.). As the religion grew, it "financed scientific exploration and inquiry, and technological creativity" (Butler, 1998, 340). Lauren's husband Bankole and daughter Larkin denounce the "blue-sky project" as an escape from reality into an immature, nonsensical fantasy on a par with *Star Trek* (Canavan, 2021, 266). Canavan agreed with the fictional family that sustainable space colonization lay beyond human abilities: "If there's any change, it's got to happen down here, not out there" (*ibid.,* 267).

See also Survivors.

Sources

Alderman, Naomi. "Dystopian Dreams: How Feminist Science Fiction Predicted the Future," London *Guardian* (25 March 2017): 2.

Andreolle, Donna Spalding. "Utopias of Old, Solutions for the New Millennium," *Utopian Studies* 12:2 (2001): 114–123.

Brown, Jayna. *Black Utopias: Speculative Life and the Music of Other Worlds.* Durham, NC: Duke University Press, 2021.

Butler, Octavia. *Parable of the Sower.* New York: Four Walls, Eight Windows, 1993.

_____. *The Parable of the Talents.* New York: Seven Stories Press, 1998.

_____. "Science Fiction Writer Octavia Butler on Race, Global Warming and Religion," (video), *Democracy Now* www.democracynow.org/2005/11/11/science_fiction_writer_octavia_butler_on (11 November 2005).

Canavan, Gerry. *Octavia E. Butler.* Urbana: University of Illinois, 2016.

_____. "Recovering Octavia E. Butler's Lost Parables," *Los Angeles Review of Books* (9 June 2014).

_____. "Science Fiction and Utopia in the Anthropocene," *American Literature* 93:2 (2021): 255–282.

Dundas, Deborah. "The Brilliance of Black Storytellers," *Toronto Star* (17 February 2018): E12.

Lievens, Laura. "The Only Lasting Truth Is Change: An Analysis of Earthseed Spirituality" (master's thesis), Université Catholique de Louvain, 2020.

Littleton, Therese. "'Black to the Future': Fest Is Mothership for African Americans in Science Fiction," *Seattle Times* (6 June 2004): K1.

Mackenthun, Gesa. "Sustainable Stories: Managing Climate Change with Literature," *Sustainability* 13:7 (2021): 4049.

Nanda, Aparajita "A Palimpsestuous Reading of Octavia Butler's *Lilith's Brood*" in *Palimpsests in Ethnic and Postcolonial Literature and Culture.* Cham, Switzerland: Palgrave Macmillan, 2021.

Turner, Jenny. "Ready to Go Off," *London Review of Books* 43:4 (18 February 2021).

"The Evening and the Morning and the Night"

Influenced by Octavia's lifelong battle with dyslexia, the title "The Evening and the Morning and the Night" summarizes a coming-of-age dilemma. The action requires two youths to review a mother's inherited psychosocial disease. Duryea-Gode Disease (DGD) has implications for their own deaths, a looming motif Octavia developed in "Crossover," *Clay's Ark,* "Speech Sounds," and the unpublished novel *Blindsight*. Jarringly violent and cynical, fifteen-year-old Lynn Mortimer's coming-of-age tale of attempted suicide depicts a spirit undermined by terror.

Most horrifying, the self-cannibalism in patients who fail to follow a restricted diet tethers Lynn to an austere regimen representing visceral incarceration, an unavoidable inheritance that overwhelms Jesusa and Tomás Serrano y Martín in the Xenogenesis series. Lynn's unease amid a hideous epidemic arouses resentment that her parents carried the dehumanizing gene, yet chose to conceive their daughter, an option that cripples Sarah's daughter Carrie in *Kindred* and threatens Keira "Kerry" Maslin's mutant baby in *Clay's Ark* and Lillian Iyapo's son Akin in *Adulthood Rites*. New Jersey activist Brittney Cooper, a specialist in gender and women's studies at Rutgers, New Brunswick, assessed the decision as "black women's intellectual commitment" to sexual self-expression and to maternal traditions evading racial and class bias (Cooper, 2017).

Inborn Infirmity

Metaphorically, the author conflates disability with blackness and greed, a two-layered allegory that receives major critical attention. Theri Alyce Pickens, an English professor at Bates College in Lewiston, Maines, characterizes the crossover between disability and race as "the plasticity of Blackness and madness in tandem" (Pickens, 2019, 26). She adds that, in past medical diagnoses, "the physically or mentally abnormal body and the racially abnormal body were understood as close cousins" (*ibid.*). The story pictures deranged victims gouging their eyes and swallowing flesh as forms of self-hate. On the downside of white-dominated capitalism, the creation and promotion of toxic chemicals that kill off humankind like Paracetco in the Parable series result from corporate greed. A frequently reissued novella, it grounds dangers to the vulnerable from commercial jeopardy in marketing the drug Hedeonco, a cancer cure derived from old money—the profits from chemicals, oil, and pharmaceuticals. As a hint at the cruelty of DGD, Octavia implies hedonism in the formulation of Hedeonco and combines root words suggesting "harsh God."

The first-person voice narrates the microbial tentacles that wrest life from both Lynn's parents. In a surreal flash, the father sickens suddenly, then murders and flays his wife before digging into his own chest, killing himself on the eve of Lynn's high school graduation. The horrendous double death is a harbinger of her own pariah status as a "double DGD" doomed to cognitive lapse and a corporeal demise (Butler, 2005, 43). A description of a low-level custodial care institution pictures patients *in extremis* gnawing at themselves among maggots, rats, and cockroaches, the vermin associated with decaying corpses.

Female Strengths

Octavia energized the denouement with outlandish details. Monstrous imagery accounts for fears in Lynn and lover Alan Chi that they are doomed to a loathsome end, the lugubrious significance of "night" in the title. To shield her son,

Naomi Chi, one of the author's self-sacrificing widows on a par with Lilith Iyapo in the Xenogenesis series and Lauren Oya Olamina Bankole in *The Parable of the Talents*, deliberately martyrs herself through isolation among the diseased. By giving victims choices, staff consultant Beatrice Alcantera lightens Naomi's affliction and identifies in Lynn a future patient advocate. Octavia raised hopes that talented people can direct their skills toward rehabilitating the sick and enfranchising minority females.

Octavia asserted that untapped originality can turn toxic. Under society's blame-the-victim philosophy, seclusion and othering further dissociate patients from normality. Allegorically, they tear from themselves the creativity that has no outlet until they enter a rest home that furthers imagination through kindness and counseling. A recipient of the 1987 Science Fiction Chronicle Reader Award, the story of womanly resourcefulness earned nominations for a 1988 Locus honor, Nebula citation, and the Theodore Sturgeon Award. In addition to appearing in *Bloodchild and Other Stories,* the narrative enticed new audiences in *The Year's Best Science Fiction, Best New SF 2, Omni Visions, Univers 1989, Escape Pod, Penguin Book of Modern Fantasy by Women, Dark Matter, Crucified Dreams,* and *Daughters of Earth,* a library of America volume.

See also Motherhood.

Sources

Butler, Octavia. "The Evening and the Morning and the Night," *Bloodchild and Other Stories*. New York: Seven Stories Press, 2005, 33–70.

Cooper, Brittney C. *Beyond Respectability: The Intellectual Thought of Race Women*. Champaign: University of Illinois Press, 2017.

Hall, Alice, ed. The Routledge Companion to Literature and Disability. London: Routledge, 2020.

Japtok, Martin, and Jerry Rafiki Jenkins, eds. Human Contradictions in Octavia E. Butler's Work. Cham, Switzerland: Palgrave, Macmillan, 2020.

Pickens, Theri Alyce. Black Madness: Mad Blackness. Durham, NC: Duke University Press, 2019.

Prakash, M., and K. Lavanya. "Transformation of the Human Race in Octavia E. Butler's *Clay's Ark,*" *European Journal of Molecular & Clinical Medicine* 7:11 (2020): 1729–1731.

"The Evening and the Morning and the Night" Genealogy

Octavia gave Lynn Mortimer a surname suggesting death, a reference to suicidal urges. For contrast, her lover Alan Chi's family name in Chinese means "life force," but the author opted to mention that the Nigerian clan identity in Ibo/Igbo signifies "a hovering custodial angel."

The concept of caretaking sets the tone of the climax, a visit to Dilg, a nursing home outside San Jose, California, where Beatrice Alcantera keeps safe ailing people like Alan's mother Naomi. In the same vein as "Alan Chi," the author selected Beatrice's names from Latin for "blessed" and Arabic for "bridge," a suggestion of Lynn's means of approaching her future mother-in-law. The given name Naomi alludes to Ruth's widowed mother-in-law, who changes her name to Mara (bitter) in Ruth 1:20–22 to acknowledge poverty and sorrow among females overwhelmed by patriarchy. Through humility and motherhood, around 1110 BCE, Ruth becomes the matriarch of the Davidian dynasty.

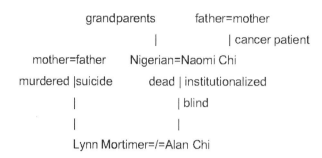

Sources

Butler, Octavia. "The Evening and the Morning and the Night," *Bloodchild and Other Stories*. New York: Seven Stories Press, 2005, 33–70.
Pickens, Theri Alyce. *Black Madness: Mad Blackness*. Durham, NC: Duke University Press, 2019.

Exotic Species

Octavia strikes at the hubris of *Homo sapiens* with a series of alternative conceptions that blend normal earth genes with peculiarities, urges, and supernatural skills. The unforeseen offspring with their abnormal appearances beg the question "What is human?" and "What is alien?," the basic query in "Speech Sounds." The quandary dogs the neophyte Gan in "Bloodchild," afflicts Lilith Iyapo's human-Oankali son Akin in the Xenogenesis series, and perplexes the amnesiac vampire Shori Matthews in *Fledgling*. More concerns bedevil Mary Larkin in *Patternmaster* and Keira "Kelly" Maslin and her mate in *Clay's Ark*. The author juxtaposes grotesque limbs, vampire teeth, and primordial torsos with identifiable emotions and sensitivities, the motivation for accepting compromises to the standard species.

The author offsets liberal views on hybridity with conservative devaluation of anomalies. Resisters of change conspire to slaughter all mutants to preserve *Homo sapiens* in its original form, even though its previous incarnation did not stop rioting in *The Parable of the Sower* or a nuclear disaster in *Dawn*. The least principled try to exterminate mutant babies or redesign their bodies through cosmetic surgery, the plot of the resister Neci in *Adulthood Rites* to reduce the child Margit's seven fingers to five. While transitioning to a bare survival, the most adaptable humans find themselves warring against hard-shell types like Neci, who equate compromisers like the human-Oankali prodigy Akin with traitors.

Accepting the "Other"

In a discussion of humankind in "Amnesty," translator Noah Cannon gently, agreeably acknowledges that "the universe has other children" besides earthlings, her validation of posthumans (Butler, 2005, 158). She struggles to indoctrinate six new recruits at a Mojave bubble on the nature of invaders, each from a community of beings having no visible shape, no sense of smell, and no need for sleep. The description suits other grotesques in science fiction:

Beast	*Title*	*Characteristics*
Aaor	*Lilith's Brood*	a non-gender human-ooloi hybrid
achti	"Bloodchild"	furry edible herd animal killed for food
Akin	*Adulthood Rites*	the half-human, half–Oankali prodigy leading humans to settle on Mars
alien employer	"Amnesty"	a gentle, supportive supervisor of translator Noah Cannon
Amber	*Patternmaster*	psionic leader who eats her own hand to foil Clayarks
An-yanwu	*Wild Seed*	a long-lived Nigerian healer who shapeshifts into tigers, eagles, and dolphins
Asa Elias Doyle	*Clay's Ark*	a black astronaut and survivor of space travel that infects him with a mania to mate
Clayarks	*Patternmaster*	furless, tailless, catlike human-headed beings who carry disease and chase Patternists at speeds of 100 kph
Dana Franklin	*Kindred*	time traveler to nineteenth-century Maryland plantation
Dehkiaht	*Lilith's Brood*	an ooloi who sires the first human-Oankali hybrid
Dichaan	*Lilith's Brood*	a ooloi who sires three human-Oankali daughters
Doro	*Mind of My Mind*	a vampiric shapeshifter 4,000 years old who cannibalizes victims
	Wild Seed	the dominator of An-yanwu, a benevolent healer who tames him
Emma	*Mind of My Mind*	a 300-year-old breeder who longs for perpetual youth
Garkohn	*Survivor*	indigenous humanoid hunters with fur colored blue, yellow, or green
God	"The Book of Martha"	a shapeshifting deity who alters gender at will
Ina	*Fledgling*	ancient vampires who thrive on darkness and symbiont human blood
Jacob Boyd	*Clay's Ark*	a mutant four-year-old quadruped with enhanced sense of smell and hearing
Jdahya	*Lilith's Brood*	Oankali parent of ooloi Nikanj
Jodahs	*Lilith's Brood*	a human-ooloi hybrid
Joseph	"Childfinder"	a psionic protector of Barbara
Josif Petrescu	*Fledgling*	vampire father of hybrid Shori Matthews
Kahguyaht	*Lilith's Brood*	ooloi parent of ooloi Nikanj
Karl Larkin	*Mind of My Mind*	a high level psionic who investigates warehouse thievery
Katherine Dahlman	*Fledgling*	a judgmental vampire who promotes persecution of Shori Matthews

Beast	Title	Characteristics
Margit	*Lilith's Brood*	a human-Oankali daughter
Mary Larkin	*Mind of My Mind*	a high-level psionic trainer of beginning mind readers
Nahtahk	*Survivor*	a vicious, arrogant hunter of Garkohns
Nikanj	*Lilith's Brood*	an ooloi who mixes genes from foreign species
N'Tli	"Bloodchild"	an impregnated caterpillar-shaped being
Oankali	*Lilith's Brood*	nomadic sea slugs with tentacles that communicate via pheromones and images for gene trading with other species
ooloi	*Lilith's Brood*	a third gender capable of altering genetic codes
Orel Ingraham	*Clay's Ark*	a diseased kidnapper of normal humans
pyros	*The Parable of the Sower*	arsonists maddened by a drug
Shori Matthews	*Fledgling*	hybrid black vampire afflicted with amnesia
Silks	*Fledgling*	racist attackers who foster with the Ina
space microbe	*Clay's Ark*	an independent virus that shares symbiosis with humans
sphinx	*Patternmaster*	a human-headed, lion-bodied beast with falcon's wings
subcontractor	"Amnesty"	a bush-shaped species that has no ears or limbs who speaks and punishes captives through electric shock
Tahneh	"A Necessary Being"	childless leader of a desert people
Tehkohn	*Survivor*	kidnappers and raiders colonized by missionaries
T'Gatoi	"Bloodchild"	velvety, multi-limbed female Tlic government official three meters long with yellow eyes and hissing voice
Tiikuchahk	*Lilith's Brood*	a human-Oankali hybrid sired by Dichaan and Nikanj
tilio	*Dawn*	Oankali vehicles traveling along slime trails like slugs
T'Khotgif	"Bloodchild"	Tlic mate of Bram Lomas, who carries her eggs to term
Tlics	"Bloodchild"	caterpillar-like parasites and dominators of Terrans
Valerie	"Childfinder"	a psionic reader of Harriet Tubman's biography
Rufus Weylin	*Kindred*	nineteenth-century Maryland native who can summon his great great granddaughter from the mid-twentieth century
wormlets	"Bloodchild"	newborn tlic bloodsuckers

Pakistani writer Ayesha Kiran, a research scholar of Communication and Media Studies at Public Sector University in Lahore, detailed the unattractive Oankali of *Dawn* as vertebrates similar to robots.

BENDING THE WILL

Octavia substantiated tolerance and compromise as the most promising methods of relieving earth's self-annihilation from superstition, hate, and violence. She incorporated these motivations in stalkers of psionic black children in "Childfinder," Silk assassins of radical vampires in *Fledgling*, and Los Angeles bus rioters in "Speech Sounds." For exotic beings in the Xenogenesis series, Kendra R. Parker, an English professor at Hope College in Holland, Michigan, allegorized the Oankali as metaphoric beings representing the "difference that humans are invited to embrace—or risk extinction by defying" (Parker, 2018). The ethics of alien clinicians like Nikanj echo the medical manipulations of black patients during colonial bondage and tests conducted by the Tuskegee syphilis experiments on 400 black males from 1932 to 1972, the cause of 128 deaths.

Octavia's speculative fiction exonerated alien hybridizers who tried to salvage post-apocalyptic humans. Through Lilith Iyapo and her mutant son Akin, earth's survivors of nuclear war learn to coexist on Mars and to sanction advanced interspecies copulation as a source of orgasmic release and conception of a third species blessed with the best traits of humans and Oankali. Critic Gerry Canavan, an English professor at Marquette University in Milwaukee, observed Octavia's daring proposition: "That interplay of attraction and revulsion is the source of what is simultaneously most utopian and most disturbing about her stories" (Canavan, 2016).

See also Adaptation; Villains.

Sources

Butler, Octavia. *Adulthood Rites in Lilith's Brood*. New York: Warner, 2000, 249–517.
_____. "Amnesty," Bloodchild and Other Stories. New York: Seven Stories Press, 2005, 147–186.
Canavan, Gerry. *Octavia E. Butler*. Urbana: University of Illinois, 2016.
Hampton, Gregory. "In Memoriam: Octavia E. Butler (1947–2006)," *Callaloo* 29:2 (Spring, 2006): 245–248.
Kiran, Ayesha. "Human Identity and Technophobic Posthumanism in Octavia Butler's Dawn," *Indiana Journal of Arts & Literature* 2:8 (2021): 1–15.
Parker, Kendra R. *Gale Researcher Guide: Octavia Butler and Afrofuturism*. Boston: Cengage Learning, 2018.

Exploitation

Octavia wrote passionately about the relationship between opportunist and prey in the alien manipulation of translator Noah Cannon in "Amnesty," the luring of Jane with wine and casual sex in "Crossover," the sexual compromising of Stephen's sister Barbara in "Near of Kin," and the demeaning of dark-skinned females in the author's book review "Black Feminism: Searching the Past" for the October

17, 1983, issue of *Washington Post*. The duping of voters in the Parable series during the 2032 election of U.S. President Andrew Jarret inflicts a blustering demagogue on naive citizens expecting great things for the country. By rationalizing his vile acts as the outgrowth of Christian America, he unleashes crusaders to destroy, seize, and subjugate victims with electronic dog collars. The author winds down the disastrous term of office with a landslide that frees contrition camps and with Jarret's death from alcoholism, a proof of corruption at the heart of a bully and flimflam artist.

A case in point from her early fiction, astronaut Asa Elias "Eli" Doyle in *Clay's Ark* survives an extraterrestrial virus that he quarantines among a desert cult before it can endanger the globe. The ranch house hideaway shelters normal human females who suffer viral contamination and, against their will, conceive the next generation of symbionts. The sect's purpose is to supply earth with an adapted generation. Sex overrides morals in another setting where Tahneh, Hao (magistrate) of a desert tribe in "A Necessary Being," signals sexual attraction to her Hao guest Diut from a mountain tribe with a bite on the throat. When he returns the seductive nip, Tahneh ponders that the ritual can signal both affection and betrayal, the future she has in mind for the outsider. In both instances, coital solutions to human dilemmas prove elusive.

Men in Peril

Physical threat generates horror in the grisly story "Bloodchild," in which hapless human men supply an extraterrestrial race of worms with inner body spaces for growing a new generation of wormlets. Reproduction requires a selfless male pregnancy that the author drolly labels an "unusual accommodation" (Butler, 2005, 32). The problem of removing the fetuses before they can devour their host's flesh and blood creates a tension in Gan, a neophyte birthing father. After he views the caesarian section of Bram Lomas, who shrieks in agony as the midwife slices open his torso, Gan realizes the extent of exploitation and his selection by T'Gatoi as the next parturient man, a role derived from family obligations.

Opportunism takes two forms in *Kindred*, Octavia's classic time travel novel set in nineteenth-century plantation times. For writer Dana Franklin, romance with Kevin, a white California author, requires clearing the air about manipulation and profiting from dating a black woman. Dana bridles at his attempts to employ her as typist. After a timeslip carries her from 1976 back to Maryland in 1819, she profits from traveling with a white husband, who poses as her owner and lover to shield her from slave era torture. The conclusion of the neo-slave narrative places the female rescuer of her great great grandfather, Rufus Weylin, in an on-the-spot rape attempt that she foils by stabbing him. Octavia built the action into a classic approach-avoidance scenario that exonerates Dana, but costs her an arm when she eludes the past by bursting through a time boundary.

The Master Rogue

In the estimation of Pravin Sonune, English department chair at R.B. Attal College Georai, India, the author contended that women in science fiction aim to reconstruct society and the ecosystem harmoniously and productively while men deserve blame for most of patriarchy's miseries by exploiting force, dominance, war, and politics. The Patternmaster series sets the deathless Nubian Doro in the role of pseudo-scientific hybridizer. During four thousand years, his life requires the murder of people he chooses as his next embodiment. To promote a projected super race, he romances An-yanwu, an immortal Nigerian healer, and dazzles her with a transatlantic voyage in the *Silver Star* magically sped by Isaac, Doro's prodigy. After repeated killings and threats, she creates her own social incubator at a Louisiana plantation where freedom and support of refugee slaves create opportunities for a satisfying life. To tame Doro's excesses, An-yanwu pleasures herself by taking the form of a dolphin, an unconstrained existence in free waters. Navle Balalaji Anandrao, English professor at Deogiri College in Aurangabad, India, corroborated Sonune's contentions by endorsing female outreach to "growth and all-round sound development unto the last" (Anandrao, 2021, 106).

In the abstract, the author denounced American capitalism for harnessing cheap labor in have-not countries, Doro's method in *Mind of My Mind* of phasing out expendables. In the judgment of Marlene D. Allen, a professor at Columbus State University in Georgia, the worst money-grubbing sins involve hazardous employee environments: "They employ people and make no provision for safety. They may be poisoned with chemicals, hurt in equipment foul-ups…. And people do tend to get used up after a certain time" (Allen, 2009, 1357). The model of the cannibalistic entrepreneur continues in the Parable series, in which limited pay and malnutrition at Olivar, an oceanfront suburb of Los Angeles, exploits West Coast panic with empty promises to employees. A proposed relief of robotic factory work and capitalization of natural resources begins at Acorn, a migrant commune at Cape Mendocino, with hand-working the soil. Simple gardening becomes a satisfying antidote to the terrors and insecurities of refugees from chaos and the breakdown of the vegetal world.

See also Capitalism; Dominance; Slavery.

Sources

Allen, Marlene D. "Octavia Butler's Parable Novels and the Boomerang of African American History," *Callaloo* 32:4 (Fall, 2009): 1353–1363, 1387.
Anandrao, Navle Balaji. "Female Characters in Science Fiction: Archetypal Messengers of Social Equity & Equality," *International Multilingual Journal for Arts and Humanities* 1:6 (August 2021): 106–118.
Butler, Octavia. "Black Feminism: Searching the Past," (review) *Washington Post* (17 October 1983): B2.
_____. "Bloodchild," *Bloodchild and Other Stories*. New York: Seven Stories Press, 2005, 1–32.
Sonune, Pravin. "Feminism, Women, and Science Fiction of Octavia Butler," *Epitome Journals* 7:4 (April 2021): 54–67.
Vakoch, Douglas A. *Dystopias and Utopias on Earth and Beyond*. New York: Routledge, 2021.

Feminism

A literary activist, Octavia viewed black feminism through the Akan-Twi lens of *sankofa,* a term from Ghana meaning "retrieving the best from the past." In National Public Radio's "Morning Edition" for February 24, 2021, Laine Kaplan-Levenson summarized the author's outreach as "Octavia, the feminist; Octavia, the

Afrofuturist; Octavia, the radical…. Octavia the prophet" (Kaplan-Levenson, 2021). The author's research developed an historical consciousness of black female endurance in the mystic past and the African diaspora. Her works charged the white world with the silencing of black female stories, adages, songs, and riddles. She obligated black feminists to explain, build, and nest in a nontraditional black reality that rebuts Western denial of nonwhite women's worth.

The author credited second wave feminism in the 1960s and 1970s for giving female authors the right to shape superwomen in science fiction the way they imagined them. In a salute to women's progress, *The Parable of the Sower* reveres Alicia Catalina Godinez Leal, an Hispanic astronaut martyred on a Mars mission, and esteems teacher Corazon "Cory" Olamina, who joins her children in rifle practice as a home defense. Horrified at a decaying corpse, Aura Moss abandons the outing and leaves the security jobs to men. The decision replicates female choices to retreat into the chivalric past and act like ladies, a romantic construct common to ballads, literature, advertising, music, and art. Protagonist Lauren Oya Olamina labels the regression a "breeding ground for resentment" (Butler, 1993, 88).

By Lauren's contrast to rash, risk-bound younger brother Keith, the author implies that girls pass through coming of age with less family disruption and more intellect, yet face certain ravaging if seized by all-male gangs, a destructive model of mob-think. To her horror, in *The Parable of the Talents,* she views electric collars and tongue cutting as means of silencing women, a policy of radical Christian Americans. Rapists force females into male subjugation because they have "lost all modesty and offered [themselves] in the streets" (*ibid.,* 212). Rumors defame Lauren's daughter, Larkin Bankole, by alleging an illicit pregnancy and abortion, the standard media character assassination of self-determined females. In a letter from her conservative brother Marcos Duran, Lauren receives scriptural direction from 1 Timothy 2:11, "Let the woman learn in silence with all subjection." Meanwhile, the Alexanders brainwash their foster daughter Larkin to "be seen and not heard … like a sheep in Christ's flock," a throwback to the censored Christian lady of Arthurian literature (*ibid.,* 239).

In a quip about sexism on the spaceship/planet in *Dawn,* repressed human Paul Titus says, "They need a little women's and men's lib up here" in a place where "women … walk noiselessly to avoid abuse" (Butler, 2000, 89). By novel's end, there is no gendered face-off: the task before Lilith Iyapo appears too much for anyone, male or female. In fear of regression in the few surviving earthlings, Paul warns her that a return to the stone age could cause males to "drag you around, put you in a harem, beat the shit out of you," the assault suffered by rape victim Marina Rivas in *Imago* and by concentration camp inmates in *The Parable of the Talents* (*ibid.,* 93). The events reflect historical surmise that Neanderthals lacked "civilized restraint" toward women and valued males for strength and control (*ibid.,* 94).

Women in Power

Octavia toyed with gender puzzles in *Wild Seed* by exemplifying the witch-like shapeshifting of An-yanwu, a Kush-Ibo/Igbo healer. In changing bodies with beasts, she learns the voracious lusts of the leopard, the soaring heights of the eagle. In the underwater traits of dolphins, she delights to be female in the only sport that favors women competitors. Reflecting over other incarnations, she recalls, "Only in her true woman-shape could she remember being seriously hurt by males—men" (Butler, 1980, 202). The rhetorical stress of the final two words carries the author's experience with human males and their penchant for harming and killing females. Lauding An-yanwu and Butler's other wonder women, British analyst Theri Alyce Pickens, a professor of English at Bates College in Lewiston, Maine, admired how they "navigate their survival in societies riddled with complex hierarchies… based on differences in gender, race, species, and mental strength" (Pickens 2014, 33).

As an example from black history, the writer relived mobs chasing sorcerers to burn at the stake, an epic scene from the Female Holocaust, the three-century mania causing some nine million murders. On the American shore, the self-centered Patternmaster Doro, who breeds witches as "good kills" to stave off loneliness and ennui, satisfies the needs of Wheatley citizens to execute necromancers and diviners—"expected it, accepted it, treated it as a kind of religious sacrifice," a backhanded swipe at historic Puritan extremism (*ibid.*, 255). An-yanwu's personal experience at eighteenth-century Wheatley garbs her in the outfit of a "real lady … a New York lady," a vast alteration from the Nigerian matriarch and priestess, a "respected and valued woman" by townspeople (*ibid.*, 245). An-yanwu derides a chameleon-like existence where "only a few pieces of cloth make me a 'real lady'" (*ibid.*). She later grouses at the demotion of women to sexual chattel "preserved for the use of owners alone," Alice Greenwood's situation with Rufus Weylin in *Kindred* (*ibid.*, 521).

OCTAVIA'S FEMALES

No longer a white male option, fantasy characterization moved away from Octavia's memories of "princesses and witches, which is the kind of role women played in the science fiction I remember when I began" (Beal, 1986, 16). In the place of fabricated heroines, she created Valerie Rye, the armed University of California at Los Angeles history professor in "Speech Sounds" who stands her ground amid a bus riot. Nnedi Okorafor-Mbachu, a Nigerian-American fantasist, accounted for fan love of the author's boldness "to create characters who had the audacity to be black and female and exist in the future, with aliens at that!" (Okorafor-Mbachu, 2008, 243). For readers, the daring recreation of the Yoruban river deity Yemonja in Alanna Verrick, the diaspora leader in *Survivor,* and the immortal matriarch An-yanwu/ Emma in *Wild Seed* and Emma in *Mind of My Mind* proved mind-stretching, soul-awakening, a major asset of Afrofuturism.

To position renewed femininity in the speculative future, the author had to rethink the past. In the death struggle of lovers Diut and Alanna Verrick in *Survivor,* Octavia stated a womanly outlook on spousal abuse: "Do you think I'll learn faster out of fear of your beatings? I won't. I can't" (Butler, 1978, 107). With human rationale, she proposes talking out man-woman differences or separating. Diut soothes mutual anguish by joining her in spreading salve on their wounds, an allegorical acknowledgment of physical and emotional hurts. Octavia rewarded the couple with a satisfying sex life and hopeful escape from tyranny, outcomes of mutual regard.

The author gravitated toward positive energies and concessions rather than man-of-the-house conflict and control, the fault of Tom and Rufus Weylin as plantation owners in *Kindred* and of humans persecuting translator Noah Cannon in "Amnesty." Unlike the spiteful skeptic and alien-hater Thera Collier, the protagonist looks for the benefits of yielding to extraterrestrial earth invaders, especially their preference for armless hugs, called "enfolding" (Butler, 2005, 149). The novel *Mind of My Mind* expands on the long-lived Nubian Doro's pairing of telepaths through marriage as a form of eugenics, the basis of a controlled super race. However, his daughter Mary's self-determination challenges his supervision of telepaths as though pulling strings on puppets. Even after the wedding to Karl Larkin, she remains her own person. Doro, who is adept at "playing God," admits: "She doesn't have a 'kind.' She's unique," a world builder who becomes Doro's rival at Patterning (Butler, 1977, 32).

WOMEN OF WONDER

For *Patternmaster* in 1976, the author developed dramatic scenarios in which Teray, son of Jansee and the Patternmaster Rayal, learns about self-defense from Amber, an independent healer. Because of her liberation from standard gendering, she defends bisexuality and demands her own house, not wedlock. Feminist and award-winning sci-fi author Pamela Sargent, the co-creator of *Star Trek* and author of the Venus series, dubbed such autonomous and inventive females "Women of Wonder" for applying distinct strengths to different situations, from healing, marriage, and military savvy to governance and peacemaking (Sargent, 1974, 11).

As models of female tenacity, examples of women with possibilities range across Octavia's canon:

AMN—"Amnesty"   Kin—*Kindred*
AR—*Adulthood Rites*   LB—*Lilith's Brood*
BC—"Bloodchild"   MMM—*Mind of My Mind*
BOM—"The Book of Martha"   NB—"A Necessary Being"
CA—*Clay's Ark*   PM—*Patternmaster*
CF—"Childfinder"   POS—*The Parable of the Sower*
Dawn—*Dawn*   POT—*The Parable of the Talents*
EMN—"The Evening and the Morning and   SS—"Speech Sounds"
   the Night"   Sur—*Survivor*
Fl—*Fledgling*   WS—*Wild Seed*
Im—*Imago*

Characters	Source	Strengths	Weaknesses
Alanna Verrick	Sur	logic, patience	renewed addiction to *meklah*
Alice Greenwood	Kin	rescuer	susceptible to her owner's seduction
Amber	PM	independent healer	unbalanced physical strength

Characters	Source	Strengths	Weaknesses
An-yanwu/Emma	WS	motherly, stubborn	daring violence in nature and disobeying her controller
Barbara	CF	innovative teacher	nonconformist, misfit, rebel, not psionic organizer
Beatrice Alcantera	EMN	professional, hopeful	prejudiced toward a female rival, territorial
Belen "Len" Ross	POT	willingness to learn	rearing in an effete environment
Cheah	NB	strong, alert, daring	loyal to males threatening a female leader
	Sur	worthy mate	a hunter who relies on her husband, Judge Jeh
Corazon "Cory" Olamina	POS	altruistic, defensive, church pianist, teacher	unequal treatment of son Keith and daughter Lauren
Dana Franklin	Kin	courageous, empathetic	lacks control of time travel and slave era laws
Emma	MMM	matriarchal grandma	lack of psionic power
Jansee	PM	motherly, loyal	risks marrying her brother Rayal
Jesusa Serrano y Martín	Im	defender of her people	attraction to Jodahs, who can cure her tumors
Jorah Maslin	CA	devoted wife and mother	dies leaving her daughter to face leukemia
Keira "Kerry" Maslin	CA	willing wife and mother	sick from the final stages of leukemia
Lauren Oya Olamina	POS	visionary, philosopher	ambivalence toward her father's faith
	POT	leader	overwhelming Christian America army
Lilith Iyapo	Dawn	logical, courageous	given to doubts about her role in educating humans
	AR	amazon	grief for her son and for crimes against Tino Lael
Lynn Mortimer	EMN	comforting, emotive	suspicious as a result of horrific memories and dread
María de la Luz	Im	resilient	a matriarch who sanctions incest with son Adan
Martha Bes	BOM	willingness to serve God	fear of catastrophic error in correcting human errors
Mary Larkin	MMM	clever, resilient, caring	combative, rude
May	POT	physician's assistant	a sharer who lost her tongue to anti-female extremists
Meda Boyd	CA	motherly, daring	risks producing a diseased child
Noah Cannon	AMN	rescuer of humankind	susceptible to rough handling by a subcontractor
Rane Maslin	CA	daring	infected with an extraterrestrial virus
Sarah	Kin	competent, energetic	cautious about risking Carrie against overseers and owner

Characters	Source	Strengths	Weaknesses
Shori Matthews	Fl	strong, aggressive	eager to learn family history erased by amnesia
Tahneh	NB	commanding authority	angered by her father's crippling by Rohkohn torturers
Tate Rinaldi	AR	child protector	needs Gabe for love and affirmation
Valerie	CF	pre-psi child	surly; not ready for group interaction
Valerie Rye	SS	armed professor, survivor	lonely and grieving for her three children
Zahra Moss	POS	experienced traveler	occasional stubbornness; small size
	POT	strong mother	dies, leaving her husband Harry to grieve

For contrast, Octavia created Margaret Weylin in *Kindred*, who leaves her son to a vindictive father, and Neila Verrick, a missionary wife in *Survivor* who lacks the rescuer's faith in foster daughter Alanna.

FEMALE CREDENTIALS

The development of woman-to-woman camaraderie illustrates the intuitive might of female friendship, an instinctive alliance based on mutual experiences rather than androcentric competition or superiority. On a night when eight white patrollers threaten Alice Greenwood's family in *Kindred*, the mother gambles on male retribution by giving protagonist Dana Franklin sanctuary in her cabin despite Dana's lack of manumission papers. On a tutorial level, to ensure Dana's safety from the lash, kitchen slave Sarah teaches her to cook and denotes her breaches of the white-black boundary. Sarah's mute daughter Carrie surprises Dana with wit and savvy in a financial plantation turnover that threatens her children with the auction block. In each instance, female backgrounds in injustice and peril sanction a reliable refuge to other women, especially loners, the disabled, and mothers.

In a discussion of justice for females, Octavia declared faulting the woman an eternal sellout. The paradigm of males cosseting women equated with imprisonment, lifetime suppression, and exoneration of men for warlike savagery, the result of sanctioning patriarchal biblical orthodoxy in *Survivor* and *The Parable of the Talents*. The author dramatized a spur-of-the-moment rage in Rane Maslin in *Clay's Ark*, where she aims an automatic rifle and sprays death on car gangs before her murder and decapitation, an iconic override of female agency. Ironically, she leaves the desert cult her twin Keira "Kerry" Maslin in a renewed state of health and eager to bear a hybrid child. In a salute to the author's recording of head shaving, branding, stoning, cutting out tongues, witch hunting, and burning alive, De Witt Kilgore and Ranu Samantrai, both on staff at Indiana University at Bloomington, credited her with commemorating black female endurance: "If humanity as a whole is subject to the fear of bodily violation and exploitation, in Butler's futures it is black women who have the longest familiarity with it" (Kilgore & Samant-rai, 2010, 355). The authenticity of her heroines raised mainstream popularity of feminist sci-fi and academic legitimacy of her characterizations of masculinity and femininity.

Sources

Beal, Frances. "Interview," *Black Scholar* 17:2 (March/April 1986): 14–18.
Butler, Octavia. "Amnesty" in *Bloodchild and Other Stories*. New York: Seven Stories Press, 2005, 147–186.
_____. *Clay's Ark*. New York: St. Martin's Press, 1984.
_____. *Dawn* in *Lilith's Brood*. New York: Warner, 2000, 2–248.
_____. *Mind of My Mind*. New York: Doubleday, 1977.
_____. *The Parable of the Sower*. New York: Four Walls, Eight Windows, 1993.
_____. *The Parable of the Talents*. New York: Four Walls, Eight Windows, 1998.
_____. *Survivor*. New York: Doubleday, 1978.
_____. *Wild Seed*. New York: Doubleday, 1980.
Canavan, Gerry. *Octavia E. Butler*. Urbana: University of Illinois, 2016.
Govan, Sandra Y. "Interview," *Obsidian III* 6:2/7:1 (2005–2006): 14–39.
Kaplan-Levenson, Laine. "Sci-Fi Writer Octavia Butler Offered Warnings and Hope in Her Work," *Morning Edition*. Washington, DC: NPR (24 February 2021).
Kilgore, De Witt Douglas, and Ranu Samantrai. "A Memorial to Octavia E. Butler," *Science Fiction Studies* 37:3 (November 2010): 353–361.
McKoy, Sheila Smith. "Yemonja/Yemoja/Yemaya Rising" in *Recovering the African Feminine Divine in Literature, the Arts, and Practice: Yemonja Awakening*. Lanham, MD: Lexington Books, 2020, 55–68.
Okorafor-Mbachu, Nnedi. "Octavia's Healing Power" in *Afro-Future Females*. Columbus: Ohio State University Press, 2008, 241–243.
Pickens, Theri. "'You're Supposed to Be a Tall, Handsome, Fully Grown White Man': Theorizing Race, Gender, and Disability in Octavia Butler's *Fledgling*," *Journal of Literary & Cultural Disability Studies* 8:1 (2014): 33–48, 126.
Pitts, Michael. *Alternative Masculinities in Feminist Speculative Fiction: A New Man*. Lanham, MD: Lexington Books, 2021.
Sargent, Pamela. *Women of Wonder*. New York: Penguin, 1974.

Fledgling

A *Bildungsroman* narrated by an experimental melanin-rich female vampire, Octavia's last novel implements seriocomic horror imitating romance and detective narratives. After a lengthy career in research and speculative fiction, the author chortled, "It's been a long time since writing was fun" (Govan, 2005–2006, 35). Drawing on precolonial West African lore, her text absorbed a wealth of material on fearful desires of the *soucouyant* (blood-sucker) and the terrors in the soul-stealing Hausa witches in Niger, the *adze* of Ghana and Togo, and the jealous Yoruba witch-wives of Nigeria. Transatlantic slave trade distributed the original lore to the *aziman* of Dahomey, *asema* of Surinam, *sukuyan* in Tobago-Trinidad, *loogaroo* (Loup-garou) of Grenada and Haiti, and the *feufollet* (will-o'-the-wisp) of Louisiana. She considered other titles: *Memory, Flesh, Bone, Blood; Blood, Flesh, Bone, Memory; Scars; Darkling; Dark Light; Blood Groups;* and *Fireweed,* but chose a baby bird image to project the stumbles and misunderstandings of the neophyte vampire.

In an interview with *Democracy Now,* the writer revealed the origins of Shori Matthews, her mutant protagonist, temporarily called Renee (reborn): "Her people managed to genetically engineer her. These vampires are a different species. They are not vampires because somebody bit them" (Butler, 2005). Devoid of magic and the supernatural, they join a global diaspora of refugees across Eastern Europe, Great Britain, Asia, and the Americas and conceal human symbionts who supply nutrients for Ina blood drinkers. The Ina evolve a species interdependence that erases boundaries separating individual types and sexualities.

Echoing Akin's sensations that begin *Adulthood Rites,* Octavia traces the protagonist's awakening through pain, tactile impressions, deer footsteps, and dark, which she prefers to risking sunburn and blisters outside her cave. Scars, like landmarks of black history, embody the dolor of human bondage from the lashings and mutilations that slave masters inflicted. Revelations broaden the trope by calling Shori's amnesia a larger disfigurement for depriving her of racial and clan belonging. Inching into a burned settlement, Shori relives the dismay of Lauren Oya Olamina in *The Parable of the Sower* upon discovering the arson that killed Alexandra Casey, her husband's sister. Essential to the theme of blackness, Shori ponders folkloric vampires—"children of the great Goddess"—who were "feared, hated, and hunted" and grieves the seventy-eight victims of arson kindled by unknown assassins (Butler, 2005, 298, 43). She concludes that killing a potential attacker "would seem almost ... just," a simplistic view of payback (*ibid.*).

Genre Mix

In conflating sexual pleasure with predation, the text incorporates elements of the mystery-romance. While Shori quizzes guard Raleigh Curtis about a helicopter landing, the action develops suspense about her connection to the burned-out ruins, which seem worthless. Octavia rounds out the genre mix with humor in Iosif Petrescu's Darwinian wisecrack about the Ina being "the more gifted cousin" to humankind than chimpanzees (*ibid.,* 73). Additional speculation about the vampire species arriving originally from space echoes pseudo-scientific surmise about earth mysteries, such as builders of the Egyptian pyramids, Stonehenge, and the Nazca lines of Peru. To thrash out Ina history and folk roots, Iosif arranges discussions in a large hall, a democratic system that Acorn residents employ in the Parable series. The clerestory at the back of the Ina conference room implies an openness to truth, the controlling theme of *The Parable of the Talents.*

Replicating the conscription of neo–Nazi and neocon factions from naive schemers, the author incorporates the Silks, whom Julian Lucas, a writer for the *New Yorker*, described as "a conservative, old-line Ina family—night-supremacist blue-blood-suckers—who consider her a threat to their species' integrity" (Lucas, 2021, 75). Their strategy parallels the tactics of Mafia goon squads—grooming of "someone's tools" into special ops to attack the Ina (Butler, 2005, 197). Victor Colon, whose name hints at the formation of mercenary squads like that of Hernán Cortés's colonialist invaders of Tenochtitlan in 1518, recounts a series of raids. By describing a failed foray on the innovative Ina, he reveals Shori's skill at ripping out throats. Ending the vampire feud with a council session at Punta Nublada, California, the author wrings wit from its translation, "Cloudy Point," a pun on elusive side issues before the judges.

CLAIMING THEIR OWN

The falling action brings to a verdict a three-night tribunal that ironically initiates Shori as a respected Ina. According to Kendra R. Parker, on the English staff of Hope College in Holland, Michigan, the dramatic face-off, like the October 1991 Anita Hill Hearings before the Senate Judiciary Committee, examines "intersectional disempowerment and know-your-place aggression" (Parker, 2018, 60). Judgment creates unity and rededication of the Ina to ancient vampire precepts by putting speciesism on trial. The author facilitated Shori's acceptance by cautiously selecting advocates and legal tactics that oust Katherine Dahlman as Silks clan spokeswoman and advocate for racial purity, a nostalgic dream of an Edenic past. By toppling liars and deceivers through testimony, the protagonist establishes both integrity and remarkable acumen in a young contender whom Silks detractors deride as a near-human "mongrel cub" disabled by amnesia (*ibid.*, 238). In defense of a hybrid species, she enhances an allegory of racism by disparaging the plot of hate crimes and championing the reward to symbionts of health and longevity.

The purpose of Octavia's rooting out monstrous evil among the Ina takes a Christian turn in repetition of I John 1:7, composed before 110 CE by the beloved disciple of Jesus. By enabling future generations to "walk in the light," an image mentioned previously in *Mind of My Mind,* Shori ends the white-skinned vampire's dependence on darkness, the source of secret sin and hidden resistance (*ibid.*, 294). The author's choice of a light/dark metaphor and the renewed vitality of the victimized female fit securely in colonial American literary tradition, particularly Nathaniel Hawthorne's *The Scarlet Letter.* The loss of librarian Theodora Harden, the symbolic bearer of literacy, costs Shori grief and martyrdom while attesting to the assembled jurors that she represents justice and the benefits of reason. Because the DNA experiment succeeds, scions of Shori can claim addictive venom and the ability to stand guard over their alternative enclave by day, a suggestion of group protection of HIV/AIDS patients.

Sources

Burt, Stephanie. "Octavia Butler Wanted to Write a 'Yes' Book," *National Republic* (27 May 2021).
Butler, Octavia. *Fledgling.* New York: Seven Stories Press, 2005.
_____. "Science Fiction Writer Octavia Butler on Race, Global Warming and Religion," (video), *Democracy Now www.democracynow.org/2005/11/11/science_fiction_writer_octavia_butler_on* (11 November 2005).
Govan, Sandra Y. "Interview," *Obsidian III* 6:2/7:1 (2005–2006): 14–39.
Jenkins, Jerry Rafiki. *The Paradox of Blackness in African American Vampire Fiction.* Columbus: Ohio State University Press, 2019.
Lucas, Julian. "Stranger Communities," *New Yorker* 97:4 (15 March 2021): 73–76.
Nayar, Pramod K. "Vampirism and Posthumanism in Octavia Butler's *Fledgling*," *Notes on Contemporary Literature* 41:2 (2011).
Parker, Kendra R. *Black Female Vampires in African American Women's Novels, 1977–2011.* Lanham, MD: Lexington Books, 2018.

Fledgling **Genealogy**

The author distinguishes patriarch Iosif Petrescu with the Romanian surname "son of the rock," a hint at the hardy Transylvanian vampire tradition that underlies

Fledgling. She identifies rescuer Wright Hamlin by a name indicating a residence builder and home lover. His efforts to resurrect Shori Matthews from amnesia suit her name, which is East African for "nightingale." Her unavoidable deer slaying and cannibalism of Hugh Tang derives depth from "intelligent" and "succeed," references to his job of locating Iosif Petrescu's missing daughter, who cost him his life.

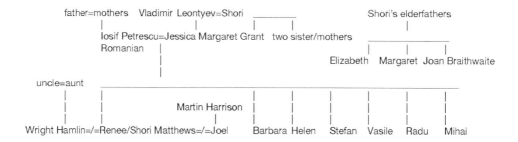

The contrast of the Petrescu and Gordon clans with Silks suggests the humility of most Ina as opposed to notions of privilege in a superior race. Various uses of "Ina" in Asian languages yields "pure" in Hebrew and "mother" in Hindi, Malay, Tamil, Javanese, and Islam. The name condones a gentle people who authorize living in harmony and mutual benefits of health and long life shared with symbionts.

Sources

Butler, Octavia. *Fledgling.* New York: Seven Stories Press, 2005.
Lucas, Julian. "Stranger Communities," *New Yorker* 97:4 (15 March 2021): 73–76.

Food

Octavia distinguished hearty menus and meals as well as the historical crumbs and dregs consumed by the disempowered peasant. She detailed the hearth-baked loaves on dying embers in *Wild Seed*, a contrast in *The Parable of the Talents* to the spoiled potatoes and boiled cabbage that prisoners eat at Camp Christian. Americans tend to savor the simple snack—Wright Hamlin's scrambled egg and ham sandwich with beer, a breakfast of sausage and waffles, and Brook's pepper-smoked salmon in *Fledgling* and the cold chicken and potato salad that Grandma Emma feeds Mary Larkin in *Mind of My Mind* (Butler, 1993).

The result of earth's apocalypse takes shape in the flavorless "lumpy cereal or stew" that prisoner Lilith Iyapo scrapes from an edible bowl in *Dawn* (Butler, 2000, 6). The ooloi Nikanj serves human raid victims nut porridge that Marina Rivas describes as uninteresting, but tasty. As rewards for accepting aliens, the Oankali rescuers offer Lilith a fruit and vegetable feast accompanied by bread and honey, rice, nuts, spices, and their own quatasayasha (cheese). Protein-rich viands in the Amazon Basin in the sequel, *Adulthood Rites,* introduce humans to farmed fish, earthworms, beetles, ants, wasps, bees, caterpillars, fungus, and small animals. Healthful spreads foreshadow Lilith's success in *Imago* as gardener of fruits and vegetables, including peanuts (*Arachis hypogaea*), a contribution from Mesoamerica predating a Peruvian strain from 5600 BCE.

For flour and french fries, the extraterrestrials experiment with cassava. Content with the substitutions for wheat and potatoes, newly awakened humans sit quietly during mealtime, a universal pacifier of communities. After building stilt houses, they share a feast of breadnut (*Brosimum alicastrum*), brazil nuts, papaya, banana, yam, breadfruit, corn, and pineapple. Another celebration includes baked fish. Lilith broadens the menu with smoked fish, palm fruit, and South American inga fruit (*Inga edulis*). In volume two, *Adulthood Rites,* the author adds plantain, the stimulant quat (*Catha edulis*), and scigee, a pork-flavored plant mutated by nuclear war. *Imago,* the last of the Xenogenesis trilogy, contributes figs and cacao pulp as an accompaniment to nuts and a fruit and nut porridge.

Food Culture

The writer stressed food sovereignty that impacted tone and atmosphere, for example, a diplomatic feast of fish and birds from a drought-ridden desert in "A Necessary Being" and Shori Matthews's rejuvenating mouthfuls of nanny goat in *Fledgling.* Octavia rewarded God with a tuna salad sandwich and sparkling cider in "The Book of Martha" and travelers Amber and Teray in *Patternmaster* with the game that fed coastal California ancestors—quail and deer, jerky, and raisins. In *The Parable of the Sower,* the gated community of Robledo, California, grows common vegetables—collards, carrots, squash, potatoes, lettuce, cucumbers, peppers, melons, corn—and vine and bush fruit, peach, plum, persimmons, fig, lemon, and grapefruit trees, the Barbadian crossbreed of pomelo and orange. Staples in starving times resemble the stores of First Peoples—citrus fruit, walnuts, and acorns, once famine meals for the ancient Greeks and Jomon Japanese and a source of flour easier to obtain than oats, barley, corn, or wheat.

In a chaotic era, survivors make bean salad, shoot birds and squirrels, and, in backyard cages, raise rabbits and chickens for stew. On the road past Salinas, clusters of grapes, sandwiches with tomatoes, and Natividad Douglas's offer of breast milk to an orphan recapture the starvation relief in *The Grapes of Wrath* given by John Steinbeck's migrant Rose of Sharon Joad, a symbolic Christ figure. Members of Acorn, the Cape Mendocino, California, commune in *The Parable of the Talents,* celebrate a fifth successful year with a menu typical of slave hearths and Native American staples: goat cheese, fried rabbit, baked potato, acorn bread, and sweet potato pie. Subsequent snacks incorporate apple juice and the fruit of palms and cacti, a source of sweet bulbs from the prickly pear for making juice and desserts.

To reclaim Afro-American food heritage, the author integrates servings suitable to time and place. Southern plantation spreads of corn meal mush, peeled potatoes, herring, cornbread, and refreshments at corn husking and Christmas parties typify the era of *Kindred,* a pseudo-slave narrative set from 1815 to 1831 on the Chesapeake Bay near Easton, Maryland. In contrast to civilized eating, planters served slaves in wood troughs to make it easier to count their chattel during meals. More balanced fare recurs as a peacemaker and alleviator of sorrows in Rufus Weylin during recovery from broken ribs. Sarah the cook sends coffee, eggs and ham, corn cakes, and biscuits with butter and peach preserves, the kind of satisfying menu drawn from fresh country produce grown and harvested by slaves. At Alice Greenwood's burial, Dana recognizes the age-old communal tradition of edible gifts and remarks "I had never thought about how far back the custom might go" (Butler, 1979, 252).

AFROFUTURIST MEALS

In the exposition of *Wild Seed,* a meal of yams and a soup of vegetables, smoked fish, and palm oil derive ingredients from Nigerian healer An-yanwu's hunting and gathering "fruit, nuts, roots" and killing birds and small animals (Butler, 1980, 14). An African wedding on the transatlantic sloop *Silver Star* lacks palm wine, a native essential attesting to loss of heritage rations. To revive An-yanwu, her lover Doro feeds her the dry meat and hard bread common to ship's larders. Another change in diet occurs as the couple navigate New York's Hudson River, where farms grow corn, barley, and oats for beer, bread, horse feed, and popcorn. The author surveys Sarah Cutler's colonial table in 1690, when hearty protein-heavy cuisine included turkey, roast venison, and a meat and vegetable soup developed from Native American succotash. Dining on dairy foods discloses the lactose intolerance of Africans like An-yanwu. For the drunken Thomas, sustenance relies "mostly on beer and cider and rum" to wash down An-yanwu's bear, fish, game birds, and venison, the "witch food" that he maligns (*ibid.,* 385, 388).

In 1840, An-yanwu views slave quarters containing a hearthside bake kettle, water bucket and gourd dipper, and overhead bunches of herbs and dried corn, models of kitchen preparation for winter cookery and healing. African American staples remain simple—nuts, raisins, rabbit stew, rice, yams, cornbread, coffee, and madeira, a Portuguese wine ferried over Triangular Trade simultaneous with African slaves. The diet causes her children to complain that "she ate like a poor woman" (*ibid.,* 598). Frances Bonner, a women's studies teacher at the University of Queensland, Australia, summarized heirloom meals as "not just a sign of the female, but, with for example the emphasis on yams, cassava and African agricultural practices, a sign of the black female of African origin" (Bonner, 1990).

For *Clay's Ark,* as a solution to California's food instability, Octavia foresaw a subsistence farm in a mountainous valley of the Mohave Desert. A rescuer's serving of ham and chickens, salad, baked potatoes, corn, carrots, green beans, and rolls references the standard home cooking of the 1800s, which employed more green foods than colonial spreads. A storage area provides beer and bread with roast beef, a rugged meal appealing to ranchers. A follow-up mention of watermelon and a raw tomato and ear of corn straight from the garden foreshadows the voracious gobbling of virus survivors, who snatch at live animals and devour them raw. To enhance mutations brought on by extraterrestrial disease, she depicted the infected with ravaging hunger and appetites for uncooked ground meat, rabbits, and unseasoned chickens. Allegorically, the massive lust for wild food indicates a microbe that resurrects sexual yearnings aroused by the smell of women in estrus as well as prehistoric human tastes for red meat, the basics of human longevity.

Sources

Bonner, Frances. "Difference and Desire, Slavery and Seduction: Octavia Butler's Xenogenesis," *Foundation* 48 (Spring, 1990): 50–61.

Brown, Jayna. *Black Utopias: Speculative Life and the Music of Other Worlds.* Durham, NC: Duke University Press, 2021.

Butler, Octavia. *Dawn* in *Lilith's Brood.* New York: Warner, 2000, 2–248.

_____. *Wild Seed.* New York: Doubleday, 1980.

Fiskio, Janet. *Climate Change, Literature, and Environmental Justice: Poetics of Dissent and Repair.* Cambridge, UK: Cambridge University Press, 2021.

Kiran, Ayesha. "Human Identity and Technophobic Posthumanism in Octavia Butler's *Dawn*," *Indiana Journal of Arts & Literature* 2:8 (2021): 1–15.

Franklin, Dana

Octavia created writer Dana Franklin as one of a series of wonder women who adapt to near impossible plights. Bearing a Gaelic-Norman given name and surname meaning fire and honest, activist Edana "Dana" Franklin lives in California during the 1970s Black Power Movement. Her civil rights philosophy echoes the beliefs of Nigerian healer An-yanwu Iyapo in *Wild Seed,* translator Noah Cannon in "Amnesty," and Laurel Oya Olamina and her husband, Taylor Franklin Bankole, in *The Parable of the Sower.* By migrating instantly outside Easton, Maryland, in 1815, she becomes a near magical transgressor of what Adwoa Afful of York University in Toronto called "all geographical/national boundaries instituted to keep (black) dislocations in place" (Afful, 2016, 98). The author spoke of her time-traveling protagonist as "determined not to tolerate the beliefs of the time, but she eventually recognizes that the whole society is set against her and that she has to put up with it to survive" (Young, 2004, 33).

Displacement into the slave era of American history forces Lauren to study the past from a twentieth-century perspective and base decisions upon map reading and analysis of bondage capitalism. Neither saintly nor cunning, she fights the internal war of situational ethics—the choice between moral ideals and everyday pragmatism in a hellish Maryland plantation scenario she observes over a seventeen-year period. Significant to intermittent appearances via timeslip, she bears the gift of literacy derived from education and a scholarly home library. In a summation of Octavia's focus in *Kindred,* critic Jayna Brown, a professor at Pratt Institute in Brooklyn, New York, specified "what humans would do when faced with a cruel environment," a statement well suited to the neo-slave narrative (Brown, 2021, 97).

Timeslip to Maryland

A bit of backstory places the Franklin biracial wedding in Las Vegas, Nevada, a hint at Dana and Kevin's gamble on marrying out of race. The author rewards Dana with wit and guile in carrying a switchblade in a backpack along with a state map, a history of slave time, aspirin, sleeping pills, antiseptic, and soap. A bicentennial quarter dated 1976 proves her time origination at the nation's 200th birthday. Tom Weylin, the Maryland planter, considers her unnatural, but identifies her normal vulnerabilities to pain and death. She hopes for a move to Philadelphia, the hub of the Underground Railroad in the free state of Pennsylvania. Details salute Quaker abolitionist Lucretia Mott, conductor Harriet Tubman, and William Still, father of the diaspora to freedom.

By analyzing stages of time travel and return to Kevin Franklin, Dana adheres to the Scots motto "Cuimhnich air na daoine o'n d'thainig thu (Remember those from whom you came)," a Gaelic version of *sankofa,* the Ghanaian Akan-Twi tenet of "Retrieve the best of the past." She realizes the time-smashing power of emotion: "Rufus's fear of death calls me to him, and my own fear of death sends me home" (Butler, 1979, 50). She willingly takes the role of domestic by cooking breakfast, cleaning the kitchen, carrying water to Rufus each morning, and kindling a fire from coals to warm his room, a symbol of black history. Her respect for other blacks increases for Sarah, the cook and housekeeper who is wise enough to accept bondage out of fear of reprisal. Dana expresses concern for Sarah's undervalued mute daughter Carrie and familial respect for former freedwoman Alice Greenwood, who suffers extreme hurts for fleeing with husband Isaac Jackson.

Shielding a Great Grandsire

The protagonist recognizes the vicious cycle that planter Tom Weylin arouses in his son and heir through belief in white superiority. Ostensibly gentle and amenable to reason, Rufus deteriorates into "a man of his time," a privileged slave owner who takes whatever satisfies his appetites (*ibid.,* 242). Unable to control impromptu rage, he lapses into momentary bluster and fury, which he expends on Alice, his bedmate. Octavia returned to owner ravishment of slave women in *The Parable of the Sower* with an employer's lustful stares at Natividad Douglas's breastfeeding of her son Domingo. To avenge Tom Weylin's death from heart attack, Rufus sends Dana to the fields with the vindictive overseer Evan Fowler, an appropriately named "bird catcher" who flogs her across the breasts, a symbolic attack on womanhood and female vulnerability. After suffering a slap in the face, Dana's attempt at suicide epitomizes her despair at random assault and the sale of blacks to appease Rufus's spite.

Octavia forces her wonder women to the edge of agency, a progression that Dana shares with Lauren Oya Olamina and Zahra Moss in the Earthseed series, Barbara in "Childfinder," and Shori Matthews in *Fledgling.* Lacking a choice, Dana must stab her tormentor and great great grandsire to avert rape. Like Connie Ramos in Marge Piercy's *Woman on the Edge of Time,* Dana accepts the risk of murdering a white man to shield her own family line, a dilemma that places her under archaic bondage law enacted in South Carolina in 1740. The text creates racial irony in a cousin's assumption that Kevin is an abusive white husband capable of lashing his black wife.

Sources

Afful, Adwoa. "Wild Seed: Africa and Its Many Diasporas," *Critical Arts* 30:4 (August 2016): 93–104.

Brown, Jayna. *Black Utopias: Speculative Life and the Music of Other Worlds.* Durham, NC: Duke University Press, 2021.

Burt, Stephanie. "Octavia Butler Wanted to Write a 'Yes' Book," *National Republic* (27 May 2021).

Butler, Octavia. *Kindred.* New York: Doubleday, 1979.

O'Neall, John Belton. *The Negro Law of South Carolina*. Columbia, SC: J.G. Bowman, 1848.
Williams, Sherley Anne. "On Octavia E. Butler," *Ms.* 14:9 (March 1986): 70–73.
Young, Earni. "Return of Kindred Spirits," *Black Issues Book Review* 6:1 (January–February 2004): 30–33.

"Furor Scribendi"

Octavia's ache to publish equipped her with advice for other neophyte authors, particularly young blacks. In "Persistence," a 2000 interview for *Locus* magazine, she urged would-be writers to study "History. Anthropology. Something where you get to know the human species a little better" as a source of character logic and action (Butler, 2000, 6). She exemplified the value of research in symbolic character names, such as the librarian Theodora (gift of God) Harden in *Fledgling* and the close-minded missionary Neila (lock) Verrick in *Survivor*. Studies in human beginnings and primitive African storytelling provided background for An-yanwu's longevity and healing power in *Wild Seed*.

From meager coming-of-age beginnings, which the author described as "crap," writers should be their own best critics and persist rather than take an easy out (*ibid.*). She joked about throwing early work away: "Where's that? There's no such place. It's going *somewhere*" (*ibid.*). The quip asserts that all beginners outgrow aspects of their first efforts, which leave a permanent mark on the psyche. From her early experience, she developed higher standards and refused to reissue *Survivor*, her debut novel, because of its shortcomings.

The author issued "Furor Scribendi" in *L. Ron Hubbard Presents Writers of the Future IX*, an anthology of promising new works. The essay title, Latin for "A Madness for Writing," restates Juvenal's satire, early second century CE, "Insanabile cacoëthes scribendi" (an incurable itch to write). Horace's version in a second collection of satires in late first century BCE declared "Tantus amor scribendi" (So great a passion for writing). The phrase characterized Octavia's mania or rage to develop speculation on paper. She drew on a background in original and unpredictable plots and characters, the sources of fan acceptance of her short stories, speeches, *Fledgling*, and the Patternmaster, Parable, and Xenogenesis series.

To the beginner, Octavia ruled out inspiration as essential and urged instead positive habits. She outlined an agenda based on a variety of positive stimuli to language development:

1. Read a variety of works and listen to others on tape.
2. Take classes that arouse comments from students and teachers.
3. Think of grammar and vocabulary as your tools.
4. Write daily.
5. Store ideas in a journal.
6. Refine the work to the best of your ability.
7. Form dependable habits.
8. Enjoy the fun side of writing.
9. Don't stop.

In the Afterword, the author stressed "persist" as that most crucial advice, a character trait of her tough heroines Alanna Verrick, Barbara, Dana Franklin, Keira

"Kerry" Maslin, Lilith Iyapo, Shori Matthews, An-yanwu, and Mary Larkin. From a devotion to personal writing, Lauren Oya Olamina, the formulator of a new religion in the Parable series, compiled her poems and aphorisms into *Earthseed,* a globally accepted scripture.

Sources

Butler, Octavia. "Furor Scribendi," *Bloodchild and Other Stories.* New York: Seven Stories Press, 2005, 137–146.

_____. "Persistence," *Locus* 44:6 (June 2000): 6.

Hanganu-Bresch, Cristina, and Kelleen Flaherty. *Effective Scientific Communication: The Other Half of Science.* New York: Oxford University Press, 2020.

Grotesque

Octavia permeated philosophy and strategy with monstrous elements. Examples reiterate concern for anatomical wholeness: the lopping of Isaac Jackson's ears for fleeing slavery in *Kindred,* the abortion of grubs who gobble pregnant males in "Bloodchild," Curt Loehr's axe murder of Lilith's husband Joseph "Joe" Li-Chin Shing in *Dawn,* and two Ina community conflagrations and the burying and decapitation of Katherine Dahlman in *Fledgling* to prevent her resurrection from the grave. For the Parable series, smoldering corpses mark the foray of teen criminal Keith Olamina, who watches while gangs blind a man and set him aflame. When the gang turns on Keith, they skin him alive, leaving his sister grieving over his atrocious torture. The outré touches set sci-fi and speculative characters apart from realistic cast members.

From legendary tropes, the author restated barbarity from world history, including the Russian pogroms in *Fledgling* that persecuted Romanians. Her Xenogenesis novels stressed snake-haired medusas with nudibranch tentacles in *Dawn* and Neci's proposal in *Adulthood Rites* that humans reclaim hybrid Oankali girls by pruning their appendages, the position of alien eyes. The unilateral scheme dramatizes the inhumanities suffered by Native American children seized by missionaries in 1897 for "civilizing" at the government-staffed Carlisle Indian School in Pennsylvania. Their braids sheared and language and religion forbidden, very young pupils coped with hunger and European clothes and lace-up shoes. Two hundred succumbed to despair and in-house epidemics.

Visual Horrors

Vermin and bestial children contribute to Octavia's reputation for specific aberrations. Gruesome rat-chewed troglodytes living in sewers and cesspools in *Clay's Ark* and the car band pedophiles who gang-rape children illustrate extremes of savagery. The fear of bearing a mutant child concerns Rane Maslin, a budding sixteen-year-old suitable for breeding the offspring of men infected by a raging extraterrestrial virus. Terror of conceiving a freak such as Jacob Boyd, a four-year-old feline quadruped endowed with rapid movement and hypersensitive smell and vision, causes Rane to consider terminating any fetus "with an old wire coat hanger," the stereotypical reliever of unwanted pregnancies in the author's time

(Butler, 1984, 34). The threat words twentieth-century fears that abortion targets the disabled.

The glimpse of Rane devouring raw steak while she "let blood run down her chin and arms" in *Clay's Ark* and flesh gnawing of patients in "The Evening and the Morning and the Night" heightens Octavia's monstrosities with perverse food images (*ibid.*, 63). Through cannibalism in *Patternmaster*, the falling action elevates the sacrifice of Amber's hand, which she amputates and eats to prevent her powers from strengthening enemy Clayarks. For control of employees in *Wild Seed*, the immortal despot Doro crops the right hand of mouthy employee Bernard Daly, then cauterizes the stump to produce a worker who respects total authority. Doro sets up such demonstrations to induce "fear or belief that [he] was a god," the essential goad to his followers (Butler, 1980, 113).

Outré Style

To establish tone and atmosphere, the author applies grotesquerie to character exposition, a visual aesthetic that politicizes age, color, size, and health. A disturbing view of An-yanwu in the shape of a leopard reveals a hunger for the flesh of Lale Sachs, Doro's barbarian son. With a slash to his shirt, she rips fragrant torso meat that amplifies her fiendish appetite, a depraved act reminiscent of legendary carnage in her early life. At the murder of son Stephen and sexual abuse of child Helen, An-yanwu in leopard form attacks villain Joseph Toler, a worthless suitor. For maximum disdain, she buries his remains in a weedy unused slaves' cemetery, Octavia's evidence of wickedness in other eras of black history. By marginalizing the protagonist, the text unjustly recategorizes the shapeshifter from beloved healer to disgusting feral sadist, a phantasm that authors Risa Dickens and Amy Torok, specialists in the occult, link to African mask art and mimetic dance.

In the prequel, *Mind of My Mind*, Grandma Emma, a 300-year-old breeder, epitomizes the female longing for perpetual youth, a portent of Ina symbionts in *Fledgling*. She reshapes her elderly form by smoothing hard venous claws, creating incongruity "on the ends of withered, ancient arms" (Butler, 1977, 10). Even less palatable, her lover/father Doro, a Nubian immortal, kills a knife wielder and engulfs his body, becoming a döppelganger of the attacker. The fluidity of body changes grows more confusing for Mary, Doro and Rina's nineteen-year-old psionic daughter. At the time that Rina conceived Mary, her father existed in a white body with "traffic-light green" eyes from "some poor guy from a religious colony ... in Pennsylvania," a ludicrous suggestion of Doro as Amish (*ibid.*, 16). The cycle of shapeshifting discloses one of Octavia's most repulsive malefactors, a despot who murders and re-inhabits corpses that allow him free movement and unlimited choice of identities over time and space.

A Repulsive Cast

To dramatize metamorphosis and hybridity, Octavia excelled at pitiable, unsightly conditions, especially those targeting infants, children, and the disabled for abandonment, disenfranchisement, and exclusion from society, such as the neurofibromatosis tumors in *Imago* on siblings Tomás and Jesusa Serrano y Martín and a potential disability in their offspring. In the story "A Necessary Being," the hamstringing of Chief Judge Ehreh, a Hao magistrate, begins with vengeful Rohkohn burning his legs behind the knees. He spends the rest of his career as a repellant warden either crawling or dependent on a sedan chair or wheeled cart for transport. The author stepped up the unbearable squalor of the lowest class of Californians in *Mind of My Mind* at the home of Miguela Daniels, whose derelict husband lies in his own excreta. Two malnourished children can barely utter cries for food. A third, a three-day-old corpse, died of mutilated limbs and torture. Less beneficent than physician Taylor Bankole's purging of gunshot wounds in *The Parable of the Talents*, maggots riddle the infant flesh in search of corruption, a hint at the rot that erodes Doro's planned empire.

For the history of black slavery in *Kindred*, the author particularized real punishments—binding naked figures to rough tree bark, dog bites, lashing and kicking, rape, sale of plantation children, and slicing the ears of Isaac Jackson before selling him to a Mississippi plantation, an agrarian hellhole. Its snaky rice swamps and fever-ridden cane fields were notorious for shortening slave work spans. Out of frustration with his heir, Maryland planter Tom Weylin layers his son Rufus with welts transversing older scars from previous beatings, a gridwork similar to that laid over plantation chattel. The child cowers from a future round of flogging, which could kill him. Reviewers of Damian Duffy and John Jennings's graphic adaptation of *Kindred* note how jagged black outlines amplify disorienting pain and exhaustion, the residue of field labor under Tom's lash.

See also Exotic Beings.

Sources

Butler, Octavia. *Clay's Ark*. New York: St. Martin's Press, 1984.
_____. *Kindred* (graphic novel), adapted by Damian Duffy and John Jennings. New York: Abrams Comicarts, 2017.
_____. *Mind of My Mind*. New York: Doubleday, 1977.
_____. *Wild Seed*. New York: Doubleday, 1980.
Dickens, Risa, and Amy Torok. *Missing Witches: Recovering True Histories of Feminist Magic*. Berkeley, CA: North Atlantic Books, 2021.
Ibrahim, Habiba. *Black Age: Oceanic Lifespans and the Time of Black Life*. Albany: New York University Press, 2021.
Rodrigues, Sara, and Ela Przybylo, eds. *On the Politics of Ugliness*. Cham, Switzerland: Palgrave Macmillan, 2018.
Vakoch, Douglas A. *Dystopias and Utopias on Earth and Beyond*. New York: Routledge, 2021.

Hybridizing

The propagation of startling experimental races and species dominates Octavia's improvements to life on earth. Ambiguity hovers over the Mohave Desert cult in *Clay's Ark,* crash site of a returning starship bearing an insidious virus, one of the perils of universal travel featured in author Michael Crichton's *Andromeda Strain*. Because infection raises astronaut Asa Elias "Eli" Doyle's libido and forces him to sniff out fecund women for mating, births reveal the deviant species known as Clayarks. Without implementing the innate talents of exotic felines like four-year-old Jacob Boyd, a bizarre cat-boy, the novel focuses on risk, a theme that Octavia reprises in the story "Amnesty" and the seriocomic dialogue "The Book of Martha."

The writer's speculative fiction proposes alterations to the human body, especially eyes, mobility, and reproductive organs. Racing about on four legs, hybrid Clayarks employ sharpened visual and olfactory acuity that could help them survive raids by mobile car gangs. A fragmentary hope resides in Keira "Kerry" Maslin, a Nigerian-American expectant mother of a mutant child. Her fetus projects an end to color bias because of its entry into a multiracial family headed by a Japanese father, Stephen Kaneshiro. The author's dabbling in futuristic inter-breeding speculates on obliteration of white ascendancy over nonwhites.

HAZARDOUS MISCEGENATION

The crossbreeding of humans with unearthly beings in Mojave Desert bubbles in "Amnesty" suggests that a superior hybrid could boost future survival across the planet. The concept motivated cross-species reproduction in *Dawn* and the DNA mixing of Shori Matthews, the first black vampire in *Fledgling*. The proposal of the Nubian tyrant Doro in *Wild Seed* to cross-fertilize a superior race of psionics involves trial and error, testing his theories of "exactly which families to breed together to get what he wants" (Butler, 1980, 250). His feral son Lale Sachs serves as selector of test subjects with "small strangenesses, buddings, beginnings of talents like his own" (*ibid.,* 253, 254). Doro the mastermind determines that "Dutch, German, English, various African and Indian peoples … were either good breeding stock or … served useful purposes." The categorizing mimics the begetting of strong black slaves in the American South through selective breeding, and, from 1933 to 1945, Hitler's attempts to propagate an Aryan master race by exterminating Jews and gypsies who threatened his plan.

The author generated menace by viewing Doro as a "wolf [who] became aware of a rabbit when the wind was right," a bestial metaphor for an amoral hybridizer who tinkers with personalities who are either worthy or expendable (*ibid.,* 255). Sometimes the experiments work to the detriment of people like Isaac's mother, who raves in anguish and kills herself, the victim of dire mind games. Mary Larkin, Doro's biracial teenager in the sequel *Mind of My Mind*, discovers latent powers that she develops into a complex ability to read minds and oversee actions. By evolving positive ethics, she outwits her evil father and begins populating earth with useful, productive telepaths. Octavia repeated the creation of a beneficent hybrid in *Fledgling* in the dark skin and tolerance for sun in Shori Matthews, an upgraded Ina vampire capable of standing guard in daylight.

POSTHUMAN WISDOM

In the author's earliest example, *Survivor,* multiple strands of race and species produce the next level of beings in the baby of Alanna Verrick and Diut.

Alanna's provenance introduces Octavia's first gene-mixing in multiple categories: an African-Asian-American outsider rescued and acculturated by Puritanic white missionaries, models of an iron-fisted religious sect. The extensive contributions to creolization augment her value to aliens and human ethnicities at the same time that an unusually scrambled background burdens her with fearful alternatives. More trenchantly, the quandary of outlandish choices assaults the alien-human hybrid Akin in *Imago*, causing him to feel like "a floating, disembodied mind" (Butler, 2000, 455). Analyst Stacy Magadanz, a reference librarian at California State University at San Bernardino, summarized his internal unrest as the result of "irreconcilable differences in his own character," predictable elements of coming of age (Magadanz, 2012, 55).

For *Lilith's Brood*, Octavia detailed a method of adding untried genes to the constantly evolving human species. The end product would suppress what Michael Pitts, a Czech gender specialist at the University of South Bohemia, termed "toxic masculinity," a traditional intent "to consolidate power and control through aggression" (Pitts, 2021, 94, 96). In *Adulthood Rites,* the author spoke through Lilith Iyapo a warning of human foibles:

> Humans persecute their different ones, yet they need them to give themselves definition and status. Oankali seek difference and collect it. They need it to keep themselves from stagnation and overspecialization [Butler, 2000, 329].

Lilith's son Akin, a dazzling prodigy, grapples with the variety of traits in his DNA and his mother's directive to "Embrace difference," an aphorism that Navle Balalaji Anandrao, English professor at Deogiri College in Aurangabad, India, calls "the epigraph for the whole Xenogenesis trilogy" (*ibid.*; Anandrao, 2021, 7). As described by Aparajita Nanda, a professor of ethnic studies at the University of California at Berkeley, Lilith's wonder boy "variously abides, rejects, combines, and even improvises traits" derived from a mix of human and Oankali gene swapping (Nanda, 2021, 221). Endowed with intellectual depth and empathy, he realizes why humans reject alien-style genetic healing if a cure costs them reproductive liberties. Favoring his human inclinations, he declares, "Let them have the freedom to do that" (Butler, 2000, 468).

The ability to delineate threats to either humans or Oankali raises Akin to ombudsman for interspecies differences based on the aliens' rejection of domination, subjugation, and aggression. His messianic purpose augments the likelihood that earthlings can escape a scorched planet and deflect past faults arising from nuclear war and racial primacy, Octavia's choice of the worst of human evils. With rhetorical ease, he foresees the struggle ahead on Mars: "All people who know what it is to end should be allowed to continue if they can continue" (*ibid.,* 471). His wisdom exemplifies the author's hopes for a lasting civilization in the stars.

See also Reproduction.

Sources

Anandrao, Navle Balaji. "Futuristic Vision of a Millennial World: Science Fiction of Octavia Butler," *Literary Cognizance* II-2 (September 2021): 3–10.

Butler, Octavia. *Adulthood Rites* in *Lilith's Brood*. New York: Warner, 2000, 249–517.

_____. "Amnesty," *Bloodchild and Other Stories*. New York: Seven Stories Press, 2005, 147–186.

_____. *Imago* in *Lilith's Brood*. New York: Warner, 2000, 518–746.

_____. *Wild Seed*. New York: Doubleday, 1980.

Magadanz, Stacy. "The Captivity Narrative in Octavia E. Butler's *Adulthood Rites*," *Extrapolation* 53:1 (2012): 47–59.

Nanda, Aparajita "A Palimpsestuous Reading of Octavia Butler's *Lilith's Brood*" in *Palimpsests in Ethnic and Postcolonial Literature and Culture*. Cham, Switzerland: Palgrave Macmillan, 2021.

Pitts, Michael. *Alternative Masculinities in Feminist Speculative Fiction: A New Man*. Lanham, MD: Lexington Books, 2021.

Imago

The concluding volume of the trilogy *Lilith's Brood* dramatizes the view in Revelation 21:1 in which a new Jerusalem, the city on the hill, replaces the old, "for the first heaven and the first earth were passed away." The post-apocalyptic narrative opens on the metamorphosis of 29-year-old Jodahs, the first ever child of human Lilith and Tino and the ooloi Nikanj. A three-source hybrid bearing an Arabic/Hebrew name meaning "partner," Jodahs describes her/his unforeseen mutation as not human but a human-born construct. "Apparently beneficent," according to *Washington Post* book critic Ted White, Jodahs warns newcomers to Mars that starfarers from earth cannot escape self-destruction because of flaws in their makeup (White, 1989, 8). He prophesies doom for the planet—"a lump of stripped rock" similar to the moon (Butler, 2000, 531). Conflict erupts as Jodahs realizes that metamorphosis has turned her/him into an ooloi awaiting exile to the mothership.

The author emphasized Oankali pacifism and their axiom "Life was treasure" (*ibid.*, 564). A shapeshifting miracle worker, Jodahs exerts healing expertise on Marina Rivas, a migrant to Mars, and reshapes her narrow pelvis to spare her a grisly demise in childbirth. On the river passage south from Lo, Jodahs undertakes a greater task in regenerating the rotted human leg of João. Jodahs' friendship with Jesusa and Tomás Serrano y Martín leads her/him to suggest a marriage of the siblings with an ooloi, who offers to rid them of neurofibromatosis, a genetic defect to which their children are susceptible. He/she explains how her/his brother Akin colonized Mars to allow earth's people "to live as themselves," an authorial blessing on transgender humans (*ibid.*, 638).

Trust Factors

Central to Octavia's themes lie suppression of human rights, rape and forced parturition, and the definition of species. Critic Charles Johnson, an English teacher at the University of Washington in Seattle, rebuked the author for a "tendency to plunge so deeply into fantasy that revelation of everyday life ... disappears" (Mehaffy and Keating, 2001, 45). Jodahs' attraction to Jesusa leads to a confession of Oankali secrets about human faults, the causes of racial self-destruction. He/she predicts that earth will devolve down to a mineral core incapable of supporting life. Because Jesusa risked her life on a journey from the mountains, Jodahs praises her for saving the last human holdouts, an example of the agency in the author's wonder women. He/she proposes that the siblings build a raft and ferry her to her family, who will oversee a second metamorphosis, the final stage of Jodahs' coming of age.

Octavia emphasizes the selfishness of colonizers who limit interaction and autonomy through power grabs that parallel white European subjugation of black slaves, Hispanics, and Native Americans. To Jesusa, mutual dependence on the Oankali is "an un–Christian thing, an un–Human thing," yet Jodahs' dedication to her welfare and healing suggests an alien reverence for mortals and a loathing of guns and bullets (*ibid.,* 648). A deeper alliance with parents and sibling Aaor elevates the tone from fear of pursuers to safety in the family camp. Confronting age-old questions about the nature of human love, the components in *Imago*—affection, friendship, gender, attraction, desire, passion—forge a complex view of Oankali-earthling relationships, one of the writer's convoluted examples of interspecies breeding.

Layered Conflicts

Late in the cliffhanging novel, Tomás recounts in mythic form the post-war sufferings of his Spanish-speaking forebears. With a Central American origin story, he calls the fifteen-year-old Mexican matriarch María de la Luz (Maria of the Light), the region's First Mother for proving fertile after years of human sterility. Impregnated by rapists, she gave birth to Adan, named for earth, three daughters, and a second son debilitated by a crippled spine. She and Adan produce the third generation. The theme of exclusion of the disabled increases in importance after climbers of the Andes Mountains reach a terraced stone city modeled on Peru's Machu Picchu and meet South Americans of variant might and ability. The motif of dissimilarity recurs in *Fledgling* in the clash between traditional Ina in the Silk and Dahlman clans and the unique black Shori Matthews, a pre-adolescent vampire who doesn't have to shun daylight.

Octavia's *Bildungsroman* stresses healing of body and spirit as the beginning of a successful Mars colony, a homecoming for fertile peoples open to enlarged sex roles and myriad identity categories. To achieve a planetary utopia, mortals must quell rampant xenophobia and accept all newcomers. In a darkened South American cave, Jodahs, the exceptional hybrid, cures the scaly skin of Santos Ibarra Ruiz, a reflection of Jesus's healing of unnamed lepers in three gospel accounts—Matthew 8:1-4, Mark 1:40–45 and Luke 5:12–16. Through altruistic treatment of other disabilities, Jodahs the miracle worker endears himself to humans and plants a town on the riverbank. The prototypical seed stirs with life, foreshadowing an open-endedness and unpredictability that anticipates the Earthseed series of parables. Speaking from a feminist perspective on the adoption of saner, more inclusive life modes, Czech critic Michael Pitts of the University of South Bohemia credits the existential resolution to "compromise within the lives of people marginalized by" patriarchy (Pitts, 2021, 17).

Sources

Butler, Octavia. *Imago* in *Lilith's Brood.* New York: Warner, 2000, 518–746.
McCaffery, Larry, ed. *Across the Wounded Galaxies.* Urbana: University of Illinois Press, 1990.
Mehaffy, Marilyn, and AnaLouise Keating. "Radio Imagination: Octavia Butler on the Poetics of Narrative Embodiment," *MELUS* 26:1 (2001): 45–76.
Pitts, Michael. *Alternative Masculinities in Feminist Speculative Fiction: A New Man.* Lanham, MD: Lexington Books, 2021.
White, Ted. "Love with the Proper Stranger," *Washington Post* (25 June 1989): 8.

Imago Genealogy

A mythic basis for a Latin American religious dynasty begins with storytelling, the world's oldest preservation of beliefs and history. A feminist slant elevates Mexican matriarch and First Mother María de la Luz (Mary of the Light) for surviving multiple rapes, a resilience based on acceptance of divine guidance.

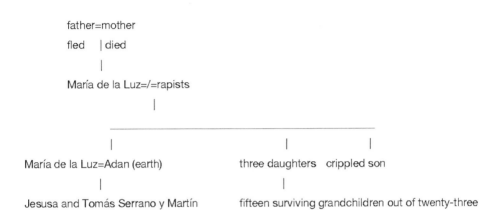

In token of her endurance of humiliation and sexual assault, the only fertile female on earth becomes First Mother, a reshaping of the Blessed Virgin and a recall of human sightings of Mary, such as those mythologized at Domremy and Lourdes, France, in 1424 and 1858; Knock, Ireland, on August 21, 1879; on May 13, 1917, at Fatima, Portugal; and Medjugorje, Montenegro, on June 24, 1981.

From the matriarch, the clan derives a past and a "second coming" or chance at improving their race. The inbreeding of mother with son, the mythologized "earth," idealizes the faithful female, maternity, and child rearing. A reference to "walking in the light" recurs in *Fledgling* as a future option for hybrid black vampires like Shori Matthews.

Sources

Butler, Octavia. *Imago* in *Lilith's Brood*. New York: Warner, 2000, 518–746.
Pitts, Michael. *Alternative Masculinities in Feminist Speculative Fiction: A New Man*. Lanham, MD: Lexington Books, 2021.
White, Ted. "Love with the Proper Stranger," *Washington Post* (25 June 1989): 8.

Kindred

An empathetic study of writer Dana Franklin's antebellum ancestry, in 1979, Octavia's neo-slave narrative rounded out twenty years of public debate of the place of African Americans in history. The text derived direction from "shame over [slave ancestors] who came before us" (Carr, 1992, 36). It employed science fiction not with aliens, but with literal truth like that of Ray Bradbury's space and race exploration story "The Other Foot."

Historian Henry Louis Gates, Jr., noted the importance of a black speaker "to posit both the individual 'I' of the black author, as well as the collective 'I' of the race" (Gates, 1985, xxvi). Dana's text spotlights black-owning forebears in biracial family trees as well as the solution to a centuries-old whodunit, crimes of arson and murder. Originally titled *To Keep Thee in All Thy Ways* from Psalm 91:11, the story haunted the author for years because "I knew it would be ugly" (Bogstad, 1978–1979, 31). In the purview of social critic Sherley Anne Williams, the novel "[launches] a startling and engrossing commentary on the complex actuality and continuing heritage of American slavery" (Williams, 1986, 72).

At age twenty-six, the protagonist and her husband, Kevin Franklin, move north from Los Angeles to Altadena, areas familiar to the author. British critic Teri Ann Doerksen, on staff at the University of Manchester, characterized the couple's story as "a literature of metaphors …. metaphorical situations that reveal contemporary social and political issues," including the education of the young in discomfiting eras of American and world history (Doerksen, 1997, 22). Symbolically, Dana hands Kevin a heap of nonfiction to shelve, a rejection of black historical fiction that lacks a basis in verisimilitude and a visible clue that her ancestor Rufus saw her in the future. The use of "river" in the first chapter heading suggests the flow of events that threaten the protagonist and Rufus. He summons her out of fear of deep water, a trope of his future as son of an abusive father and heir to a slave-owning Maryland plantation.

When Dana clutches at the past, she loses her left arm to time travel in token of a spiritual and personal investment in victims of the antebellum South. By her dedication to a grandsire, she risks lashings, exhaustion, rape, or sale to another white owner. By opening the prologue in 1976 on a grisly limb amputation, the price of a reunion with ancestors, the narrative establishes the immediacy of timeslip as well as a tie to primal earth. Dana's soiling in thick river mud and brackish water proves her story of rescuing Rufus Weylin, her great great grandfather. The lost left arm becomes the inherent sacrifice, a legacy of bondage south of Easton in coastal Maryland on the Chesapeake Bay "over a century in time and three thousand miles of space" (Butler, 1979, 46). The mystic arm exemplifies the pull of past injustice on a twentieth-century Californian.

By crossing time and distance, a time gap from June 9 to July 4, 1976, Dana arrives under pine trees to save Rufus, a pre-school white boy, from drowning in a river, a loss that would have cost Dana her earthly existence. She succeeds at artificial respiration, a symbolic act that shares life and breath with whites. After examining the amputation, with the speaker's hesitance in Karl Shapiro's poem "The Leg," she slowly adapts to an inexplicable handicap. Integral to the plot, Dana's self-protection requires that Rufus survive to sire her branch of the family tree. Octavia emphasizes apprehension for her great grandfather with the title *Kindred*/kin dread, meaning ancestral condition, and the family name Weylin/wailing, which indicates land by a road. Both puns hint at the griefs caused by human trafficking and anticipate the post–Civil War night riding of the Ku Klux Klan. When the French translation appeared in 2000, the title changed to *Liens de Sang* (Bloodlines), an affirmation of miscegenation.

DOUBLE IDENTITY

By forcing Dana in and out of the nineteenth and twentieth centuries, Octavia introduced clues to the villain Tom's uncontrolled anger at intellectuals and "uppity niggers" (Allison, 1989, 67). He demonstrates handiness with the whip against nine-year-old Rufus, a budding thief and pyromaniac. On June 9, 1831, the wrath of an armed father and hysterical mother cause Dana to dematerialize and search for a term naming "the thing that happened to me" (*ibid.*, 17). When she informs Kevin of the events, he suspects delusions or dreams but can't deny her disappearance and return in wet, muddy clothes. The extent of violence from Margaret Weylin's fists hammering her shoulders is also undeniable. On a second lapse in time, she fears patrols because "paperless blacks were fair game for any white," a familiar peril for Central American migrants in the twentieth century (*ibid.*, 34).

By adding attempted rape to multiple crimes, Octavia commiserated with female slaves, whose bodies offer sexual indulgence for their captors. As commercial investments, black women produce valuable offspring for sale, even the biracial children of white owners. Dana uses the cookhouse as a getaway from the Weylin residence and a freer space to converse with slaves and prepare food, a standard womanly microcosm in feminist literature such as Amy Tan's *The Kitchen God's Wife* and Kaye Gibbons' *On the Occasion of My Last Afternoon*. Sarah, the widowed cookhouse manager, regrets Tom Weylin's sale of her three children, leaving her only Carrie, a teen mute who has little monetary value compared to Dana. Because Kevin joins her time travel and begins tutoring Rufus, Dana expresses maternal love by rearing the boy in tolerance, lenience, and literacy, a gift replicated in *The Parable of the Seed* in Lauren Oya Olamina's reading lessons for Zahra Moss. Ironically, Dana feels safer by posing as Kevin's kept woman and by relying on his inside discoveries about the Weylins.

PART OF THE SYSTEM

A central issue, acclimation to bondage, creates a rift between Kevin and Dana. She realizes that a white man like Kevin views slavery as a less urgent socioeconomic infraction than history portrays. Dana's severe beating for book theft elevates reading as a contentious asset to liberation. The sacrifice for literacy recurs in Octavia's introduction of Harriet Tubman to Valerie in "Childfinder" and in "Speech Sounds" via University of California at Los Angeles history professor Valerie Rye's retrieval of a boy and girl from a speechless population to train for a more promising future. In *The Parable of the Talents,* Lauren Oya Olamina enacts the simple alphabet training of author Gary Paulsen's *Nightjohn*, a young adult historical novel dramatizing primitive writing in the dirt with a stick. Dana states an inner obligation to remain in a milieu of bondage and slave illiteracy: "I've got to try ... if trying means taking small risks and putting up with small humiliations," including sleeping on a rag pallet in the attic (*ibid.*, 83).

At age twenty-five, as Rufus turns into a clone of Tom Weylin, Octavia exemplified the Southern plantation system's effect on generations of male slave owners as they matured from heir to owner. Dana recognizes the virulent personality shift as the son replaces his deceased father and launches a free-floating grudge for Tom's death from cardiac disease, a satiric jab at the heartless planter. In the pattern of the serial female abuser, Rufus experiences remorse, but doesn't apologize for his ruthlessness or petty payback to Alice or Dana. Alice detects the effectiveness of physical battery: "Marse Rufe really put the fear of God in you, didn't he?" (Butler, 1979, 220). Even more effective is the contemplation of transport in a coffle of bondsmen bound for the auction block.

Octavia's skill at mixing literary styles turns *Kindred* into more than allegory and fictional memoir. Described for *Callaloo* by critic Gregory Hampton, the novel exemplifies the author's "ability to blur the genres of science fiction, historical fiction, and slave narrative" (Hampton, 2006, 245). By reversing time travel, the action carries Dana through a doppelgänger nightmare with Alice Greenwood, her mirror image, a character named for Lewis Carroll's Alice Liddell, the English girl whisked underground to Wonderland. The suicidal hanging of Dana's slave double provided Octavia with a means for ending Margaret Toler's life in *Wild Seed*. Dana flees Rufus's sexual gropings and stabs him with a pocketknife. The raw conclusion of timeslip inspires her to research more about her family's Maryland beginnings, a hunger for past knowledge that locates only tatters of the plantation's collapse.

See also Dana Franklin; *Kindred* (graphic novel); Rufus Weylin.

Sources

Bogstad, Janice. "Interview," 14:4 *Janus* (Winter, 1978–1979): 28–32.

Butler, Octavia. *Kindred*. New York: Doubleday, 1979.

Carr, Elston. "Jump-Start the Time Machine," *LA Weekly* (19 March 1992): 36–37.

Doerksen, Teri Ann. "Octavia E. Butler: Parables of Race and Difference" in *Into Darkness Peering*. Westport CT: Greenwood, 1997, 21–34.

Gates, Henry Louis, Jr. *The Slave's Narrative*. New York: Oxford University Press, 1985.

Hampton, Gregory. "In Memoriam: Octavia E. Butler (1947–2006)," *Callaloo* 29:2 (Spring, 2006): 245–248.

Kearse, Stephen. "The Essential Octavia Butler," *New York Times* (15 January 2021): 12–13.

Keyes, Allison. "Octavia Butler's *Kindred* Turns 25," *Tavis Smiley Show, NPR* (4 March 2004).

Magadanz, Stacy. "The Captivity Narrative in Octavia E. Butler's *Adulthood Rites*," *Extrapolation* 53:1 (2012): 47–59.

Parker, Kendra R. *Gale Researcher Guide: Octavia Butler and Afrofuturism*. Boston: Cengage Learning, 2018.

Williams, Sherley Anne. "On Octavia E. Butler," *Ms.* 14:9 (March 1986): 70–73.

Kindred Genealogy

The carefully interwoven episodes of *Kindred* reveal to Californian Dana Franklin her historical and blood ties with the Weylin household outside Easton, Maryland, where she becomes one of her own ancestors. Her two times great grandfather Rufus is "still vaguely alive in the memory of my family" because Rufus's daughter, Hagar Weylin Blake, inscribed family names and dates in a large bible protected by a wood chest, a sacred relic paralleling the Israelite Ark of the Covenant as described in Exodus 37:1–9, compiled around 600 BCE. The relationships become more personal after Dana assists Alice in February 1831 at Hagar's birth.

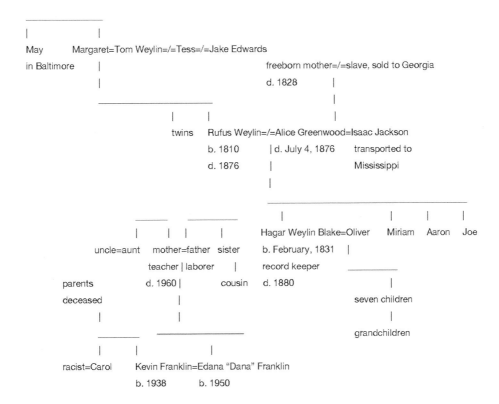

The accumulation of bible names—Joseph, Miriam, Aaron, Hagar, Hannah, Isaac, Luke—heightens the connection between a Southern plantation and the Exodus, the flight of Israelites from bondage in Egypt to the Promised Land, possibly begun in 1260 BCE under Pharaoh Rameses II.

Sources

Butler, Octavia. *Kindred*. New York: Doubleday, 1979.
Lackey, Tyler. "Afrofuturism and Spirituality," https://ssrn.com/abstract-3906952 (12 August 2021).

Kindred (graphic novel)

The posthumous encapsulation in visuals of Octavia's 1979 neo-slave narrative *Kindred* aroused delayed praise for the author and for the use of kinetic graphics to resonate with youth reading black fiction. Ronald L. Williams, a teacher of African American literature at Temple University in Philadelphia, summarized the compelling nature of the story, which "asks you to look back in time and at the present simultaneously" (Young, 2004, 30). The cell-by-cell revelations of Dana Franklin's out-of-control time travels to a Maryland plantation energized the narrative pace and dramatized passion and frantic interaction between owners, white teacher Kevin Franklin, and agricultural chattel, including his enslaved black wife. The adaptation required collapsed characters and a loss of language to prune a leaner text. The use of shackles as an infinity symbol accommodated both the timeslip sub-genre and the effects of slavery today. With streamlined plot, the reader bypassed the emotional nuances and authorial philosophy of the fictional version.

The adaptors, 2018 Eisner-winning editor John Jennings and artist Damian Duffy, felt touched and honored to depict in the graphic medium Afrofuturism, biracial ancestry, and classic speculative fiction by a respected black female forerunner. Jennings stated, I never lost sight of how much this woman's work means to us all and that

> her voice deserved the best that I could muster. It was required of me as an illustrator to channel her rage and pain into this book. It was a duty [Batiste, Boelcskevy, and Lewis, 2018].

He legitimated the use of phenotype (inherited behaviors) and skin tones for "sheer visibility of race" (*ibid.*). After tear-filled sessions, he added, "It's a rough book, and it will leave you hurting" (*ibid.*).

The stream of kudos from such authorities as *Booklist, New York Times, O: The Oprah Magazine, Social Justice Books, University of Texas Libraries,* and a starred review in *School Library Journal* remarked on traumatic images of pre–Civil War bondage. Modern readers gained accessibility through alternating sepia and color episodes with Gothic shadow figures. In a review for *Comics Bookcase,* Ariel Baska legitimated the visual transformation: "Once Dana is drawn into the past, … the danger is palpable on the page" (Baska, 2010). *Kirkus Reviews* and *Common Sense Media* applauded the thick, urgent black outlines and visceral immediacy dramatizing brutal punishments and uncertainties among progenitors of all Americans.

Although a visual version is not a substitute for the original novel, *Huffington Post* acknowledged that the drawings complement and enhance dialogue through body language and facial expression. *Slate* called attention to the darkening of the past as an alert to the present. On May 4, 2017, the graphic novel won an ICA Reads from the Institute of Contemporary Art, Boston, and recognition at the Third Annual Black Comics Arts Festival. By intersecting antebellum history with the flesh trade and diminution of women, the work found a place in classrooms and family bookshelves as well as the *New York Times* bestseller list.

Sources

Baska, Ariel. "Review," *Comics Bookcase*, www.comicsbookcase.com/reviews-archive/kindred-graphic-novel-adaptation (10 November 2020).

Batiste, Stephanie L., Mary Anne Boelcskevy, and Shireen K. Lewis. "Interview," *Journal of Black Studies and Research* 48:4 (6 November 2018).

Butler, Octavia. *Kindred* (graphic novel), adapted by Damian Duffy and John Jennings. New York: Abrams Comicarts, 2017.

Royal, Derek Parker. "Introduction: Coloring America: Multi-Ethnic Engagements with Graphic Narrative," *MELUS* 23:3 (2007): 7–22.

Young, Earni. "Return of Kindred Spirits," *Black Issues Book Review* 6:1 (January–February 2004): 30–33.

Language

Octavia's ease at compact, un-ornamented dialogue derived from an organic style trimmed of excess verbiage and sentiment, an asset of "Near of Kin," *Dawn,* and "Crossover." To characterize coming-of-age angst in the Parable series, she denoted insolence and flippancy in the hip slang, swearing, and teen vernacular of Lauren Oya Olamina, her younger brother Keith, and friend Zahra Moss, a seasoned outsider in *The Parable of the Sower.* In a strict fundamentalist household, Lauren's impudent diary style veils discontent and the stirrings of revolt. With a touch of wit, she puns on suspect neighbors: "Payne and Parrish. What perfect names" (Butler, 1993, 35). The drug of choice, pyro, gets trimmed to 'ro in the style of methamphetamine/meth. In the sequel, *The Parable of the Talents,* the writer depicts discernment and maturity in Lauren, whose aphoristic verse introduces converts to her insightful Earthseed philosophy.

For *Dawn,* Octavia teased sci-fi conventions for macaronic names the length of "Kaaltediinjdahya lel Kahguyaht aj Dinso" and ridiculed would-be rapist Wray Ordway with a phallic name meaning "nook" and "man with a spear." The text satirized the adverbs "badly" and "well," the pronoun "ourselves," multiple meanings for "rear," and the noun/adjective pair "anger/angry" (Butler, 2000, 15). Until a spinal puncture alters Lilith Iyapo's brain, a sketchy vocabulary assists her with such terms as *kaizidi,* Swahili for "helper," and *Fukumoto,* a Japanese surname meaning "blessed beginning." By melding global languages in names and places, the text promotes multicultural awareness and acceptance of nontraditional terms.

For emphasis on forceful characters, the author clipped formal spellings to Joe, Curt, Tate, Pete, and Gabe, monosyllabic names filling the cast with punch and vigor. After the jungle fight with axe-wielding humans, the alien Oankali celebrate through nerve stimuli, "a whole language of sensory images and accepted signals that took the place of words" (*ibid.,* 238). In *Imago,* the third volume of Xenogenesis, the author created honorifics—ooan (parent), eka (child), oeka (son), lelka (mated child)—and the ooloi storage unit yashi (glory, success), a source of information and memory.

In addition to the author's skill with alien patois, during a 1991 interview for *Callaloo,* Randall Kenan acknowledged her ability to write wise, majestic, epigrammatic character speech. She incorporated aphorism in the historic Ina speech and writing of *Fledgling* and the ancient imperial language shared by tribes in "A Necessary Being." For Diut, an outsider to the Rohkohn, the language of writing and conversation seems ironic, slightly comic and mocking. The speech learning of the infant Akin in *Adulthood Rites* imparts intuitive knowledge, causing the baby's "picture of the world" to expand (Butler, 2000, 258). Supplementing his precocious verbiage, Ahajas injects him with sensory pressures and images requiring no words. In "The Evening and the Morning and the Night," Octavia explains the Nigerian etymology of "Chi," an Ibo/Igbo term for "guardian angel or personal god" (Butler, 2005, 40). The diction derives from academic research into vernacular and standard languages and their etymologies, an issue for the indigenous Garkohn humanoids in *Survivor.*

Words in Milieu

The author strove to let a few words set tone and atmosphere. In the capture scene of *Adulthood Rites,* an estimation of raider size and armaments takes shape in short, jerky sentences suited to the child Akin. For Jodahs, the ooloi in *Imago,* hesitance to touch his sibling Aaor extracts negativity from the English translation of the Hindi "come on." The placement of slaves in *Wild Seed* finds compatible lingo in some homes in Wheatley, New York, and unfortunate pairings with people unfamiliar with African languages. The initial division leaves newcomers "apprehensive, uncertain, reluctant to leave" a friendly shipboard group who communicated well through known vocabularies (Butler, 1980, 254). Over Triangular Trade, the separation of abductees by tribe and language family became a means of suppressing collaboration among runaways.

The writer acknowledged the demand for communication, with or without speech. For Shori Matthews, the amnesiac Ina in *Fledgling,* recognizing the sound and sight of her species language speeds "an oddly comfortable shifting of mental gears" (Butler, 2005, 193). Development of vampire history reveals that a secret language helped the new arrivals to adapt to earth through "directional signs, territorial declarations, warnings of danger, and mating needs" (*ibid.,* 194–195). The mute California citizens in "Speech Sounds" make do with physical symbols and signals. Octavia joked that, in antagonistic situations: "Loss of verbal language had spawned a whole new set of obscene gestures" (Butler, 2005, 95).

The writer specified levels of language as marks of refinement. Mary's trash talk in *Mind of My Mind* is relevant to a nineteen-year-old in the 1970s "working like hell to get out of" a neighborhood of "poor bastards from any race you want to name" (Butler, 1977, 14). To illustrate the set pattern of family squabbles, the text pits mother Rina against Grandmother Emma on the subject of Mary's options to deter an opportunist—"either hit him or screw him" (*ibid.*). Her father Doro speaks like a normal authoritative parent: "You don't listen, girl. I talk to you and you don't listen," a typical rebuke from older generation to younger (*ibid.,* 16).

In "Amnesty," the absence of a common medium forces deaf aliens to "put together a code—the beginnings of a language—that got communication started" by body language and touch-sign (Butler, 2005, 161). Thus need forced compromise between extraterrestrial overlords and human survivors, who underwent lab analysis—"not cruel, but very thorough," a hint at the importance of language between species (*ibid.*). For translator Noah Cannon, a human abductee, relationships with aliens require careful examination. Any fears of captivity disperse when her employer strokes and calms her, "pleasing itselves," a reflexive pronoun suited to an exotic, multiperson mutant (Butler, 2005, 155). Before Noah communicates with the hominids at the Mojave Desert bubble, indigenous people create a code to circumvent the need for torturing humans.

Nuanced Communication

By varying tone and diction, Octavia suited language to atmosphere and context, particularly for Valerie Rye, the mute University of California at Los Angeles history professor in the story "Speech Sounds." For the cook's daughter Carrie, a mute teen slave in *Kindred*, hand gestures replace voicing everyday communication with her mother Sarah, an exemplar of unrecoverable history. As often happens to the voiceless, she appears retarded, an example of the demotion of all chattel to backward children. Sarah regrets the sale of her other children and the fact that "people think [Carrie] ain't got no sense" (Butler, 1979, 76). Critic Aisha Matthews, an independent sci-fi scholar, points out that muteness becomes an asset: it "contributes to [Carrie's] operation as a moderately autonomous subject in less fear of being sold" (Matthews, 2021, 14).

Octavia attached dialect to locale, as with Margaret Weylin's Southern accent, a clue to the slave state setting. Her husband Tom uses the obsolete term "cipher" to refer to math computation (*ibid.,* 91). To combat her use of "nigger," a pejorative common to the plantation South, Dana Franklin suggests he would feel offended by the term "white trash," a class-related insult to the poor and uneducated (*ibid.,* 61). Less offensive, "Aunt Sarah" becomes a desultory recognition of a cookhouse slave manager, who ranks above field hands on the "mammy" level. At the warehouse where Dana Franklin takes inventory while writing a book, Buz, an ignorant laborer, suggests she join Kevin and "write some poor-nography together," a moronic assumption about fiction (Butler, 1979, 54). By observing an eight-man patrol interrogating blacks, the protagonist hears something worse—the crude man-talk common to white males who consider black women a sexual job benefit.

In the tense, post–World War III atmosphere of emerging epidemic, characters in *Clay's Ark* speak knowingly of an otherworldly microorganism. On arrival by starship, it threatens to spread globally from California through a mobile populace. To enlarge on danger, Octavia equipped a car gang with a Mercedes the color of red wine, a combination of images suggesting the mercy and sacrifice symbolized by Christian communion. She heightened a conversation between Dr. Blake Maslin and daughter Keira by typing in all caps on a computerized prescription pad. The internist, out of humanitarian fears, informs her "WE MUST GIVE WARNING, GET TREATMENT!" (Butler, 1984, 21). The change in typography builds drama around Keira's terminal leukemia, which makes her a living sacrifice to earth's rescue. Later, when Blake falls victim to a female predator's scent, he tolerates her lewd humor about the size of his penis, "big old rifle or little handgun," a combination of phallic jest with firepower (*ibid.,* 57).

See also Diction; Names; Scripture.

Sources

Butler, Octavia. *Adulthood Rites* in *Lilith's Brood*. New York: Warner, 2000, 249–517.
_____. "Amnesty," *Bloodchild and Other Stories*. New York: Seven Stories Press, 2005, 147–186.
_____. *Clay's Ark*. New York: St. Martin's Press, 1984.
_____. *Dawn* in *Lilith's Brood*. New York: Warner, 2000, 2–248.
_____. "The Evening and the Morning and the Night" in *Bloodchild and Other Stories*. New York: Seven Stories Press, 2005, 33–70.
_____. *Fledgling*. New York: Seven Stories Press, 2005.
_____. *Kindred*. New York: Doubleday, 1979.
_____. "Speech Sounds" in *Bloodchild and Other Stories*. New York: Seven Stories Press, 2005, 87–110.
Kearse, Stephen. "The Essential Octavia Butler," *New York Times* (15 January 2021): 12–13.
Kenan, Randall. "Interview," *Callaloo* 14:2 (Spring, 1991): 495–504.
Matthews, Aisha. "Give Me Liberty or Give Me (Double) Consciousness," *Third Stone* 2:1 (2021): 1–21.

Lilith

The widowed matriarch from Los Angeles in the trilogy *Lilith's Brood*, Lilith Iyapo becomes a First Mother and mythic progenitor. Her backstory derives from Semitic Mesopotamian and Israeli lore that claims Adam's first wife as Eve, the garden keeper, and New Testament exposition of the Virgin Mary. Depicted in folklore as the night hag who eats her own children, a parallel of the Central American La Llorona, who wails in the dark as she attempts to kidnap babies, Octavia's version depicts her more as mediator and storyteller than she-demon. The Oankali enhancement of her wellness, stamina, and memory confers hybridity. Amanda Boulter, a language professor at the University of Winchester, England, viewed Lilith's unique gene map as a "genetic symbiosis that disturbs the relationship between 'self' and 'other'" (Boulter, 1996, 171). Consequently, resisters of hybridization consider her a "traitor to Humanity" (Butler, 2000, 560).

Octavia pictured Lilith in the role of wonder woman. In the 2007 treatise *Bodies of Tomorrow*, Sherryl Vint, a specialist in speculative fiction at the University of California, Riverside, identified Lilith as a threat to "the constructed boundary between human and non-human" (Vint, 2007, 65). Her abduction by aliens from a ruined planet resets scenarios with the limited choices found in standard captivity narratives, especially her attempt to escape the spaceship/planet. She impugns obligatory reproduction with aliens and requests pen and paper to record her kidnap. To the end of confinement, she bolsters her spirits with an action motto, "Learn and run!," a watchword suitable to refugees on the Underground Railroad (Butler, 2000, 248).

The fictional character resembles the history of Cynthia Ann Parker, a nine-year-old white Texan kidnapped from Fort Parker on May 19, 1836, by Comanche warriors. Like Lilith, Cynthia adapted to tribal life and married Chief Peta Nocona (Lone Wanderer). Over a quarter century of domesticity as an Indian wife, she bore daughter Topsana and sons Pecos and Quanah. After Texas Rangers shot Nocona at his hideout on Mule Creek, officers recovered Cynthia and Topsana in December 1860. Quanah's federal appointment to Comanche war chief parallels Akin's centrality to the Phoenix village resisters as leader of the human resettlement on Mars.

Educator of Aliens

In *Dawn*, the first of the trilogy, the fictional Lilith, an Eve-like earth mother, sets herself a task of saving all life. To that end, she educates earthlings, the job of Noah Cannon in "Amnesty," and breeds with the slug-like Oankali in "Bloodchild." Of their alien shape and behavior, she accepts species traits: "We need to know them for what they are" (*ibid.*, 170). Her human daughter, Ayre, and hybrid children, Margit and Akin, a human-Oankali born in *Adulthood Rites*, and Jodahs, an amorphous ooloi, instruct others on the inevitability of change. The author's theme of planetary survival depends on a tolerance of nonconformity and exotic species, which Lilith at first questions, then exuberantly accepts, even sexual relations with a non-human being.

The opening pages add the Nigerian surname Iyapo, Yoruban for "difficult situations," which Lilith overcomes by enduring, a female strength acknowledged by Patricia Melzer, a gender studies specialist at Temple University in Philadelphia. Octavia deliberately imagines the protagonist as a glass-half-full type who "had learned to savor any pleasure, any supplement to her self-esteem" (Butler, 2000, 6). The citation depicts her as a gleaner like Ruth, a scriptural matriarch not too proud to scour a harvested field for leftover grainheads (Ruth 2:2). Upon meeting Paul Titus, the first human male adult she has encountered on the mothership/planet, Lilith parries his attempted rape with an insult—a suggestion that the aliens have used his semen to impregnate his own mother. The Oedipean revulsion at son/mother sex succeeds in turning Paul's lust into assault that breaks Lilith's wrist.

Proponent of Equality

Releasing sleeping humans a few at a time, Lilith becomes a female Moses at age two hundred—a universal savior endowed with superhuman strength. She builds shelters elevated on pilings, an indigenous Austronesian and Central American home style. She gracefully introduces the newcomers to a terrifying alien world and stifles their blame with ease. In the rescue of Allison Zeigler from rape by five males, Lilith dubs them "cavemen.... *Fools*.... Human garbage" (*ibid.*, 177). Reminiscent of John the Baptist's humility, her rebuke reasserts the humanistic ideal: "Nobody here is property.... We stay human" (*ibid.*, 178).

Volume two, *Adulthood Rites,* concentrates on a *stabat mater* scenario— Lilith's maternal grief after raiders steal son Akin. During his year as the captive of resisters, she searches distant villages and finds the three-year-old in the Phoenix community near the recycling pit. Still concerned for his welfare, she draws others to her for storytelling and raiders to her vegetable and fruit garden, but leaves Akin to his solitary roaming. Like the pensive sea nymph Thetis, the mother of Achilles in Greek myth, Lilith senses a redemptive future for her son "giving life to a dead world" (*ibid.*, 467). *Imago* pictures her motherly concerns and a creative side, painting scenes on bark cloth with black ink "to make herself feel Human" (*ibid.*, 689). The overall profile endears her to readers as one of Octavia's captivating wonder women.

See also Dawn; Feminism; Reproduction.

Sources

Boulter, Amanda. "Polymorphous Futures: Octavia E. Butler's Xenogenesis Trilogy" in *American Bodies: Cultural Histories of the Physique*. Washington Square: New York University Press, 1996, 170–185.
Butler, Octavia. *Dawn* in *Lilith's Brood*. New York: Warner, 2000, 2–248.
Hampton, Gregory. "In Memoriam: Octavia E. Butler (1947–2006)," *Callaloo* 29:2 (Spring, 2006): 245–248.
Holden, Rebecca J., and Nisi Shawl, eds. *Strange Matings: Science Fiction, Feminism, African American Voices, and Octavia E. Butler*. Seattle, WA: Aqueduct, 2013.
Melzer, Patricia. *Alien Constructions: Science Fiction and Feminist Thought*. Austin: University of Texas Press, 2021.
Vint, Sherryl. *Bodies of Tomorrow: Technology, Subjectivity, Science Fiction*. Toronto: University of Toronto Press, 2007.

Lilith's Brood

A trilogy presenting the DNA workings and reproductive interdependence of Xenogenesis, *Lilith's Brood* honors the pacifist Oankali, who collect and splice sources of endowment rather than kill and waste genetic tissue. Octavia maintained suspense by slowly revealing vital information about earth's attempt at recovery from nuclear war. Essayist Judith Lee identified the titles *Dawn, Adulthood Rites,* and *Imago* as adaptations of the biblical myths "Creation, Incarnation, and Apocalypse" (Lee, 1996, 175). She added a link between Jesus's duality as human and divine to Akin's human appearance and his perception of human and ooloi sense impressions. As a result of double intelligence, Akin, a creole uniting alien with human, becomes mediator between Oankali and the resisters and savior of the holdouts.

In the first volume, *Dawn,* the title figure gradually learns about the tentacled Oankali race and their living spaceship. Octavia conceals until volume two, *Adulthood Rites,* the ship's identity, *Chkahichdahk,* an onomatopoetic name suggesting machinery. The extraterrestrial Oankali gene traders comb the universe for hybridizing material they can exploit. Analyst Gerry Canavan uses the Oankali genetic engineers as models of adaptation for abandoning identity and superiority to "[achieve] special immortality" (Canavan, 2016). After scrutinizing human behavior, they puzzle over resisters—intellectuals who cling to competition and status, two sources of strife and world war that cause earth's nuclear immolation. To neutralize both faults, the Oankali orchestrate extinction by sterilizing resisters.

A major detriment to Octavia's writing, her obsession with maturation stultifies action with too much anguish and fear, a flaw in Mary's metamorphosis in *Mind of My Mind* and Aaor's transition in *Imago,* a coming-of-age treatise. The theme of ripening affects all characters, especially the biracial infant Akin in *Adulthood Rites,* the child of Lilith, Joseph "Joe" Li-Chin Shing, Nikanj, and two Oankali. While he ages beyond twenty, he facilitates the *Homo sapiens* side and befriends earthlings, whom he believes should have a chance at restoration. In the background, humankind settles in the Amazon Basin and picks through rubble to understand how earth failed. They determine what sherds can be recycled in Phoenix, a village ironically named for the mythic bird that reclaimed itself from ashes by its own efforts.

Extending the metaphor of reprocessing old into new, Octavia elevated disability and healing to major themes. She concluded the trilogy in *Imago* with reclamation of Jesusa Serrano y Martín and her brother Tomás from neurofibromatosis, a severe birth defect causing tumors. Their sibling Jodahs ministers to a distant clan, ostensibly Peruvian Inca, by an arduous trek up Andean mountain trails and escarpments to the humans in greatest need of medical treatment and cultural stimulation. The author's 1976 journey to the ruins of Machu Picchu, Peru, provided eyewitness details of the ancient Inca settlement as an embodiment of Andean inbreeding and fear of change.

The high mountains provide an unfamiliar setting for the resolution of *Lilith's Brood.* By demonstrating benevolence to those encumbered with genetic defects, Jodahs, the first ooloi construct, gathers a throng of sickly mountaineers, a suggestion of Jesus's appeal to those suffering leprosy and blindness. In the estimation of James Campbell of Linköping University, Sweden, *Lilith's Brood* "highlights the benefits of xenophilia and consequently condemns xenophobia" (Campbell, 2020, 21). The formation of a riverside village portends a home-grown shuttle that will eventually carry a fertile population to a Martian colony, the terraformation that hovers on the horizon above a ruined earth. The utopian outreach recurs in *The Parable of the Sower* after an Hispanic astronaut Alicia Catalina Godinez Leal dies a martyr on a Mars mission, a model for refugees seeking a safe homeland.

Sources

Butler, Octavia. *Lilith's Brood*. New York: Warner, 2000.
Campbell, James. "Variable Otherness in Octavia Butler's Xenogenesis," www.diva-portal.org/smash/get/diva2:1436640/FULLTEXT01.pdf (Spring, 2020).
Canavan, Gerry. *Octavia E. Butler*. Urbana: University of Illinois, 2016.
Dillon, Sarah. *The Palimpsest: Literature, Criticism and Theory*. London: Bloomsbury, 2007.
Holden, Rebecca J., and Nisi Shawl, eds. *Strange Matings: Science Fiction, Feminism, African American Voices, and Octavia E. Butler*. Seattle, WA: Aqueduct, 2013.
Lee, Judith. "'We are All Kin': Relatedness, Mortality, and the Paradox of Human Immortality" in *Immortal Engines: Life Extension and Immortality in Science Fiction and Fantasy*. Athens, GA: University of Georgia Press 1996, 170–182.
Magadanz, Stacy. "The Captivity Narrative in Octavia E. Butler's *Adulthood Rites*," *Extrapolation* 53:1 (2012): 47–59.
Nanda, Aparajita "A Palimpsestuous Reading of Octavia Butler's *Lilith's Brood*" in *Palimpsests in Ethnic and Postcolonial Literature and Culture*. Cham, Switzerland: Palgrave Macmillan, 2021.

Lilith's Genealogy

Octavia excelled at describing females who overcome obstacles. She chose Lilith Iyapo, a widow bereft of her Nigerian husband Sam, father of their child Ayre, as well as her parents, sister, and two other siblings. In grief, she ponders how quickly an unlicensed Los Angeles driver wiped out her household and altered her forever. After adapting to alien Oankali, who rescue her from a radioactive earth, she resolves to endure on an alien planet. Upon reuniting with other humans, she loses a second mate, Joseph "Joe" Li-Chin Shing, a Chinese-Canadian slain by Curt Loehr, a human axe murderer whose surname means "powerful."

The author created irony from character fears of aliens and the aggression of Lilith's own kind. As a breeder with the Oankali, she becomes a "partner-species" revered for her accomplishments, personality, and uniqueness (Butler, 2000, 153). Outsider Tino reverts to scriptural myths of Lilith that impart an "unusual name loaded with bad connotations" (Butler, 2000, 36). Union of earthlings with extraterrestrials enables the Oankali to "[save] the few remaining fragments of humanity" as part of the DNA of mixed species children (*ibid.*, 207). Augustino "Tino" Leal and Lilith plus Nikanj, Dichaan, and Ahajas become Akin's parents.

Sources

Allison, Dorothy. "The Future of Female," *Village Voice* (19 December 1989): 67–68.
Butler, Octavia. *Adulthood Rites* in *Lilith's Brood*. New York: Warner, 2000, 249–517.
_____. *Dawn* in *Lilith's Brood*. New York: Warner, 2000, 2–248.
Nanda, Aparajita "A Palimpsestuous Reading of Octavia Butler's *Lilith's Brood*" in *Palimpsests in Ethnic and Postcolonial Literature and Culture*. Cham, Switzerland: Palgrave Macmillan, 2021.

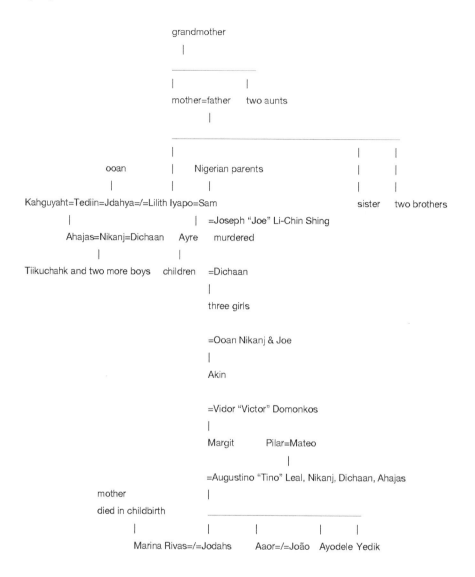

Mind of My Mind

A prequel to *Patternmaster* and explanation of Patterning through selective breeding, Octavia's *Mind of My Mind* surpasses *Survivor* as compelling fiction about desires, psychic battles, and fulfillment. The themes also structure *Wild Seed* and *Clay's Ark* and anticipate the transitioning of Oankali to full potential in the Xenogenesis series. In an interview with Janice Bogstad, a women's studies specialist at the University of Wisconsin at Eau Claire, the author identified the character Emma Daniels as an Amyambo, an Ibo/Igbo shapeshifter named Atambusee (Bogstad, 1978–1979, 31). She becomes so revered by the citizens of Unicha, Nigeria, that she remains immortal in their mythology in the same mode as Shori Matthews, a phenomenal black vampire in *Fledgling*.

Mind of My Mind builds suspense of a father-daughter clash that silences Doro, a long-lived Nubian telepath, from the comeuppance of his clever daughter Mary. The author considered *Prepattern* and *Psychogenesis* as possible titles for the origins of conscious and unconscious mental processes that impact the outward self and behavior of a woman produced by eugenics and miscegenation. The immortal father's plan to engender a race of super mind readers takes shape over four millennia, involving centuries of human experiments and the jettisoning of failures who can't survive the massive input of terror and mental furor. By transposing his being from body to body, Doro survives from the ancient Sudanese in Gash and Khartoum in the 2930s BCE until the 1970s. Because he develops no magnanimity, critic Caitlin O'Neil, an English professor at the University of Massachusetts, Dartmouth, surmises that his egotism makes "material conditions of black women across the globe … all too painfully real" (O'Neil, 2021, 63).

Mary, the unprecedented biracial daughter of Rina and the creator Doro, actualizes his scheme to broaden human receptivity to thought, an augmentation that Octavia foresaw as essential to survival. The author enhanced Mary's latent will by transitioning her from teenage mouthiness to independence. Knowing what's at stake, Mary challenges her egocentric father, who had tried "to build a race around himself" (*ibid.*, 9). The illusion of supremacy disregards the incest of Doro's immense family who have advanced to "actives," one of whom she marries (*ibid.*, 17). A fault in the project forbids Mary "permission to kill" other actives, especially any person who aids her transition to adulthood (*ibid.*, 68).

Octavia incorporated the Western profit motive in *Mind of My Mind* by adding to the long-lived Nubian Doro's robotic families the owners of the Whitten Coleman chain, a conglomerate he possessed for seventy years. Although the family had asked for assistance in the past, gradual profitability freed them "to handle their own problems," one of the perquisites of democratic capitalism (Butler, 1977, 30). One of their challenges, worker theft, proves easy for Doro's son Karl Larkin to circumvent with a brain empowered by psionics. Through telepathy, he identifies thieves and the location of stolen goods, a common warehouse crime.

Mistress of Telepathy

At Palo Verde, a deceptively vernal "greensward" in Forsyth, California, Doro watches Mary's maturation out of curiosity. She lives in a polyamory household with husband Karl Larkin and his lover Vivian and survives an excruciating transition to full clairvoyant Patternist. By staffing a household with five leashed telepaths, she forms a "First Family" of channelers who merge into "a single clawing hand" (Butler, 1977, 36, 97). To shield her human web from Doro's takeover, she launches a community of fifteen hundred and trains five thousand telepathic children in a private school. Although a tyrant herself, she becomes what *Village Voice* essayist Dorothy Allison termed "a more benevolent one" (Allison, 1989, 67).

Into murderous group confrontation, Mary savors superiority—"my ambrosia—power, sustenance, life itself," a stimulant to her vampirish essence (Butler, 1977, 81). The climax arrives with Clay Dana's transition from latent to active, a metamorphosis that Doro had failed to complete. After curtailing years of submission to brother Seth, Mary endows Clay with psychokinesis, by which he can move objects and himself without effort. The author applies psionics to the Dana Drive, a mechanism that activates the starship *Clay's Ark*. The implications of "clay" suggest a malleable mind that Mary renders free of pain by grasping fragile threads of the psionic network. The strategy also draws in her cousins Christine and Jamie Hanson and lifts them out of petty crime, an implication of Mary's good will toward society's least reputable rung.

REACHING THE PINNACLE

Provocative ironies envelop Doro's masterplan, notably Mary's ability to repair his failures. Advanced to "some sort of mental queen bee," for two years, she recruits more cousins for her "Patternist society" (*ibid.,* 95). Nonviolent methods guide the worker bees toward worthwhile professions—Rachel to healing, Ada toward teaching the next generation, Karl supporting his wife's eugenic project, and Jan reimagining art, a personal trait that Octavia revisits through Leah in *Wild Seed* and Naomi Chi in "The Evening and the Morning and the Night." Execution is Doro's only solution to thwart Mary's community and to obliterate what analyst Kendra R. Parker, a teacher of black literature at Hope College in Holland, Michigan, terms Mary's "ethics of care over dominance" (Parker, 2018, xxxiv).

The author begins dismantling the plot in Chapter Ten by breaking apart the First Family from Larkin House in Palo Verde, an agrarian term suggesting a green eden or utopia. The ongoing resentment of a female overseer keeps husband Karl Larkin on edge around his wife until intimacy reunites them. Because of group unity, Doro considers Mary a serious competitor for boss of a master race. In the estimation of Kendra R. Parker, Mary chooses a "politics of respectability" and empathy as a means of dominance (Parker, 2018, 9). The family's community at Santa Elena bears an iconic meaning—a holy point of light, a guidance system for the 1,538 Patternists whom Octavia revisited in *Fledgling*. At a cognitive war between Mary and Doro, burning fibers signal a showdown. Empowered by her Patternists, the rebel daughter consumes her father/lover/rival at the cost of 154 weak telepaths and her grandmother Emma. Untrammeled by Doro's narcissism, Mary's collaborative world-making bodes well for the future.

See also Doro; Slavery.

Sources

Allison, Dorothy. "The Future of Female," *Village Voice* (19 December 1989): 67–68.

Bogstad, Janice. "Interview," 14:4 *Janus* (Winter, 1978–1979): 28–32.

Butler, Octavia. *Mind of My Mind.* New York: Doubleday, 1977.

McCaffery, Larry, ed. *Across the Wounded Galaxies.* Urbana: University of Illinois Press, 1990.

O'Neil, Caitlin. "Towards an Afrofuturist Feminist Manifesto" in *Critical Black Futures.* London: Palgrave Macmillan, 2021.

Parker, Kendra R. *Black Female Vampires in African American Women's Novels, 1977–2011.* Lanham, MD: Lexington Books, 2018.

Trafford, James, and Pete Wolfendale, eds. *Alien Vectors: Accelerationism, Xenofeminism, Inhumanism.* Abingdon, UK: Routledge, 2020.

Miscegenation

The author filled speculative fiction with the possibilities of blended beings—black, white, and Asian in *Clay's Ark,* Hispanic and Asian with white and black in the Parable series, and black with white in *Kindred* and *Fledgling.* In *Survivor,* interspecies marriage with Tehkohn husband Diut arouses friction between Alanna and her missionary rescuers, Jules and Neila Verrick. Fanatic preservers of pure DNA, the missionaries condemn miscegenation because they lack Alanna's practicality and skill at mediation. By highlighting the relation of sex to race in the Xenogenesis series, particularly the three-way origins of Akin, sci-fi author Samuel R. Delany stated that, "on any absolute level, race doesn't exist" (Delany, 2021, 252). He typified the circular logic of heredity, which "always turns out to be its own pollutability—sometimes called purity" (*ibid.,* 280). Because of its "fracturing trauma on the body politic," he determined that race can kill or ennoble the individual (*ibid.*). An ambiguity for global history, Delany observed, "like nature, race has much to answer for" (*ibid.*)

For Cheah and Jeh, Garkohn members of differing mountain castes in "A Necessary Being," the protests of challengers arouse pride in the stable marriage of a hunter with a judge. When the couple visits the Rohkohn, their union stirs prejudice in Judge Ehreh, who prevents permanent alliances among desert tribe members. Octavia indicated that the successful proliferation of liberalized marriages ended confrontations and fostered mixed race children. In the backstory, the author stressed that both races derived from the same ancient empire and once spoke the same language, a reflection of the Abrahamic beginnings of Jews, Christians, Druze, and Muslims.

MIXING SPECIES

Octavia's radical notion of human genes permeated with exotic hybrids raised issues of extraplanetary life and the standard earthly mating of male with female. Outcomes resulted in unpredictable exoticism, some offering enlarged psionic intelligence, psychokinetics, and hyper-sensitivity to sights, smells, tastes, and sounds, the qualities shared by Clayarks and by human–Oankali mixes in *Lilith's Brood.* For an outside opinion in *Adulthood Rites,* a chance meeting in the Amazon Basin with miscegenation resister Augustino "Tino" Leal raises questions of Akin's traits, which appear completely human. Without verbalizing bias, Tino stops short of querying the child's extrasensory and physical makeup, which pleases humans because he looks "So Human. So beautiful," a judgment that equates white people with esthetic primacy (Butler, 2000, 385).

Octavia escalated reactions to interbreeding with socially objectionable entanglements such as community scrutiny of Diut's liberal views in "A Necessary Being" on the cross-caste union of Jeh and Cheah. Her fiction examined the hybridization of humans in "Amnesty" with unearthly beings living in Mojave Desert bubbles and Tino Leal's repudiation in *Adulthood Rites* of interspecies children and their benefits to humankind. Of the interracial marriage in *Kindred,* the French translation published the title as *Liens de Sang* (Bloodlines), in which Dana Franklin incurs family scorn for wedding Kevin, a white man. In her residence as a slave on a Maryland plantation, she encounters Tom Weylin, a nineteenth-century patriarch, who flaunts pure whiteness as both privilege and exoneration for his purchasing and brutalizing dark-skinned people. His entitled wife, Margaret Weylin, affirms superiority by sanctioning the cult of Southern womanhood, based on domesticity, submission, piety, and chastity. The self-replicating pattern recurs in heir Rufus Weylin, who violates anti-miscegenation laws by dehumanizing his property, Alice Greenwood.

Dismantling Boundaries

The author ventured into controversial areas of incest, pedophilia, and bestiality. A problematic mating in *Wild Seed* causes the immortal Doro to observe the Nigerian An-yanwu's joyous swimming and flying with his blond son Isaac. The controller determines that the Ibo/Igbo female and the white man would make a strong pair producing "desirable, potentially multitalented children" (Butler, 1980, 221). The conclusion veers from social rejection in the 1960s of racially mixed marriages and biracial offspring, when conservative forecasts for the global family envisioned confused traits. Before Doro leads An-yanwu on a New York City tour in 1690, he intends to reshape himself as a white male to prevent having to prove he is a freedman. His reasoning relates to the seventeenth-century laws and customs: "This is not an easy place to be black. Soon it will not be an easy place to be Indian" (*ibid.*, 227). In opposition to his adaptive thinking, An-yanwu favors her black heritage.

Octavia's last novel, *Fledgling,* hypothesized vampire Shori Matthews's hybridity and her compelling love for Wright Hamlin, a normal white male enamored of a child. The mutant protagonist represents a one-time experiment in species mixing, a strengthening of human and vampire traits to provide longevity, potent venom, and light resistance, an allegorical theme that sets her free from ancient Romanian traditions. More to the point of the Ina esthetic, elderfathers equate miscegenation with an offense to social equilibrium and the stability of homogeneity. Shori's uniqueness and possible marriage to Wright unearth a secret insecurity in the Silks and Dahlmans about their clannish pride in pure versus mulatto bloodlines. The issue of amounts of melanin in black and white bodies rebuts Katherine Dahlman's court testimony and brands her a liar and fabulator of human pollution. Her decapitation epitomizes an end to white-only self-glorification and the indefensible notion of color supremacy.

Sources

Butler, Octavia. *Wild Seed.* New York: Doubleday, 1980.
Delany, Samuel R. *Occasional Views Volume 1.* Middletown, CT: Wesleyan University Press, 2021.
Jenkins, Jerry Rafiki. *The Paradox of Blackness in African American Vampire Fiction.* Columbus: Ohio State University Press, 2019.
Montgomery, Maxine Lavon. *The Postapocalyptic Black Female Imagination.* London: Bloomsbury, 2021.

"The Monophobic Response"

Octavia's short essay "The Monophobic Response," a reissue of her October 1995 PEN speech "Journeys" at Quill & Brush, Rockville, Maryland, esteemed her interest in cosmic life. Her themes proposed a long overdue reckoning for human egotism, which she equated with juvenile behavior. Hazel Carby, the University of Rochester's 2018/2019 Distinguished Visiting Humanist, cited Butler's acceptance of "other possibilities of thinking about the human" ("Knowing," 2020). Regardless of the individual's sophistication or learning, each *homo sapiens* labors to grow up and rid the self of hostility, skepticism, "prickly pride," and terror of the unknown, such as the challenges threatened by climate change "a potential for a massive, paradigmatic shift in the social order" (Butler, 2000, 416; "Knowing" 2020).

The author posed the fundamental query "What if things were different?," the basis of all science fiction (*ibid.*). For example, the burdens of Dr. Blake Jason Maslin, an internist in *Clay's Ark,* besets him with a daughter he can't cure of leukemia and captors who threaten to unleash a viral havoc worldwide by mating the infected with normal humans. Because earthmen fixate on earthly shoving matches, speculative writers like Octavia created "other life elsewhere in the universe" (*ibid.*, 416). The extension enables readers to "project alienness onto one another," the outcome of breeding caterpillar-human offspring in "Bloodchild" and Clayarks in the Mohave Desert in *Patternmaster* (*ibid.*, 415). The possibility of vast differences also underlies the recurrent theme in "Speech Sounds," "The Evening and the Morning and the Night," "A Necessary Being," "Childfinder," and *Survivor.* All scrutinize the author's imaginative proposals of far-flung divergence.

Octavia projected the unconventionality of fictional beings onto anyone who could be victimized, harmed, or exterminated because they claimed, "another culture, country, gender, race, ethnicity," the basis of human-vampire mating in *Fledgling* (*ibid.*). At odds with the *homo sapiens* fascination with space exploration lies the problem of communication with the "other," the subject of Miami Date College's November 2015 series "Aliens Among Us." Like combative brothers and sisters, the characters in Octavia's writings encounter a rivalry that confounds the notion of universal oneness, the theme of "Amnesty." More serious than alienating an exotic adversary, proponents of "alternative modes of belonging" contemplate the controlling theme of the Xenogenesis series—a "new way of seeing" the spawning of races to replace our dubious generation (Carby, 2020).

See also Dominance; Race.

Sources

Butler, Octavia. "The Monophobic Response," *Dark Matter: A Century of Speculative Fiction from the African Diaspora*. New York: Aspect/Warner Books, 2000, 415–416.
Carby, Hazel. "Knowing Yourself, Historically" www.invisibleculture*journal.com/pub/* knowing-yourself-historically/release/1 (15 November 2020).
Johnson, Clifton Zeno. *Race in the Galactic Age: Sankofa, Afrofuturism, Whiteness and Whitley Strieber*. Albany: State University of New York, 2019.

Motherhood

Octavia commended mothers as humanizers, a quality found in Lilith Iyapo, mother of the infant male mutant Akin in *Adulthood Rites.* Additional exemplars included kindergarten teacher and child rescuer Lauren Oya Olamina Bankole in *The Parable of the Sower* and Choh's surrogate mother in "A Necessary Being," the weaver who shields children from a showdown between Rohkohn fighters and a Hao guest. Paradoxically bearing no offspring, Tahneh represents the nation's "necessary being" and all-mother. The scenario foreshadows Tahneh's decision-making as maternal guardian of her people and reliever of their drought.

On the personal level, Naomi Chi, stricken with the self-destructive DGD disease in "The Evening and the Morning and the Night," withdraws into a rehabilitation center for the diseased. She intends isolation to protect son Alan from a grotesque self-annihilation. Encouraging Naomi's recovery, staff counselor Beatrice Alcantera heartens patients with a natural mothering based on acceptance of the handicapped. In an overview of Octavia's selfless females, novelist Dorothy Allison, a writer for *Village Voice,* admired the author for "making sure that the contradictions and grief her women experience are as powerfully rendered as their decision to sacrifice autonomy" (Allison, 1989, 67).

Octavia had strong reason for internalizing the strength in maternal figures, each based in part on her own widowed mother, Octavia Margaret Guy Butler, and widowed maternal grandmother, Estella Edna Haywood Guy. The author's fictional offshoots civilize the human realm with empathy and compassion as well as self-sacrifice, some leading to martyrdom. Her supreme Madonna figure, Lauren Oya Olamina Bankole, tries for two years in *The Parable of the Talents* to conceive a child by her husband, Taylor Franklin Bankole. At the enclave of Acorn, she excels at what Patricia Hill Collins, a sociologist at the University of Maryland, terms "othermothering," a communal childcare by neighborhood females, older children, aunts, grandmothers, and black church organizations. The expansive model often coincides with the birth mother's work as a domestic caring for white children, the irony of Pecola Breedlove's yearning for female attention in Toni Morrison's *The Bluest Eye* (Collins, 2015, 13). The beloved Larkin Bankole, a kidnapped toddler, becomes the protagonist's Holy Grail, the source of stress and detective work until the adult daughter locates Lauren. The author permeated scenarios with Lauren's ache for her baby, the only remnant of an intense relationship with a father who adored his child.

Love and Loss

Octavia fleshed out the mother-child relationship with mortal qualms. In a get-acquainted conversation with Oankali captive Paul Titus in *Dawn,* Lilith Iyapo reflects on her only child, Ayre. Paul surmises that Lilith's choice of natural childbirth impressed the aliens as a sign of courage and determination. Consequently, they groom her for a special purpose. She rejects the idea of bearing a hybrid or a "human child to tamper with" in laboratory experiments (Butler, 2000, 94). To her surprise, Kahguyaht accepts her as the most fitting parent "to teach, to give comfort, to feed and clothe, to guide," an outline of mother love as defined by the Greek στοργή (*storge* or dependency-based affection) (*ibid.*, 111). In *Adulthood Rites*, the second volume of *Lilith's Brood*, Lilith proves him right in her reunion with Akin, the three-year-old abductee of raiders. She provides her son "the security of flesh" by "bending, lifting him, hugging him so hard it hurt," a paradox foretokening potential loss (*ibid.*, 412).

The priorities of loving and losing in *Wild Seed* forced the author's African all-mother to accept the inevitable. Analyst Ruth Salvaggio, a language and literature expert at the University of North Carolina, Chapel Hill, characterizes the Nigerian herbalist An-yanwu as a generous, loving ancestral prototype: "Maternity ... is the main source of her being, the principal reason for her existence" (Salvaggio, 1984, 81). She takes in stray or neglected children; her daughter Margaret Nneka, an augury of the future, bears an Ibo/Igbo name meaning "mother is great." The long-lived healer allows the Greek concept of ἀγάπη (*agape*, unconditional love) to shape a concluding relationship with the Nubian Doro, her fiendish companion. To his charge that she shields children, she claims, "I only allow them to be children for as long as they will," before they learn "sorrow and evil," the result of incestuous union with Doro (Butler, 1980, 574).

As matriarch and mother, An-yanwu represents "the great African ancestress. She encompasses and epitomizes defiance, acceptance, compromise, determination, and courage," the traits of Octavia's wonder women (*ibid.*). Variant characteristics contribute to parental and clan relationships, from Karl Larkin's sadistic mother in *Mind of My Mind* and Lauren Olamina's addict mother in *The Parable of the Talents* to the volunteer foster mom Valerie Rye in "Speech Sounds" and the reliable Grandmother Emma, Mary Larkin's standby mom:

Character	Title	Child	Parenting Style
Ahajas	*Dawn*	Tiikuchahk	loving parent
Alanna Verrick	*Survivor*	Tien	mourner of bi-species child killed in a raid
Alice Greenwood	*Kindred*	Aaron, Joe, Miriam, Hagar	mother driven to suicide by forced concubinage
Amber	*Patternmaster*	unborn child	feminist wife to Patternmaster Teray
An-yanwu	*Wild Seed*	Stephen, Peter	ferocious avenger of her son's murderer
Barbara	"Near of Kin"	daughter	concealer of incest with brother Stephen
Cheah	"A Necessary Being"	two children	a hunter who marries a judge
Cory Doran	*The Parable of the Sower*	Keith, Gregory, Bennett, Marcus, Lauren	protector of four sons and a stepdaughter against invaders
Denice	*Wild Seed*	Leah	normal African mother
Emma	*Mind of My Mind*	Mary Larkin	accepting, generous, wise grandmother
foster mother	"A Necessary Being"	Choh	a weaver who shields children from invaders
Gwyn	*Clay's Ark*	daughter	polyamorous mother
Hagar Blake	*Kindred*	Dana's lineage	the family record keeper

Character	Title	Child	Parenting Style
Inez	*Imago*	nine children	dedicated South American parent
Iye Ifeyinwa	*Wild Seed*	son	widowed by murder
Jansee	*Patternmaster*	Coransee, Teray	hovering over sons she hasn't seen in two years
Jorah Maslin	*Clay's Ark*	Keira, Rane	a deceased mom who survives in her children's principles
Keira Maslin	*Clay's Ark*	unborn	hopeful of starting a hybrid nuclear household
Lauren Olamina Bankole	*The Parable of the Talents*	Larkin Bankole followers	adoring, frenzied parent of an abducted child and guide urging residents to leave earth
Lea Westley	*Mind of My Mind*	Vaughn	foster mother of a psionic son
Leah Ordway	*Adulthood Rites*	twenty children	mother rearing family in a South American jungle
Lien	"Bloodchild"	Gan, Xuan Hoa, Qui	a cherisher of an immature son
Lilith Iyapo	*Dawn*	Sharad, nursery of humans, Ayre	patient loving English teacher; widow of Sam; cautious breeder of mutants and fosterer of Sharad
	Adulthood Rites	Akin, Margit, Jodahs, Aaor, Ayodele, Yedik	skin-to-skin contact and language instruction
Margaret Nneka	*Wild Seed*	two sons	faithful wife of a wastrel
Margaret Weylin	*Kindred*	Rufus, twins	ineffective buffer between son and vengeful father
María de la Luz	*Imago*	Adan, daughters, crippled son	rape survivor who mates with her son
Mary Larkin	*Mind of My Mind*	Karl August Larkin	parent of a promising psionic son
Mateo	*Lilith's Brood*	Augustino Leal	committed mother
Meda Boyd	*Clay's Ark*	Jacob, Joseph	desperate to save her four-legged sons from caging
Naomi Chi	"The Evening and the Morning and the Night"	Alan Chi	isolates herself in an institution to protect her son from DGD, a cannibalistic disease
Natividad Douglas	*The Parable of the Sower*	Domingo	successful mother of a biracial son
Neila Verrick	*Survivor*	Yahnoh, Alanna	parent of a foster daughter and birth son
Rina	*Mind of My Mind*	Mary Larkin	breeder of psionic daughter
Sarah	*Kindred*	Carrie, sons	protector of a disabled daughter and mourner of three sons sold at auction
suicide	*Mind of My Mind*	Isaac, Lale	despairing breeder with Doro
Tehkorahs	*Adulthood Rites*	two daughters	raises human-ooloi children
T'Khotgif	"Bloodchild"	infant	breeder with human Bram Lomas
Valerie Rye	"Speech Sounds"	two toddlers	mourner of three dead children; rescuer of two precocious siblings

Character	Title	Child	Parenting Style
wife	*Clay's Art*	Christian, Meda	wife of patriarchal husband Gabriel Boyd
Zahra Moss	*The Parable of the Talents*	Tabia, Russell	devoted wife and strong family defender

PARENTAL PRIORITIES

Obstacles test Octavia's mothers for endurance and pragmatism. In the falling action of *Kindred,* Dana Franklin awaits the birth of Hagar, daughter of Alice Greenwood and the matriarch of Dana's genealogy and of the Abrahamic religions as outlined in Genesis 16:1–16 and the Koran 14:37. The breaking point for Alice and Sarah, sale of their children guts the will to live. Octavia reflects on an opposing view of maternity in Keira and Rane Maslin, sixteen-year-old twins in *Clay's Ark.* Inflicted with maternal absence since the death of mother Jorah, the girls rely on memories of the invisible mother's steadying example, which bolsters Keira during treatment for terminal blood cancer. Among diseased isolates, Meda Boyd bears Asa Elias "Eli" Doyle's children, whom the extraterrestrial virus turns into hyper-sensitive quadrupeds Jacob Elias Boyd and Joseph. To Eli's discomfort at having a freakish son, he silently loves him and longs to make him human, but considers euthanasia as an alternative. Meda shields Jacob, a toddler who refuses to walk on two legs, in fear that the boy will be captured and caged like an animal.

Octavia presented other alternatives of nourishing and parenting. For contrast, she created Kayce Alexander, a parent bearing a name meaning "watchful defender of men." As Larkin Bankole's foster mother, Kayce favors birth child Kamaria to the detriment of Larkin's self-esteem. In a journal on May 24, 1995, the author characterized an even-handed all-mother, Lauren Oya Olamina Bankole, protagonist of *The Parable of the Talents.* As a kindly pastor and "other-mother," she exemplifies what Maxine Lavon Montgomery, a specialist in African diaspora at Florida State University at Tallahassee, called "enabling figures in Africana literature and culture," beginning with Côte d'Ivoire folklore about Mami Wata or Mother Water, a guardian of past and future (Montgomery, 2021, 127, 141).

The loss of motherland for black slavewomen, like Sarah and Carrie in *Kindred,* introduced the scourges of compulsory motherhood, denial of maternalism, and reproductive dispossession when children become the commercial products of bondage, the core crime in Toni Morrison's *Beloved.* The author's double use of Lauren in two volumes of the Parable series provides a model savior and comforter. A proponent of Afrofuturism, she "struggles to seduce, scare, lash her people on to the fulfillment of the Earthseed destiny" (Brown, 2021, 104). As a pacifier of troubled children, she lessens distress on followers with scriptural recitation from her verse, a feminist doctrine opposing violence, sexism, racism, and classism. Her benevolence and focus on a starry future inhibit the human penchant for self-destruction and infighting and press outcast Californians toward collective prosperity.

See also Lilith; "Speech Sounds" Genealogy.

Sources

Allison, Dorothy. "The Future of Female," *Village Voice* (19 December 1989): 67–68.
Brown, Jayna. *Black Utopias: Speculative Life and the Music of Other Worlds.* Durham, NC: Duke University Press, 2021.
Butler, Octavia. *Adulthood Rites* in *Lilith's Brood.* New York: Warner, 2000, 249–517.
_____. *Dawn* in *Lilith's Brood.* New York: Warner, 2000, 2–248.
_____. *Wild Seed.* New York: Doubleday, 1980.
Collins, Patricia Hill. *Black Feminist Thought: Knowledge, Consciousness, and the Politics of Empowerment.* New York: Routledge, 2015.
Cox-Palmer-White, Emily. *The Biopolitics of Gender in Science Fiction: Feminism and Female Machines.* New York: Routledge, 2021.
Lilvis, Kristen. "Mama's Baby, Papa's Slavery? The Problem and Promise of Mothering in Octavia E. Butler's 'Bloodchild,'" *MELUS* 39:4 (Winter, 2014): 7–22, 220.
Montgomery, Maxine Lavon. *The Postapocalyptic Black Female Imagination.* London: Bloomsbury, 2021.
Salvaggio, Ruth. "Octavia Butler and the Black Science-Fiction Heroine," *Black American Literature Forum* 18:2 (Summer, 1984): 78–81.

Names

Octavia's attention to etymology shapes her lists of objects, places, and characters with extensive nuance. For *Dawn,* a contrast of human vs. alien names exemplifies the vast difference in language, motivation, and physiology. By giving Victor Dominic a belligerent surname on a par with Victor Colon in *Fledgling*, she formed an impression of a colonial male who wins by command. For Leah Bede, the first name meaning "weary" fits the family name "prayerful." The combination suggests a religious devotee who, unlike eighth-century CE English ecumenical writer the Venerable Bede, trusts in passive piety, a character trait common to colonial era captivity lore. In the same tone as Victor Dominic, the name Joseph "Joe" Li-Chin Shing in the Xenogenesis series connotes the prosperity of a people through triumph, in his case, the posthumous conception of Akin, a unique mutant and guide to settlement in the stars. Josh Stricklin, University of Southern Mississippi scholar and author of *Jokes from the Gallows,* listed the name as an example of the author's whimsy in a pun of "I can," a verbal gesture to his galactic mission.

In the same vein, the author identified other Oankali prisoners by prominent traits. Celene Ivers acquires mystic worth from a Greek/Hindi identity meaning "heavenly zeal," a set of religious traits that Lilith Iyapo translates into "harmless" (Butler, 2000, 122). The trend toward strength in males identifies Gabriel Rinaldi as "strong councilor," Derick Wolski as "village ruler," and Conrad Loehr as "bold force." A pet name, "Nika," a short form of Nikanj, recalls the Greek goddess of victory who poses in the Parthenon on Athena's outstretched palm. Women's names appear less aggressive in Tate Marah, a "cheerful sea creature," and Beatrice Dwyer bearing "dark blessing." At the salvage pit in volume two, *Adulthood Rites,* the insertion of the Sanskrit pronoun "eka" typifies Akin as "the one" (*ibid.,* 415, 416). Fulbright teaching fellow Aparajita Nand, on the staff of English and black studies at the University of California at Berkeley, notes that the child is equally "akin" to the Oankali and humans.

Name Integration

In 1976, the writer peopled the Patternist series with subtle designations, for example, Patternmaster Rayal, husband of Jansee (Jan's son). The final syllable of

Coransee designates her boy with a north European combination implying "son of the crescent moon," a female symbol reflecting Jansee's maternal instincts. Their son Teray takes the first syllable of Rayal for himself, producing a sound-alike to the biblical patriarch Abraham's father Terah (wanderer). Teray adds it to his first wife, Iray, whose naming echoes the Hebrew for "watchful." After Iray's disloy-alty, Teray takes as second wife the healer Amber, an Arabic term for "fierce or jewel." Other choices link characters with significant persons, places, and allusive qualities:

Goran—Scots Gaelic for highlander or mountaineer
Jackman—French for a servant
Joachim—Hebrew for a Housemaster named for the Virgin Mary's maternal grandfather
Kai—Scandinavian or Welsh for earth woman, keeper of the keys
Lady Darah—Hebrew for wise
Laro—French for rock
Michael—Hebrew for God's gift
Suliana—Latin for a mute seeking independence

For Clay Dana, the mythic English name attached to the starship *Clay's Ark* and, by extension to enemy mutant Clayarks, indicated a mortal closeness to bare earth. In the novel *Clay's Ark,* the explorer ship's psychokinetic drive, named Dana Drive for the inventor, symbolizes the genius revealed in a reclaimed loser. Clay recurs in *Mind of My Mind* as a malleable farm worker dependent on overbearing brother Seth, a third son of Adam in Genesis whose name means "appointed" for his replacement of Abel, the brother whom Cain murdered in Genesis 4:1–18.

Octavia dropped paratextual nuance into fictional exposition, such as Dar-rington for the secretive enclave of vampire Iosip Petrescu (son of the rock) in *Fledgling.* Wright's surname, Hamlin, alludes to the piper who lures the rats from Hamelin town, a medieval setting in the folkloric verse of German poet Johann Wolfgang von Goethe. A complex implication attaches to Lauren Oya Olamina and Christopher Morpeth Donner, a presidential candidate in *The Parable of the Sower.* Belgian scholar Laura Lievens at the Université Catholique de Louvain noted the connection of Lauren Oya Olamina to distress in nature through Oya, a Yoruba warrior-queen and weather goddess capable of summoning change through fire, lightning, tornadoes, gales and hurricanes. The inferences build up with Christo-pher (Columbus) and Morpeth, a Scots road and site of a murder. Donner, the pat-ronymic of pioneers snowbound in the California sierras, lost 34 members between December 1846 and April 1847 to cold and starvation, relieved in part by canni-balism. A black hero, David "Day" Turner, bears the royal Hebrew name of King David, Jerusalem's warrior-ruler, and the family name of Nat Turner, a visionary slave who tried to free Africans in Virginia. The addition of "Day" links the survi-vor to Jamaican-American composer Harry Belafonte's "Banana Boat Song" derived from the folk chant "Day-o," an Afro-calypso paean to the islander loading fruit for export.

ALLEGORICAL RHETORIC

In "Speech Sounds," the writer's inventiveness adds complexity to interpretation of "obsidian," a volcanic rock that could refer to black, rock, or Peter, from the Greek *petros* for rock. All three possibilities impart reasons for University of California at Los Angeles history professor Valerie Rye to trust her rescuer. She bears a name implying a complex duality, strong and discontented (Govan, 2005–2006, 26). The coupling of strength with grievance extends the theme of survival in a California setting flawed with havoc, ruin, and possible extinction. Fortunately for the pair at the end, the possession of speech and memory implies a means of renewing the original meaning of "family" for Valerie's two foster children.

The author assured interviewer Sandra Y. Govan that "Names do matter," a belief she actualized in *Survivor* with the addictive fruit *meklah*, Hebrew for sacrificer, and in *The Parable of the Sower* with the town of Robledo, derived from the Latin *robor* for oak. The names Naomi (pleasant), the self-sacrificing mother, and Beatrice (blessed), the kind asylum guide in "The Evening and the Morning and the Night," embed a somber tone with hope. On a deeper level, Barbara, the title rescuer in "Childfinder," represents the "foreign woman" eluding a repressive organization to save another Valerie. The staunch Jordan, already identified as a telepath, recalls the biblical Jordan River, in which evangelist John the Baptist immersed Jesus, thus recognizing his divine promise.

In 1996, Octavia disclosed to Marty Crisp, a book reviewer for the Lancaster, Pennsylvania, *Sunday News,* a clever way of creating names for space beings from "cheesy little dictionaries…. Japanese, Spanish, Hebrew, Swahili, Arabic" (Crisp, 1996, H3). In *Mind of My Mind,* Mary's husband Karl Larkin's name means "manly" and "fierce," a fitting moniker for an unwilling mate of a psionic woman. The gunman Palmer Landry bears a two-part identity as pilgrim land ruler. For the protagonist of "The Book of Martha," the author picks the housewife from Luke 11:40–42 rather than her more studious sister Mary and infuses domesticity in the Aramaic meaning of "Martha" as house mistress. Similarly, Alan Chi, a pre-med student in "The Evening and the Morning and the Night," bears an Ibo/Igbo name from southeastern Nigeria indicating a guardian deity. Calling on her dyslexic tendency to read what isn't there, she attached syllables from different sources: for "Bloodchild," she made the most of Chinese terms, choosing "humane" for the mother Lien, "dry and empty" for son Gan, "subordinator" for son Qui, and "well chosen" for daughter Xuan Hoa. Octavia heightened allegory by naming the wild beast *achti*, which is Tamil for agile, and calling the victim Bram, a connection to Bram Stoker, the Irish author of the horror classic *Dracula*.

For Doro, the immortal Nubian in *Mind of My Mind* and *Wild Seed*, the author chose a word that meant east, the direction of sunrise as a token of his grand plan to build a super species of mind readers. His New York seed village of Wheatley contains symbolic surnames: Cutler (knifemaker), Strycker (tester), Sloane (raid), Lann (sword), Croon (crooked), and Waemans, Scots Gaelic for "serious man." An-yan-wu's slave husband, Mgbada, bears the Nigerian Ibo/Igbo name "deer." An-yanwu's name means "sun," a visual icon in the 1690s for a West African healer that Doro anglicizes to "Sun Woman," an apocalyptic icon in Revelation 12 (Butler, 1980, 269). A less clear choice, her attacker Lale Sachs bears an identity formed of "lullaby" and "Saxon," a paradox similar to potential rapist Paul Titus, a seemingly harmless human in *Dawn* whose names recall St. Paul and his missionary associate Titus.

Sources

Butler, Octavia. *Dawn* in *Lilith's Brood*. New York: Warner, 2000, 2–248.
_____. *Wild Seed*. New York: Doubleday, 1980.
Crisp, Marty. "Interview," (Lancaster, PA) *Sunday News* (11 February 1996): H3.
Govan, Sandra Y. "Interview," *Obsidian III* 6:2/7:1 (2005–2006): 14–39.
Kenan, Randall. "Interview," *Callaloo* 14:2 (Spring, 1991): 495–504.
Mao, Douglas. *Inventions of Nemesis*. Princeton, NJ: Princeton University Press, 2020.
Nanda, Aparajita "A Palimpsestuous Reading of Octavia Butler's *Lilith's Brood*" in *Palimpsests in Ethnic and Postcolonial Literature and Culture*. Cham, Switzerland: Palgrave Macmillan, 2021.
Qadeer, Haris, and P.K. Yasser Arafath, eds. *Sultana's Sisters: Genre, Gender, and Genealogy in South Asian Muslim Women's Fiction*. London: Routledge, 2021.

"Near of Kin"

A study of secret incest written for *Chrysalis 4* in 1979, Octavia's "Near of Kin" creates a subtle humor out of the phrase "next of kin" and teases out through niece-uncle dialogue the lacunas in clan consanguinity. She took the title from a biblical injunction against taboo sexual encounters in Leviticus 18:6, a prohibition intended to prevent inbred defects to mind and body like those inherent in the pagan royal dynasties of Egypt and Persia and the European Hapsburg line. Interbreeding may have caused Pharaoh Tutankhamun's clubfoot and congenital jaw defects in Charles II of Spain. Metaphorically, Octavia's niece and uncle pour through a muddle of memorabilia, papers that question the authenticity of documentation by revealing all but the truth of the girl's uncertain fathering.

The author examined sex with relatives from multiple perspectives. She reprised the blood kin affinity in *The Parable of the Talents* in niece Larkin Bankole's adoration of "Uncle Marc," a Christian America evangelist "so good-looking, and a beautiful person" who also ensnares the love of his sister, Lauren Oya Olamina "in spite of herself" (Butler, 1998, 279). His dramatic encounter with niece Larkin, renamed Asha Alexander by her foster parents, a Sanskrit name meaning hope or wish, delighted her. She exclaims to the wanderer, "my uncle … *my uncle!*" (*ibid.*, 318). Octavia stressed the irony of Larkin's mother hunger and a kinship that "restores love and harmony within a family" previously destroyed by religious fanaticism (Rouillard, 2020, 38).

Anticipating the disclosure in the Parable series, the earnest conversation in "Near of Kin" with the unnamed niece reveals Stephen's off-limits affair with sister Barbara when he was thirty-five and she, thirty. Conceived out of love, the 22-year-old protagonist gains a nuclear family when Stephen comforts sister Barbara for her four miscarriages and abandonment by a faithless husband. By clarifying his relationship with a beloved niece, the narrative relieves her fears that Barbara was reluctant to rear a daughter. Octavia created situational irony from the college student who approaches truth through personal inquiry rather than academic research.

The crux compares to a three-way squabble of *Mind of My Mind* in which Mary scorns her sister/mother Rina's incest with relatives while ignoring her own birth to the long-lived Nubian Doro, the father and exploiter of related experimental communities. The resolution frees the niece of gnawing suspicions about Uncle Stephen, whom she resembles like a twin, a commonality that brings down Camelot in Arthurian lore from the brother-sister siring of the villain Mordred. Analyst Linda Marie Rouillard, a world cultures specialist at the University of Toledo, Ohio, described incest as "claustrophobic ... [depriving] the family ... of the potential richness and material wealth, to say nothing of the generic diversity, that can result from broad social connections" (*ibid.*, 45). Her description corroborates Octavia's building of strength in the Patternist genealogy following the marriage of Rayal to his sister Jansee and her bearing of sons Coransee and Teray. By marrying a rebel feminist, Teray forms an exogamous family with pregnant wife Amber, a bisexual healer.

The two-gender doppelgänger concludes with Stephen's firm insistence that his niece/daughter accept her inheritance, a stern order delivered in fatherly fashion. An unusually candid addition to the author's canon, the story, based on biblical accounts of incest between Abraham and Sarah (Genesis 20:12), Lot's daughters' seduction of their drunken father (Genesis 19:30–38), and the unions of Adam's sons with Eve's daughters (Genesis 5:4), examines taboo behaviors and their implications for genetic continuity in the human family tree. For the defamed college student, acceptance of her parents' sins disburdens her of Barbara's troubled life and rewards her with the designation of "father" for a man she already loves.

Sources

Butler, Octavia. "Near of Kin in *Bloodchild and Other Stories*. New York: Seven Stories Press, 2005, 73–85.
_____. *The Parable of the Talents*. New York: Seven Stories Press, 1998.
Eisenberg, Ronald L. *Jewish Traditions*. Lincoln: University of Nebraska Press, 2020.
Jackson, Michael. *Coincidences: Synchronicity, Verisimilitude, and Storytelling*. Berkeley: University of California Press, 2021.
Rouillard, Linda Marie. *Medieval Considerations of Incest, Marriage, and Penance*. Cham, Switzerland: Springer Nature, 2020.

"Near of Kin" Genealogy

Through name choice, Octavia creates a troubling backstory of identity and parentage. By leaving the protagonist unnamed, she implies the predicament of a niece/daughter in conversation with her uncle/father. Like the main character in James Hurst's insightful story "The Scarlet Ibis," the protagonist lacks a clear identity, a reflection of his role as "brother."

The author heightens the puzzle by naming the mother Barbara, the Latin *nomen* meaning both strange and foreign, an intimation of the disjointed mother-daughter relationship. The choice of Stephen's name allies him with a king of England, nine popes, and the first Christian martyr, murdered by stoning in Jerusalem in 34 CE.

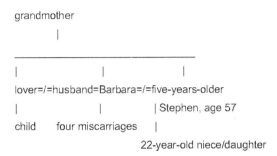

```
grandmother
     |
 _____
 |               |              |
lover=/=husband=Barbara=/=five-years-older
 |               |         | Stephen, age 57
child    four miscarriages  |
                 22-year-old niece/daughter
```

Sources

Butler, Octavia. "Near of Kin" in *Bloodchild and Other Stories.* New York: Seven Stories Press, 2005, 73–85.

Rouillard, Linda Marie. *Medieval Considerations of Incest, Marriage, and Penance.* Cham, Switzerland: Springer Nature, 2020.

"A Necessary Being"

Six years after Octavia's death in 2006, her agent Merrilee Heifetz saved the novella "A Necessary Being" from a massive scrap heap of the author's ephemera. It reads like a prequel—an ancillary chapter of nonhuman antipathies in *Survivor.* The title reflects an eighteenth-century belief in priorities: God is a necessary being who had to exist; humankind is a contingent or dependent being who must rely on deity for origination. According to backstory, Tahneh, the Rohkohn Hao (magistrate; Chinese for "Good") and mother figure of a desert people, regrets that Rohkohn sadists had disabled her father. According to Kristen Lillvis, an English researcher at Marshall University in Huntington, West Virginia, his wounding left her immobilized as both queen and thrall. Well indoctrinated in desert life, she had once dared explore caverns within passages leading to the Pacific Ocean, a female version of the Greek hero Theseus's exploration of Crete's underworld.

Unlike the author's string of wonder women, Tahneh functions at a physical disadvantage and substitutes reason for force. Despite her blue skin tone and courage, she grieves that her aristocratic body conceives no blue child to provide the next tribal judge. In a masterful panorama of tone and atmosphere, she flinches at the arrival of Diut, a handsome blue mountain Hao striding from the east across the arid badlands. Through a tribal merger, he becomes a possible inheritor to replace the barren magistrate in the Hao succession. The iffy future explains Octavia's title designation of Diut as an essential figure to two ethnic groups and to Queen Tahneh.

The story echoes previous motifs before plunging into more diplomatic directions. A black martyr to tribal longevity in the style of Barbara in "Childfinder," Lilith Iyapo in *Lilith's Brood,* and Shori Matthews in *Fledgling,* Tahneh shrewdly extends courtesy and a simple feast on birds and fish while sizing up the obviously inexperienced young visitor. Welcome to guests involves an outward display of changeable body colors and luminescence, biological displays of emotion. Libido compels her to nip the throat of her guest, a gustatory sampling that Shori repeats on Wright Hamlin in *Fledgling*. When Diut's playful nibble advances ritual love play, Tahneh contemplates whether oral aggression could signal both sexual willingness and the treachery she plans to overwhelm the rival outlander.

The tone of an ancient imperial language gives place to romance with a night of lovemaking followed by the queen's conspiracy to capture Diut. Tahneh needs the outsider as a hostage to ransom Rohkohn hostages Jeh and Cheah. Bearing a Chinese surname meaning "thank," Cheah is a tough, wary female hunter mismatched to Judge Jeh, a member of another mountain caste. Octavia segued from an outdoor fight between tribes to the hamstringing with burns behind the knees of Ehreh, a Hao chief judge bearing the German name "honor." He remains prejudiced against mixed marriage, even though the desert tribes claim descent from the same prehistoric empire.

The author darkens the atmosphere to symbolize limited choices for the drought-ridden desert, a metaphor for Tahneh's barren womb. Unlike medieval quest stories set in castles, the action diverts to a subterranean tussle among children who practice camouflage tactics until rescued from guards by maternal weavers, epitomes of shared labor and union. The juvenility of the feud anticipates the mature negotiation between fighters Tahneh and Diut to renew the kingdom. At a verbal climax, she claims to have returned Diut's life. The story dramatizes Octavia's belief that earth's people must mature from ancient savagery to a cerebral means of avoiding a pyrrhic war in which no one wins.

See also Dominance; *Survivor*; Tone.

Sources

Butler, Octavia. "A Necessary Being" in *Unexpected Stories*. New York: Open Road Media, 2014, 11–76.

Kearse, Stephen. "The Essential Octavia Butler," *New York Times* (15 January 2021): 12–13.

Lillvis, Kristen. *Posthuman Blackness and the Black Female Imagination*. Athens: University of Georgia Press, 2017.

Wanzo, Rebecca. "The Unspeakable Speculative, Spoken," *American Literary History* 31:3 (Fall, 2019): 564–574.

Whiteside, Briana. "Blogging about Octavia Butler," *CLA Journal* 59:3 (March 2016): 242–250.

"A Necessary Being" Genealogy

A complex interaction of nonhuman desert dwellers, Octavia's posthumous story returned to figures and situations in *Survivor*. Set against a primitive backdrop, the feminist study depicts Tahneh as hierarchical figurehead in an ineluctable position as Hao (magistrate) and barren queen in a stymied dynasty.

To increase tensions between tribal adversaries, the author set the events during

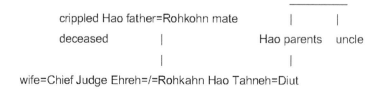

crippled Hao father=Rohkohn mate | |

deceased | Hao parents   uncle

                            | |

wife=Chief Judge Ehreh=/=Rohkahn Hao Tahneh=Diut

drought, a geographic crisis that forces Diut to seek a solution to water shortages. As speculative fiction, the subject of water distribution characterizes Octavia's projections that future wars will involve peoples in questions of sharing.

Sources

Butler, Octavia. "A Necessary Being," *Unexpected Stories*. New York: Open Road Media, 2014, 11–76.
Lillvis, Kristen. *Posthuman Blackness and the Black Female Imagination*. Athens: University of Georgia Press, 2017.

Olamina, Lauren Oya

For the teen teacher/evangelist of *The Parable of the Sower,* Octavia endowed her own personality with the super traits of the quest hero. Habiba Ibraham, a Seattle English professor at the University of Washington, compares Lauren to the aged black female witnesses in Ernest Gaines's *The Autobiography of Miss Jane Pittman* and Alex Haley's *Roots.* In a coming-of-age story set on post-apocalyptic terrain, Lauren mimics the autobiography of a fugitive slave and toys with episodes of bisexuality, a mind-expanding characteristic of the priest Teiresias in Sophocles' tragedy *Antigone.* Blessed with spiritual energy, she emerges as a complicated, introspective, but tender-hearted California diarist. On the cusp of womanhood, she battles in a daybook religious misgivings and despair. Teri Ann Doerksen, a British teacher at the University of Manchester, compared the figure to the martyred Christ because "her mother was an addict of a drug [Paracetco] that made Lauren hyperempathetic" (Doerksen, 1997, 22). The psychosomatic syndrome forced Lauren and fellow "sharers" Emery and Grayson to experience the collective trauma of others, often collapsing in agony when they most needed strength. The trigger is vision, a glimpse of suffering.

Similar experiences with empathy and a free-flowing skepticism forge oneness in the Olamina diaspora, a pilgrimage for which the company evolves a common language and coping strategy. In an essay for the *New York Times,* writer Samantha Hunt pities a girl bearing "so much feeling in a world that does not value feeling" (Hunt, 2021). Fortunately, the delusional gift readies her to resist community anarchy launched by "paints" and "pyros." Lauren's family rapport leans away from her stepmother, Cory Duran, toward males—her deceased father and brother Keith, younger brothers, and boyfriend Curtis Talcott. With the warmth of lovers Emily Webb and George Gibbs in playwright Thornton Wilder's *Our Town,* Lauren and Curtis advance from puppy love to sexual involvement and serious discussion of wedlock. The choice pushes Lauren to reveal misgivings that her boyfriend can fit into plans for Earthseed's enlightened doctrine and a destiny in the stars.

Formulating a Message

Named for the Latin for "crowned with honor," Lauren insists that the doctrine of Earthseed revealed itself to her over a lengthy study. According to Canadian writer David Morris, a philosophy professor at Concordia University in Montreal, she "[pushed] back against religious fundamentalisms that enshrine hierarchy" (Morris, 2021). A *Los Angeles Sentinel* book review described her as "a single-minded force, a seer, a poet, and black woman with a vision of God, goodness, and change in the broken world of 2032" ("Octavia," 1999, A9). In the night sky, the visionary regards "a whole other world" (Flood, 2021). For conflict, the plot depicts her abnormal tenderness of heart, an anomaly the author called "a kind of biological conscience" (Butler, 1998, 99). During an epoch of invasion, theft, arson, rape, and murder, she stands watch and kills intrusive pyros quickly, neatly to stave off debilitating empathy, the compassion that stifles action.

The diarist voices *The Parable of the Sower* at a teen level fraught with smart-mouth criticisms of life as the preacher's oldest child and sister of the sociopath Keith and the heartthrob Marcus. Glenn Grant, a reviewer for the Montreal *Gazette*, blamed the rush of mature thoughts on youth "forced to grow up too quickly" (Grant, 1995, H4). By age eighteen, she imagines becoming a teacher like her parents, but she elevates pedagogy from the mundane to the celestial. Her theory credits biracial children like Domingo Douglas with the ongoing search for truth. Transition from fundamentalist to versatile ecclesiastic and shepherd to her followers refutes the purpose of prayer to sway God, the inexorable creator. Even though the Reverend Olamina believes she lacks humility, the prophetic daughter admits "how many things I've got to learn" and wonders what source will direct her thinking (Butler, 1998, 26).

Like most professional teachers, Lauren devotes herself to planning by studying the topography ahead and collecting maps of Oregon and Washington. With brief, pithy verse "more useful to me when I'm afraid," she composes "Earthseed: The Book of the Living," original epigrammatic scripture defining a Deistic theology based on an indifferent god (Butler, 1993, 125). Her frank assessment of human terrors replicates the poet's words in Psalm 130, the "De Profundis (Out of the Depths)," a ninth-century BCE cry to the Almighty for support and mercy. When criminals run amok in her gated community, she has no choice but to bolt. On the way north from Robledo, she chides herself for being "full of books and ignorant of reality," a coming-to-knowledge common to teens and idealists (*ibid.,* 156). Flight exposes her to the need for caution, armaments, food security, and sentries to patrol during the night, when refugees feel more vulnerable.

A Stable Community

In *The Parable of the Talents,* Lauren Oya's journal reveals a more cunning influence. In northwestern California, she founds Acorn on September 26, 2027, on Cape Mendocino facing the Pacific coast. She states Octavia's profound belief that emotional healing and coping "will break the old cycle, even if it's only to begin a new one, a different one" (Butler, 1998, 321). She reasons with her lover, physician Taylor Franklin Bankole, "If I had to die … shouldn't it be while I was trying to help the community?" (*ibid.,* 45). Her skeptical daughter, Larkin Bankole, sneered that her mother had already been "a missile, armed and targeted" at brother Marcos Duran, a revivalist whom she set up to fail at a group sermon (*ibid.,* 5).

With tepid enthusiasm, the author endorsed her heroine as "someone who was coming up with solutions of a sort" (Butler, 2005). After the maggot (armored vehicle) attack by President Andrew Steele Jarret's Crusaders, the seventeen-month prison narrative orchestrates liberation and her short, pithy commands. She calmly calls the roll and determines that nineteen females have survived. The losses include her baby daughter Larkin, Zahra Moss Balter, and Taylor Bankole. The mudslide that frees captives from electronic dog collars leads to a resounding victory with guns and hand-to-hand reprisal against guards that devolves into an "orgy of destruction" (*ibid.*, 233).

A Second Conflagration

Similar in deliberate arson to the razing of Robledo and the fire-bombing of Shori Matthews's family in *Fledgling*, the burning of Acorn becomes the second phoenix reduced to ashes, an augury of renewal. The author pictures Lauren comforting companion Harry Balter as he views his children's fingerprints. Weeping and physical embraces release their exhaustion and sorrow. To maintain secrecy, she adopts a male guise and renames herself Cory Duran after her dead stepmother. The nuanced etymology suggests "hard core" as proof of a fearless heart. Octavia diverted attention to Lauren's sharing of suffering and focused on obsessive searching for daughter Larkin. After reuniting with brother Marcos, Lauren experiences a bitter betrayal—his lies about Larkin's parents' deaths.

By ending the novel on Lauren at age eighty-one, the author elevates the protagonist from grieving parent to martyr awaiting transfer to destiny in the stars. Of Lauren's value to the writer's objectives, an author interview in *Locus* stated that the neophyte evangelist is the "one person who decides this is what religion should be doing, and she uses religion to get us into interstellar space" (Butler, 2000, 6). The concept reprises Octavia's leader Alanna Verrick in *Survivor,* a prototype for Lauren's idealistic pilgrimage. In *Adulthood Rites,* the middle volume of the Xenogenesis series, the author heightens mutant Akin's influence as leader during the readying of earthlings for migration to Mars. The novels anticipate the youthful enthusiasm of black vampire Shori Matthews, the spearhead of another rejuvenation of a dying society.

See also Earthseed.

Sources

Butler, Octavia. "Devil Girl from Mars: Why I Write Science Fiction," *Media in Transition,* MIT (19 February 1998).
_____. *The Parable of the Talents.* New York: Seven Stories Press, 1998.
_____. "Persistence," *Locus* 44:6 (June 2000): 6.
_____. "Science Fiction Writer Octavia Butler on Race, Global Warming and Religion," (video), *Democracy Now* www.democracynow.org/2005/11/11/science_fiction_writer_octavia_butler_on (11 November 2005).
Canavan, Gerry. "Science Fiction and Utopia in the Anthropocene," *American Literature* 93:2 (2021): 255–282.
Doerksen, Teri Ann. "Octavia E. Butler: Parables of Race and Difference" in *Into Darkness Peering.* Westport CT: Greenwood, 1997.
Flood, Alison. "Perseverance Martian Landing Point Named after Octavia E. Butler," London *Guardian* (10 March 2021).

Grant, Glenn. "Review: *The Parable of the Sower*," (Montreal) *Gazette* (4 March 1995): H4.

Holden, Rebecca J., and Nisi Shawl, eds. *Strange Matings: Science Fiction, Feminism, African American Voices, and Octavia E. Butler.* Seattle, WA: Aqueduct, 2013.

Hunt, Samantha. "What Is a Teenage Girl?," *International New York Times* (27 January 2021).

Morris, David. *Public Religions in the Future World: Postsecularism and Utopia.* Athens: University of Georgia Press, 2021.

"Octavia E. Butler at African American Museum Tonight," *Los Angeles Sentinel* (24 March 1999): A9.

Turner, Jenny. "Ready to Go Off," *London Review of Books* 43:4 (18 February 2021).

The Parable of the Sower

In 1993 and 1998, Octavia produced an illustrative diatribe—two Parable books drawn from the discord and jeopardy of her own times from humankind's predisposition to self-destruct. On National Public Radio's *Morning Edition,* producer Laine Kaplan-Levenson called the work "the-apocalypse-is-right-now coming-of-age story" (Kaplan-Levenson, 2021). The Dublin *Irish Independent* declared the imaginative series an urgent and invigorating view of eco-political erosion, the cause of splintered families and gang formation. Much like Laguna Pueblo author Leslie Marmon Silko's *Almanac of the Dead,* the narratives lacerate the era's homelessness, violence, greed, racism, and misogyny that threaten the American southwest. In an introduction to a boxed set of Parable novels, activist Gloria Steinem acclaimed the author's "seeds of warning" about a fictional future "that has already begun to come true" (Steinem, 2019).

For maximum terror, the author set the first volume during the Pox, a medieval term for apocalypse. She projected peril and sacrifice of the dutiful in the death of Mars astronaut Alicia Catalina Godinez Leal, whose names carry adjectival hints of noble, pure, godly, and loyal. Glenn Grant, a book critic for the Montreal *Gazette,* summarized the allegory as a "depressing picture of America in terminal decline" from "siege mentality" summarized in Revelation 18:2 with a comparison to Babylon, the nexus of apostasy (Grant, 1994, I3). The text predicts California's doom from new forms of capitalistic slavery and indenturing, malnutrition, fires, drug and gun obsessions, and water shortages. Worsening the action, Lauren Oya Olamina weathers a delusional affliction, an empathy for suffering that seizes her at critical moments. At age eleven, she hemorrhaged when her brother Keith tricked her into empathizing with a flow of fake blood. Later, the debility boomerangs in her favor, enlightening her to other people's reactions to racism and injustice.

Octavia characterized the Earthseed doctrine as Lauren's work in progress. Like the protagonist, the author labored to perfect a religious tenet in a period of juvenile bloodshed and doomed childhood. Contributing to urgency, a fortress mindset poses a short-term solution to risk that leaves locals unprepared for a frontal assault. For the rural saga, she chose the title *The Parable of the Sower* after much debate: "It was a perfect title; it was the kind of title that just made me feel good because I knew it was right" (Govan, 2005–2006, 29). In the running, she listed *Justice; Judgment; Godshaper; Gods of Clay; Daughter of Mourning; Olamina*; and *Girasol*, an Italian term for "sunflower" based on the Greco-Roman *gyre* (to turn) and *sol* (sun). The latter names the heliotroping movement of a blossom toward sunlight, a metaphor for Lauren's contemplation of God.

Precarious Society

By situating fifteen-year-old Lauren Oya Olamina in 2024 in middle-class Robledo, California, the story introduces a gated community amid a lush vegetable and fruit garden secured by firearms, patrols, and security dogs. Her first and last names, a blend of French and Yoruban, identify a wise northwest African and Brazilian Orisha (warrior goddess) who fosters business profits. Her middle name Oya recalls the mythic death queen who rules the Niger River and dispatches whirlwinds and lightning. The glint of fire from her sword or machete reflects complicity with a mate, the blacksmith Ogun, in imposing harrowing change or death. Ironically, Lauren's voicing of the narrative through diary entries lists the unspoken frustrations of a P.K. (preacher's kid) with Baptist ritual. She blames the Reverend Olamina for the growing validation of violence, particularly rebel son Keith's beating for theft and running away (Butler, 1993, 173).

According to critic Gerry Canavan, the Parable novels and their "slow motion apocalypse" became the author's "most predictive works of science fiction" (Canavan, 2021, 264, 263). Self-arming increases in response to gun deaths, disappearances, and invasions. The edenic setting gives place to the Mormon style polygamy of *Fledgling*, financial ruin, and bedlam from arson, pedophilia, suicide, rape, atrocities. Lauren extracts from Keith the monstrous extremes of "paints," orgasmic drug maniacs who set people and buildings on fire. Octavia echoed the motif in the collapse of Phoenix in *Imago* and with gasoline bombs and deaths in *Fledgling* (Butler, 1993, 110). Lauren's peers Joanne Garfield and Harry Balter fantasize a reinvention of the Underground Railroad by proposing to migrate over the Washington border into Canada, but Joanne lacks Lauren's reliance on self and sense. Because Lauren's father has "blind spots" and a heavy punitive hand, she must depend on logic to make the pilgrims "something other than beggars" (*ibid.*, 57).

Pilgrimage

Lauren expects another biblical Jericho, the first permanent West Bank settlement which Joshua and his Israelites crushed at the conquest of Canaan around 1200 BCE in Joshua 6:1–27. On July 30, 2027, mobocracy led by demonic "paints" forces her to flee with a "grab and run pack" down Durant Road to Meredith Street, names redolent with "hardship" and "tyranny" (*ibid.*, 58). Her diary and the sardonic description of her 57-year-old lover Taylor Franklin Bankole of an "installment-plan World War III" mocks the failings of police, fire, and water departments and the rising of Pacific tides (Butler, 1993, 8; 1998, 4). By gulping "pyro," addicts fuel the urge to set fire to objects and people and become "human maggots" by picking valuables from wreckage (*ibid.*, 159). In the pattern of Lauren's generation, the young devalue strict ritual and dogma and embrace spirituality, a balm to hearts gashed by pandemonium.

Lauren internalizes the massive disjuncture of civilization by classifying change as an emerging truth, which she calls Earthseed. A female Moses disguised in men's haircut and attire, she pairs with Harry Balter, a white neighbor, and tours

Hanning Joss, a "security conscious" emporium mocking the American worship of commerce (*ibid.,* 174). Among a heterogeneous scrum of travelers, she, Harry, and Zahra Moss trudge U.S. 101 north along the Pacific Coast toward Santa Barbara, a diaspora mirroring Dust Bowl traffic through inhospitable "stay on the road" towns in John Steinbeck's *The Grapes of Wrath* (*ibid.,* 240). The trek to northwest California yields a Noah's ark of human rejects for their racial/ethnic diversity.

Along the northeastern route, within what Mary Louise Pratt, a 2019 American Academy of Arts and Sciences Fellow and president of the Modern Language Association, labels a "contact zone," refugees avoid privatized cities and reshape society to suit the needs of marginalized people (Pratt, 1992, 23). Gabriela Bruschini Grecca of the Universidade Estadual Pauli in São Paulo, Brazil, outlined the divergences in a transcultural cavalcade:

Refugee	Ethnicity	Characteristics
Allie Gilchrist	white	girl prostituted by her father
Doe Mora	Hispanic	daughter of single father
Domingo Douglas	black/Hispanic	biracial baby
Emery Solis	black/Japanese	wife of a Mexican man and a former debt slave
Gloria Natividad Douglas	Hispanic	wife of a black man and mother of Domingo, a mixed-race son
Grayson Mora	Hispanic	single father of Doe and former debt slave
Harry Balter	white	the only white male, educated, but naive
Jill Gilchrist	white	prostitute who pairs with sister Allie
Lauren Oya Olamina	black	educated leader posing as a male
Taylor Franklin Bankole	black	son of a man who took an African surname
Tori Solis	black/Hispanic/Japanese	tri-racial daughter of a single mother
Travis Charles Douglas	black	son of a cook for a rich household
Zahra Moss	white	former homeless person and wife of a polygamist; she sympathizes with Lauren's hyperempathy

Lauren teaches Zahra to read and discusses Earthseed with Harry and the convert Travis Douglas, a name suggesting a bridge over a black stream resembling the "river of the poor … flooding north" (Butler, 1998, 223). Lauren's stress on action alludes to another Douglas, black abolitionist and orator Frederick Douglass, a proponent of black education who taught himself to read and write.

A Hybrid Homeland

The decision to transform Earthseed into a reality grips Lauren at the same time as the earthquake on August 27, 2027, and the discovery of $2,400–$3,600 in hundred-dollar bills. An instant affinity for Bankole acquaints her with a physician named in Yoruban "build my house," a foreshadowing of his cabin at Acorn, the commune to come. His given names imply an honest hands-on crafter. Outside Salinas, the ragged troop rescues sister prostitutes Allison and Jillian Gilchrist, a surname indicating "servant of Christ." To avoid Bay Area chaos, they press on to San Juan Bautista (Saint John the Baptist) and the San Luis Reservoir, a monument to a thirteenth-century French king beloved for mercy and human rights. Beyond Sacramento, the refugees witness cannibalism. Octavia's allegorical naming continues with two more needy females, Tori (bird) and her mother, Emery Tanaka Solis (brave, rice paddy, comfort). By helping former Latino agricultural slaves Doe and Grayson Mora, Lauren and Bankole declare themselves "the crew of a modern Underground Railroad" (*ibid.*, 292).

After two months on the road, on September 26, 2027, Taylor Bankole generously provides access to three hundred acres in northwestern California at Cape Mendocino. The emblematic total of thirteen pilgrims recreates a Christ figure and twelve apostles. Lauren guides the enlightened travelers to Acorn, a Gothic name for "fruit of open land." They find Bankole's family and home lying in ash and rubble with no indication of who killed them or why they torched the residence. Octavia recreated the charred scenario in *Imago's* Phoenix village and the Silks' revenge killings in *Fledgling*. The farmland on which Lauren sows vegetables and fruit seeds from her go-bag promises sustenance for all. To balance hope with letting go of the past, enclave members grieve for their dead and perpetuate future hopes with a stash of acorns, a source of new, strong trees.

See also Capitalism; Coming of Age; Earthseed.

Sources

Butler, Octavia. *The Parable of the Sower.* New York: Four Walls, Eight Windows, 1993.
_____. *The Parable of the Talents.* Seven Stories Press, 1998.
Canavan, Gerry. "Science Fiction and Utopia in the Anthropocene," *American Literature* 93:2 (2021): 255–282.
Doerksen, Teri Ann. "Octavia E. Butler: Parables of Race and Difference" in *Into Darkness Peering.* Westport CT: Greenwood, 1997.
Govan, Sandra Y. "Interview," *Obsidian III* 6:2/7:1 (2005–2006): 14–39.
Grant, Glenn. "Black Woman Author Is Rarity in SF," (Montreal) *Gazette* (26 March 1994): I3.
Grecca, Gabriela Bruschini. "'A Racist Challenge Might Force Us Apart': Divergence, Reliance, and Empathy in *Parable of the Sower* by Octavia Butler," *Ilha do Desterro* 74:1 (January–April 2021): 347–362.
Guerrero, Paula Barba. "Post-Apocalyptic Memory Sites: Damaged Space, Nostalgia, and Refuge in Octavia Butler's *Parable of the Sower*," *Science Fiction Studies* 48:1 (2021): 29–45.
Kaplan-Levenson, Laine. "Sci-Fi Writer Octavia Butler Offered Warnings and Hope in Her Work," *Morning Edition.* Washington, DC: NPR (24 February 2021).
Pratt, Mary Louise. *Os Olhos do Império: Relatos de Viagem e Transculturaçao.* London: Routledge, 1992.
Steinem, Gloria. "Octavia Butler's Parable of the Sower" in *Parable of the Sower & Parable of the Talents Boxed Set.* New York: Seven Stories Press, 2019.
Turner, Jenny. "Ready to Go Off," *London Review of Books* 43:4 (18 February 2021).

The Parable of the Sower (graphic novel)

Adapted by artist Damian Duffy and 2018 Eisner-winning editor John Jennings into what *Essence* called a "prophetic odyssey," the graphic version of the first Parable novel visualized a surreal havoc that drives residents of Robledo, California, to safety in the northwest (Butler, 2021, back cover). Unlike the denser development of *Kindred,* the initial novel opens on inset lines from an original verse collection, "Earthseed: The Books of the Living," composed by visionary Lauren Oya Olamina. As epigrams and dialogue usher in the conflicts that disrupt normal families and congregations within the walled community, precipitous action follows characters on bicycles, a representation of flight by determined survivors through hellish lawlessness. Wordless panels dramatize a climactic point—brother Keith's fight with the Reverend Olamina, a letdown for the close-knit household. The feud affirms that, during a cataclysm, righteous characters face a moral slump despite Baptist beliefs.

Readers applauded poignant portraits and the shortening of dreamscapes and lengthy dialogue from the original narrative. Others admired the potent arson scenes and insightful portrayals of disease among the street have-nots set against a lined notebook paper motif. Some recoiled from horizons ablaze with orange and red and welcomed a rewrite that cleared up confusions from the original character-heavy novel. Reviewer Paul Lai, on staff at Ramsey County Library in Minneapolis, felt hurtled into "a gothic monstrosity of circumstances" by mad-dash crisis (Lai, 2020). The symphonic disasters parry Lauren's deeply thought-out "construal of God and religion she is creating on her own" (*ibid.*). A choice for the Graphic Novel Club discussions in Cheyenne, Wyoming, and candidate for a sequel, *The Parable of the Talents* (graphic novel), the work earned nomination for a 2021 Hugo Award for Best Graphic Story.

In an interview with Frederick Luis Aldama, an English professor at Ohio State University, Damian Duffy promoted the Octavia Butler renaissance and an urgency to repackage her artistry. John Jennings favored comic form as "an ever-flexible storytelling medium," a visual subgenre that balances the iconic with the surreal (Aldama, 2021). Crucial to the formation of a new religion, the positioning of verses by Lauren Oya Olamina esteems her creed for inspiring a debilitated populace. Duffy revealed to Los Angeles public librarian Andrea Bochert that he researched headline events in California for immediacy. Through panels generating the story, the dominance of rust red epitomizes the murder of the ecosystem. He added hopes to transcribe in visuals two more of Butler's novels—*Wild Seed* and *The Parable of the Talents*.

Out of admiration for the author, Duffy provided a cover for *Octavia's Brood: Science Fiction Stories from Social Justice Movements*, a survey of fantasy as a source of political appraisal and change, major themes in *The Parable of the Sower* (Bradley, 2021, 3). Publisher Harry N. Abrams offered teachers a guide featuring topics on coming of age, beliefs, disabilities, predictive dystopia, and tainted earth, which forces humans to seek an extraterrestrial retreat on Alpha Centauri, the closest planets and constellations to the solar system. To the author, Mars may be stony, empty, airless, and cold, but it is the nearest the future comes to heaven.

Critiques from *Kirkus Reviews* and *USA Today's* journalist Felecia Wellington Radel acknowledged a shrewd examination of socioeconomic rot. *Publishers Weekly* reviewer Nicole Audrey Spector praised the story's qualms about gangs, water crisis, and isolation. The colors of terrain and flame caught the attention of a *Library Journal* critic for visualizing eco-disaster; an endorsement from *School Library Journal* recommended the novel's realism for teen patrons. To critic Alison Flood, a book reviewer for the London *Guardian,* the notion of exploring and colonizing distant planets constituted one of the few beneficial concepts of the twentieth century.

Sources

Agranoff, David. "Interview," https://podcasts.apple.com/gb/podcast/pfdw-20-octavia-butlers-parable-sower-interview-damian/id1524359471?i=1000495542300.

Aldama, Frederick Luis. "Anatomy of a Panel: John Jennings, Damian Duffy, and *Parable of the Sower,*" http://www.comicosity.com/anatomy-of-a-panel-john-jennings-damian-duffy-and-parable-of-the-sower/.

Bochert, Andrea. "A Talk with Comic Creator Damian Duffy," https://www.lapl.org/collections-resources/blogs/lapl/talk-comic-creator-damian-duffy (15 June 2021).

Butler, Octavia. *The Parable of the Sower* (graphic novel), adapted by Damian Duffy and John Jennings. New York: Abrams Comicarts, 2021.

Doerksen, Teri Ann. "Octavia E. Butler: Parables of Race and Difference" in *Into Darkness Peering.* Westport CT: Greenwood, 1997.

Flood, Alison. "Perseverance Martian Landing Point Names after Octavia E. Butler," the London *Guardian* (10 March 2021).

Hammie, Jessica. "Learn or Die," https://www.smilepolitely.com/arts/learn_or_die_a_review_of_parable_of_the_sower/ (23 April 2020).

Lai, Paul. "Review: *Parable of the Sower,*" http://www.multiversitycomics.com/reviews/parable-of-the-sower/ (17 February 2020).

Radel, Felicia Wellington. "Timely 'Parable' Gets a Bit Graphic," *USA Today* (9 February 2020): C2.

Spector, Nicole Audrey. "John Jennings and Damian Duffy Are Disturbing the Peace," *Publishers Weekly* 266:44 (4 November 2019): 33–34.

The Parable of the Talents

Dubbed a pessimist during composition of the Parable series in the mid–1990s, Octavia foresaw that humankind is "not really that long-term" (Due, 2019). In her musings on global lapses, she charged *Homo sapiens* with migrating back to the dark ages, a lapse envisioned in the rioting and crime of *The Parable of the Talents,* her major cautionary tale. To matters as obvious as climate change on the Pacific coast, she questioned how humanity can make itself more survivable. Reflecting the thrust of her bluesy lament of the 2030s, she reflected through the words of 63-year-old physician Taylor Franklin Bankole on the world's "repeating cycles of strength and weakness, wisdom and stupidity, empire and ashes," a veiled reference to the author's allusions to the phoenix myth (Butler, 2000, 164).

In an historic flashback to "post–Pox America," Octavia's allegory introduced a militia uniformed in black tunics with white crosses, a recreation of the Knights Hospitallers, who supported European conquest of the Holy Lands in 1113 during the First Crusade (Butler, 1998, 278). The color scheme also marked the cross-bearing Ku Klux Klan of the 1860s and Nazi SS of the late 1930s, both enforcers of carnage and societal disintegration. The author found more recent parallels of fascism in Bosnia, East Timor, Kosovo, Germany, and Rwanda. She warned, "We forget history at our peril," a rewording of the 1905 alert from Spanish philosopher George Santayana (*ibid.*). For a title, she tweaked a punitive message in the New Testament original, found in Matthew 25:14–30. Instead of hoarding talents, the wise receiver puts them to work.

Challenges from Octavia's time besiege the original thirteen characters. In the critique of Naomi Alderman, a journalist for the London *Guardian,* "People are hungry for change because the old ways haven't worked, the U.S. is plagued by deadly weather patterns that kill hundreds, and civilisation has collapsed to the point that it's 'crazy to live without a wall to protect you'" (Alderman, 2017, 2). The only succor is mutual dependence. To Carolyn Alessio, a book critic for the *Chicago Tribune,* the author explained, "Where you have a lot of people who have lost members of their families, it's not that surprising that they join some other family or other group and wind up forming a whole different entity or community" (Alessio, 1998, F3). The regrouping policy served Native American tribes during the Indian Wars, abolitionists in the 1850s and 1860s, and migrant Okies to California during the Depression. The author patterned the diaspora after pathfinder Mormons, who carried belongings in handcarts in 1856 and increased their cult membership by birth, adoption, and conversion, which return to the novel as propaganda and brainwashing tools of Christian America indoctrinators.

Lauren's Acorn

The idealistic leader, Lauren Oya Olamina, chose the name Acorn to forecast the vigor and durability of Humboldt County, an area named for German explorer Friedrich von Humboldt, the original biogeographer. In 1799, he described human-induced climate change, which analyst Avi Brisman, on staff at Eastern Kentucky University at Richmond, termed "anthropocentric myopia" (Brisman, 2019, 49). Language and trade learning emulated the slave era method of "each one teach one," a philosophy based on mutuality and reciprocity among the sixty-seven Acorn members. The protagonist's daughter, Larkin Bankole, scorns the Earthseed doctrine and accuses her mother of worshipping an unconscious, indifferent deity. According to Larkin, her mother evolved into a harmless eccentric given to spouting "grand words" (Butler, 1998, 48). The loss of her daughter to the influence of Marcos Duran sealed Lauren's fate as a martyr of Earthseed.

Social restructuring through salvaging, truck farming, schools, barter, and banking precedes a New Age political platform. Among the wealthy, in 2032, Belen "Len" Ross's mother retreats into fantasy provided by Dreamasks and a V-bubble, a virtual escapism that Octavia borrows from Ray Bradbury's techno-fantasy *Fahrenheit 451.* In the view of Roger Keil, a critic for the Toronto *Canadian Press,* the narrative promises the skeptic that "humans, nature, technology, environments, and the relationships between them are malleable" (Keil, 2020). More destructive to Lauren's doctrine than brother Marcos's sermons, demagogue Andrew Steele Jarret batters religious tolerance and drafts a reactionary crusader army to reclaim traitorous Alaskans and defiant women. On September 26, 2033, Lauren reports how maggots (armored vehicles) overrun Acorn with gas canisters, a tactic echoing the German use of 2-chloroethyl sulfide (mustard gas) during World War I. The terrorist attack shatters refugee dreams of occupying an isolated Eden.

The Fall of Acorn

Destruction is absolute. After abducting Larkin, the invaders seize phones and computers, lock Acorn residents in two school rooms, and rename the enclave Camp

Christian, a snide implication of righteous acts. The corrupt concentration camp brainwashes survivors with a stringent protocol involving parroting chapters of scripture. After imprisoning Lauren, crusaders name her Asha Vere, a Swahili/Latin combination suggesting "true life." The original Asha Vere was a fictional character promoting the subjugation of audacious women. To suppress altruism, prison lackeys teach Lauren that "human decency is a sin," yet she clings to Earthseed altruism (Butler, 1998, 225). Upon her escape, the travel motif resumes, a symbol of migrant determination.

Lauren Oya Olamina emulates pioneers as exemplars of persistence. Intent on "what we could be, what we could do," she ventures north up I-5 toward Portland, Oregon, a former Mecca for settlers in the 1840s traveling the Oregon Trail (*ibid.,* 321). She campaigns for a space program that transfers humankind to the stars, a salvation that the author described as "a destination that isn't something that we have to wait for after we die" (Butler, 2005). Lauren accepts adult dilemmas in her intent to spread "all the strong religious faith we human beings can muster to make it happen" (Butler, 1998, 165).

To supply the moon with migrants, space shuttles blast off from earth with adults in suspended animation. Cargo bays carry embryos, farm equipment, and seeds, a form of Underground Railroad into space on a par with the great Western migration. Against the aged matriarch's advice, earthlings name the rocket the *Christopher Columbus,* an ironic salute to the Catholic-sponsored New World discovery that introduced Indian genocide, African slaves, and the lust for Eldorado to enrich the Spanish monarchs Ferdinand and Isabella. In her notes on the Parable novels, Octavia regretted earth's agony, which she described as a phantom pain resulting from a failed amputation of Terran obsessions.

Sources

Alderman, Naomi. "Dystopian Dreams: How Feminist Science Fiction Predicted the Future," London *Guardian* (25 March 2017): 2.

Alessio, Carolyn. "Review: *The Parable of the Talents,*" *Chicago Tribune* (20 December 1998): F3.

Allen, Marlene D. "Octavia Butler's 'Parable' Novels and the 'Boomerang' of African American History," *Callaloo* 32:4 (Winter, 2009): 1353–1365.

Brisman, Avi. "The Fable of 'The Three Little Pigs': Climate Change and Green Cultural Criminology," *International Journal for Crime, Justice and Social Democracy* 8:1 (2019): 46–69.

Butler, Octavia. "Brave New Worlds: A Few Rules for Predicting the Future," *Essence* 31:1 (1 May 2000): 164.

_____. *The Parable of the Sower.* New York: Four Walls, Eight Windows, 1993.

_____. *The Parable of the Talents.* New York: Seven Stories Press, 1998.

_____. "Science Fiction Writer Octavia Butler on Race, Global Warming and Religion" (video), *Democracy Now* www.democracynow.org/2005/11/11/science_fiction_writer_octavia_butler_on (11 November 2005).

Doerksen, Teri Ann. "Octavia E. Butler: Parables of Race and Difference" in *Into Darkness Peering.* Westport CT: Greenwood, 1997.

Due, Tananarive. "Interview," *Essence* 50:4 (4 October 2019): 72–75.

Keil, Roger. "Global Urbanization Created the Conditions for Current Coronavirus Pandemic," (Toronto) *Canadian Press* (19 June 2020).

Parable Series Genealogy

Octavia managed a massive cast of characters for the Parable series and detailed their actions against issues that "we're brewing for ourselves right now" (Butler, 2005). Drama begins with Keith Olamina's sneaking away from home with his stepmother Cory Duran's keys and continues in the Reverend Olamina's punitive sermon on the Ten Commandments. As violence worsens in the early 2030s, no single strategy halts criminal invasions.

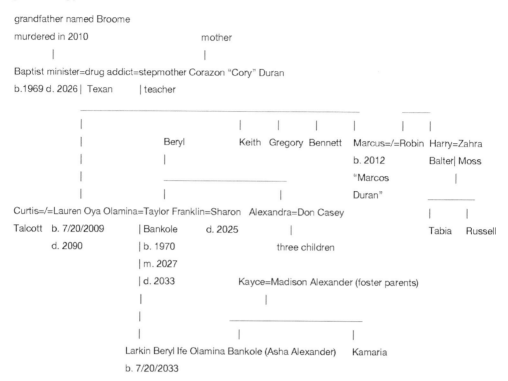

After raiders burn the Olamina corpses in their house, a matrilineage like the author's family draws strength from the examples of stepmother Cory Duran and teen evangelist Lauren Oya. In the next generation, Lauren's daughter Larkin Bankole grows up in the home of Kayce, a foster mother ironically named "watchful." Her foster father, Madison Alexander, bears the name of a founding father of America and the surname of the great Macedonian conqueror Alexander III the Great. Their names imply the guardianship of a daughter they treat like an inmate.

Sources

Butler, Octavia. *The Parable of the Sower.* New York: Four Walls, Eight Windows, 1993.
_____. *The Parable of the Talents.* New York: Seven Stories Press, 1998.
_____. "Science Fiction Writer Octavia Butler on Race, Global Warming and Religion," (video), *Democracy Now* www.democracynow.org/2005/11/11/science_fiction_writer_octavia_butler_on (11 November 2005).
Doerksen, Teri Ann. "Octavia E. Butler: Parables of Race and Difference" in *Into Darkness Peering.* Westport CT: Greenwood, 1997.

Patternmaster

The first of five volumes of dystopic tales about betrayal and male-against-male battle of wills, *Patternmaster* got its start in 1959 when the author was twelve. Her

story of psychic networking surveyed rabid antipathies between blood kin, a resetting of the biblical rivalry of twins Jacob and Esau in Genesis 27:1–41 to replace their
blind father Isaac. Simply put by critic Gregory J. Hampton, a specialist in black
studies at Howard University in Washington, D.C., the plot "is an Arthurian tale of
two brothers seeking the throne of their father," an archetype as old as King David
and his traitorous son Absalom in II Samuel 17–18 (Hampton, 2006, 245). The plot
complication relies on a psionic link or Pattern between characters that seems as
effortless as "clasping hands" (Butler, 1976). Protecting individuals from outside
incursions are "shields ... very much like digital firewalls that provide a measure of
protection from unauthorized access" (Hampton, 2006, 26).

Family unity emerges as a coalescing element of the realm and household
against mental encroachment. Ruling over the network with declining strength, the
elderly Rayal becomes the ideal king—"that core where all the people came together"
(*ibid.*, 155). The long-lived Patternmaster clings to control during a stereotypical fight
of envious brothers. The author set up a dramatic bid by the older son, Coransee, a
facile liar and phallocentric manipulator, to buy his younger brother Teray, who has
just left Redhill School, a color clue to struggles ahead. Like other coming-of-age
characters in "Bloodchild," "A Necessary Being," *Mind of My Mind, Fledgling, Adulthood Rites,* and *The Parable of the Sower,* the boy has much to learn, more by experience than academics.

Hands-Free Fighting

Grappling on a psychic plane, the characters have little need of standard weaponry. The wrangle with Housemaster Joachim over an exchange of Teray for artist
Laro involves shielding inner thoughts from eavesdropping and countering potential enslavement. The multi-level affray costs Teray his freedom because Coransee
intends to control his brother's mind and assign him to muteherding, a desultory
name for the indoctrination of a low caste. Other signs of tyranny over less important beings alert Teray that the guard Jason abuses the mutes, specifically Suliana.
Jason demotes Patternist superiority by asserting that mutes are not so stunted as
the elite class believes.

The novel eludes the oneupmanship of the opening scenes to follow Teray away
from former wife Iray, an unworthy life partner seduced by Coransee. In Octavia's
usual style, she inserted a feisty, clever female, the biracial healer Amber, a nomad
named for the Arabic for "fierce." In the backstory, society forced her into exile
because she refused to accept an arranged marriage. With Teray, she gallops south
along the California coast through clashes with quadruped enemy Clayarks and the
rival Patternists of Lady Darah, the incarnation of the Hebrew for wisdom. Ultimately, the wise overwhelm the bestial.

Claiming the Throne

The author dotted a tense narrative with moments of beauty at sea and on land
before danger encroaches. Amber flourishes at military strategies and confrontations

that conclude Chapter Six with Coransee's reclaiming of his brother. At a suspenseful moment, the Clayarks shoot Amber through the throat, a temporary silencing of a self-determined female. The ramped-up tension enacts a three-way regency struggle with unsubstantiated threats and dealmaking. Reflecting on dominant themes, Octavia revealed multiple thoughts on titles: *Bondage, The Reign of Mind, Midpattern*, and *Birthright*, a variety based on the concepts of enslavement, human rights, and hierarchy.

A liberated spirit and bisexuality distance Amber from the standard future wife, the type of women who would be useless to Teray. A touch of humor derives from her riposte to his offer of making her lead wife. She quips, "How interested would you be in becoming my lead husband?" (Allison, 1989, 67). Because he reveals an all-out dedication to Amber and their unborn child, the trio engage in wearying mind games. By ending the day's bloodbath with a union of Outsiders, Octavia foresaw a community devoted to Teray, the new Patternmaster, and reliant on the agency of Amber, a co-ruler and healer who takes female lovers.

Sources

Allison, Dorothy. "The Future of Female," *Village Voice* (19 December 1989): 67–68.
The Bloomsbury Handbook to Octavia E. Butler. New York: Bloomsbury, 2020.
Butler, Octavia. *Patternmaster.* New York: Doubleday, 1976.
Colmon, Clayton D., Jr. *On Becoming: Afrofuturism, Worldbuilding, and Embodied Imagination.* Newark: University of Delaware, 2020.
Hampton, Gregory. "In Memoriam: Octavia E. Butler (1947–2006)," *Callaloo* 29:2 (Spring, 2006): 245–248.
McCaffery, Larry, ed. *Across the Wounded Galaxies.* Urbana: University of Illinois Press, 1990.
Williams, Algie Vincent, III. *Patterns in the Parables: Black Female Agency and Octavia Butler's Construction of Black Womanhood.* Ann Arbor: University of Michigan, 2011.

Patternmaster Genealogy

Patternmaster required a tight lineage to illustrate Octavia's ventures from stereotypical sexuality and polyamorous family formation. The original Patternist, Rayal, takes to wife his sister Jansee and kills his siblings, a dynastic clash based on

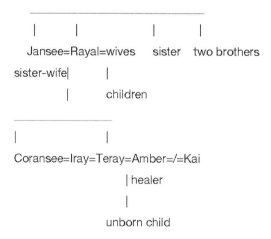

the Greco-Roman myths of Zeus and sister-wife Hera and Saturn and his sister-wife Ops. Saturn's son Jupiter extended the incestuous marriage motif by uniting with his sister Juno, the goddess of wives and childbirth.

Amber and Teray's aims for a future of realm sharing gained possibilities from their hopes for their unborn child.

Sources

Butler, Octavia. *Patternmaster.* New York: Doubleday, 1976.
Doerksen, Teri Ann. "Octavia E. Butler: Parables of Race and Difference" in *Into Darkness Peering.* Westport CT: Greenwood, 1997.

"Positive Obsession"

Submitted to *Essence* under the heading "Birth of a Writer," the May 1989 speech "Positive Obsession" presented Octavia's career credo at a conference for black women authors. She adapted the title from the first page of *The Parable of the Sower* and applied socratic method to questions of race. Her memories revealed the mother-to-daughter tutelage of kitchen conversations anticipating a satisfying future. The inset verse for Lauren Oya Olamina's "Earthseed: The Books of the Living" warned that artistic output requires persistence and adaptability lest obsession lead to dwindling enthusiasm or fanaticism. Octavia concluded, "Without positive obsession, there is nothing at all" (Butler, 2021, 1). Her 1988 jottings in a notebook declared that her works, like Lauren's, would be bestsellers and her beliefs would influence millions of readers.

While viewing writing obsessions from a personal perspective, the author admitted to "[wondering] whether as a Black person, a Black woman, you really might be inferior—not quite bright enough, not quite quick enough, not quite good enough to do the things you want to do" (Butler, 2005, 132). From a rocky early girlhood marred by her father's death and the family's poverty, she fought personal misgivings about her size, stutter, and dyslexia, obstacles to public speaking, reading, and driving a car. Saluting her intent to move beyond disabilities, the illustration of Damien Duffy and John Jennings, adapters of the graphic versions of *Kindred* and *The Parable of the Sower,* recaptured the prehistoric study of constellations, in which global stargazers saw animals and mythic characters as disparate as Ursa Major and Orion the hunter, models of individualism and agency.

In debates with self, Octavia advanced from intellectual evaluations of speculative fiction to questions about the lack of black representation among science fiction writers. A posthumous rise rewarded her canon for inspiring a new generation of blacks to persist in the creative arts despite repeated rejections. Significant female achievers among her characters—An-yanwu, Shori Matthews, Amber, Lilith Iyapo, Valerie Rye, Keira Maslin, Alanna Verrick, Dana Franklin—became classic standard bearers for change enabled by community formation, time travel, telepathy, mind reading, and telekinesis. Mystery writer Walter Mosley typified Octavia's fictional environments in *Wild Seed* as places where "African Americans and other people of color were present and significant in ways they had not been before" (Stewart, 2006,

B10). Pravin Sonune, English chair at R.B. Attal College in Gevrai, India, concluded, "If civilization is to survive, Butler's work implies, it will be the strong, black feminists such as those who dominate her fiction who will assure society's salvation" (Sonune, 2021, 64).

Specifically, Octavia valued the potential of science fiction to spawn progressive sociopolitical transformation. Her canon revealed a perseverance that brought her monetary success and fame. By generalizing, she puzzled over the purpose of most genres: "What good is any form of literature to Black people? … to alternative ways of thinking and doing?" (Butler, 2005, 134–135). Her speech implied that speculative fiction, a genre built on open-ended ideas, can inspire debate on black culture and Afrofuturist feminism, a philosophy she pioneered. Acorn, the brainchild of Lauren Oya Olamina, the poet-guide in the Parable series, profited from her belief that a positive obsession is "sweet and powerful." Single-minded pursuits make sense of events and blunt pain, fear, and rage while engaging disciples in projects valuable to community wellbeing (Butler, 1998, 47).

Sources

Butler, Octavia. "*I shall be a bestselling writer…,*" www.huntington.org/sites/default/files/styles/photo_gallery/public/photo-gallery/octavia-butler_4_0.jpg?itok=pqacPQbT, 1988.
_____. *The Parable of the Sower* (graphic novel), adapted by Damian Duffy and John Jennings. New York: Abrams Comicarts, 2021.
_____. *The Parable of the Talents.* New York: Seven Stories Press, 1998.
_____. "Positive Obsession" in *Bloodchild and Other Stories.* New York: Seven Stories Press, 2005, 123–136.
Sonune, Pravin. "Feminism, Women, and Science Fiction of Octavia Butler," *Epitome Journals* 7:4 (April 2021): 54–67.
Stewart, Jocelyn Y. "Obituary," *Los Angeles Times* (28 February 2006): B10.
Vakoch, Douglas A. *Dystopias and Utopias on Earth and Beyond.* New York: Routledge, 2021.

Race

Reared during racial segregation, Octavia wrote fiction, essays, and speeches that challenged mid-twentieth-century thinking on exclusion-based on skin color. In retrospect, in the words of English professor Frann Michel at Willamette University in Salem, Oregon, the author recalled clues to bias in girlhood readings when "a lot of people wrote about going to another world and finding either little green men or little brown men, and they were always less in some way" (Michel, 2013, 103). The author began her career by refutating faulty logic about human value: "Science fiction, extrasensory perception, and black people are judged by the world elements they produce" (Williams, 1986, 70). She examined a future crisis with the assumption that blacks have the fortitude to "survive the present and participate in shaping the future," an affirmation of worth (*ibid.,* 72).

Octavia aroused sympathies for pariahs. According to Dorothy Allison's essay in *Village Voice,* the author applied the term nigger in "matter-of-fact handling of racism in the everyday lives of her characters … lesser people who are treated with contempt, bred like animals (or slaves)," the fate of Maryland bondswomen Sarah and mute daughter Carrie in *Kindred* (Allison, 1989, 67). In a survey of law, Achille Mbembe, a Cameroonian racial theorist, placed the safety of nonwhites like the

Weylin laborers on a single issue, biopolitics based solely on color, which he judged "almost insurmountable," the destiny of runaway slave Isaac Jackson (Mbembe, 2017, 22, 82). Much of Octavia's subjectivity revealed ways of treasuring bold, savvy, life-loving nonwhiteness, a theme in "Amnesty" in the employment of Piedad Ruiz, "a small, brown woman" bearing a name meaning "dutiful renowned ruler" (Butler, 2005, 158). The author confided to Janice Bogstad, an interviewer for *Janus,* that she intended to make readers "comfortable with characters who are not all male, who are not all white, and who just don't fit" (Bogstad, 1978–1979, 30). The statement echoed biographical comments about her own past as a too-tall, black, shy dyslexic.

THE WORST OF THE PAST

The author incorporated the nadir of black history—enslavement as a motivation for Triangular Trade over the Atlantic from the sixteenth to the nineteenth centuries, a tragic era that elitist vampire Katherine Dahlman in *Fledgling* recalls from her advanced age. The alliance of European piety with colonial commercialism set nonwhites apart from greedy, money-mad whites, who cited scripture to exonerate a cruel labor system. Set in 1690 on Africa's west coast in *Wild Seed,* glimpses of slave managers scorn the overseeing and branding that leaves a "blackened, crooked gouge" on chests (Butler, 1980, 22). On the Bight of Benin, agent Bernard Daly, named for the German "hardy bear," warns the shapeshifter Doro that his appearance at the slave depot in the body of a black man leaves him open to gunmen who disapprove of his race and his association with black companions, the healer An-yanwu and her grandson Okoye.

The face-off at the departure point places abductor and abductee within range of each other. Okoye rewords the racist slurs by calling Daly a "white animal" (*ibid.,* 23). Daly's retort carries the seventeenth-century European prejudice that Africans are "Heathen savages…. They're like animals. They're all cannibals," an ethnic smear worsened by the taboo against consuming human flesh (*ibid.*). Doro's snide retort about learning "symbolic cannibalism" from missionaries refers to transubstantiation during Holy Communion, an iconic recreation of Christ's flesh and blood in bread and wine (*ibid.*). Agent John Woodley's ironic malediction—"Godless animals"—repeats the European justification of enslaving non-believers to convert them to Christian ideals.

BOUNDARIES

Because the author focused on othering, she constructed real and imaginary boundaries between "our kind" and people of different skin color, gender, language, culture, and ethnicity. In 1961, the sci-fi author added species, an element of outer space abduction fiction that set new standards for injustice. Teri Ann Doerksen, an English specialist in speculative fiction at Manchester University, found reasons to chastise Time Warner Popular Library for representing Octavia's black character Lilith Iyapo on the cover of *Dawn* as a Caucasian. The extraterrestrial Nikanj stirs her revulsion at a mutant's "alienness, his difference, his literal unearthliness," which divided Oankali genders into male, female, and flexible (Butler, 2000, 13). For Doro's blond son Isaac in *Wild Seed*, the pilot village of Wheatley, New York, profits by the absence of artificial castes in 1690, when European settlers of the New World considered themselves superior to blacks and Indians. Isaac, being "white and black and Indian," feels no racial burden among Doro's multiracial seed people, whom he chooses to "mix and stir" to create a master race (Butler, 1980, 246–247).

Mentioning the Great Negro Plot of March 18, 1741, the narrative indicated greater white vs. black prejudice in New York City, where thirty African arsonists and robbers went to the gallows or burned at the stake. On the basis of questionable trials, another eighty entered exile in the Caribbean. For the fictional An-yanwu, the oracular Nigerian healer, her drunken mate Thomas agrees with demoting Africans to useful serfs. He shouts, "You're a black bitch brought here for breeding and nothing more" (*ibid.*, 384). After forming an agrarian colony in Louisiana in 1840, she rids her household of such color bias. Because of antebellum prejudice, her five white residents pretend to be octoroons, a less subordinate caste than full-blood blacks.

From east to west, Euro-American superiority promoted antagonism against First Peoples, many of them interbred with Hispanics, blacks, and whites. During writer Dana Franklin's fictional time travels to a Maryland plantation in *Kindred*, history's urgency impinges on her thoughts. Mention of the frontier causes her to compare Native American crises with those of African slaves: "West…. That's where they're doing it to the Indians instead of the blacks!" (Butler, 1979, 97). The comment vilified early American imperialism, which victimized any resident not suited to expansionism. Under the doctrine of Manifest Destiny, white colonists carried God's blessing to profit exclusively on North America resources.

Defining Citizenry

In the purview of analyst Jayna Brown, author of *Black Utopias,* "Dominant social formations have denied African diasporas the rights and freedoms associated with being defined as human" (Brown, 2021, 7). Octavia's speculative fiction offered an out. The convoluted story of the Nubian immortal Doro in *Mind of My Mind* features a master manipulator of eugenics who casually changes forms and identities with felons, youths, whites, and blacks of either gender. The author deftly limited overt racism, allowing an occasional confrontation to develop. When Jan Sholto encounters Rachel "Rae" Davidson and Mary, the chief mind reader, Jan's thoughts give away the hidden aversion: "She had taken one look at Rachel and me and thought, Oh, God, *niggers*!" (Butler, 1977, 69). In the essay "The Monophobic Response," a reissue of the October 1995 speech "Journeys," Octavia mocked white ostracism of blacks: "No wonder we're so good at creating aliens" (Butler, 2000, 415).

In the 1978 novel *Survivor,* color variances range across human shades to alien blue, a mark of superiority. To express the urge for transformation, analyst Christopher Castiglia, an English professor at Pennsylvania State University, characterized the standard captive as "cunning, physically fit … and willing to revise their racial, gender, and national identifications" (Castiglia, 1996, 25). A rebel, Alanna Verrick, a foundling residing with white missionaries Jules and Neila Verrick, resists ethnic categories after she overhears Beatrice Stamp's bigoted proposal that she return to her "own kind" (Butler, 1978, 28). The aspersion states an impossibility for the only Afro-Asian.

Temporarily rid of earth's colonial and patriarchal bonds, Alanna realizes the reciprocity of entrenched racism when Diut, her mate, stereotypes missionaries. She conceals disapproval that "He could be as condescending, as patronizing, towards the Missionaries as most Missionaries were toward [his race]" (Butler, 1978, 100). He exonerates himself for expressing color preference from boyhood with a faulty statement of nature vs. self-identity: "Respect for the blue was inborn with us" (*ibid.*, 103). The role of furthering a proud race caused Swedish critic Maria Holmgren Troy, an English professor at Karlstad University, to view *Survivor* as a model of patriarchal "control of women for the reproduction of race purity" (Troy, 2010, 1122–1123). Because of her racial blend, Alanna is not eligible to be tribe matriarch.

Accepting Otherness

Because of Octavia's uniqueness as a black, female sci-fi writer, she led a lonely existence. Her keen interest in news, as explained by Ed Park, writer for *Harper's Magazine,* kept her "intimately attuned to this country's racial fault lines" that included mixed neighborhoods, miscegenation, integrated schools, and biracial adoption (Park, 2021, 94). Her review of novelist Alice Walker's *In Search of Our Mother's Gardens* for the October 17, 1983, issue of the *Washington Post,* broached the subject of dark-skinned mothers' envy of their light-skinned children, who encountered less bias than their parents. In widower Blake Jason Maslin's memories of his steely-voiced Nigerian wife Jorah in *Clay's Ark,* she appears "smooth and dark as bittersweet chocolate, soft and gentle," a beauty and goodness reflected in her twin daughters Keira and Rane (Butler, 1984, 57). To contrast the contentment of the biracial Maslin family, the novel concludes on manic murder of "anyone who seems a little odd…. Asians, blacks, and browns" (*ibid.*, 73). In the aftermath of global chaos and the impending birth of Keira "Kelly" Maslin's multiracial mutant child, the narrative anticipates a new species after whites become obsolete.

The writer became adept at transposing color opposites. Drawing on the misrepresentation of African slaves by whites, in *Patternmaster* in 1976, she reset racial history with Patternists and quadruped Clayarks. The bitter opponents view "each other across a gulf of disease and physical difference and comfortably told themselves the same lie about each other"—that their enemies are not human (Butler, 1976, 25). In 2025, residents of Robledo, California, in the Parable series prolong the nation's history of bias for a nonsense reason: "People are expected to fear and hate everyone but their own kind," a description of the "Paints" whom Octavia modeled after skinheads, neo–Nazis, and white nationalists (Butler, 1993, 36).

Amid a stream of ragged poor and homeless, *The Parable of the Sower* dramatizes the additional peril of color bias. During social disintegration about Los Angeles, Octavia champions leader Lauren Oya Olamina's realization that a mixed bag of followers "are all I have left" (Butler, 1993, 178). Lauren's journal records examples of an American apartheid: At seaside Olivar, the conglomerate Kagimoto, Stamm,

Frampton (KSF) promotes commerce in water. The firm promises employment, but rejects black and Hispanic applicants. At the discovery of interracial sex between Craig Dunn and Siti Moss, Lauren Oya Olamina observes rising racial tensions: "I thought someone was going to get killed. Crazy" (Butler, 1993, 87). Zahra Moss warns Lauren that traveling north with Harry Balter, a white man, can stir racists to homicidal mania. Lauren admits the growth of social volatility: "Mixed couples catch hell" (*ibid.*, 203).

In volume two, *The Parable of the Talents,* Lauren accepts the challenge of a compound of "you name it: Black, White, Latino, Asian, and any mixture at all" (Butler, 1998, 45). To her delight, newborn citizens of Acorn accept blended backgrounds as normal, a fictional representation of assumptions that the youngest Americans would outgrow mid-twentieth-century bigotry. The rise of a Nazi style Christian America army targets blacks via false charges that they promote violent crime and vagrancy. Under the guise of punishing the heathen, the minions of U.S. President Andrew Steele Jarret return to antique religious justification of bondage by capitalizing on nonwhites through indentured servitude or donation of organs. Octavia placed her last hopes for parity on the Internet and Lauren's electronic issuance of her Earthseed scripture for all to consider. Lacking visible ties to color, her poetry arouses the nation to solidarity.

See also "The Monophobic Response," "Why Is Science Fiction So White?"

Sources

Allison, Dorothy. "The Future of Female," *Village Voice* (19 December 1989): 67–68.

Bogstad, Janice. "Interview," 14:4 *Janus* (Winter, 1978–1979): 28–32.

Brown, Jayna. *Black Utopias: Speculative Life and the Music of Other Worlds.* Durham, NC: Duke University Press, 2021.

Butler, Octavia. "Amnesty" in *Bloodchild and Other Stories.* New York: Seven Stories Press, 2005.

_____. *Clay's Ark.* New York: St. Martin's Press, 1984.

_____. *Dawn* in *Lilith's Brood.* New York: Warner, 2000, 2–248.

_____. *Kindred.* New York: Doubleday, 1979.

_____. *Mind of My Mind.* New York: Doubleday, 1977.

_____. "The Monophobic Response," *Dark Matter: A Century of Speculative Fiction from the African Diaspora.* New York: Aspect/Warner Books, 2000, 415–416.

_____. *The Parable of the Sower.* New York: Four Walls, Eight Windows, 1993.

_____. *The Parable of the Talents.* New York: Seven Stories Press, 1998.

_____. *Patternmaster.* New York: Doubleday, 1976.

_____. "Positive Obsession" in, *Bloodchild and Other Stories.* New York: Seven Stories Press, 2005.

_____. *Survivor.* New York: Doubleday, 1978.

_____. "Why Is Science Fiction So White," *Garage* 15 (4 September 2018).

_____. *Wild Seed.* New York: Doubleday, 1980.

Castiglia, Christopher. *Bound and Determined: Captivity, Culture-Crossing, and White Womanhood from Mary Rowlandson to Patty Hearst.* Chicago: University of Chicago Press, 1996.

Doerksen, Teri Ann. "Octavia E. Butler: Parables of Race and Difference" in *Into Darkness Peering.* Westport, CT: Greenwood, 1997, 21–34.

Magadanz, Stacy. "The Captivity Narrative in Octavia E. Butler's *Adulthood Rites,*" *Extrapolation* 53:1 (2012): 47–59.

Mbembe, Achille. *Critique of Black Reason.* Durham, NC: Duke University Press, 2017.

Michel, Frann. *The Female Face of Shame.* Indianapolis: Indiana University Press, 2013.

Park, Ed. "Parable of the Butler," *Harper's Magazine* 342:2049 (February 2021): 93–97.

Stewart, Jocelyn Y. "Obituary," *Los Angeles Times* (28 February 2006): B10.

Troy, Maria Holmgren. "Negotiating Genre and Captivity: Octavia Butler's *Survivor,*" *Callaloo* 33:4 (Fall, 2010): 1116–1131.

Williams, Sherley Anne. "On Octavia E. Butler," *Ms.* 14:9 (March 1986): 70–73.

Reproduction

Octavia's ingenuity at propagating living beings attests to her skill at one of the most exploited aspects of science fiction. She opened the 1987 novel *Dawn* with the chapter "Womb," an introit to an imprisoned female and strong authorial opposition to rape and the coopting of women's reproductive rights. By broadening the fears of pregnant women to include conception of an "other-than-human" being, the narrative enhanced views on abortion and the right of females to end chancy conceptions (Butler, 2000, 163). Throughout the Xenogenesis trilogy, the questionable rejection of the incest taboo, pedophilia, and attraction to the same-sex parent upends human respect for reproductive heritage, a revered biological linkage that Pakistani writer Ayesha Kiran, a research scholar of Communication and Media Studies at Public Sector University in Lahore, calls the "web of kinship" (Kiran, 2021, 12). In its place, the nomadic aliens propose conception by two humans, two gendered Oankali, and one neuter ooloi, an idealistic innovation on sexual norms and longevity that disgusts humans.

Earthling Paul Titus warns Lilith Iyapo that long periods of suspended animation gave the alien Oankali opportunities to clone, incubate fetuses in animal wombs, or harvest reproductive cells without human consent, thus producing seventy offspring from Paul's semen. Lilith's feisty response admits she can't fight alien exploitation "but we don't have to help them" by sharing sex, the Oankali term for polyamorous coupling (*ibid.*, 95). In an erotic trio, she joins the ooloi Nikanj and her Chinese-Canadian mate Joseph "Joe" Li-Chin Shing for a delightfully intense union "ablaze in sensation, lost on one another" by sharing each other's orgasm (*ibid.*, 162). Those who fall in love with an ooloi incur constant desire that causes pain and eventual death, a yearning similar to symbionts for vampires in *Fledgling*.

In the second volume, *Adulthood Rites,* Octavia particularizes conception and birth among Oankali. In an alien form of coitus that Augustino "Tino" Leal accepts as a "splash of icy-sweet pleasure," Nikanj describes his assignment as "mixing" Lilith's children like alchemists in medieval laboratories (*ibid.*, 302). Octavia pictured the "sexually precocious" Nikanj and his Lego building blocks "constructed gene by gene, chromosome by chromosome ... the work of our ooloi parent" (*ibid.*, 551, 552). Such daring heroines as Lilith Iyapo, in the purview of *Village Voice* author Dorothy Allison, "survive to mother the next generation—literally to make the next world" (Allison, 1989, 67).

Mutant Birthing

At the delivery of Ahajas' infant, the text describes a peremptory opening in the left side and the emergence of head tentacles, evidence of mutation. The author repeated the theories of English anthropologist Ashley Montagu: "The child knew now that it was coming into an accepting, welcoming place" (Butler, 2000, 333). She contrasted tolerant Oankali with the humans of Phoenix village, who procure biracial girls and plot to shear off their tentacles and extra fingers to make them resemble human females. She summarizes a racist impasse: "Their kind is all they've ever known or been and now there won't be any more" (Butler, 2000, 377).

A view of Nigerian Ibo/Igbo in 1690 in *Wild Seed* pictures traditional West African birthing to oracle and healer An-yanwu, mother of forty-seven children. She states that none arrived under the taboos on twins, breech birth, deformity, or neonatal teething, all causes for abandonment. They survive under the aegis of a supernatural mother whose power fosters independence rather than enslavement by a husband. The long-lived Nubian Doro, An-yanwu's new mate, observes that infanticide is wasteful of human potential. Refuting his logic, critics Rebecca J. Holden, an English teacher at the University of Maryland, and Nisi Shawl, a journalist for *Ms.* Magazine and the *Seattle Times,* contend that "such matings produce or lead to … the inevitable crossing and blurring of boundaries" (Holden & Shawl, 2013, 1). Obscure origins "often bring with them physical and emotional pain," even if they guarantee species longevity (*ibid.*).

The author described anticipation of unnatural sex lives in *Clay's Ark* and of offspring born in space or on the moon. In a discussion of reproduction at the July 12–14, 2002, Readercon in Burlington, Massachusetts, she surprised male panelists with a blunt question: "How much of this speculation about a post-human future has to do with men's desire to control reproduction?" (Devney, 2002, 14). One example, astronaut Asa Elias "Eli" Doyle, leaves frozen sperm on earth and delights that negative speculation proves spurious. He is glad his pre-flight contraceptive implant before the starship *Clay's Ark* took him to Proxi Two has worn off, refuting gossip about astronauts "playing Adams and Eves on some alien world" (Butler, 1984, 55).

The Artificial Family

Ironically, Octavia saves alternatives for earth rather than Proxima Centauri, a constellation named for the Greek man-headed horse. The fear of contamination triggers a suspenseful escape of father Blake Jason Maslin and daughters Keira and Rane from diseased Californian raiders. Because he has fought private battles apart from the girls, Blake lacks knowledge of Jacob, the catlike son of Meda Boyd and Eli. To deepen mystery, the dialogue between Blake and daughters ends, leaving the girls exchanging meaningful glances. A similar exchange in *Fledgling* between vampires Shori Matthews and her father, Iosip Petrescu, places her in a dilemma: whether to remain with lover Wright Hamlin or settle near Iosip's people. Among the Ina, she learns her people's history and the difficulty producing viable children. Their adoption methods resemble those of Native Americans: "Everyone took in orphans and tried to weave new families from remnants of the old" (Butler, 2005, 195).

According to critic Jayna Brown, a media specialist at the Pratt Institute in Brooklyn, New York, in *The Parable of the Talents*, the author remained skeptical of artificial wombs, computerized eggs, clones, and the "technological advances … designed to serve only privileged first worlders" (Brown, 2021, 97). Under President Andrew Steele Jarret, Christian fanatics accept parentage of orphans and children seized from "wicked" mothers and rename adoptees to erase their birth homes. Characters respect their limitations, even those doomed from innate genetic faults, the burdens of Lynn Mortimer and Alan Chi, lovers in "The Evening and the Morning and the Night." Alan realizes that a single sterilized generation could rid society of DGD, an inborn compulsion toward suicidal cannibalism. He explains to Lynn the power of libido: "People are still animals when it comes to breeding. Still following mindless urges, like dogs and cats," a description of Valerie Rye's impromptu backseat romance with Obsidian in "Speech Sounds" (Butler, 2005, 42).

The author's October 1995 speech to the PEN/Faulkner Awards ceremony at Quill & Brush, Rockville, Maryland, "Journeys," retitled "The Monophobic Response" in 2000, anticipated the question of hybrid reproduction. The chief hindrance, human revulsion by interspecies sex, becomes an issue for the Ina in *Fledgling*. Equating distaste with racism in missionaries, the novel *Survivor* thrives on melodrama as Jules and Neila Verrick turn their backs on their foster daughter Alanna, who carries a human-Tehkohn fetus. In simplifying her relationship with Diut, she explains her adaptation to a furry-maned hominid: "We were at least equally strange-looking to each other," a witty put-down to intolerance (Butler, 1978, 163).

THE NEW SPECIES

Bizarre unions enable Octavia to apply imagination to the possibilities of human mating with aliens. In the words of analyst Karen Joy Fowler, a *New York Times* bestselling writer, her masterly story "Bloodchild" creates a human–Tlic clan "intertwined in an intimate sexual history" that she describes as "consensual, loving" (Fowler, 2006). For the humanoids in "Amnesty," translator Noah Cannon regrets the caging of pregnant women and the loss of newborns through lab experiments, stillbirths, and miscarriages, two of them Noah's. The one hundred infants who survive "live outside in secret, and some will never leave the bubbles," a peril for mutants (Butler, 2005, 165). The isolation of variant lifestyles recurs in *Fledgling* with the seclusion of vampires and their symbionts from prying eyes.

Almost as an afterthought, Noah claims that the best of the experimental babies become excellent translators and a possible future salvation of the planet, Octavia's prime motivation for speculative fiction. The scandalous births leave others susceptible to abductors, incarcerators, torturers, and rapists. For maximum protection, parents sequester the hybrid infants underground. For her liberal attitude, alien recruit James Adio accuses her of betrayal with the biblical allusion of Judas's receipt of "thirty pieces of silver" in Matthew 26:15 for betraying Christ (*ibid.*, 168). To the translator, the metamorphosis of procreative acts to rescue humankind demand no forgiveness.

See also Couples; Motherhood; Parenting.

Sources

Allison, Dorothy. "The Future of Female," *Village Voice* (19 December 1989): 67–68.

Brown, Jayna. *Black Utopias: Speculative Life and the Music of Other Worlds*. Durham, NC: Duke University Press, 2021.

Butler, Octavia. *Adulthood Rites* in Lilith's Brood. New York: Warner, 2000, 249–517.

_____. "Amnesty" in *Bloodchild and Other Stories*. New York: Seven Stories Press, 2005, 147–186.

_____. *Clay's Ark*. New York: St. Martin's Press, 1984.

_____. *Dawn* in Lilith's Brood. New York: Warner, 2000, 2–248.

_____. "The Evening and the Morning and the Night" in *Bloodchild and Other Stories*. New York: Seven Stories Press, 2005, 33–70.

_____. *Fledgling*. New York: Seven Stories Press, 2005.

_____. *Imago* in *Lilith's Brood*. New York: Warner, 2000, 518–746.

_____. *Survivor*. New York: Doubleday, 1978.

_____. *Wild Seed*. New York: Doubleday, 1980.

Devney, Bob. "Orbita Dicta," *The Devniad Book 82B:* www.devniad.com (July 2002).

Fowler, Karen Joy. "Remembering Octavia Butler," *Salon* www.salon.com/2006/03/17/butler_3/ (17 March 2006).

Holden, Rebecca J., and Nisi Shawl, eds. *Strange Matings: Science Fiction, Feminism, African American Voices, and Octavia E. Butler*. Seattle, WA: Aqueduct, 2013.

Kiran, Ayesha. "Human Identity and Technophobic Posthumanism in Octavia Butler's *Dawn*," *Indiana Journal of Arts & Literature* 2:8 (2021): 1–15.

Sarah's Genealogy

The source of Octavia's reprise of black history retreats to the House of Slaves on Africa's Gorée Island, Senegal, and the hapless captives forced through a door of no return. Sarah, the cook and housekeeper of the Weylin family outside Easton, Maryland, represents a repository of racial experience and liberation through dietetic service to the entire household. From plantation savvy, she admits to being "the frightened powerless woman who had already lost all she could stand to lose," a slave mentality advanced by brutal discipline (Butler, 1979, 145). Sarah's biracial family illustrates the close connection of whites and their black minions/relatives, including Carrie, the mute domestic and seamstress. Repulsed by literature, she finds wholeness in the research of time traveler Dana Franklin, who completes her project in the future.

The cook's name points to the biblical Sarai, the sister-wife of Abram, a scion of Noah, and daughter-in-law of Terah. She journeyed west with her husband around 2150 BCE from the port of Ur at the fertile crescent. They settled at Hebron west of the Dead Sea in Canaan, where he served the Israelites as prophet and patriarch. An Old Testament matriarch renamed Sarah (princess), she won hearts with her piety and welcome, the hallmark of the Weylin plantation kitchen. From her descended grandson Jacob, sire of Israel's twelve tribes, a sign of longevity awaiting the Weylin's slaves and the rest of American history.

To recoup Africa's regal queens, Octavia endowed the plantation cook with *sankofa*, the Akan-Twi term for "retrieval of the best from the past." She selected the name Sarah to designate the black matriarch and foremother of plantation chattel,

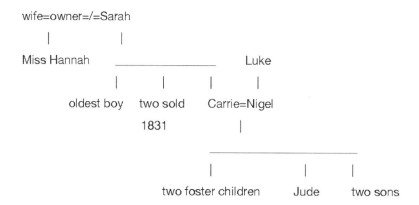

a complicated female figure of cunning and endurance after "Marse Tom took my children all but Carrie" (*ibid.,* 14). The writer reprised the *ad hoc* style of family formation in the Parable series, in which unrelated former slaves and captives unite in workable clans. Sarah's cookhouse, a standard site of regeneration and womanly influence in feminist literature, becomes a sanctuary for bondsmen and for Dana Franklin, great great granddaughter of Rufus Weylin from the twentieth century.

Esteemed as family nourisher, caregiver, authority, and manager of domestic labor, Sarah dictates a survival manual for black women. Through intergenerational memory, she coaches Dana on the use of period kitchen tools to make cherished recipes. She treasures Carrie, a mute mother of sons sold after the master's death. Through mother and daughter, Octavia generated a line of trust that saved Dana from the jealousy and spite of disapproving field hands. The hierarchy of the omnipresent mother figure survived in post–Civil War family structure, notably in the author's mother and grandmother, who replaced Octavia's deceased father as heads of household.

Sources

Butler, Octavia. *Kindred.* New York: Doubleday, 1979.
Hobson, Janell. *When God Lost Her Tongue.* London: Routledge, 2022.
Matthews, Aisha. "Give Me Liberty or Give Me (Double) Consciousness," *Third Stone* 2:1 (2021): 1–21.
O'Neill, Caitlin. "Towards an Afrofuturist Feminist Manifesto" in *Critical Black Futures.* Singapore: Palgrave Macmillan, 2021, 61–92.
Yerman, Forrest Gray. "Finding the Superhero in Damian Duffy's and John Jennings Graphic Novel Adaptation of Octavia Butler's *Kindred*" in *The Bloomsbury Handbook to Octavia E. Butler.* London: Bloomsbury, 2020, 259–273.

Scripture

Much of Octavia's plotting and character building relied on written authority from "the Bible, the Talmud, the Koran, or some other religious book that helps ... deal with the frightening changes" (Butler 1993, 221). She revered biblical myths of the persecuted Job, Old Testament patriarchs Abraham and Noah, and the eighth-century BCE prophet Isaiah and seer Malachi from the fifth century. Her texts revered female archetypes, such as Naomi (pleasant), the mother-in-law in "The Evening and the Morning and the Night," Alanna Verrick's Old Testament beliefs in *Survivor,* and the traits of mediator Lilith Iyapo, the Madonna/Moses in the trilogy *Lilith's Brood.* From Genesis I, the Parable books extolled cooperative garden work as an ecofeminist reclamation of humans from diaspora back to the soil.

The second eco-critical volume, *Adulthood Rites,* particularizes relics of earth after nuclear war and a lamentation for the apocalypse—a museum collection of Christ images "to remind them of what we were" (Butler, 2000, 389). For specifics of disastrous earth stewardship, the author combined metaphors by picturing the biracial child Akin sickened from the taste of a plastic cinema of the Sermon on the Mount from Matthew 5–7. He identifies the material as poison, Octavia's charge against her era's spiritual and physical defilement of the planet with long-lived man-made detritus. Still learning human shortcomings, Akin marvels at "more poison packed tight together in one place than I've ever known" (*ibid.*, 388).

The grand finale of *Adulthood Rites* resembles a palimpsest formed from the Sodom and Gomorrah episodes in Genesis 19:28, Deuteronomy 29:23, Jeremiah 49:18, Amos 4:11, Luke 17:29, II Peter 2:6, and Jude 1:7 and the phoenix myth, a pervasive combustion and replenishment allegory recorded by Greek historian Herodotus, encyclopedist Pliny the Elder, and Roman poet Ovid. Like the disobedient wife of Lot in Genesis 19:26, resisters to change who turn back toward Phoenix village disappear. Novelist James Baldwin's 1963 title *The Fire Next Time* reset a slave-era freedom song, "Mary, Don't You Weep," as a source of a divine prophecy of earth's second cataclysm. Baldwin incorporated arson in "the Negro's past, of rope, fire, torture, castration, infanticide, rape, death and humiliation" as outcomes of "rage, hatred, and murder, hatred for white men" (Baldwin, 1963, 105). Unlike Noah and the flood in Genesis 6:17, which the Reverend Olamina interprets in *The Parable of the Sower,* the next destruction of human evil, as stated in Hebrews 12:29, would reveal god's recompense as a "consuming fire," a terrorist ploy by racial purists in *Fledgling.*

Octavia characterized flame as an extension of gun violence. Total annihilation by arsonists Neci and Macy "would destroy Human chances at a new world because they were drunk and out of their minds" (*ibid.*, 509). The stagy passage depicts Akin languishing in bed and anticipating death as fire consumes the building. For accuracy, his rescue by Gabriel creates literal truth about the archangel of Jewish, Christian, and Islamic lore from a translation of his Hebrew name, "God is my strength." At a theatrical encounter, Gabe says "Jesus Christ!" at the approach of agitator Gilbert Senn, a pun on "sin." Dialogue enhances an armed showdown with Akin's declaration, "Humanity will live or die by what you do now" (*ibid.*, 514). Appropriately, "witnesses for their people" flee the burning village by following the river to the east, toward the rising sun, a veiled reference to the Second Coming (*ibid.*, 517).

SCRIPTURAL DICTION

To Octavia, rearing in biblical history and wisdom became a fulcrum to speculative fiction. The Nigerian seer An-yanwu in *Wild Seed* summarizes Hebrew creation in terms of race: "Whites believe their god made the first people of clay" (Butler, 1980, 299). For Udenkwo, a childless slave, the undying Nubian Doro states, "My people will be your people," a menacing inversion of the widow Ruth's vow to her mother-in-law Naomi in Ruth 1:16–17 (*ibid.*, 136). A later citation from Romans 12:16 reminded listeners to be humble, preceding Deuteronomy 23:15, a caution about returning refugee slaves to their masters. To authenticate the fantasy setting in "The Book of Martha," protagonist Martha Bes displays knowledge of Jonah, Noah, and Job, whose example of strength returns in *Wild Seed.* The almighty receives Martha's request for green grass, which the author authenticated with the biblical okay "And it was so" (Butler, 2005, 195). The scriptural tone heightened the humor of a one-to-one verbal debate between deity and mortal.

Titles of the author's published works incorporated the terms ark, pruning hook, and parable, as well as bits of scripture, e.g., "The Evening and the Morning," God's rounding out of day one of creation with a balance of light and dark. She completed the title with "and the Night," a metaphor for the dark future for humankind beset by an epidemic (Butler, 2005, 33). In *Kindred*, the existential verse from Job 14:1–2 reminds survivors of their mortality. For commercial impact, "Servants, be obedient to them that are your masters" (Ephesians 6:5) proved handy for slave owners rationalizing human trafficking. Even more scriptural, her uncompleted canon added to the list amen, Eden, Jesus, God, Potiphar's wife, Sodom and Gomorrah, Beatrice, heavens, Jericho, believers, Ruth, Canaan, Elisha, shepherds, pottage, Good Samaritan, Thomas, Stephen, Judas, Eli, Jesse, Rachel, Hagar, Mary Magdalene, Miriam, Leah, Cain/Kane, Jezebel, two Josephs, and two Isaacs, Doro's son in *Wild Seed* and the son of Abraham and Sarah who recurs in *Kindred*.

The author expressed to interviewer Sandra Y. Govan, an English professor at the University of North Carolina at Charlotte, an admiration for the 1611 and 1901 editions of the bible: "I read the King James for the beauty of it, and I read … the American Standard Version for understanding" (Govan, 2005–2006, 28). Her appreciation of religion esteemed an institution that dragged self-interested humans from their destructive urges. She recalled James Adio's charge of "thirty pieces of silver" in "Amnesty" against translator Noah Cannon, implying betrayal of her species. Ramping up the theatrics, James bears a Yoruban surname from Nigeria meaning "righteous." His vile retort implies that exterminating hybrid babies is essential to blood purity, a species impossibility.

STORYTELLING

With biblical allegory, Octavia filled *Clay's Ark* with bible names—Eli, Gabriel, two Jacobs, Joseph, Asa, Adam, Eve, Stephen—and remarked on a late twentieth-century resurgence of religious fanaticism laden with political overtones. The black astronaut Asa Elias "Eli" Doyle outpaces the average Californian in scriptural knowledge, a fact that impresses employer Gabriel Boyd. At Gabriel's burial, Eli chooses verses from Job and Lamentations, dismal chapters that deepen sorrow. A retrospect to 1990s films mentions the Second Coming of Christ and Sodom and Gomorrah, wicked cities that God mysteriously obliterated for their sins. The mass annihilation hinted at the car gangs and ranch holdouts who attempted to free themselves of an interstellar virus.

In contemplating change, Octavia cited a patchwork of scripture as an outgrowth of social collapse. She quoted John 1 and Acts 2 as liturgy to accompany Lauren's ritual emersion baptism and borrowed from Judeo-Christianity, Yoruba orishas, Buddhism, Hinduism, Taoism, and Greek myth to stitch together a less rigid doctrine. At key moments, Lauren retrieves Nehemiah 4:14 as a refutation of "Thou shalt not kill" and recites the classic of parallelism, "To everything there is a season" (Ecclesiastes 3:1–8). The author also extracted drama from crucial scenes, as with Cory Olamina's citation of Revelation 18:2 bewailing Babylon's fall in 689 BCE to Assyria and again to Persia in 539 BCE. As Lauren journeys from Los Angeles up the stream of poor migrants along U.S. 101 toward Oregon, she adopts Christ's identification of fishers of men and resolves to begin "fishing that river" for converts to Earthseed, her new faith (Butler, 1993, 223).

The author began the second novel, *The Parable of the Talents,* with a vision of the Reverend Olamina reading from Christ's teaching in Matthew 25:14–30, which concludes with "weeping and gnashing of teeth." During the 2032 election of President Andrew Steele Jarret, he reinterpreted Jesus driving money changers from the temple as a sanction of violence, a revision that encourages oppression and spiritual paralysis through obsessive memory work. After listing Hindus, Muslims, Buddhists, Jews, and pagans as equals of the money changers, Jarret whips listeners to a peak by restating Jesus's question, "Why have we forsaken thee?" and by denigrating other faiths as "lovers of Satan" (Butler, 1998, 84). At Christian America concentration camps, his menials legitimize torment by citing Proverbs 13:24, which they reduce to "Spare the rod and spoil the child" (*ibid.,* 224). In standard demagoguery, his glib restatements reduce alternate beliefs to weeds, viruses, worms, and cancers. Lauren Oya Olamina nullifies his rabble rousing by accusing him of divide and conquer, an algorithmic gambit dating to the Babylonians and Julius Caesar. In an echo of her father's sermons, she ponders Jarret's self-annihilation in Proverbs 16:18, "Pride goeth before destruction" (*ibid.,* 335).

See also Names.

Sources

Baldwin, James. *The Fire Next Time.* London: Michael Joseph, 1963.
Butler, Octavia. *Adulthood Rites* in *Lilith's Brood.* New York: Warner, 2000, 249–517.
_____. "Amnesty" in *Bloodchild and Other Stories.* New York: Seven Stories Press, 2005, 147–186.
_____. "The Book of Martha" in *Bloodchild and Other Stories.* New York: Seven Stories Press, 2005, 189–214.
_____. "The Evening and the Morning and the Night" in *Bloodchild and Other Stories.* New York: Seven Stories Press, 2005, 33–70.
_____. *The Parable of the Sower.* New York: Four Walls, Eight Windows, 1993.
_____. *The Parable of the Talents.* New York: Four Walls, Eight Windows, 1998.
Govan, Sandra Y. "Interview," *Obsidian III* 6:2/7:1 (2005–2006): 14–39.
Morris, David. *Public Religions in the Future World: Postsecularism and Utopia.* Athens: University of Georgia Press, 2021.

Shori

A merger of nonhuman cross-breeding and preadolescent bisexuality, Renee/Shori Matthews, an outsider at age fifty-three, humanizes and socializes the vampire myth at the core of *Fledgling.* Her Americanized diaspora story topples seduction fiction with a cheerful flexing of the wings and endorsement of polyamorous attentions between vampires and their symbionts. Although she looks like an ultra-black grade-school girl with an immature, hairless body, she exhibits catlike night vision and speed and a lust for blood in her attacks on deer. She delights in Wright Hamlin, a tantalizingly furry human similar in traits to Alanna Verrick's Diut in *Survivor.* Octavia wrested humor out Shori's need to bite her man, an urge that both satisfies and arouses him. He demands, "Do you love me, Shori, or do I just taste good?," a flippant jest at the grimness of Romanian vampire lore dating to 1431 (Butler, 2005, 139).

Octavia probed the protagonist's part-human, part-Ina origin and her admission of a Renaissance-style passion for Wright. The pattern of Mormon polygamy allows her father Iosip Petrescu to satisfy four female symbionts without disharmony or jealousy, a domestic arrangement in the Richard Moss family that the author scrutinized in *The Parable of the Sower*. For variety, the plot explores Theodora Harden's lesbian devotion to Shori, the protagonist's attraction to Joel Harrison and Daniel Gordon, and her half-hearted union with Brook and Celia, former symbionts of Iosip and his son Stefan. By killing an adversary and returning adamantly to Wright, Shori energizes her role as the lure to a heterosexual relationship.

By questioning Daniel Gordon in Punta Nublada, California, Shori begins detective work on the mystery of arsonists, night raids, and serial mass slayers attacking Arlington with gasoline bombs and expunging all family ties. An instinctive inspection of familiar places eases a longing to know the past and her connection to vestiges of a burned-out ruin where she was born, symbols of fragmented belonging to Ina society. For security from sunlight, Wright walls her into debris, a representation of global efforts to halt refugees from infiltrating communities. Her identity as the lone survivor repeats a literary trope of romanticist James Fenimore Cooper's *The Last of the Mohicans* in the melancholy loss of the sachem Uncas to Magua, a vengeful Huron. To the racist Silks, Shori represents a threat to species superiority via the conception and birth of black vampires.

In the final chapters, Octavia settles criminal and moral issues by dramatizing vampire jurisprudence and death penalty. After quibbling and blatant animosities, the Council of Judgment finds Katherine Dahlman and the Silks guilty of blindsiding Shori's family with onslaughts of racial genocide. Daniel Braithwaite esteems her for endurance and truth telling: "You not only survived twice, but you came to us with what you knew and you led the fight to destroy most of the assassins and to question the survivors" (Montgomery, 2021, 30). Exonerated in public, Shori attains esteem for probity.

The court's judgment—beheading Katherine Dahlman and isolating grown Silk males in separate clans—solves the quandary on a somber note, the destruction of a renegade Ina sept and Shori's alliance with the Braithwaites. Left only partially settled, Shori's attempt to extend cohabitation with Wright despite her nutritional/sexual ties to Joel, Daniel, Celia, and Brook poses an ongoing dilemma for humans attracted to vampires and for possessive men like Wright. In calling a "Council of the Goddess," Shori summons strengths of feminism, divinity, and her future motherhood (*ibid.*, 292). The greater theme highlights precocious female sexuality and the efforts of white society to suppress a vigorous, cohesive ethnic matrilineage.

Sources

Butler, Octavia. *Fledgling*. New York: Seven Stories Press, 2005.
_____. "Science Fiction Writer Octavia Butler on Race, Global Warming and Religion," (video), *Democracy Now* www.democracynow.org/2005/11/11/science_fiction_writer_octavia_butler_on (11 November 2005).
Govan, Sandra Y. "Interview," *Obsidian III* 6:2/7:1 (2005–2006): 14–39.
Lucas, Julian. "Stranger Communities," *New Yorker* 97:4 (15 March 2021): 73–76.
Montgomery, Maxine Lavon. *The Postapocalyptic Black Female Imagination*. London: Bloomsbury, 2021.

Nayar, Pramod K. "Vampirism and Posthumanism in Octavia Butler's *Fledgling,*" *Notes on Contemporary Literature* 41:2 (2011): 6–10.

Slavery

Octavia employs U.S. history as a means of instructing readers on racism and dehumanization, an encroachment that suppresses Native Americans, compromises low-paid factory workers, and leaves African Americans biologically whole, but socially defunct. As a model of bio-capitalism, bondsmen are subject to forced reproduction, murder, sale, beatings, and mutilation. Critics around the world make connections between the Parable series and nineteenth-century enslavement, an overlay of literary types that Italian analyst Raffaella Baccolini, a professor at the University of Bologna, terms "genre blurring" (Baccolini, 2003, 520). Gabriela Bruschini Grecca of the Universidade Estadual Pauli in São Paulo, Brazil, characterized *The Parable of the Sower* as a "counter-narrative of resistance" to subjugation (Grecca, 2021, 348). She identified race as a determiner of how "corporatist capitalism revives aspects of slavery in Butler's California of 2025" through neo-slave narratives about flight to freedom (*ibid.*). Teri Ann Doerksen, a British teacher at the University of Manchester, summarized citizen plight: "People are bought and sold as life becomes cheapened; race and gender become determinants of who will survive the night in the open," the most dangerous time for refugees and the homeless (Doerksen, 1997, 23).

Analysts drew on historical injustice toward nonwhites for comparisons, but regretted that, because of delayed justice, witnesses of collective trauma are no longer alive. To survey continued subjugation, analyst John Hall, on staff at Presentation Academy in Louisville, Kentucky, listed post-abolition echoes of slave misery in

> forced labor, false imprisonment, involuntary biological testing, and compulsory sterilization, … police brutality, the school to prison pipeline, concentrated poverty, and voter suppression, a meticulous, systematic, and heinous destruction of black cultural vestiges [Hall, 2021].

According to analyst Marlene D. Allen, on staff at the United Arab Emirates University at Al Ain, the author speculated how capitalism and technology can still cause "a 'boomeranging' of history … so that *anyone* who is vulnerable to exploitation … will be subject to slavery" (Allen, 2009, 1356).

GLOBAL SERVITUDE

Octavia's fiction investigated Afrofuturism through ancient lore, mythic beliefs, and the wisdom and preliminary science of North Africans from Nubia and Egypt. She applied imaginative plotting to an encounter with child kidnap, abductee disorientation, and involuntary thralldom to a master race, the plight of Tomás Serrano y Martín in *Imago,* indentured and agrarian slaves and stolen children wearing dog collars in *The Parable of the Talents,* and translator Noah Cannon in the alien tale of extensive interrogation in "Amnesty." Enslavement causes vassalage to psionics in *Patternmaster* and writer Dana Franklin's impromptu bondage during time travel to an antebellum Maryland plantation in *Kindred,* featuring "real women caught in impossible situations" (Allison, 1989, 67). For the opening lines of *Wild Seed,* the kidnap of an entire Ibo/Igbo village in 1690 depicts the early years of enslavement when stalkers "with their guns and their greed … herded away" the choicest merchandise and slaughtered the culls (Butler, 1980, 4). To acquire more goods for sale, they "waged war to get slaves to sell to the Europeans," who fostered the flesh trade on the flimsy excuse "to teach them civilized religion" (*ibid.*, 65, 104).

The author made authoritative judgments on a "country where blacks were under constant obligation to prove they had rights to even limited freedom" (*ibid.*, 629). Without bodily and reproductive liberties, a home and common language, and residential status, in the description of Adwoa Afful, on staff at York University, Toronto, bondsmen became "mere shadow figures" robotized into tools of production and erotic pleasure (Afful, 2016, 101). Octavia satirized the white definition of "civilization," which required females to smother themselves in Western clothing and shoes, an outward show of sexual subjugation (Butler, 1980, 230). To the homemaker An-yanwu, the best way to rear free children is in the Nigerian homeland, "where blackness was not a mark of slavery" (Butler, 1980, 277).

To undo the harm, An-yanwu must redefine gender and race as well as community, the key stabilizer that the long-lived tormentor Doro lacks. By 1840, she relocates to a Louisiana plantation in Avoyelles Parish, a former Native American enclave snuffed out by European settlers. She reports the ill luck of her insane mate, a strong muscled man the New Orleans auctioneer displayed by hands, teeth, and penis. To Doro, she characterizes the importance of parenthood to Ibo/Igbo clansmen as opposed to the commercialized offspring of male slave breeders, who sire black children like herd animals. The extensive story adds an observation about white men fathering brown children as opposed to white women, who merit disgrace for producing biracial offspring, a subject that characterizes the blended diaspora in *The Parable of the Sower*.

CALCULATED MISERY

In a 1990 interview, editor Larry McCaffery described the author's works as urgent surveys of human trafficking, torment, and reproductive captivity—the treatment of human offspring as agrarian products of female breeding stock like Sarah and Carrie in *Kindred* and Lilith Iyapo in *Dawn*. For those caught in escapes, the punishments threatened dismembered fingers, docked ears, or death—"starving, 'bout naked, whipped, dragged, bit by dogs" (Butler, 1979, 145). In a reflection on New England bondage in 1690, German historian Dominik Nagl of the University of Mannheim described Boston's property law, which equated seventeenth-century Africans with moveable goods "not much different from tools or livestock" when 11 percent of homes had slaves (Nagl, 2013, 5). In a year that saw the kidnap of 30,000 West Africans, each bondsman brought a price of £17–22 ($4,661.11–$6,032.04 in current value), which doubled by 1790 to £40–50 ($6,459.52–$8,074.39).

The author debated the wrong of pervasive ethnic victimizing, including agrarian thralldom in the Parable series. Dana, the Californian in *Kindred*, strikes a nerve in Sarah, an enslaved cook who nurtures hatred for mistress Margaret Weylin for selling Sarah's three sons to finance "new furniture, new china dishes, fancy things you see in that house" (Butler, 1979, 95). By watching children playing a game of auction, Dana's husband Kevin realizes how easily people acclimate to servitude and the sale of black chattel. A later realization in Dana reframes planter Tom Weylin from a cold-natured brute to "an ordinary man who sometimes did the monstrous things his society said were legal and proper" (*ibid.*, 134).

BONDAGE PATTERNS

Through speculative fiction, Octavia expanded on opportunities for vassalage. Mary Larkin's physical and psionic servility in *Mind of My Mind* results from latent human experiments by her father/lover, the immortal Nubian Doro. Success depends on the achievements of active Patternists, the relationship of Seth Dana with brother Clay and faith healer Rachel "Rae" Davidson with minister Eli Torrey. To Mary, Rachel's controller, the healer condemns the telepathic violation of "our mental privacy as well as our freedom" (Butler, 1977, 71). Of forced wedlock to experienced clairvoyant Karl Larkin, Mary declares her wish to "be one of the owners instead of one of the owned," a verbal recognition of Third World angst (*ibid.*, 29).

Octavia spoke her perspective through Doro's instruction of Mary on the basics of subjugation. He reminds her "to accept your own proprietary feelings as legitimate and demand that your people accept you on your terms," a twisted rationalization justifying human exploitation (*ibid.*, 61). Karl views the in-house situation for five additional telepaths as a parallel of slaves learning the regimen of a plantation—to "find some way to live our lives this way and make the best of it," a statement embedded with capitulation to a master (*ibid.*, 74). A sexist outburst from Jesse Dana injects misogyny: "A woman, for Godsake! The biggest damn thing about her is her mouth," a standard complaint from custodial males who would disempower women with silencing (*ibid.*, 78).

SLAVE TRANSPORT

The author's comparison of African populations forcibly moved and bred for service to satisfy a profit motive reminded readers that "at least ten million blacks were killed … during the Middle Passage," a deadly sea voyage that deported captives between 1525 and 1859 (Beal, 1986, 17). Lynell George, a journalist for the *Los Angeles Times,* compared the abduction to seizure by aliens: "You're put in the hold of a ship for months. You're separated from your family. You're robbed of your language. What does that sound like if not science fiction?" (George, 2004). By setting Okoye's wedding aboard Doro's sloop *Silver Star,* the author proposed a black utopia with adequate food, blankets, and freedom to enjoy the cool sea air. "There were no whips, no guns. No woman was raped," a summary of the lawlessness aboard slaving vessels (Butler, 1980, 162). Of the suffering of Triangular Trade, Octavia continued envisioning slaves packed so compactly "that they could hardly move and chained in place so that they had to lie in their own filth, beatings, the women routinely raped, torture … large numbers of slaves dying," ironically, a model of poor business practices (*ibid.*, 163).

The author disparaged the methods of slave dispersal. Her description of plantation customs identified patrollers in the act of sexual battery, "a little fun terrorizing people who weren't allowed to fight back" (Butler, 1979, 46). From 1508 to 1859, the mass abduction enriched in-country trade with Ashanti, Ibo/Igbo, Mandinka, Akan, Yoruba, and Bantu—human goods from Senegambia, Biafra, Guinea, Benin, Ivory Coast, and Angola. She stressed the similarity of the Great Migration of American blacks to the North from 1916 to 1970 to sci-fi stories of alien diasporas transplanting newcomers to earth by spaceship, a relocation offering opportunities for self-betterment.

On another positive note, the story "Speech Sounds" retrieved from Underground Railroad history the formation of black constable patrols in Boston and Philadelphia in the rescuer's name "Obsidian," a raw-edged black glass formed from igneous lava blasted from volcanos. Africans, Asians, indigenous Mediterranean and Pacific islanders, and Native Americans valued the naturally sharp scree extruded under high heat as a trade item useful for blades, medical lancets, arrowheads, dinnerware, decorative gems, and mirrors. The character Obsidian's attention to duty that he once owed the Los Angeles Police Department saves two children, emblems of hope for future normality. By martyrdom through intervention against a murderer, he hails self-sacrifice to black liberty.

See also "Amnesty"; "Crossover"; *Kindred*.

Sources

Afful, Adwoa. "Wild Seed: Africa and Its Many Diasporas," *Critical Arts* 30:4 (August 2016): 93–104.

Allison, Dorothy. "The Future of Female," *Village Voice* (19 December 1989): 67–68.

Baccolini, Raffaella, and Rom Moylan, eds. *Dark Horizons: Science Fiction and the Dystopian Imagination.* London: Routledge, 2003.

Beal, Frances. "Interview," *Black Scholar* 17:2 (March/April 1986): 14–18.

Brown, Jayna. *Black Utopias: Speculative Life and the Music of Other Worlds.* Durham, NC: Duke University Press, 2021.

Butler, Octavia. *Kindred.* New York: Doubleday, 1979.

_____. *Mind of My Mind.* New York: Doubleday, 1977.

_____. *Wild Seed.* New York: Doubleday, 1980.

Doerksen, Teri Ann. "Octavia E. Butler: Parables of Race and Difference" in *Into Darkness Peering.* Westport CT: Greenwood, 1997.

George, Lynell. "Black Writers Crossing the Final Frontier," *Los Angeles Times* (22 June 2004).

Grecca, Gabriela Bruschini. "'A Racist Challenge Might Force Us Apart': Divergence, Reliance, and Empathy in *Parable of the Sower* by Octavia Butler," *Ilha do Desterro* 74:1 (January–April 2021): 347–362.

Hall, John. "Parable of the Sower: A Positive Afrofuturist Obsession," https://sites.middlebury.edu/bltnmag/2021/05/28/4749/ (28 May 2021).

McCaffery, Larry, ed. *Across the Wounded Galaxies.* Urbana: University of Illinois Press, 1990.

Nagl, Dominik. "The Governmentality of Slavery in Colonial Boston, 1690–1760," *Amerikastudien/American Studies* 58:1 (2013): 5–26.

Space

About the time that Octavia investigated leaving the Butler nest to establish independence, she began following star-faring exploration from the late 1950s to John Glenn's three laps around the earth on February 20, 1962, in Friendship 7 to the Apollo 11 moon landing on July 20, 1969. Her vision of the future prophesied a rapid colonizing of the moon, Proxima Centauri, and Mars, the destination of starship passengers from Phoenix village in *Imago*. Universal travel provided escapes from what idealist Lauren Oya Olamina in *The Parable of the Sower* calls "this dying place ... the rotting past," the ravaged hardscrabble of Robledo, California (Butler, 1993, 78, 79). In explaining the emergence of the first vampires in *Fledgling*, the author repeated theories that arrivals from space "needed time to adjust to living on Earth" (Butler, 2005, 194).

According to the June 11, 2004, sci-fi convention Black to the Future in Seattle, space travel reiterated the black experience of the Middle Passage to "make the invisible visible"—a time when African abductees "traveled somewhere on a dark vessel, not knowing where they're going and deciding at some point, no matter where we're going, we're going to survive" (Littleton, 2004, K1). As Marlene D. Allen, a professor of English Literature at United Arab Emirates University, proposed in an article for *Callaloo*, the Parable series "[asserted] an Afrocentric aesthetic .. to find freedom in outer space, as an innovative futuristic 'rememory' ... of the African American experience" (Allen, 2009, 1354). In the falling action of the sequel, *The Parable of the Talents*, the protagonist fears that humanity might "destroy the ability of our world to sustain us" and proposes "new ways to cope" (Butler, 1998, 321, 322).

WORTHY EXPLOITS

To Lauren, the future holds "the Destiny," a venture from failed lifestyles to new planets (*ibid.*, 326). Her optimism convinces followers to extend the diaspora of the 2030s to the stars. She learns from the news in 2032 that multicellular beings on Mars can eat through rocks and move along slime trails like slugs. Research on minute life forms ends because President Andrew Steele Jarret sells space research to Euro-Japanese profiteers, a typical error in planning from a short-sighted, money-obsessed hack. She denounces capitalists for being "hungry for profit, short- and long-term" and puts her trust in a new religion that encourages self-sufficiency (*ibid.*, 322–323).

The writer involved herself in the challenge "because it was taking us away from Earth, away from home, away to investigate the mysteries of the universe and, I thought, to find new homes for humanity out there," a positive venture for a crowded, contaminated planet (Butler, 2000, 164). She turned technological advances into motifs for her works: a pilgrimage to the north on foot in *Survivor*, supplying the world with a psionic species in *Mind of My Mind* and *Wild Seed*, and the sabotaged space flight opening *Clay's Ark*. The sparse topography of the latter novel returned briefly to Proxima Centauri and described "Proxi Two" as a "cool red star with its three planets hugging in close," a hint at the benefits of human collaboration (Butler, 1984, 29).

ASSESSING RISKS

The author feared for the future of the National Aeronautical and Space Administration: "I keep hearing people say manned space travel is not necessary, that we can send our robots to do the investigating. Near-space yes, but deep-space, no"

(Alessio, 1999, Q2). In *Dawn*, she originated an orbiting space home that carried unfortunate earthlings from an unlivable world before they "died of injury, disease, hunger, radiation, cold" (Butler, 2000, 15). To stabilize rescues, the Oankali brace humans in extensive hibernation, a semi-permanent transfixation that requires awakening and introduction to spaceship life. In an interview for Obsidian III with Sandra Y. Govan, on the English staff at the University of North Carolina at Charlotte, Octavia debated the possibilities of travel to another world where "we might have to pay the rent," a witty reference to demands on homo sapiens in a non-human milieu (Govan, 2005–2006, 33).

For *Imago*, the third volume of *Lilith's Brood*, Octavia gradually introduced humans to the kind of habitat they could expect on Mars. As Earthseed ritual prefaces migration from Acorn, the text bears warning of commercial self-interest in the name of its rocket ship. Canadian writer David Morris, a philosophy professor at Concordia University in Montreal, observed, "The name Christopher Columbus does not undercut it so much as remind that the human contradiction remains, and it can't be undone by Olamina or by travel in space" (Morris, 2021). Preceded by migrants from earth's Amazon Basin, the travelers face self-destruction once more because of "inherent flaws"—their intelligence and an ancient penchant for status (*ibid.*, 530).

Octavia chose the mutant Jodahs as a future Paul Revere. He warns Marina Rivas that the distant planet is cold, dry, and not green. The lack of verdure symbolized a future that the author predicted for displaced earthlings too self-indulgent to profit from their errors. She alerted venturers to a test of time: "We can't afford to go someplace else and make the mistakes we make here, here in the nest … taking, and putting back nothing—or putting back poisonous waste" (Canavan, 2014). An ecofeminist summation of fouling the nest, her warning held little hope for earth's future as a sustainable habitat.

Sources

Alessio, Carolyn. "Talking with Octavia E. Butler," *Philadelphia Inquirer* (10 January 1999): Q2.

Allen, Marlene D. "Octavia Butler's 'Parable' Novels and the 'Boomerang' of African American History," *Callaloo* 32:4 (Winter, 2009): 1353–1365.

Butler, Octavia. "Brave New Worlds: A Few Rules for Predicting the Future," *Essence* 31:1 (1 May 2000): 164.

_____. *Clay's Ark*. New York: St. Martin's Press, 1984.

_____. *Dawn* in *Lilith's Brood*. New York: Warner, 2000, 2–248.

_____. *Fledgling*. New York: Seven Stories Press, 2005.

_____. *Imago* in *Lilith's Brood*. New York: Warner, 2000, 518–746.

_____. *The Parable of the Sower*. New York: Four Walls, Eight Windows, 1993.

_____. *The Parable of the Talents*. New York: Seven Stories Press, 1998.

Canavan, Gerry. "Recovering Octavia E. Butler's Lost Parables," *Los Angeles Review of Books* (9 June 2014).

Govan, Sandra Y. "Interview," *Obsidian III* 6:2/7:1 (2005–2006): 14–39.

Littleton, Therese. "'Black to the Future': Fest Is Mothership for African Americans in Science Fiction," *Seattle Times* (6 June 2004): K1.

Morris, David. *Public Religions in the Future World: Postsecularism and Utopia*. Athens: University of Georgia Press, 2021.

"Speech Sounds"

In 1983 at a nadir of Octavia's energy and optimism, a fictional bus riot in "Speech Sounds" took shape while she was "feeling little hope or liking for the human species" (Butler, 2005, 109). The story dramatizes the regression of human-kind to a simian state. Analyst Jayna Brown, a media specialist at the Pratt Institute in Brooklyn, New York, typified the discord of the author's stories. "Speech Sounds" reaches a calamitous state: "Without cohesive social infrastructure, life is a constant state of crisis ... from violent conflict and power struggle" (Brown, 2021, 101). Similar to the civil and moral breakdown in "The Morning and the Evening and the Night," *Survivor, Dawn, Imago, The Parable of the Sower*, and *Fledgling*, the milieu omits the chivalric backstory of *Patternmaster* by setting combat on a California bus route.

By placing writer and university history teacher Valerie Rye in plague literature where people lose verbal and written communication "by something like a small, very specific stroke," Octavia analyzed the human penchant for hostility and aggression in the aftermath of viral pandemic (Butler, 1998). According to Candra K. Gill, on staff at the University of Michigan, the microbial background precipitated an apocalypse: "A total breakdown of communication ... as cataclysmic as any bomb" (Holden & Shawl, 2013, 136). The selection of contagion as a silent killer previously served Daniel Defoe's *Journal of the Plague Year*, Edgar Allan Poe's "The Masque of the Red Death," Jack London's *The Scarlet Plague*, Albert Camus's *The Plague*, and Michael Crichton's *The Andromeda Strain* as a threat to civil behaviors.

In the purview of Eileen Hunt Botting of the University of Notre Dame, women, too, have selected pestilence as the starting point of philosophical narrative on the post-apocalyptic world:

> Modern feminist political science fiction writers such as Octavia Butler and Margaret Atwood ... have used plague as a setting and a metaphor for theorizing the deeper political pathologies of human societies—past, present, and future [Botting, 2021].

In a wordless urban street scene, ambiguous physicality, symbols, snarls, and hand signals substitute for verbal expressions of human complexities. The woman-centered perspective enabled Octavia to turn short fiction into an allegory on isolation, disability, and disintegrating humanity in Los Angeles as pointed and powerful as Shirley Jackson's "The Lottery," as compelling as the daring of survivor Connie Ramos in Marge Piercy's *Woman on the Edge of Time*.

A Precipitous Time

Hardened by loss during a medical catastrophe and shielded by an obdurate exterior, protagonist Valerie Rye, a mute University of California at Los Angeles history professor, drops her guard to ponder a lack of motivation so profound that suicide and murder had become possibilities for ending three years of ennui. With the transfixing tone of Carmac McCarthy's end-of-time novel *The Road*, she arms herself with a .45 for the twenty-mile bus ride from Virginia Road in Pasadena to Los Angeles along Washington Boulevard, two verbal connections to America's Virginia-born founding father and first president. Still possessed of verbal intelligence, she studies the body language of male scrappers, the stereotypical victimizers who exploit vulnerable women and children. By trusting her projection of a normal male-female relationship with a former city cop, she risks her safety to a kind stranger who drives a blue car, a color linked to loyal service and police protection. In the background, impaired males make indecent gestures and throw rocks at the vehicles, indicators of juvenile incivility.

The story compares the hunger for conversation to sexual aridity, a need that Valerie Rye satisfies in casual coitus with Obsidian, a left-handed pseudo-rescuer in a police uniform who supplies condoms. Lacking heterosexual comforts or continued employment in the helping professions, the pair make do with a map and body language and consider a sharing of the basics—shelter, food, transportation, intimacy. Unlike the unnamed passenger who solicits help from the bus driver, the professor initiates agency and quick thinking to save a woman threatened with an unidentified knife wielder by thrusting only broken glass as a weapon. The street violence that ends an ad hoc relationship involves Valerie in an instinctive shooting of the male attacker to halt further killing. English author Glyn Morgan, an affiliate of the University of Liverpool, applauds the application of "a pandemic to write about survival, and to cast new light on how we communicate and how slender the thread is that separates us from animals" (Morgan, 2021).

Speech for Life

An ironic or "wry" flip of events, the triple death scene turns serendipitous by overriding Valerie Rye's physical needs with a penchant for the maternal side of classroom teaching. The story acquaints her with needy children who can still verbalize rational thought, a prototype that the author added to Dana Franklin's reading to Rufus Weylin and her literacy work with Maryland slaves in *Kindred*. In *The Parable of the Sower*, Lauren Oya Olamina salutes the daring of black readers who risked "whipping, sale, or mutilation for their efforts" (Butler, 1993, 218). Taking charge of a small, orphaned brother and sister, Valerie accepts a glimmer of promise in their coherent words and reclaims the propriety of burying Obsidian and the dead mother.

Purpose and autonomy in the professor replace a damaged outlook stripped of language: teaching the boy and girl directs Valerie toward a past identity, her former non-libidinous self. Harvard English professor Stephan Burt notes, "As usual in Butler, raising the young is the only unproblematic good" (Burt, 2021). Like Dana, Valerie acquires one of the benefits of teaching by learning from her pupils, a sub-theme in "Childfinder." From the Latin for "under waves," the title verb "sound" implies positive results of a whale's dive to probe great depths. The adjectival meaning prophesies wholeness and wellbeing.

Sources

Botting, Eileen Hunt. "Predicting the Patriarchal Politics of Pandemics from Mary Shelley to Covid-19," *Frontiers in Sociology* 6 (24 March 2021): 61.

Burt, Stephanie. "Octavia Butler Wanted to Write a 'Yes' Book," *National Republic* (27 May 2021).

Butler, Octavia. "Devil Girl from Mars: Why I Write Science Fiction," *Media in Transition, MIT* (19 February 1998).

_____. *The Parable of the Sower*. New York: Four Walls, Eight Windows, 1993.

_____. "Speech Sounds," *Bloodchild and Other Stories*. New York: Seven Stories Press, 2005, 87–110.

Gale, Nikita. "After Words: On Octavia Butler's 'Speech Sounds,'" *Resonance* 1:4 (2020): 462–466.

Holden, Rebecca J., and Nisi Shawl, eds. *Strange Matings: Science Fiction, Feminism, African American Voices, and Octavia E. Butler.* Seattle, WA: Aqueduct, 2013.

Morgan, Glyn. "New Ways: The Pandemics of Science Fiction," *Interface Focus* 11:5 (12 October 2021).

"Speech Sounds" Genealogy

Octavia chooses unusual settings in which to unite foster families and culture, the backstory of Alanna Verrick in *Survivor*. Valerie Rye, a widow grieving three children lost during an epidemic, lives apart from her siblings and two nephews. A bizarre set of events thrusts her into civil disorder and a happenstance relationship with Obsidian, a Los Angeles policeman. Thomas Vernon Reed, an expert in American Studies at Washington State University, characterized the situation as "realism-disrupting literary techniques to make interventions into the real social conditions of our time," such as orphaning exacerbated by AIDS and Covid (Reed, 2021, 34–35).

At the deaths of Obsidian and two more victims of random violence, the appearance of preschoolers miraculously ends Valerie's sorrow and provides pupils for language teaching, the task that Dana Franklin begins in *Kindred*.

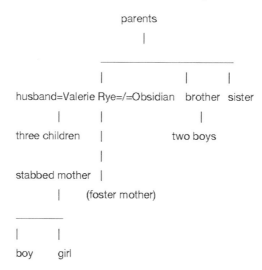

Sophie Lewis, a teacher at Philadelphia's Brooklyn Institute for Social Research, notes that the formation of a matriarchal foster family advocates a Cameroonian and Nigerian pattern of village-based surrogacy. The concept anticipates Octavia's verse in *The Parable of the Talents*:

> We can,
> Each of us,
> Do the impossible
> As long as we can convince ourselves
> That it has been done before [Butler, 1998, 177].

The mom-headed household reprises similarly ad hoc maternity in An-yanwu's plantation clan in *Wild Seed*, Barbara's shielding of clairvoyant children in "Childfinder," a weaver's rescue of mutant playmates in "A Necessary Being," Lillian Iyapo's indoctrination of human survivors in *Dawn*, and Lauren Oya Olamina's kindergarten classroom in *The Parable of the Sower*.

Sources

Butler, Octavia. *The Parable of the Talents*. New York: Seven Stories Press, 1998.
———. "Speech Sounds" in *Bloodchild and Other Stories*. New York: Seven Stories Press, 2005, 87–110.
Lewis, Sophie. *Full Surrogacy Now: Feminism against Family*. London: Verso, 2021.
Morgan, Glyn. "New Ways: The Pandemics of Science Fiction," *Interface Focus* 11:5 (12 October 2021).
Reed, Thomas Vernon. *The Bloomsbury Introduction to Postmodern Realist Fiction: Resisting Master Narratives*. New York: Bloomsbury, 2021.

Survivor

Octavia originally proposed entitling *Survivor*, her premiere novel, either Alanna, the focal character of the author's first captivity narrative, or Canaan. The latter Old Testament setting in Israel, Jordan, Lebanon, and Syria names a utopian commune at Quincy, Massachusetts, founded as Merrymount on June 25, 1624, by anti-gun, anti-liquor Puritan separatists from Plymouth Colony. *Survivor*'s action dramatizes the concept of an exodus to a new land. The author contextualizes the intent of Moses, a thirteenth-century BCE prophet, to expel Canaanites from Jordan to make room for Israelites near Mount Nebo.

Protagonist Alanna Verrick, who bears a Gaelic name meaning "precious child," displays the chutzpah of an agent similar in adaptive and leadership skills to Lilith Iyapo in the Xenogenesis series, Barbara in "Childfinder," and Shori Matthews in *Fledgling*. Alanna untangles the four-way political maneuverings of unearthly Kohn races with missionaries, iconic models of Puritans blinded by colonist Thomas Morton's rebellion at Mount Wollaston, in Quincy, Massachusetts. To communicate, Alanna decodes "light speech," flashing signals that replace verbalization (Butler, 1978, 139).

For ethnic reasons, the text presents the nonwhite orphan in pseudo-frontier warfare in which biracial people became ambassadors for cultural extremes—white Indians, black Indians, Hispanic blacks, and other mixes. The hybrid race redefines family, much like the occluded identity of Johnny Butler/True Son, a dual outcast in Conrad Richter's young adult classic *Light in the Forest*. Because of rescue and acceptance by missionaries, she feels obligated to save from Garkohn enslavement Jules and Neila Verrick, her foster parents. At the time of their escape, the missionaries must trust the Hao or magistrate of the humanoid Tehkohn (mountaineer), their former foes. The author chose Hao, the Chinese word for "good," to identify a fount of wisdom and guidance. For expedience, Alanna tempers "wild human philosophy"—knowing "when to fight and when to give way"—to the logic of compromise (*ibid.*, 110). Part of her heroism stems from re-addicting herself to meklah, a narcotic that she fights in silence.

MEDIATING RACISM

For a story that stressed the accommodation of the "other" after smooth-skinned earth people mated with hirsute hominids, the author anticipated Afrofuturism, a more significant disparity than the historical "cowboys and Indians or Englishmen and Africans" (Govan, 2005–2006, 32). Essential to the indigenous furry Tehkohn society lies a system of rigid castes—fighters, Hao, judges, and hunters and nonfighting artisans and farmers. A spontaneous shift of somatic color expresses emotion, with blue the most revered and white the happiest. Like zoologist Desmond Morris's naked ape, Alanna becomes the "furless one" (Butler, 1978, 111). To tap into nonhuman thinking, she learns to evaluate blue-green, yellow, white, gray, and iridescent color changes, a task similar to that of translator Noah Cannon in "Amnesty" and indoctrinator Lilith Iyapo in *Dawn*. By interpreting skin color, Alanna eases inter-species relations with beings lashing out with "violence, madness, and unreasoning hatred" (*ibid*., 121; Allison, 1989, 67).

In the opinion of Crystal S. Anderson, a specialist in transnational studies at George Mason University in Fairfax, Virginia, Octavia creates Alanna Verrick as a model negotiator for American blacks who reside in the complex race-conscious society of the 1970s. Similar in tone and atmosphere to *Justice and Her Brothers* by young adult author Virginia Hamilton, the first Black Newbery medalist, Octavia's plot elucidates tokens of civility in friendship, gratitude, and acceptance of differences in size, skin type, sexual orientation, and color. Essential to Alanna's success lies her caution in the proximity to Diut's monstrous shape and her control of condescension to or terrorizing smaller beings.

Savagery Within

Octavia dramatizes elements of human versus bestial uniqueness, the core of Robert Louis Stevenson's story "Dr. Jekyll and Mr. Hyde." A significant battle with a huge jerhuk extends the contrasts in a scene fraught with Alanna's wielding the weapons of jungle war, a Tarzan-like prowess that reprises the militance of Queen Penthesilea and the Amazons, female warriors in Homer's Iliad and Virgil's Aeneid. Cheah, the Tehkohn rescuer of Alanna, the lone human, offers sound advice: "Don't use your differences to isolate yourself" (Butler, 1978, 51). The command foreshadows Alanna's physical response to mating with Diut and her postcoital stroking of his mane, a non-threatening erotic lure like Wright Hamlin's hairy body in *Fledgling*.

Based on American frontier narratives of Indian captives Mary Jemison and Mary Rowlandson and on Victorian quandaries of orphans of color such as the dark-skinned gypsy Heathcliff in Emily Brontë's *Wuthering Heights*, Octavia's novel incorporates debates of moral consciousness. Founded on European imperialism, the plot relaxes racist notions of "your own kind" and promotes reception of Tien, the bi-species child of Alanna and Diut (*ibid*., 176). The Tehkohn, once an inclusive tribe, declare the need for new blood: "We are a new people.... In each child we welcome, we are reborn," a repopulation surrogacy the author develops in the Xenogenesis series, *Fledgling*, and "Speech Sounds" (*ibid*., 171). An act of kindness for Beatrice Stamp, a former community bigot, allows Alanna to boost unity and tolerance. In pagan ritual style like that of *Adulthood Rites*, Octavia uses fire to cleanse the settlement of previous animosities, but she leaves unassuaged Jules Verrick's rigorous zealotry and renunciation of his foster daughter.

See also "A Necessary Being."

Sources

Allison, Dorothy. "The Future of Female," Village Voice (19 December 1989): 67–68.

Anderson, Crystal S. "'The Girls Isn't White': New Racial Dimensions in Octavia Butler's *Survivor*," *Extrapolation* 47:1 (Spring, 2006): 35–50, 53.

Butler, Octavia. *Survivor*. New York: Doubleday, 1978.

Govan, Sandra Y. "Interview," *Obsidian III* 6:2/7:1 (2005–2006): 14–39.

Magadanz, Stacy. "The Captivity Narrative in Octavia E. Butler's *Adulthood Rites*," *Extrapolation* 53:1 (2012): 47–59.

McCaffery, Larry, ed. *Across the Wounded Galaxies*. Urbana: University of Illinois Press, 1990.

Troy, Maria Holmgren. "Negotiating Genre and Captivity: Octavia Butler's *Survivor*," *Callaloo* 33:4 (Fall, 2010): 1116–1131.

Survivor Genealogy

With *Survivor,* her first novel, Octavia introduced concepts of miscegenation that she later developed in extraterrestrial speculative sci-fi. The linkage of disparate characters develops notions of inter-species blood kin like Tien and the resulting mutant offspring, the focus of *Dawn*, the initial Xenogenesis novel, *Adulthood Rites,* and *Fledgling,* an examination of biracial prejudice among vampires.

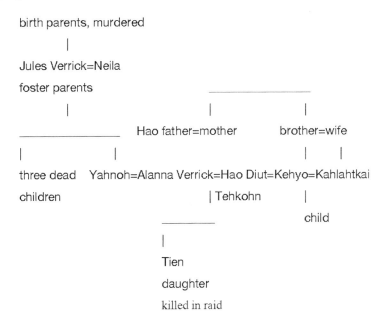

Joshua L. Miller, on staff at the University of Michigan, Ann Arbor, framed a question arising from the movement of Tehkohn survivors from collective trauma among Rohkohn: "Will migration crises continue to inflict mass cruelty on those surviving under the conditions of the most severe precarity?" (Miller, 2021, 3). As a result of what Miller calls Octavia's "awful radiant truth," the Tehkohns survive (*ibid.*). Their stamina impacts "A Necessary Being," a desert story retrieved posthumously in 2012 by the author's agent, Merrilee Heifetz (*ibid.*, 49).

See also Miscegenation.

Sources

Butler, Octavia. "A Necessary Being," *Unexpected Stories*. New York: Open Road Media, 2014, 11–76.
_____. *Survivor*. New York: Doubleday, 1978.
Miller, Joshua, ed. *The Cambridge Companion to Twenty-First Century American Fiction*. Cambridge, UK: Cambridge University Press, 2021.

Survivors

At a critical height resulting from the popularity of the Parable series, Octavia earned accolades from *Ms.* magazine for creating a "literature of survival" ("Octavia," 1999, A9). The controlling motif derived from the writer's background of poverty, fatherlessness, and poor school performance hampered by dyslexia. With a canon fraught with the worst of menaces and natural disasters, she rewarded tough, durable females like disabled South American Jesusa Serrano y Martín in *Imago*, University of California at Los Angeles history professor Victoria Rye in "Speech Sounds," gunner Rane Maslin in *Clay's Ark*, childless tribe leader Tahneh in "A Necessary Being," and matriarch Emma in *Mind of My Mind* for their refusal to yield to foes or obstacles.

Speaking through the Afro-Asian hero Alanna Verrick in *Survivor*, Octavia graced her missionary foster parents with dedication to task: "They could win a struggle against the elements as they and their ancestors had won many such struggles on Earth" (Butler, 1978, 98). Her wonder women endured by adopting the strategies of white male heroes, as with the archetypal Rayal, title figure in *Patternmaster*, whose sons—the power-tainted Coransee and the more plausible Teray—battle for an inheritance. Because Teray loses wife Iray to his brother and chooses Amber for a mate, the healer bears their child as the next generation's Patternist. More resourceful, An-yanwu, the drone of Doro in *Wild Seed*, escapes his control and founds a successful Louisiana commune of runaways and former slaves.

Inborn Traits

Journalist Stephen Kearse, in a summation for the *New York Times Book Review*, pictured the qualities of Octavia's survivors. They persist because of "resourcefulness and compromise … community and resilience," an apt description of herbalist and homemaker An-yanwu in *Wild Seed*, widow and indoctrinator Lilith Iyapo in *Dawn*, nurse Beatrice Alcantera among critically ill patients in "The Evening and the Morning and the Night," and writer and slave educator Dana Franklin in *Kindred* (Kearse, 2021, 12). Dana's use of logic and knowledge of American history enables her to outwit Maryland planter Tom Weylin, a wily slave owner who is handy with the lash.

The writer turned chaos into a multi-combat challenge in *The Parable of the Sower*. For fifteen-year-old protagonist Lauren Oya Olamina, preparation for a rugged future requires map collection, target practice with BB guns, and books on First Peoples and their development of herbalism. The collection of garden produce and the amassing of seeds, manuals, and oddments equip her for the pilgrimage to Acorn, a commune in Cape Mendocino, California, established in 2027. In her name, the first settlers on Mars board rocket ships bearing earth's people and culture into a destiny in the stars. Along the way, a secondary plot involving the kidnap of her toddler Larkin Bankole bifurcates survival into struggles for mother and daughter.

BACKUPS

The writer made meaningful use of secondary characters. The resilience of Lady Darah in *Patternmaster* parallels the staying power of Corazon "Cory" Olamina, the kindergarten teacher and stepmother in *The Parable of the Sower* who endorses community defense. As a model of resistance, physician's aid May survives the loss of her tongue to anti-female extremists. Another stout-hearted female, Tate Rinaldi, a child protector in *Adulthood Rites*, turns to lover Gabe for affirmation of her beliefs and altruism. From peasant lore, Octavia exalts María de la Luz, the sullied matriarch who produces Adan, sire of the next generation of Mexicans. A futuristic survivor, Martha Bes in "The Book of Martha" illustrates stewardship to God and to humankind by formulating and discarding unlikely corrections to inborn faults. With a similar open-mindedness toward family deviations from the norm, the college student in "Near of Kin" absorbs difficult episodes in the lives of her mother and Uncle Stephen, whom she must accept as her unknown birth father.

To contrast the best of the lot, Octavia inserted literary foils lacking the integrity and backbone of heroes. Jane, the dispirited factory worker in "Crossover," gives in to alcoholism and carnal time wasting. Compared to Alice Greenwood, a suicide in *Kindred*, Sarah runs a cookhouse as social center and mentors Dana Franklin in plantation protocol. In the final hours of Phoenix village in *Imago*, Neci, the arsonist and racial purist, disappears in the harrowing fire. Marcos Duran contrasts the spunk and idealism of his sister Lauren in *The Parable of the Talents*, who ignores his self-aggrandizing religious career to spread Earthseed to the world. In her final novel, the author contrasted Shori Matthews, a black vampire endowed with no need for darkness, to her tormentor, Katherine Dahlman, a fomenter of racism among the Silks. Because her elitist beliefs collapse in a court trial, Octavia exalts her defeat in a grisly beheading to prevent resurrection. The burial of head and body leaves Shori free to unite with vampire clans and to fill in family background that amnesia erased.

See also Feminism.

Sources

Butler, Octavia. *Survivor.* New York: Doubleday, 1978.
Kearse, Stephen. "The Essential Octavia Butler," *New York Times* (15 January 2021): 12–13.
"Octavia E. Butler at African American Museum Tonight," *Los Angeles Sentinel* (24 March 1999): A9.
Salvaggio, Ruth. "Octavia Butler and the Black Science-Fiction Heroine," *Black American Literature Forum* 18:2 (Summer, 1984): 78–81.

Time Travel

For *Kindred, Mind of My Mind,* and *Wild Seed,* Octavia provoked reader curiosity with chronoportation or timeslip travel over continents, skyways, and historical periods. The treks varied over her canon from Neolithic and antebellum autobiography in *Wild Seed* to the return of a twentieth-century starship from Proxima Centauri, the backstory of *Clay's Ark*. Episodic memory of earlier times dramatizes the Akan-Twi tradition of *sankofa*, retrieval from the past anything useful to the future. In the reasoning of Kristi Miller, a philosopher at the University of Sydney, Australia, the extrapolation of useful events from a spatial trajectory is a two-edged sword. Trying to blame earlier societies for their misdeeds—slavery, misogyny, racism, war, genocide—leads to faulty observations of reality. She declared the worth of both positive and negative happenings: "It is not rationally permissible to discount the value of past events" which continue to impact personhood, even the woeful and cataclysmic (Miller, 2021).

Among the treasures of time-loosed ventures, characters access the wisdom and learning of older eras, particularly ritual, beliefs, foodways, and village-wide mothering, a Cameroonian and Nigerian fostering system. The reclamation of orphans within an inclusive motherland inspired the writer's transfer of culture and language to two toddlers in "Speech Sounds." The concept of repossession applied to An-yanwu's homeless and runaway slaves in *Wild Seed* and to amnesiac Shori Matthews newly arrived at her ruined birthplace in *Fledgling*. In both instances, characters have lost ties to their tribal foundations and struggle to re-identify their belonging in time and place. However, Suzanne Kord, a specialist in women's literature at University College London, insisted, "You can't start over. You can't change a reality that already occurred. You may be able to go back in time, but you can't turn it back" (Kord, 2019, 15).

VIEWING OLD REALITIES

Adjustment to situational reality presents characters with complex choices, such as those perplexing the title character in Vita Sackville-West's time travel classic *Orlando*. Critic Stephanie Burt, a Harvard English professor, compared the motif of time travel in the neo-slave narrative *Kindred* to the action of Mark Twain's fanciful *A Connecticut Yankee in King Arthur's Court*. In the latter, Hank Morgan, the nineteenth-century munitions worker in the title, exits from a bump on the head and views a cavalcade of humankind from Camelot's royalty to England's most hopeless and pox-ridden. Because the nation based its success on slavery and white empowerment similar to the plantation South, she concluded that neither protagonist, Dana Franklin or Hank, located an easy fix: "In both novels, an American goes back to the past, tries to make it better, and sees how stubbornly privilege maintains itself, how hard it must be to direct any change" (Burt, 2021).

Octavia's coalescing of Ibo/Igbo cosmology with sporadic time travel in *Kindred* allows a modern liberal to confront plantation bondage. Personally introduced to field harvesting with a corn knife, twentieth-century protagonist Dana Franklin accepts the wisdom of experienced laborers to "Slow down! Take a lick or two if you have to. You kill yourself today, he'll push you to kill yourself every day" (Butler, 1977, 6). A slide into unconsciousness takes Dana three thousand miles from Maryland back home to her own time in Altadena, California, but does not end subsequent soul-killing obedience to white masters. The price of witnessing snippets of the Afro-American past, an arm wrenched out of place maims Dana's body with a "hurt-remembering" ache and evokes muscle memory of working to appease savage overseers and owners (*ibid.*, 9). By pushing back decades to scan the Weylin household, she reconciles her family's ligature to antique racism that history overlooked or only touched on, especially sexual bondage and the auctioning of children. Missing from her retrogression are ways to counteract personal pain by preventing Alice Greenwood's suicide and Rufus Weylin's murder.

WISHFUL THINKING

Unlike the pessimistic survey in *Kindred,* fluid century-hopping in *Wild Seed* rewards fictional characters with opportunities to air colonial grievances. For the undying Nubian mutant Doro and Nigerian shapeshifter An-yanwu, millennia mean nothing. An-yanwu gains metaphysical ease from gliding with eagles and swimming with dolphins. On return from romps in the ocean, she finds her dominator Doro refitted with a new body, a temporary housing that enables him to survive passages of eras dating to his birth in ancient Sudan. In addressing miraculous spans, he writes an obsolete language while An-yanwu adopts new womanly forms and continues bearing children to her lovers. A sci-fi dreamscape, the affinity for timeslip suggests the author's projection of full equity on generations of disenfranchised blacks.

Jan Sholto, an unusual telepath capable of psychometry and alternative forms of memory in *Mind of My Mind,* turns the author's imaginative time fluidity into art projects. To learn the provenance of relics, she fondles solid objects to read them like archives. A shard of 6,500-year-old crockery and a Sumerian clay tablet allow her and Mary Larkin, her controller, to perceive the experience of a female artisan from Mesopotamia, the name of Neolithic Iran east of the Tigris and Euphrates rivers in the fourth century BCE. By refining telepathic skills, Jan reformulates the components of female ingenuity. A specialist in African diaspora at Florida State University at Tallahassee, Maxine Lavon Montgomery interpreted Afrofuturistic genius as a source of "potential to bring the Afrodiaspora experience to life in new ways" (Montgomery, 2021, 8).

Sources

Burt, Stephanie. "Octavia Butler Wanted to Write a 'Yes' Book," *National Republic* (27 May 2021).
Butler, Octavia. *Mind of My Mind.* New York: Doubleday, 1977.
Kord, Susanne. *12 Monkeys.* Bedfordshire, UK: Auteur Press, 2019.
McCaffery, Larry, ed. *Across the Wounded Galaxies.* Urbana: University of Illinois Press, 1990.
Melzer, Patricia. *Alien Constructions: Science Fiction and Feminist Thought.* Austin: University of Texas Press, 2021.
Miller, Kristie. "What Time-Travel Teaches Us about Future-Bias," *Philosophies* 6:2 (2021): 38.
Montgomery, Maxine Lavon. *The Postapocalyptic Black Female Imagination.* London: Bloomsbury, 2021.

Tone

In writings and speeches, Octavia charged humankind with hubris, the Greek stumbling block to greatness in the myths of Icarus, Narcissus, Phaethon, and

Niobe. In *Lilith's Brood,* the author discredited boasting of direct lineage to a pure origin, which German feminist Christa Grewe-Volpp at Universität Mannheim labeled "total regression" (Grewe-Volpp, 2003, 161). Octavia's examples of pride span human society from politicians, capitalists, and pulpit evangelists to prison guards and vampires. Aparajita Nanda, an expert in ethnic studies at Santa Clara University, asserted that "Unfettered human pride which often goes together with the dangerous assumption that human progress depends on it, may well be a precursor to the destruction of the species," an ominous utterance summarizing the deracination and disinheritance of Californians in the Earthseed series (Nanda, 2021, 11).

In opposition to arrogance, the author developed a following for stories of tolerance, mercy, decorum, and resilience, four of the character behaviors in the resolution of *Imago.* In *Adulthood Rites,* mother figure Lilith Iyapo jokes about her communication with the alien Nikanj: "You say such god-awful things in such a gentle voice … the only voice you've got" (Butler, 2000, 259). The quip rationalizes an innate approval that encourages mediation with the nomadic Oankali. She affirms the extraterrestrial race that rescues humans for a toxic earth, but keeps them captive for sampling and manipulating their DNA. The ambiguity, typical of the author's fiction, leaves the reader to determine friend from foe.

Commending the author's concern that humanity's foibles may prove terminal, Stephen Kearse, in a reflective essay for the *New York Times Book Review,* summarized a leery tone in the author's bleak fiction and essays. He stated, "She deeply distrusted utopias, saviors, power brokers and escapism," a focal concern for the immortal Grandma Emma in *Mind of My Mind,* the biracial hero Alanna Verrick's lover Diut in *Survivor,* council appointees judging Shori Matthews in *Fledgling,* and Teray and Amber, a fleeing couple in *Patternmaster* (Kearse, 2021, 12). The doubts of An-yanwu in *Wild Seed* echo the author's suspicion of dominance by the duplicitous immortal Doro, who deviates at will from affable companion to the murderous mutant at the core of his being.

CHARACTER CONTRADICTIONS

For the *London Review of Books,* author and editor Jenny Turner described Octavia's texts as clean, calm, crisp, and laidback, an acknowledgment of American insouciance in speech and action that characterizes Mary Larkin in *Mind of My Mind,* rescuer Wright Hamlin in *Fledgling,* and Lauren Oya Olamina, protagonist of *The Parable of the Sower.* With teen flippancy, Lauren fills her journal with sassy, satiric comments, for example, "Family fights are neighborhood theater" (Butler, 1993, 114). Her runaway brother Keith saturates his criminal episodes with obscenities, a flimsy proof that, at age thirteen, he is his own man. The cheeky descriptions of murdering an elderly migrant and watching gangs set rich people on fire betoken his own torture—skinning and cautery—by the delinquents he frequents, a poignant extermination of youthful bluster and daring. In place of casualties like Keith, Lauren codifies a blunt, non-theistic belief to safeguard the remainder of humanity.

Octavia's tenacious Lauren and other wonder women left no doubt that feminism shaped an upbeat canon. In an essay for *Village Voice,* journalist Dorothy

Allison honored the author for being "a realist, writing the most detailed social criticism and creating some of the most fascinating female characters in the genre," notably, Beatrice Alcantera, Jesusa Serrano y Martín, Noah Cannon, and Alanna Verrick (Allison, 1989, 67). One protagonist, Rohkahn Hao Tehreh in "A Necessary Being," exemplifies the outward show of hospitality to a newcomer through variations of body color and luminescence. Beneath intertribal courtesies, she conceals a dubious state: a mass of concern for Diut, the young Hao from the east, and for herself, a barren magistrate incapable of producing the next generation of judges except through tribal merger. Through eye contact, she extends an invitation that quells his stress and seduces his body, a feminist answer to male coercion.

Resonating Balance

Out of distress with unalterable conditions, Octavia fashioned salubrious sci-fi islands that contrasted blight. In *Clay's Ark,* she spoke through internist Dr. Blake Jason Maslin the squalor of "vast, crowded, vulnerable" districts permeated by "sewers of utter lawlessness connecting cesspools—economic ghettos," which spew dwellers into less decadent residential areas (Butler, 1984, 12). A later description from Lupe, a former long-haul trucker, characterizes gang warfare in an urban "no-man's land" scorched by arson and bombing (*ibid.*, 30). To defend her truck from "bike packers, car bums, rogue truckers, every slimy maggot crawling over what's left of the highway system," Lupe arms herself, a self-protective mentality repeated in the Parable series (*ibid.*). The resultant shootout and explosion, like Old West paradigms, wipe out raiders, but not before killers decapitate sixteen-year-old Rane Maslin and toss her skull out the door. The insertion of gruesome death reminds the reader that the author avoided blue-sky endings to serious anarchy.

Later descriptions in *Clay's Ark* ramp up negativity with mention of car gangs, "body-parts dealers, arms smugglers" (*ibid., 37*). A touch of humor accompanies a kidnapping party seeking a male breeder, a reproductive gamut usually forced on women. The narrative applies a more respectful tone by pressuring starship crews to keep females out of space and by honoring Lorene, a midwife creating options for poor women. The choice of female victors shuns undue adulation. For strong women like Lorene, according to critic Sherley Anne Williams, a Fulbright scholar and English department chair at the University of California at San Diego, the author rewards "those who see and act upon possibilities" beyond the ordinary (Williams, 1986, 72).

Sources

Allison, Dorothy. "The Future of Female," *Village Voice* (19 December 1989): 67–68.
Butler, Octavia. *Clay's Ark*. New York: St. Martin's Press, 1984.
Grewe-Volpp, Christa. "Octavia Butler and the Nature/Culture Divide" in *Restoring the Connection to the Natural World*. Hamburg, Germany: LIT, 2003.
Kearse, Stephen. "The Essential Octavia Butler," *New York Times* (15 January 2021); 12–13.
Nanda, Aparajita "A Palimpsestuous Reading of Octavia Butler's *Lilith's Brood*" in *Palimpsests in Ethnic and Postcolonial Literature and Culture*. Cham, Switzerland: Palgrave Macmillan, 2021.
Turner, Jenny. "Ready to Go Off," *London Review of Books* 43:4 (18 February 2021).
Williams, Sherley Anne. "On Octavia E. Butler," *Ms.* 14:9 (March 1986): 70–73.

Transition

The nature of human advancement from locale to locale or persona to persona invests Octavia's headier fiction with models of conciliation, bargaining, and redemption alongside disorder and barbarity. The widow Lilith Iyapo, a compassionate earthling in *Dawn,* develops sensitivity to Nikanj, her immature alien companion. When he begins to evolve sexually, she feeds him fruit and nuts and remains close by, observing tremors in his shapeless body, the emergence of new tentacles, and deep sleep that precedes metamorphosis. Likewise imaginative, for survivors of apocalypse in the Parable novels, earth's retrogression results from technological invention of artificial wombs, an evolution commercializing the fetus. Conservatives denounce tampering with nature to yield robotized hatching and disparage assisted reproduction as "another toy of the rich" rather than a godsend to childless couples (Butler, 1998, 83). In both instances, the author applies humane criteria to her judgments of what Cajetan Iheka, a Yale University English professor, calls advancement to a "state of possibility" (Iheka, 2021).

The motif of change incorporates martyrdom and risk into paradoxical decision making. Terror of transforming into a disease carrier in *Clay's Ark* drives Andrew to struggle against alien sexual impulses by cutting his own throat. The idealist, Dr. Blake Jason Maslin, races to a California hospital to combat the extraterrestrial epidemic that haunts his family. The most progressive alternative derives from his daughter Keira, whom the contagion cured of acute myeloblastic leukemia. Because of her willingness to build a family around Japanese mate Stephen Kaneshiro and their mutant child, the novel rounds out an anarchic desert cult with hope for a changeover from human earthmen to an interspecies populace.

SMOOTHING THE WAY

Octavia views the subjective source of marital prejudice as one stage in the evolution of harmony. The biracial human Alanna Verrick's rescue by missionaries Jules and Neila Verrick in *Survivor* from alien Garkohn enslavers precedes community appraisal of an outsider. For Tahneh, the arrival at old age without bearing Hao Diut's children introduces feminist issues of barrenness and ageism for a high-born Hao woman replaced by Alanna, the young pariah. The story elevates a change in her self-important mate Diut, who concedes that pleasure and happiness are elements of loving a wife for herself. He acknowledges "a strong beauty to Alanna when one did not try to fit her into the Kohn image," a concession verifying his growth as lover and leader (Butler, 1978, 142).

Diut's progression from masculine dynast to tender husband anticipates the revamping of couples Lauren Oya Olamina and her older lover Taylor Franklin Bankole in *The Parable of the Sower* and Wright Hamlin and his underage vampire mate Shori Matthews in *Fledgling.* Both pairs confront real obstacles requiring altered thinking. For the Bankoles, differences in age foretell a solitary widowhood for Lauren. Wright, a human enchanted by an elfin girl, realizes late in his hasty affair that commitment to a vampire requires sanction of symbionts who supply her blood feedings. In each example, resolution of doubts to certainty eases for mates the differences that threaten stability.

Minor Compromises

A stumbling block for other of Octavia's characters lies in learning new languages, values, and customs in unfamiliar settings, the challenge for Nigerian captives traded to New World enslavers in *Kindred* and for An-yanwu in colonial Wheatley, New York, in *Wild Seed*. Among Dutch settlers in 1690, she begins that multiple tasks of eating American style and wearing seventeenth-century female dress, a confinement far less comfortable than her West African wraps. Similarly out of fashion, writer Dana Franklin of *Kindred* reaches a Maryland plantation in the early 1800s wearing slacks, an unheard-of adaptation to men's clothes encouraged by U.S. feminists after the 1960s. The transformation to plantation worker demands lies and evasions by claiming that she wears clothes suited to Kevin, her white owner. More troubling than physicality, her language discloses an educated mind from a liberal era, a deadly tell in her abrupt time slips into nineteenth-century patriarchy to complete what Dutch editor Eliza Steinbock and German zoologist Marianna Szczygielska termed "imagining a new world order" (Steinbock & Szczygielska, 2021, 5).

Near a Los Angeles jail, a troubling transformation in *Mind of My Mind* consumes Mary, whose brain fills with a "concentration of emotions"—a cacophony of thoughts streaming from the tortured cellmates inside (Butler, 1977, 15). Because her father/lover Doro intends her to marry Karl Larkin, an active telepath, and produce psionic children, she must experience the squabbles of sexual predators with Rina, her prostitute mother. On the way to telepathic fruition, over seventeen hours, Mary deals with "the pain and the craziness of it.... I felt like hell all the time ... about to blow" (*ibid.*, 12–13). The sudden seizure and delusions recur at transition, when she undergoes a grotesque feeling of slimy yellow worms gnawing her body. Because husband Karl's mind is entangled with hers, he suffers the same fantasy until she returns from clairvoyance to "sanity, reality" (Butler, 1977, 31). Much of Mary's transition derives from adjusting her shield to keep out predators and to screen noise while she intercepts others' thoughts. In the overview of what Barnabe Sebastian Mendoza, a Ph.D. candidate in comparative literature at Rutgers University, described as "creolizing methodology," Octavia lauds Mary's practicality and stoic acceptance of psionic woes as she reformulates the Patternist network.

Sources

Butler, Octavia. *Mind of My Mind*. New York: Doubleday, 1977.
_____. *The Parable of the Talents*. New York: Seven Stories Press, 1998.
_____. *Survivor*. New York: Doubleday, 1978.
Fry, Joan. "Interview," *Poets & Writers* (March/April 1997): 58–69.
Iheka, Cajetan. *African Ecomedia: Network Forms, Planetary Politics*. Durham, NC: Duke University Press, 2021.
Mendoza, Barnabe Sebastian. "Mythic Fertility, Impurity, and Creolization in the Works of Octavia E. Butler," (doctoral thesis), https://rucore.libraries.rutgers.edu/rutgers-lib/64065/, 2020.
Steinbock, Eliza, and Marianna Szczygielska, eds. *Tranimacies: Intimate Links Between Animal and Trans* Studies*. London: Routledge, 2021.

Villains

Octavia's deft creation of antagonists adds color and edge to personae and conflicts to journeys, the crisis in "Speech Sounds" when an unidentified knife-wielder stabs a woman and, in *Clay's Ark,* as Dr. Blake Jason Maslin attempts to save his twin daughters Keira and Rane from Mohave carjackers. In both instances, the author counters bold villainy with commendable actions by black heroes. Additional menacers reinforce the concept of perpetual danger from the everyday to the mythical and surreal:

AR—*Adulthood Rites*
AMN—"Amnesty"
BC—"Bloodchild"
BOM—"The Book of Martha"
CA—*Clay's Ark*
CF—"Childfinder"
Dawn—Dawn
EMN—"The Evening and the Morning and
    the Night"
Fl—*Fledgling*
Im—*Imago*

Kin—*Kindred*
LB—*Lilith's Brood*
MMM—*Mind of My Mind*
NB—"A Necessary Being"
PM—*Patternmaster*
POS—*The Parable of the Sower*
POT—*The Parable of the Talents*
SS—"Speech Sounds"
Sur—*Survivor*
WS—*Wild Seed*

Name	Source	Description	Target
aliens	AMN	experimenters on human anatomy and nutrition	humans
aliens	*Dawn*	captors and prison guards	Paul Titus
Andrew Steele Jarret	POS	bullying demagogue who subverts the U.S. presidency	poor, heathens
	POT	dispatcher of a Christian America militia	Acorn
Asa Elias "Eli" Doyle	CA	kidnapper	healthy people
Badger	CA	member of a desert raiding family kidnapping for ransom	vulnerable people
Blake Jason Maslin	CA	child molester	Keira Maslin
Christian America army	POT	suppressors of Acorn	Acorn, Lauren
Clayarks	PM	power mongers who pursue Coransee's rival	Teray, Amber
Coransee	PM	son of the Patternmaster and greedy brother	Iray, Teray
Cougar	POT	a crusader in the army of President Andrew Steele Jarret	children
Curt Loehr	*Dawn*	anti-alien axe murderer who kills Lilith Iyapo's husband Joe	Oankali, Joseph
Diut	NB	leader of Rohkohns to Tahneh's realm	Tahneh
Doro	MMM	barbarous rapist and killer of experimental hybrid telepaths	Mary Larkin

Name	Source	Description	Target
Doro	WS	constant threat to the children of his mate	An-yanwu
Eve	CF	opponent of black child psionics	Barbara
ex-con	Cross	former prisoner stalking his girl-friend	Jane
Gabriel Boyd	CA	patriarchal father	Media Boyd
gang	POS	deceivers and arsonists torturing outsiders	Keith Olamina
Garkohn	Sur	adversaries of Tehkohns	Alanna Verrick
humans	AMN	adversaries of aliens and their collaborators	Noah Cannon
Joseph Toler	WS	conniver and murderer of An-yanwu's son	Stephen
Karl Larkin's mother	MMM	alcoholic who burns Karl's hand into a stump	Karl
Katherine Dahlman	Fl	spokeswoman for racist Silks	Shori Matthews
knife wielder	SS	savage attacker	lone woman, Obsidian
Lale Sachs	WS	a potential rapist and marauder	women
maggots	POT	armored vehicles carrying gas canisters	Lauren, Acorn
Marcos Duran	POT	egotistical pulpit speaker	Larkin Bankole
Nahtahk	Sur	arrogant, vicious, untrustworthy First Hunter of Garkohns	Diut
Neci	AR	conniving enemy of aliens and arsonist at Phoenix	Oankali
Orel Ingraham	CA	diseased kidnapper	healthy people
paints	POS	exotic hair and skin coloring to promote terror	Californians
Paul Titus	Dawn	attacker and potential rapist	Lilith Iyapo
pyros	POS	arsonists maddened by the drug 'ro	Californians
Rachel "Rae" Davidson	MMM	deceiver of a minister about his supernatural power	Eli Torrey
Raleigh Curtis	Fl	rifleman who shoots at Shori Matthews and Wright Hamlin	Shori Matthews
resisters	AR	anti-migration group that threatens an earth diaspora	Lilith Iyapo, Akin
Rufus Weylin	Kin	manipulator of black women	Alice Greenwood, Dana Franklin
Shori Matthews	Fl	strong, agile vampire hungry for blood	Wright Hamlin, Theo-dora Harden
Silks	Fl	raiders who hurl gasoline bombs	Shori Matthews
Stephen	NK	incestuous exploiter of sister	Barbara
T'Gatoi	BC	seducer of a naive boy	Gan
T'Khotgif Teh	BC	breeder with a human male	Bram Lomas
Tlics	BC	caterpillars who threaten human males with pregnancy	Gan

Name	Source	Description	Target
Tom Weylin	Kin	plantation owner and slave master	blacks
		abuser of wife and child	Margaret, Rufus
tyrants	CF	enemies of childfinders who harbor psionic kids	Barbara
"Vee" Vivian	MMM	rival for affections of Karl Larkin	Mary

For Octavia's skill at the ramifications of human morality, author Samuel R. Delany admitted, "She may well be the best of us" (Delany, 2021, 42).

CHARACTERIZING EVIL

In the style of John Milton's Adam and Satan in *Paradise Lost,* the author crafts villains to match wily protagonists and heroes, for example, an obnoxious wino leering at Jane in "Crossover," Barbara outfoxing Eve's stalkers in "Childfinder," and history professor Valerie Rye staring down an obscene bus passenger in the story "Speech Sounds." An abstract evil, Christian America, a rigid theocracy under President Andrew Steele Jarret in the Parable series, conceals torture under "mindless rigidity" and soul cleansing (Butler, 1998, 250). Octavia relates the method of brainwashing to "medieval inquisitors," especially Castilian monk Tomás de Torquemada, the zealous fifteenth-century Catholic executioner of some two thousand alleged heretics during the Spanish Inquisition (*ibid.*). The methods compare to Jarret's—a pretense of piety as a reason for persecuting and immuring free citizens.

Extreme behaviors elevate physical and philosophical determiners, as with the reputation of Nubian mutant Doro, the Gothic villain in *Mind of My Mind* and *Wild Seed,* for raping and murdering people without remorse. In describing her prototype, Octavia told Janice Bogstad, an interviewer for *Janus,* that he was a "mindless villain ... villainous and rotten and evil" (Bogstad, 1978–1979, 31). His choice of the wastrel Joseph Toler as a husband for Margaret in *Wild Seed* illustrates a disrespect for family ethics. To characterize the dastardly Rohkohn Nahtahk, the author of *Survivor* posed enemy threats of painting enemy Garkohns red and of burning eyes, hands, and ham-strung legs before tethering victims like house pets. Villains in *Fledgling* appear less detailed during gas-tossing nighttime raids, which obscure identities until Shori Matthews pinpoints them in a vampire Council of Justice. The punishment ensures an end to the Silks clan and their spokeswoman, Katherine Dahlman, who goes to her grave headless.

OVERT DEVILTRY

Devoid of the supernatural, a nineteenth-century mortal in *Kindred,* greedy Maryland plantation owner Tom Weylin, brutalizes family and slaves, forcing his wife Margaret to escape to Baltimore. The action spotlights impromptu lashing against a "man stripped naked and tied to the trunk of a dead tree" for blows from a six-foot whip, a serpentine icon of a barbaric abuser (Butler, 1979, 92). Tom bears responsibility for hiring managers capable of cowing slaves. Atrocities derive from overseers Evan Fowler and Jake Edwards, who belabor farm workers with unrealistic expectations. Forced labor requires strokes of the lash, the symbol of slave tribulations that, according to California theologian Patrick B. Reyes, "will always be with us" (Reyes, 2021, 36). The neo-slave narrative, according to Scott Timberg, book reviewer for the *Los Angeles Times,* preceded a sea change in Octavia's image of evil from pseudo-medieval villainy to "'70s elements—environmental concerns, drugs and mystical experiences," the hallmarks of Octavia's Xenogenesis and Earthseed series (Timberg, 2010, E8).

Less clear than *Kindred's* slave era atrocities are the workings of ooloi Nikanj, the gene mixer in *Dawn,* a shapeless, tentacled alien who woos reluctant humans with intense sexual pleasure. Stephen Kearse, a book critic for the *New York Times,* explicated the novel's ambiguous galactic overlords:

> Many critics read the Oankali as benevolent saviors and Butler certainly does not make them outright villains, but the first book renders clearly their manipulation. Chemical essentialists, the Oankali see reality in narrow terms that ignore verbal consent and are always patronizing [Kearse, 2021, 13].

Octavia leaves in doubt Nikanj's rationalization for forcing earthlings to accept bi-species reproduction, his Oankali means of purifying human urges and exterminating the earthly race. In a retrospect of the Earthseed series and its attempt at rectifying human foibles, Gabriela Brischini Grecca of the Universidade Estadual Pauli in São Paulo, Brazil, agrees with Kearse that Octavia's perusals of evil "are not always obvious to the reader who is accustomed to binaries like villains (bad)/victims (good)," the embodiments of harm in early sci-fi (Grecca, 2021, 348).

Sources

Bogstad, Janice. "Interview," *Janus* 14:4 (Winter, 1978–1979): 28–32.
Butler, Octavia. *Kindred.* New York: Doubleday, 1979.
Delany, Samuel R. *Occasional Views Volume 1.* Middletown, CT: Wesleyan University Press, 2021.
Goodwin, Matthew David. *The Latinx Files: Race, Migration, and Space Aliens.* New Brunswick, NJ: Rutgers University Press, 2021.
Grecca, Gabriela Brischini. "'A Racist Challenge Might Force Us Apart': Divergence, Reliance and Empathy in *Parable of the Sower,*" *Ilha do Desterro* 74:1 (January–April 2021): 347–362.
Kearse, Stephen. "The Essential Octavia Butler," *New York Times* (15 January 2021): 12–13.
Reyes, Patrick B. *The Purpose Gap: Empowering Communities of Color to Find Meaning and Thrive.* Louisville, KY: Westminster John Knox Press, 2021.
Timberg, Scott. "A Timely, Timeless Appeal," *Los Angeles Times* (18 April 2010): E8.

Weylin, Rufus

The preschool white child whom Octavia's heroine saves from drowning in *Kindred* becomes a mystic obsession with time traveler Edana "Dana" Franklin. Because of what Janet Fiskio, on staff at Oberlin College in Oberlin, Ohio, calls an "affective connection" or telepathic link with Rufus, Dana repeatedly rescues her white great great grandfather and aids his character development to ensure her family's siring (Fiskio, 2021, 66). One of Octavia's dedicated teachers alongside Valerie Rye in "Speech Sounds" and Cory Duran and Lauren Oya Olamina in *The Parable of the Sower,* Dana reads aloud to the boy and guides his future "through a focus of books as survival guides" (*ibid.*). By modeling twentieth-century literacy, she risks scourging "until she is convinced that she might die," but she retains the role of Rufus's mentor in the belief that ten generations of "history must be told by the enslaved" (*ibid.*, 107, 70). The text accounts for current cultural conditions and attitudes with force and immediacy.

Like an old friend, Rufus acts the part of parent to an Ibio/Igbo *ogbanje* or *abunje*, a Nigerian child born and reborn to the same mother. Stella Setka, an English teacher at West Los Angeles College, explained that the "repetitive loop of the ogbanje life cycle mirrors the cycle of trauma, which, unless addressed and worked through, returns time and again" like a punitive ghost (Setka, 2020, 46). Like Lilith Iyapo's trusting son Akin in *Adulthood Rites,* Rufus trusts Dana's vague explanations of time travel, swimming and CPR, short hair, educated diction, and modern clothes and offers her advice on sanctuary. He reveals misgivings about his unique visitor: "I never know how to treat you. You confuse everybody … the kind of black who watches and thinks and makes trouble" (Butler, 1979, 255). As her guide to early nineteenth-century social and racial customs, he informs her of the use of "niggers" and "master" to denote the antebellum Maryland plantation hierarchy that he will soon join.

Parental Models

The contradictory parenting of Tom and Margaret Weylin sets antithetical examples for the boy's character. From Tom, the boy receives rough handling and arbitrary judgments preceding threats and lashes across the back with a six-foot whip, a brutal dominance similar to Tom's belaboring of slaves. Lacking his heavy hand, Margaret, like other of Octavia's maternal figures, sweet-talks the boy and shields him from outsiders, but remains secondary in child control to her prominent husband. During a doctor's realignment of Rufus's leg broken in a fall from a tree in 1819, she claws at Kevin Franklin, who holds the boy steady. Just as Rufus heals from Tom's verbal and physical flogging, his spirit acquires stamina and an unfortunate adoption of his father's truculent outbursts that corrupt his boyhood love of the black children he grew up with.

The influence of literacy instills in Rufus a new route to dominance. Because Dana reads aloud from Daniel Defoe's *Robinson Crusoe,* a sea adventure of a shipwrecked English sailor marooned on an island overrun by cannibals, Rufus craves more stories that reveal individual resistance to villainy. Rather than make an analogy between cannibals and his father's barbarous treatment of agrarian slaves, he chooses to "get somebody who makes her living by writing to write some very persuasive letters," his indirect grasp at aid from the outside world (Butler, 1979, 227). The ploy fails after Tom's death, a loss that leaves Rufus angry at the doctor who failed to save his patient, a psychological transference of blame to the innocent.

An Aberrant Model

Octavia pinpoints how Tom Weylin's reduction of Rufus to obedient factotum predisposes the boy to mimic Tom's autocracy in his adult life. She replicates the domestic situation in the Parable series with the sexist gender roles that polyga-mist Richard Moss demands of his three wives. Living in an androcentric household reflecting Mormon bondage of female Ina vampires in *Fledgling*, the Moss women in *The Parable of the Sower* endure home chores, raising rabbits for sale, and a sex-ual slavery that produces cyclical pregnancies. Sherley Anne Williams, a Fulbright scholar and English department chair at the University of California at San Diego, noted the paradox: "Dana's relationship with Rufus is a brutal reversal of her mar-riage in her own time" (Williams, 1986, 72). Like father, like son, Rufus mistreats and impregnates his once-free black mistress, Alice Greenwood, the mother of his children Hagar, Miriam, Aaron, and Joe.

Because Rufus menaces his future scion with sexual violence, the author legit-imates the knifing of Dana's ancestor, who is incapable of erasing Tom, the model tyrant, from his son's impressionable youth. Martin Japtok, an English teacher at Palomar College in San Marcos, California, added that "absolute power over Alice and his pathological relationship to power negate the possibility of love" toward family, mistress, or Alice's children (Japtok, 2020, 51). Mystic violence to Dana, the witness, permeates the toxic relationship with transformative scarring. Haitian-Canadian scholar Myriam J.A. Chancy stated that the arm amputation essentially etches the plantation experience on her flesh, a testimonial to permanent damage to black Americans by ancestral abuse and sexual exploitation.

See also Dana Franklin; *Kindred*.

Sources

Butler, Octavia. *Kindred*. New York: Doubleday, 1979.
Chancy, Myriam J.A. *Autochthonomies: Transnationalism, Testimony, and Transmission in the African Diaspora*. Champaign: University of Illinois Press, 2020.
Fiskio, Janet. *Climate Change, Literature, and Environmental Justice: Poetics of Dissent and Repair*. Cam-bridge, UK: Cambridge University Press, 2021.
Grecca, Gabriela Bruschini. "'A Racist Challenge Might Force Us Apart': Divergence, Reliance, and Empa-thy in *Parable of the Sower* by Octavia Butler," *Ilha do Desterro* 74:1 (January–April 2021): 347–362.
Japtok, Martin, and Jerry Rafiki Jenkins, eds. *Human Contradictions in Octavia E. Butler's Work*. Cham, Switzerland: Palgrave, Macmillan, 2020.
Setka, Stella. *Empathy and the Phantasmic in Ethnic American Trauma Narratives*. Lanham, MD: Lexing-ton Books, 2020.
Williams, Sherley Anne. "On Octavia E. Butler," *Ms.* 14:9 (March 1986): 70–73.

"Why Is Science Fiction So White?"

In "Why Is Science Fiction So White?," an essay for the art magazine *Garage*—originally called "The Lost Races of Science Fiction" in a 1980 edition of *Trans-mission Magazine*—Octavia demanded to know why "Blacks, Asians, Hispanics, Amerindians, minority characters in general have been noticeably absent from most science fiction" (Butler, 2018). She credited refugees and migrants with being mem-bers in the human race and, therefore, a constant global presence. Comparing cin-ema with sci-fi books, she championed the normality of brown and black humans among "the tall, furry people; the lumpy scaly people; the tentacled people; etc." (*ibid.*).

The author reasoned that white dominance resulted from habit and custom, laziness and ignorance: thus, an increase in black writers and black-authored books might entice more black samplers of science fiction. In the estimation of Clifton Zeno Johnson of State University of New York at Albany, Octavia focused world-changing fiction on the post-colonial issue of inclusivity and how "skin color remains a polarizing topic" (Johnson, 2019, iii). She warned in the 1995 essay "The Monophobic Response" that rejecting other humans leads to the snobbish rejection of "they, them, this people," the undesirables "relegated to a lower place in the social hierarchy" (Butler, 1995, 416; Johnson 2019, 18). She illustrated the workings of exclusion by creating Clayarks and feline children in *Clay's Ark* and *Patternmaster,* psionic children in "Childfinder," a black vampire in *Fledgling,* and the Oankali in the Xenogenesis series.

To enhance authenticity, Octavia's stance on equity proposed the Ghanaian-Nigerian Akan-Twi belief in *sankofa,* retrieval of useful beliefs from the past, which Johnson summarized as "reach back and embrace" (*ibid.,* 1). She urged authors to treat minority races as people, not the stereotyped "uncle" or "mammy." Such stereotypes violated realism with "unbelievable, self-consciously manipulated puppets, pieces of furniture" like the slaves in Margaret Mitchell's *Gone with the Wind* (*ibid.*). She provided exemplary models of inclusion in Patternmaster Mary Larkin, the superior telepath in *Mind of My Mind,* astronaut Asa Elias "Eli" Doyle in *Clay's Ark,* Martha Bes in "The Book of Martha," and writer Dana Franklin in *Kindred.*

See also Afrofuturism.

Sources

Butler, Octavia. "The Monophobic Response" in *Dark Matter: A Century of Speculative Fiction from the African Diaspora*. New York: Aspect/Warner Books, 2000, 415–416.
———. "Why Is Science Fiction So White?," *Garage* 15 (4 September 2018).
Dee, Nat. "Octavia E. Butler and Inclusivity in Science Fiction," acriticofeverything.wordpress.com/2020/08/11/octavia-e-butler-and-inclusivity-in-science-fiction/ (11 August 2020).
Johnson, Clifton Zeno. *Race in the Galactic Age: Sankofa, Afrofuturism, Whiteness and Whitley Strieber*. Albany: State University of New York, 2019.

Wild Seed

To revive the African feminine divine as a deterrent to twentieth-century patriarchy and racism, Octavia created a "black feminist urtext" that parallels shapeshifting with a vampiric body snatcher as opposites (Ibrahim, 2021, 46). She set the time travel plot of *Wild Seed* among the colonial Ibo/Igbo, whom award-winning Nigerian writer Chinua Achebe examined in *Things Fall Apart*. To Janice Bogstad, an interviewer for *Janus,* the author explained the Ibo/Igbo myth of the *ogbanje* or *abunje,* an evil child spirit who persecutes a mother by killing her children. Doro, the immortal Nubian mastermind, takes the role of child slayer by winnowing the best Africans to serve as lab rats. They do his bidding in "seed villages" for breeding experiments on telepaths who read thoughts and intentions, the genesis of a bio-genetically altered society (Butler, 1980, 4). Because of his disregard of human morality, he ignores the taboo of incest with his daughters by what Canadian scholar

Ella Boccara of the University of Montreal termed "la tyranny intime (intimate tyranny)," a crime specifically against women of his family (Boccara, 2020, i).

Applying an Afrocentric folk concept of cyclical time, Octavia moved effortlessly through millennia. After tracking an unusual person west from Sudan over millennia, Doro meets the oracular healer An-yanwu in what Adwoa Afful, an affiliate of York University in Toronto, calls "fictionalised pre-colonial Igboland" (Afful, 2016, 95). Doro witnesses her re-embodiments through metamorphoses into younger, more vigorous forms of male and female. The monumental encounter of undying male with shapeshifting female recasts the gentler Genesis myth of Adam and Eve into a vampiric war of wills and resistance. In the analysis of *New York Times Book Review* author Stephen Kearse, "They traverse present-day Nigeria, the Atlantic Ocean and then colonial and antebellum North America, seducing and conning each other the whole way like competing spies" (Kearse, 2021, 12–13).

Hybrid Variants

Complicating the mythic foundations, Octavia listed elements of the flesh trade and slave sale in 1690 as a lesson in black history by itemizing the crowding and filth of typical slave ships. She featured talented captives as the "seed" of Doro's American experiments in New York and Virginia, notably, newlyweds Udenkwo and Okoye, named for Nigerian villagers in *Things Fall Apart.* Eluding coarse charges of heathenism and cannibalism, Okoye ironically rebuts the white North American myth of a ship's loadmaster that black Africans fatten whites for eating. To elevate Doro's sons as models of courage, the narrative orchestrates a fearsome storm at sea and piloting by the blond, triracial Isaac, Doro's best son, whom Octavia models on the late-in-life child of Sarah and Abraham from Genesis 21:1–2. With superhuman psychokinesis, he wills the small, hardy sloop *Silver Star* rapidly through the gale. His multiple skills imply that migrants of mixed heritage offer great worth to new territories.

The author toyed with gendered and ethnic variant characters alongside alternative species. The addition of shapeshifting trials reveals An-yanwu's intractability and her curiosity about the lives of leopards, eagles, and sharks. She favors dolphins, a seagoing species she compared to "friendly people" for their individualized touch (Butler, 1980, 203). In an oceanic ode to sexuality, Octavia rhapsodizes on dolphin leaps, circles, and parallel swimming in courting couples, which critic Nisi Shawl, a journalist for *Ms.* Magazine and the *Seattle Times,* credited with a "strange, beautiful urgency" (Butler, 2014, 7). The poetic transmigration of a dolphin into a naked woman precedes caressing of flippers, ears, beak, tail, and fin and introduces the mystic possibilities of An-yanwu's offspring, the object of Doro's attraction to her and his fear of her feral brawn.

Debating Right and Wrong

At the climax of the An-yanwu-Doro love story, Octavia enumerated Doro's weaknesses in controlling a far-flung mongrel clan of his own breeding. Because he longs to possess a "wild seed," he recognizes limitations in omnipotence and in trouncing An-yanwu's shape-changing prowess. Ironically, he knows that she "had to be destroyed eventually" and share the doom of all his novelties (Butler, 1980, 49). His immoral logic bumps up against An-yanwu's query of incest: pledging her to his multitalented son Isaac, a blond human. In godless, self-willed fashion, Doro declares that "right and wrong were what he said they were," a pigheadedness more suited to toddlers and banana republic despots (*ibid.*, 222).

DORO'S DOWNFALL

In Chapter eight, another change involves An-yanwu with Thomas, a scabby, alcoholic hermit, an unlikely nemesis for Doro. To the Nubian's surprise, she chooses to heal rather than annihilate him and takes him to bed, coaxing intimacy as an antidote to his addiction. The standoff against Doro presses both Thomas and An-yanwu toward execution for disobedience, the oppressor's standard punishment of rebels. Octavia turned Doro's instant metamorphosis into a demonic being with bestial eyes and the former physique of Thomas. Saving An-yanwu from execution by sacrificing himself, Thomas endears himself, causing her to loathe more deeply the autocratic schemer. The narrative crowns her wifely love with a need to escape the too settled life in Wheatley, New York, and to rejoin the dolphins, the wild-scape of sea, and a soothing marine ambience.

Doro's search for An-yanwu in 1840 reveals his seed villages in Canada, Brazil, Mexico, and Kentucky, a spare outline of black diaspora throughout the Western Hemisphere. At Avoyelles Parish plantation in Louisiana, according to interpreter Theri Alyce Pickens, an English professor at Bates College in Lewiston, Maine, An-yanwu finds "the opportunity to look to others for healing, and to build solidarity with those similarly outcast," a compassion and diversity lacking in Doro's proposed utopias (Pickens, 2014, 33). The threat of his takeover of the "strange collection of misfits" begins with the introduction of Joseph Toler, a layabout known for wenching, gambling, boozing, and physical beauty (*ibid.*, 596). As Doro's choice of a prospective husband for Margaret Nneka, Joseph inserts evil into the family. His extinction by An-yanwu's leopard fangs to the throat suits the conniver and slayer of An-yanwu's son Stephen. The loss of Margaret to suicide illustrates the extensive suffering caused by a worthless lout to his family, an echo of the Weylin household's disorder in *Kindred* under the charge of either Tom or Rufus.

Building momentum on the interplay of gender strengths, Octavia highlighted how Doro transforms An-yanwu to bring her close to infinitude. A tumble into light causes her to feel spiritual balm from his lordly presence and his need for a mate. Paradoxically, the epiphany discloses a new masculinity in Doro. More than the previous four thousand years, he savors an affinity with An-yanwu actualized by his drinking her sweet, nourishing breast milk. By dispatching his lover on a clipper ship to the Pacific coast, he keeps his "Sun Woman" safe, an indication of humanity in the one being he cannot foil. Their compromise, which undermines patriarchy and colonialism, designates California, a modern Eldorado, as a setting for a unique, but imperfect family.

See also An-yanwu; Doro; Doro's Genealogy; *Mind of My Mind.*

Sources

Afful, Adwoa. "Wild Seed: Africa and Its Many Diasporas," *Critical Arts* 30:4 (August 2016): 93–104.

Boccara, Ella. "Female Identity and Race in Contemporary Afrofuturist Narratives: *Wild Seed* by Octavia Butler" (dissertation) University of Montreal, December 16, 2020.

Bogstad, Janice. "Interview," *Janus* 14:4 (Winter, 1978–1979): 28–32.

Butler, Octavia. *Unexpected Stories*. New York: Open Road Media, 2014.

_____. *Wild Seed*. New York: Doubleday, 1980.

Ibrahim, Habiba. *Black Age: Oceanic Lifespans and the Time of Black Life*. Albany: New York University Press, 2021.

Kearse, Stephen. "The Essential Octavia Butler," *New York Times* (15 January 2021): 12–13.

McCaffery, Larry, ed. *Across the Wounded Galaxies*. Urbana: University of Illinois Press, 1990.

McKoy, Sheila Smith. "Yemonja/Yemoja/Yemaya Rising," *Recovering the African Feminine Divine in Literature, the Arts, and Practice: Yemonja Awakening*. Lanham, MD: Lexington Books, 2020, 55–68.

Pickens, Theri. "'You're Supposed to Be a Tall, Handsome, Fully Grown White Man': Theorizing Race, Gender, and Disability in Octavia Butler's *Fledgling*," *Journal of Literary & Cultural Disability Studies* 8:1 (2014): 33–48, 126.

Pitts, Michael. *Alternative Masculinities in Feminist Speculative Fiction: A New Man*. Lanham, MD: Lexington Books, 2021.

Xenogenesis

The author's Xenogenesis series set a human precedent for tolerance with a simple motto, "Embrace difference" (Butler, 2000, 329). The text directed characters and readers to respect a companionate species that produced offspring different from their parents. Journalist Therese Littleton of the *Seattle Times* endorsed Octavia's creation of "a genre standard for portrayal of literary extraterrestrials as truly alien, and not just humans in disguise" (Littleton, 2004, K1). In betterment of sci-fi, her beings procreate the first interspecies, intergender race. The concept carried toward completion H.G. Wells' attraction to otherness in *Island of Dr. Moreau,* yet fell short of a utopian conclusion. At issue lay the threat of exterminating human individualism within an overwhelming mutation.

At the opening of the Southern Alberta Art Gallery exhibition Xenogenesis, the Otolith Group, a Canadian art collective, displayed works completed from 2011 to 2018 on themes of alien nomads. The assembly featured xenophiles attracted to genetic variation such as the DNA mixer Nikanj in *Dawn,* the caterpillar T'Gatoi seducing the human Gan in "Bloodchild," and the vampire reception of Shori Matthews, a human-Ina mutant in *Fledgling.* The Lethbridge, Alberta, *Herald* summarized the trilogy's subjects as "human extinction, racial distinction, planetary transformation, enforced mutation, generative alienation and altered kinship," all found in Octavia's future speculations ("Exhibitions," 2020, A4). British scholar Sarah Wood, a sci-fi specialist at Birmingham City University, depicted the Xenogenesis series as a rewrite of Judeo-Christian myth and biblical authority and an exploration of liberated black defiers of patriarchy, Octavia's *sui generis* wonder women. At the pinnacle of action, Wood admired her conflicts of will within a Euro-structured caste system that fictional Afro-amazons had to endure and neutralize from within.

Begun with one of the author's spunky mother figures, the omnibus publication *Lilith's Brood* pictures Lilith Iyapo, a 26-year-old black widow who bears the laurels of all-mother and the scorn of Judas. On a dynamic spaceship, alien Oankali overlords preserve recovering earthlings 250 years after a devastating nuclear war. They plot special uses for Lilith, whose courage they admire. The noun "brood" signifies her experimental offspring and the heavy cloud of discontent and apprehension that precedes a mass pilgrimage to Mars. She exemplifies a female internee under cultural imperialism, a resetting of Wright Hamlin's encounter with a provocative vampire in *Fledgling* and interpreter Noah Cannon's translation of an alien language in "Amnesty." In an essay for *Extrapolation,* reviewer Karina Vado, an English professor at the University of Florida at Gainesville, chose a more controlling theme for *Lilith's Brood:* "the inseparability of biology and culture" as they apply to cloning (Vado, 2019, 214).

Accepting an Alien Species

The influx of Butler criticism derived from academic debates of her intent. In London at Brunel University, media director Johannes Birringer, author of *Kinetic Atmospheres,* related Octavia's fanciful setting to the enchanted forests of fairy tales, the ideal locale for otherworldly encounters and outré creature. For example, because of genetic tinkering without her consent, Lilith is capable of weathering incarceration by tentacled aliens and of disciplining and training post-war human survivors, whom the Oankali store in perpetual sleep. The end product is a reformed human unafraid to crossbreed with aliens. Her offspring Jodahs, a Dracula parallel, introduces an unprecedented being capable of suppressing earth's adversaries of change or of leading the more compliant to Mars, Octavia's choice of a future homeland among the stars.

Critic Gerry Canavan described the amoral Oankali as genocidal in the style of nineteenth- and twentieth-century imperialists. For source material, the author based the Xenogenesis trilogy on the story of Virginia native Henrietta Lacks, the unknowing contributor of aggressive cervical cancer cells in 1951 to Johns Hopkins research labs. In her honor, scientists named the tissue HeLa, the identity of the Norse goddess of the underworld. Eventually repopulating the Amazon Basin on an otherwise unlivable earth, Octavia's hopeless settlers force their captors to release the rest of humankind. Survivors revere the philosophical concept of *zoe* (the Greek ζωή, life), a disembodied and zesty force wielded by Jodahs, the benevolent diplomat. As healer, he adapts human cancer to anatomical regeneration, Octavia's reflection on defective human blood cells immune to AIDS. He convinces Phoenix villagers to banish disgust at tentacled beings and accept a human–Oankali race, a fictional parallel of black Africans assimilated into colonial America.

Mixed Reviews

Compared to the Patternist series, *Lilith's Brood* earned less critical attention because of its reverse momentum. In an essay for *Village Voice,* Florida-born feminist writer Dorothy Allison regretted that the dynamic maneuverings in *Dawn* give way to tediously detailed reproductive results in *Adulthood Rites* and *Imago* of three genders:

Human	Ooloi Ooan	Oankali Mate	Offspring
Ahajas	Nikanj	—	human-Oankali hybrid
Ahajas	Nikanj	Dichaan	Tiikuchahk, a sexless Oankali hybrid and Akin's sibling
Jesusa & Tomás Serrano y Martín	—	—	Javier and Paz
Lilith Iyapo	—	Dichaan	three human-Oankali hybrid daughters
Lilith Iyapo	Nikanj	—	human-Oankali hybrid
Lilith Iyapo & Joseph	Dehkiaht	Dichaan	Akin Iyapo, the first human-Oankali hybrid, who adopts Tino as a human father
Lilith Iyapo & Sam	—	—	Ayre, a human son and Akin's sibling
Lilith Iyapo & Tino Leal	—	—	Aaor, a non-gender human-ooloi hybrid
Jodahs, a human-ooloi hybrid	—	—	
Lilith Iyapo & Vidor Domonkos	Nikanj	Dichaan	Margit, a human-Oankali daughter
Nigerian parents	—		Sam, a human son
Mateo & Pilar	—		Augustino "Tino" Lael, a human son
Paz & Santos	—		human children died
Tediin	Kahguyaht	Jdahya	Nikanj, an ooloi

Allison applauded Oankali morals, which promote an idealized family unity through joyful sexual relations, childbearing, and rearing, "the fine line between compromise and betrayal" of human traits (Allison, 1989, 68). Unlike the dogged human resistance in the first novel, the ongoing attitude of nay-sayers in *Adulthood Rites* resembles "more stubbornness than xenophobia" (*ibid.*).

The last two volumes focus on the coming of age of pro–Mars evangelist Akin, Lilith's bi-species son, and his sibling Jodahs, the evolving ooloi mediator who ushers a fertile clan of South American Andeans onto a shuttle bound for Mars for terraforming and settlement. Without citing details and outcomes of an open-ended resolution, *Imago* portends a future of beings dependent on approval of mutant merger, a parallel of slaves accepting biracial children sired by their masters. In a negative review for the *Washington Post*, critic Ted White charged Octavia with overwriting while omitting the immorality of the parasitic Oankali, who conspire to destroy earth's remains. From a symbolic perspective, Rikk Mulligan, a digital specialist at Carnegie Mellon University in Pittsburgh, finds the trilogy "oddly triumphal, celebrating the spirit of the individual who overcomes surveillance and the failure of scientific control" (Mulligan, 2018, 209).

See also Lilith; *Lilith's Brood*.

Sources

Allison, Dorothy. "The Future of Female," *Village Voice* (19 December 1989): 67–68.

Birringer, Johannes. *Kinetic Atmospheres: Performance and Immersion*. Abingdon, UK: Routledge, 2021.

Butler, Octavia. *Adulthood Rites* in *Lilith's Brood*. New York: Warner, 2000.

Canavan, Gerry. *Octavia E. Butler*. Urbana: University of Illinois, 2016.

Dunkley, Kitty. "Becoming Posthuman: The Sexualized, Racialized, and Naturalized Others of Octavia E. Butler's *Lilith's Brood*" in *The Bloomsbury Handbook to Octavia E. Butler*. New York: Bloomsbury, 2020, 95–116.

"Exhibitions Open at SAAG," *Lethbridge* (Alberta) *Herald* (26 September 2020): A4.

Littleton, Therese. "'Black to the Future': Fest Is Mothership for African Americans in Science Fiction," *Seattle Times* (6 June 2004): K1.

Mulligan, Rikk. "Renewing the Sense of an Ending," *Extrapolation* 59:2 (2018): 205–209.

Pough, Gwendolyn D., & Yolanda Hood. "Speculative Black Women: Magic, Fantasy, and the Supernatural," *Femspec* 6:1 (June 2005): ix.

Vado, Karina. "On Genomics and Identity," *Extrapolation* 60:2 (2019): 210–215.

White, Ted. "Love with the Proper Stranger," *Washington Post* (25 June 1989): 8.

Aphorisms
by Octavia Butler

- All struggles/Are essentially power struggles. (*The Parable of the Sower*)
- Be Good to one another. (*The Parable of the Talents*)
- Choose your leaders with wisdom and forethought. (*The Parable of the Talents*)
- Civilization is the way one's own people live. Savagery is the way foreigners live. (*Wild Seed*)
- Consider—/We are born/Not with purpose,/But with potential. (*Earthseed*)
- Don't Matter what ought to be. Matters what is. (*Kindred*)
- Down through history, in myth and even in science, we've kept putting ourselves in the center, and then being evicted. ("Amnesty")
- Education is the most direct pathway to God. (*The Parable of the Talents*)
- Embrace difference. (*Adulthood Rites*)
- Everyone has something that they can do better than they can do anything else. ("Positive Obsession")
- Everything truly alive dies sooner or later. (*Wild Seed*)
- Getting a rejection slip was like being told your child was ugly. ("Positive Obsession")
- God exists to be shaped. (*The Parable of the Sower*)
- Habit is persistence in practice. ("Furor Scribendi")
- Have faith and work your ass off. (*The Parable of the Talents*)
- Have your fun, then come up with a wonderful-sounding reason why it was the right thing for you to do. (*Adulthood Rites*)
- How many times can you have everyone taken from you and still have the will to start again? (*Dawn*)
- How much of what we do is encouraged, discouraged, or otherwise guided by what we are genetically? ("The Evening and the Morning and the Night")
- Human babies are ugly even when they're normal, but we love them. If we didn't the species would die. (*Clay's Ark*)
- Human beings ought to be able to behave better than a bunch of rats. ("Amnesty")
- I consider protecting an unborn child a responsibility for two. (*Patternmaster*)

245

- If you have to do something, it might as well feel good. (*Dawn*)
- If you work hard enough at something that doesn't matter, you can forget for a while about the things that do. ("The Evening and the Morning and the Night")
- Leaving children illiterate is criminal. (*The Parable of the Talents*)
- Life was treasure. (*Imago*)
- A lot of solid-looking things can be destroyed quickly. (*Survivor*)
- Make a habit of doing your best. ("Furor Scribendi")
- The more educated, the more sophisticated, the more thoughtful we are, the more able we are to conceal the child within us. ("The Monophobic Response")
- No part of me is more definitive of who I am than my brain. (*Dawn*)
- Not all children let themselves be molded into what their parents want them to be. (*Kindred*)
- Not all feelings are reasonable. ("A Necessary Being")
- Nothing ever works smoothly with humankind. ("The Book of Martha")
- The only lasting truth/Is Change. (*The Parable of the Sower;* "Brave New World")
- Our only help is ourselves and one another. ("The Monophobic Response")
- Our record in dealing with each other does not bode well for any nonhuman species we might discover, no matter how peaceful we believe our intentions to be. ("Future Forum")
- People are still animals when it comes to breeding. ("The Evening and the Morning and the Night")
- People must be their own gods and make their own good fortune. (*Wild Seed*)
- Reality was whatever happened, whatever she perceived. (*Dawn*)
- Rejections are … every writer's rite of passage. ("Furor Scribendi")
- Religions are no more perfect than any other human institutions. (*The Parable of the Talents*)
- Slavery was a long slow process of dulling. (*Kindred*)
- Sometimes it's a good thing to scare people. (*Adulthood Rites*)
- Sometimes, one must become a master to avoid becoming a slave. (*Wild Seed*)
- Suspicion is more likely to keep you alive than trust. (*The Parable of the Sower*)
- Take care of one another. (*The Parable of the Talents*)
- There are so many tiny things within even one cell of a human body. (*Wild Seed*)
- There are times when people need religion more than anything else. (*The Parable of the Talents*)
- There're worse things than being dead. (*Kindred*)
- There's more to healing than just closing wounds. (*Imago*)
- There's nothing wrong with being stoic when you have to be. (*The Parable of the Talents*)

- We are unable to get along with those aliens who are closest to us, those aliens who are of course ourselves. ("The Monophobic Response")
- We are vastly more self-centered than is necessary for our survival and our progress. ("Future Forum")
- When men have absolute power over women, the men rape. (*The Parable of the Talents*)
- Who knows what we humans have that others might be willing to take in trade for a livable space on a world not our own? ("Bloodchild")
- Worship is no good without action. (*The Parable of the Sower*)
- Writing has been my way of journeying from incomprehension, confusion, and emotional upheaval to some sort of order. ("The Monophobic Response")
- Writing is communication. ("Furor Scribendi")
- You don't have to beat people to treat them brutally. (*Kindred*)

Glossary

Note: Abbreviations in parentheses refer to titles of the author's works

AMN—"Amnesty"
AR—*Adulthood Rites*
BC—"Bloodchild"
CA—*Clay's Ark*
CF—"Childfinder"
CO—*"Crossover"*
Dawn—Dawn
DCC—"Discovery, Creation and Craft"
EMN—"The Evening and the Morning and the Night"
Fl—*Fledgling*
Im—*Imago*
Kin—*Kindred*

LB—*Lilith's Brood*
MMM—*Mind of My Mind*
MR—"The Monophobic Response"
NB—"A Necessary Being"
NK—"Near of Kin"
PM—*Patternmaster*
PO—"Positive Obsession"
POS—*Parable of the Sower*
POSg—*Parable of the Sower* (graphic)
POT—*Parable of the Talents*
SS—"Speech Sounds"
Sur—*Survivor*
WS—*Wild Seed*

---

abunje See *ogbanje.*

abyss (POS, 66) a bottomless chasm

acolyte (POT, 354) assistant to a priest

acute myeloblastic leukemia (CA, 2) a rapidly advancing cancer in white blood cells

Ado (WS, 3) town in Ekiti, Nigeria

adrenaline (Im, 677) a hormone that readies the body for exertion or stress

adz (WS, 419) a right-angled wood refining tool that dresses timber

affinity (*Dawn*, 35) a natural affection or sympathy

agave (POT, 31) a desert plant that produces fiber, sweetener, arrow points, and a stem for roasting

agouti (AR, 337) edible rodent from Central or South America

ague (Kin, 202) malaria

AK-47 (POT, 110) an assault rifle designed in 1941 in the Soviet Union

albino (WS, 17) lacking pigment in the skin and eyes

Al-Can (POT, 201) Alaskan-Canadian

Alpha Centauri (POS, 222; POT, 310) the closest star system to earth

altered consciousness (AMN, 163) a change in brain function through sleep, hypnosis, meditation, disease, or drugs

altruism (MMM, 89) moral concern for the well-being of others

amoeba (POT, 81) free-moving single-celled beings

anachronistic (CA, 34) belonging to a different time or milieu

anaconda (AR, 319) a South American water boa

ananas, bohnen, bananen, mangos (AR, 338) "pineapple, beans, bananas, mangos" in German

androgynous (AR, 371; *Dawn*, 11, 97; POT, 303) genderless

antebellum South (Kin, 32) the slave culture that enriched Southern states before April 1861

anthropology (*Dawn*, 87) the study of

---

humankind, its behavior, culture, and society

antibodies (CA, 19) proteins in the immune system that isolate and neutralize microbes

antioncogenes (EMN, 71) a protein that shrinks cancer

antiseptic (Kin, 146) a germicidal or antimicrobial liquid or salve

arigato gozaimasu (*Dawn*, 68) "thank you" in Japanese

Armageddon (POS, 67) location of the last earthly battle between good and evil

asexual (*Dawn*, 35) reproduced without sexual union

asphyxiation (*Dawn*, 5) suffocation

asteroid (PO, 126) a minor planet in the Solar System

atavistic (CA, 8) savage

autoimmune disease (Fl, 69) a condition causing the body's resistance to attack itself

Avoyelles Parish (WS, 478) a county in east central Louisiana named for Native Americans

bake kettle (WS, 534) bake oven or Dutch oven shaped in 1850 with three legs and a rimmed lid

bark cloth (Im, 689) fabric beaten from fibrous inner tree bark

baroque (EMN, 47) heavily detailed, grandiose European art or architecture from the 1600s to 1740s

bayou (WS, 525) a swamp, marsh, or slow-moving streamlet carrying lake or river water

BBC (Fl, 152) the British Broadcasting Corporation, a media conglomerate in London

Bela Lugosi (Fl, 140) Romanian film actor who played Dracula in 1931

Benin (WS, 3) West African country between Nigeria and Togo

Benjamin Franklin (POS, 15) a founding father of the U.S.

Bhagavad Gita (POT, 58) Hindu scripture written around 500 BCE

bigotry (Kin, 111) bias or prejudice against an

identifiable group, such as women, gays, blacks, the obese

bioelectric (AR, 262) a live organism containing electric currents

bioluminescent (AR, 262) a live organism that makes and emits light rays

bipedal (*Dawn*, 131; Im, 681) two-legged

blue-collar agency (Kin, 109) a bureau that grooms workers for employment

Bonny (WS, 26) a town of enslavers in southern Niger east of the Niger River, where 20,000 mostly Ibo/Igbo bondsmen were shipped out to the Americas in 1790

The Book of Common Prayer (POT, 58) an Anglican prayer book compiled in 1549

Botswana (AR, 366) a south African country

bravado (DCC, 1) swagger, audacity

bromeliad (*Dawn*, 199) spiny-leafed tropic plants of the pineapple family centered with stiff blossoms

buck nigger (Kin, 123) slang for a black male

Buddhism (POS, 261) a religion based on impermanence

bushmaster (AR, 346) poisonous pit viper

caesarean (*Dawn*, 92; Im, 585) delivery of a baby through an abdominal incision

caiman (AR, 319; *Dawn*, 238) a reptile in the alligator family

carbine (CA, 3) a firearm shorter than a rifle

cardiopulmonary resuscitation (Kin, 209) emergency chest compression to restore breathing

Carnegie Mellon (Fl, 266) a university in Pittsburgh, Pennsylvania

carnivorous (*Dawn*, 54; Im, 652) nourished on meat

carob (POS, 210) a natural substitute for chocolate

Cassandra (*Dawn*, 236) the Trojan princess in Homer's Iliad whose warnings went unheeded

catatonic (AMN, 173, *Dawn*, 193) abnormally immobile

cauterize (WD, 19) burn a wound to halt bleeding

cecropia (Im, 568) a tropical tree of South America bearing palmate leaves

celibacy (CA, 46) voluntary abstinence from coitus

Centauri (CA, 15) one of three stars in a constellation near the sun

cerebral hemorrhage (PM) a stroke or brain bleed

chaos theory (POT, 47) a study of disorder that locates patterns

chica (CA, 29) Spanish for "friend"

choke-cuffs (CA, 52) tight restraints for arms or legs

chromosome (AR, 257; Im, 551) strand of genetic formulation in a cell nucleus

chronoportation (Kin, xi) time travel, temporal voyage, or timeslip

Churchill (POT, 169) royal appointee to England's war minister from May 10, 1940, to May 23, 1945

cipher (Kin, 91) an antique term for computing math problems

civility (*Dawn*, 109) courtesy or respect

coati (AR, 441) a South American animal related to the raccoon

coco yam (WS, 1) a common tropical root vegetable; taro or eddo

coffle (Kin, 221, 238) a line of slaves chained or bound together and traveling toward buyers

coke (Fl, 187) cocaine

Communist Revolution of 1917 (Fl, 240) the overthrow of Tsar Nicholas II and the end of the Russian empire

composting toilet (POT, 104) a self-contained latrine that uses aerobic bacteria to decompose waste

composure (Kin, 187) self-control

conditioning (*Dawn*, 201) training or accustoming a living creature to certain circumstances

conscripted (MMM, 97) recruited or drafted into the military

consensus (AR, 277, 414; *Dawn,* 154; Im, 540) a harmonious agreement

contralto (Kin, 171) low female voice

cosmological (POS, 83) relating to the beginning and growth of the universe

cull (AR, 267; MMM, 106) to remove a dangerous or inferior object or strip trash from a group

Dachau (MMM, 120) location of a Nazi concentration camp in southern Germany from March 22, 1933, until liberation in late April 1945

Darwinism (EMN, 69) belief that nature selects the best strains to reproduce

Deist (POS, 15) a believer that God creates, but has no influence on life

demagogue (Palwick interview) an agitator or rabble rouser

dengue fever (Kin, 225) a flu-like disease borne by the Aedes mosquito

Denmark Vesey (Kin, 141) a black leader of a South Carolina rebellion in July 1822

diaphoresis (CA, 10) excessive sweating

dichotomy (NB, 40) a division into opposites

DNA (Fl, 153) deoxyribonucleic acid in hereditary tissue

Easton Point (Kin, 253) a Maryland town in Talbot County dating to 1662

Egyptian Book of the Dead (POS, 125) chants and spells dating to 2670 BCE guiding the spirit through the underworld

eidetic memory (*Dawn*, 60, 218) a precise photographic recall

El Camino Real (POS, 223) the roadway connecting Spanish missions with Baja California in 1683 and with East Texas in 1691

electrochemical (*Dawn,* 169) relating to chemical reactions caused by electric charge

electromagnetic radiation (AR, 455) light traveling in waves of energy

Elisha (Kin, 24) an Old Testament prophet who performed the equivalent of mouth-to-mouth resuscitation on the son of the wealthy woman of Shunem, Israel, in II Kings 4:18–37

Elizabeth I (Fl, 215) last Tudor ruler of England after her father, Henry VIII

embryonic (*Dawn*, 257) of a fetal or pre-birth state

endorphin (AR, 454; POT, 80) a pituitary or nerve secretion that reduces pain and imparts pleasure and a sense of well-being

entropy (POS, 218) gradual decline to

disorder; degeneration or collapse. *SEE ALSO* second law of thermodynamics.

epicanthic fold (Sur, 6) a fold in the upper eyelid

epigenetic (CA, 7) of inherited traits that don't involve DNA

epilogue (Kin, 262; WS, 69) a concluding comment

epiphyte (*Dawn,* 234) a plant growing from a tropical tree; a bromeliad or orchid

epithet (Sur, 36) a description or character of a human trait or characteristic

ESP (Pl, 252; POS, 11) extrasensory perception or clairvoyance

Español? Português? Sim, senhor. Falo Português. (Im, 597) "Spanish? Portuguese? Yes, sir. I speak Portuguese" in Portuguese.

ethics (MMM, 130) moral principles

ethnology (*Dawn,* 108) a study and analysis of cultures

etymologist (*Dawn*, 75) a specialist in word histories

eugenics (*Dawn*, 143; MMM, 1) improvement of humankind by breeding people for desirable traits

eulogize (POS, 134) honor or praise the dead

eunuch (*Dawn*, 89) an emasculated male

euphemism (POT, 89) pleasing or nonthreatening words that conceal shocking or unacceptable terms

euphoria (AR, 512) overwhelming happiness

existentialism (POS, 261) a belief system based on acts of free will

extrasolar (BC, 31; POT, 83) beyond the solar system

fallopian tube (Im, 680) the passage that directs ova (eggs) into the uterus

fascist (POT, 145) of a doctrine based on nationalism or ethnicity rather than the worth of the individual

fatalism (Sur, 22) a belief that destiny is predetermined and unavoidable

feral (POS, 36) wild, untamed

Ferdinand and Isabella (Fl, 237) king and queen of Spain after they wed in 1489

fire-and-brimstone (POT, 136) the sulfurous flames of hell

Fourteenth Amendment (Kin, 263) a constitutional amendment granting citizenship to anyone born in the U.S.

Frederick Douglass (Kin, 140) a Maryland-born orator and abolitionist who escaped slavery

fuego (POS, 143) Spanish for "fire"

fungi (AMN, 149) organisms that reproduce by spores

Gaia hypothesis (Palwick interview) a belief that living things feed on the planet and regulate it

gene map (*Dawn*, 99; Im, 551) a schematic arrangement of genes on a chromosome

genetics (EMN, 37; Im, 542) the study of inherited traits

Georgian colonial (Kin, 67) a common brick dwelling style during the reigns of the Hanoverians displaying classical design, convex dormer windows, and book-ended chimneys on the two-and-a-half story side walls.

germ line (Fl, 224) cells that pass inherited material to offspring

gestational (POT, 83) concerning development of a fetus in the uterus

godlings (WS, 400) miniature deities

gopher wood (POS, 67) cypress timber, which Noah used in Genesis 6:14 to build the ark

Hajji (PM, 5) a Muslim male who has completed a pilgrimage to Mecca, Mohammed's birthplace

hallucination (Kin, 17) an illusion, apparition, or mirage

Harriet Tubman (Kin, 141) a Maryland abolitionist who led seventy slaves to freedom

Hatfield and McCoy family feud (Fl, 154) antagonism between two families after the Hatfields ambushed McCoys on January 1, 1888, at the Big Sandy River between Kentucky and West Virginia

hedonism (CA, 55) a life purpose based on pleasure

herbivore (CA, 66) a being that eats plants

hermaphroditic (Im, 712) marked by male and female traits

hierarchical (*Dawn*, 39) of a social order structured on rank or authority

hieroglyphics (MMM, 73) a preliterate Egyptian writing system employing pictures

Hiroshima (POT, 169) a Japanese city that the U.S. bombed on August 6, 1945

Hitler (POT, 169) German dictator who started World War II on September 1, 1939

humanicide (*Dawn*, 8) slaughter of all living people

humanoid (Sur, 5) a being that resembles a human

Huntington's disease (AR, 363) a degenerative disorder of the nerves

hyperempathy syndrome (POS, 11) an intense sensitivity to pain and death

hypocrisy (POS, 24) deceit, fakery

hypocrite (NK) a deceiver who criticizes beliefs or practices that he engages in

hysterics (Kin, 158) frenzied overreaction

idiot savant (EMN, 110) a mentally impaired person gifted with a particular skill, such as mental calculation

Idu (WS, 3) town in northwest Nigeria

Igbo (AR, 434) people of southern Nigeria, also called Ibo

imago (Im, 519) the post-larval stage of insect life

implantation (BC, 13) an insertion in the body of mechanical devises or materials

imprinting (*Dawn*, 191) the biological identification of young with another being or parent

Inca (AR, 409) the largest native empire in pre–Columbian America

incontinent (Kin, 153) unable to control bowels and bladder

incubation period (Kin, 153) the time from microbial exposure to the appearance of the first symptoms

inertia (EMN, 41) a resistance to movement, speed, or direction

infrared (AMN, 152) invisible radiation

James Monroe (Kin, 63) the fifth U.S. president

Jericho (POS, 55) a Canaanite city west of the Jordan River that Joshua and the Israelites destroyed in 1550 BCE

Jezebel (POT, 223) the Tyrian wife of Israel's King Ahab, around 850 BCE, she imported the worship of Baal to replace Yahweh

João (Im, 597) Portuguese for "John"

John Donne (POT, 58) sixteenth-century English clergyman and poet

John Quincy Adams (Kin, 63) the sixth U.S. president and eighth Secretary of State

joist (POS, 161) timber or beam

jojoba (POT, 185) a shrub in the southwestern U.S. that produces a waxy oil

Jonathan Edwards (POT, 63) an eighteenth-century New England revivalist

journeyman (PM, 1) an apprentice or associate

Judas goat (*Dawn,* 67, 152) a leader of herds to slaughter

jump the broomstick (Kin, 123) slave equivalent of marriage

kaleidoscopic (MMM, 36) changeable in color or pattern; variable

keloid (Kin, 149) thick scar tissue common to black skin

King James Bible (POT, 202) an English translation of the Bible completed in 1611

Knott's Berry Farm (EMN, 77) a theme park in Buena Vista, California

kola nut (WS, 9) a caffeine-rich nut of a West African evergreen

konichiwa (*Dawn*, 68) "hello" in Japanese

Ku Klux Klan (Kin, 37) white vigilantes and terrorizers of newly emancipated slaves in Pulaski, Tennessee, in 1866

kung fu (*Dawn*, 148) a disciplined Chinese martial art based on quickness

Kush (WS, 3) an ancient kingdom in the Nile Valley on the Egypt-Sudan divide, dating to 2450 BCE

larynx (Fl, 312) the voice box, holding centers of speech and a passage to the lungs

las estrellas son gratis (POSg, 2) Spanish for "the stars are free"

latent (*Dawn,* 156; Im, 535; WS, 494) dormant, concealed, or inactive

laudanum (Kin, 217) a common opium-based painkiller standardized in the 1660s

Lazor wire (POS, 14; POT, 205) thin optical glass

leach (WS, 41) to dissolve ash or soil with water

Lear (AR, 408) the British title figure in William Shakespeare's tragedy *King Lear*

liana (*Dawn*, 201; Im, 630) a woody forest vine

limbo (Kin, 18) a state of oblivion or confinement

Llama (POS, 41) a Spanish firearms brand

London (POT, 169) the target of the German Blitz, a bomb siege on England's capital from September 7, 1940, to May 11, 1941

loup-garou (WS, 486) French for the shape-shifting, blood-drinking "werewolf"

luminescent (NB, 14) glowing

Machu Picchu (*Dawn*, 88) an Inca citadel built in the Andes Mountains of Peru in the mid–1400s.

Mandarin (Im, 742) the Chinese language of northern and southwestern China

Margaret Mead (*Dawn*, 87) an American anthropologist who studied sexual maturation in Samoa in the 1920s

matriarchy (Fl, 115) a tribe or society dominated by women

Medusa (*Dawn*, 20) a death-dealing Gorgon with snaky hair who turned people to stone at a single glance

melanin (Fl, 153; Keyes interview) dark pigment of eyes, skin, and hair

Meribah (Kin, 193) a town north of Mount Sinai along the Israelite exodus from Egypt

metabolism (*Dawn*, 206) the body's processing of food into useable energy

metamorphosis (AR, 352; *Dawn*, 82; Im, 523) transition into adulthood

microbe (CA, 13) a bacterium, virus, or other disease-causing microorganism; a germ

Middle Passage (Kin, xi) the middle segment of Triangular Trade that took enslavers to Africa, across the Atlantic, and into ports such as Charleston, South Carolina, and New Orleans, Louisiana, for auctioning Africans to the white moneyed class.

miho/mijo (CA, 13) a Spanish endearment for "my son"

Missouri Compromise (Kin, 63) legislation on March 6, 1820, halting the spread of slavery into the West

mitochondria (AR, 427) small independent organs within cells that govern energy and breathing

Mohawk (WS, 276) an Indian nation and member of the Iroquois League living in New York and along the Great Lakes

morning star (WS, 617) a common name for the planet Venus

multisensory (Im, 53) involving more than one bodily perception

mutualistic symbiosis (Fl, 69) a shared relationship that benefits both parties

muzzleloader (Kin, 65) a one-shot Kentucky rifle requiring priming by shoving a metal rod against powder and wadding toward the end of the barrel

myeloblastic (CA, 7) referring to immature white blood cells.

myeloma (SS, 109) cancerous blood plasma

Nagasaki (POT, 169) a Japanese city that the U.S. bombed on August 9, 1945

Nat Turner (Kin, 141) a rebel slave who led a revolt in Southampton County, Virginia, in February 1831

Nazis (Fl, 196) fascists who incorporated racism, eugenics, anti–Marxism, anti-gay, anti-gypsy, and antisemitism in their philosophy

neoteny (AR, 283) retaining immaturity in an animal or plant

Nero (Kin, 25) Rome's fifth emperor, a ruler famed for viciousness

neurochemical (Im, 637; POS, 144) related to the makeup and use of chemicals in the nervous system

neurofibromatosis (Im, 665) a genetic disorder that raises tumors on nerve tissue.

neurosensory (*Dawn*, 168; Im 567) relating to functions of the nervous system

neurotransmitter (POS, 12) a chemical bearing an impulse from one nerve to another

New Calabar (WS, 26) an eastern Nigerian slave depot on the Bight of Biafra up the Cross River, where African kings sold black captives for 30 to 36 copper bars each

niño (AR, 345) Spanish for "little boy"

nirvana (POT, 49) in the faiths of India, a concept of total happiness

nock (Sur, 164) to fit an arrow to the bowstring

nonbiodegradable (AR, 388) impermeable by living organisms

nonpeople (Kin, 53) expendable employees

North Star (Kin, 143) a celestial guidance system for refugee slaves via the pole star, the point in the night sky that aligns with earth's axis

nova (BC, 198) a star that quickly flares, then loses its glow

nucleotide (AR, 257) compounds forming DNA

nudibranch (*Dawn*, 14) soft mollusk

obsidian (SS, 97) black glass formed from igneous rock extruded from a volcano

octoroon (WS, 527) a biracial person having black forebears and one white grandparent

ogbanje (WS, 5, 425) an Ibo/Igbo term for a Nigerian evil spirit born from a human body

olfactory (*Dawn*, 196; Fl, 116) relating to smell

olijkoecks (WS, 443) Dutch for "doughnuts"

Onitsha (WS, 3. 463) city north of the Niger River delta in Nigeria

ophidiophobe (MMM, 34) a person afraid of snakes

opium (Kin, 78) poppy juice used as a painkiller

optic (Im, 643) of the eye and vision

organelle (Im, 544) a specialized part of a cell

orifice (*Dawn*, 28) opening

Orion nebula (EMN, 110) a bright star cloud in the Milky Way

Orumili (WS, 3) Ibo/Igbo for "great water," their designation of the Niger River

os rouge (WS, 547) French for "red bone," a Louisiana native who is half black and half Indian

ovipositor (BC, 18) a tube through which a female fish or insect exudes eggs into a male

oxbow lake (AR, 313) a U-shaped lake that forms when an arc of a river erodes into a separate body of water

Oze (WS, 3) a tiny planet

ozone layer (AR, 290) a gas shield that stops ultraviolet radiation from damaging earth

palisade (POT, 106) a defensive enclosure or wall

palmprint-voiceprint (EMN, 48) a biometric identifier of hands or voices

papists (WS, 278) Catholics under the sway of the Vatican pope

parable (POS, 134) an illustrative story stressing morality or spirituality

parapsychological (CA, 55) supernatural

parasitize (*Dawn*, 225) exploit or infect

pariah (NB, 64) outcast

pass (WS, 595) a vernacular term for a non-white person's infiltration of white society by posing as white

patois (WS, 488) vernacular or common language of a region

pecking order (MMM, 84) a hierarchy based on rank or authority

Pelican Bay State Prison (POT, 199) a notoriously punitive U.S. penitentiary in Crescent City, California

peripatus (AR, 306) a velvety worm

pheromone (AR, 262; EMN, 67; Im, 690) a hormone that triggers a response in the senses of others

photovoltaic (CA, 8) converting light into electric current

physiology (*Dawn*, 12, 78) the study of body parts and their functions

plasmid (CA, 18) a round strand of DNA

plaster of Paris (*Dawn*, 129) a gypsum powder that hardens after moistening

polemic (DCC, 6) a bitter written or oral attack on an opinion or belief

poop deck (WS, 37) a roof over a ship's rear cabin

porphyria (Fl, 39) a blood disease that affects skin and nerves

postpartum (POT, 166) of emotions emerging in a mother after she gives birth

potable (POS, 13) drinkable

pottage (POS, 122) the one-pot lentil stew for which Esau sold his birthright to brother Jacob in Genesis 25:29–34

Praying Indians (WS, 277) Christian Indians from New England and Canada

precocity (AR, 258) early growth of teeth or development of language or motor skills

prefiero tener las estrellas (POSg, 2) Spanish for "I prefer to have the stars"

prefiero tener las luces de la ciudad de vuelta (POSg, 2) Spanish for "I prefer to have the lights from the edge of the city"

prickly pear (POT, 34) a nopal cactus that produces seeded fruit for juice or jelly

primordial (CA, 7) at the beginning of creation

profaned (*Dawn*, 192) tainted

prologue (Kin, 9) introduction

prototype (CA, 56) a model of a starship

Proxima (CA, 7) Latin for "closest"

psis (MMM, 57) clairvoyants; mind readers

psionic (CF, 77; MMM, 57) paranormal or psychic

psychiatrist (Kin, 241; MMM, 109) a doctor who treats mental disorders

psychohistorical (Kin, x) concerning reasons for behaviors and attitudes

psychokinesis (MMM, 94) moving objects by psionic mind power

psychologist (MMM, 109) an expert in mental dynamics

psychometry (MMM, 107) using touch to determine the history of a person or object

pummelo (AR, 361) the largest citrus fruit

Punta Nublada (Fl, 139) Spanish for "Cloudy Point"

pyromania (POS, 143) an impulse to set fires

quadroon (WS, 595) a biracial person having one biracial parent

quarter (Kin, 93) slave barracks

quasi-human (AR, 422) seemingly genuine human

querulous (SS, 109) whining or whimpering

quicklime (Fl, 207) calcium oxide, which speeds tissue dehydration and decay

reactionary (Kin, 111) an opponent of reform or progress

relativity theory (POT, 47) a study of gravity and its effect on phenomena

repressive societies (Kin, 141) a reference to Nazi book burners

rhetorical question (*Dawn*, 109) a question that expects no answer

roll-top (Kin, 135) a sliding desk cover made of retractable slats

Rose Bowl (Kin, 247) a stadium at Pasadena northeast of Los Angeles, California

Royal African Company (WS, 17) an African mercantile and slave depot established by England's King James II on the Gambia River from 1660 to 1708

saboteur (AMN, 170; CA, 27) a terrorist or subversive agent

sadistic (Kin, 94) seeking pleasure by harming or intimidating others

-san (*Dawn*, 68) a polite recognition of a person or family in Japanese

sanctuary (PM) a place of safety and rest

São Paulo (Im, 603) the financial center of Brazil

savanna (WS, 1) open grassland

sayonara (Dawni, 68) "goodbye" in Japanese

schizoid (POT, 212) an eccentric personality disorder that causes a person to withdraw from social interaction

scrip (POS, 175) a company's substitute for legal cash

scut work (CO, 120) servile, boring labor

sealing wax (Kin 136) hot wax used to seal flat sheets of paper into envelopes

sea urchin (AMN, 162) a spiny, spherical sea creature

Second Coming (CA, 8) the Christian anticipation of Jesus's return to earth

second law of thermodynamics (POS, 218; POT, 48) as energy is transferred or transformed, more goes to waste and degenerates into disorder

semiarid (PM, 93) a region rarely watered with rain or snowmelt

serial mass murder (Fl, 153) group murders repeated in multiple incidents

Sermon on the Mount (Kin, 218) the idealistic doctrine of Jesus Christ about Christian ethics as found in Matthew 5–7

Sierra Nevada (Fl, 239) mountains between California and Nevada

silt (AR, 318) fine dirt or sand that settles on a riverbank or harbor bottom

siphon pump (POT, 202) a tube that pulls liquid from one source and deposits it in another

slag (POS, 164) melted metal

sleeper ship (Govan interview; AMN, 182) a starship holding crew hibernating in suspended animation

slime mold (POT, 80) a fungus that joins independent cells to form kingdoms

sloop (WS, 251) a two- or three-masted warship topped with square rigging

smithing (WS, 264) shaping metal over a forge

sociopathic (POS, 115) antisocial, unrepentant

Sodom-and-Gomorrah (CA, 61; POT, 223) two cities north of the Dead Sea that God destroyed with fire for their wickedness

Sojourner Truth (Kin, 140) black abolitionist orator

solar plexus (NB, 45) a networks of arteries and nerves at center of the human abdomen

Spanish Florida (WS, 344) in 1741, the first major European land claim in North America

spectroscopic (POS, 83; POT 149) relating to measuring radiation

sphincter (AR, 445; *Dawn*, 52) a muscular, reflexive opening of a tube

spiritual essence (Fl, 43) a mental repository of peace and positive thoughts

sporangia (CA, 66) the casing holding fungal spores

squatted in (POS, 10) resided illegally in a vacant house or building

Stalingrad (POT, 169) site of a battle from August 12, 1942, to February 2, 1943, that caused two million Russian casualties

Stone Age (*Dawn*, 91) a general term for 3.4 million years of prehistory, which ended around 2,000 BCE

straight razor (Kin, 92) a folding shaving tool consisting of a sharpened steel blade set in a handle

subatomic particle (AR, 454) a particle smaller than an atom

subcontractor (AMN, 150) a smaller business performing labor on a large project

submachine gun (Fl, 131) a magazine-fed, automatic carbine

subsistence farming (CA, 8) agrarian efforts that feed the owner and family

subvocalization (AR, 296) speaking words in your head while you read

Sufism (POS, 261) a Muslim belief system proclaiming mystic union with God

suggestible (Fl, 79) impressionable, malleable

surrogate motherhood (BC, 198; *Dawn*, 60) bearing an artificially inseminated child for another woman

suspended animation (*Dawn*, 129) dormancy or hibernation

Swahili (AR, 434; POS, 230) an East African language in Burundi, Kenya, Rwanda, South Sudan, Tanzania, and Uganda

symbiont (AR, 427; CA, 11; Fl, 69; Govan interview) an organism living in close cooperation with another being

symbiosis (POT, 125) productive interaction between two organisms

symbiotic (AR, 313, 427; *Dawn*, 35) a beneficial interaction between organisms

synergy (Im, 549) the combined efforts of two or more agents

synthesize (AR, 463) manufacture

tactile (Im, 633) related to touch

tai chi (*Dawn*, 148) a defensive Chinese martial art

Talmud (POS, 221) Jewish teachings originated in the second century CE and compiled in 500

Tau Cetians (MR, 415) residents in the Tau star of the constellation Cetus

telekinesis (Kin, xi) time travel or chronoportation

telepath (POS, 128) a person who communicates or reads thoughts through mind-to-mind interaction

telepathy (*Dawn*, 107) wordless communication through thought interaction

terraforming (Palwick interview; POS, 21) turning property into a facsimile of earth

Thomas Jefferson (POS, 15) third U.S. president

Tibetan Book of the Dead (POS, 125) an eighth-century CE compendium guiding spirits through obstacles to the afterlife

Tigris and Euphrates (Fl, 194) southwest Asian river system where earth's first civilizations began

Tojo (POT, 169) the Japanese general of the Imperial Japanese Army hanged on December 23, 1948, for war crimes and deaths of five million

Tokyo (POT, 169) Japanese industrial center bombed by the U.S. from November 17, 1944, to March 10, 1945, with 210,000 casualties

Tourette's syndrome (POT, 250) a nervous condition that causes repeated twitches, jerks, sniffs, or coughs

Tower of Babel (POT, 144) an origin myth in Genesis 11:1–9 from 3500 BCE based on the Hebrew for "confuse"

tracheostomy (*Dawn,* 13) a surgical opening through the neck into the windpipe

traction (Kin, 86) grip or adhesion of a wheel on a road or rail

trundle bed (Kin, 153, 219, 534) a low cot that slides under a bigger bed

Twi (AR, 372) the language of Ghana

Typhoid Mary (CA, 48) Mary Mallon (1869–1938), a servant infected with typhoid fever

ultraviolet (AMN, 152; AR, 290) radiation present in sunlight

umbilical (POS, 83) relating to a line or cable carrying life necessities

vampire (Fl, 18) the reanimated body of a dead person who comes from the grave at night to suck the blood of sleepers

vampire theater (Fl, 94) drama based on the uniqueness of vampires

Van Rensselaers (WS, 253) seventeenth-century Dutch migrants to New York state

Vayase! Ahora mismo! (CA, 30) Spanish command, "Go! Right now!"

verisimilitude (DCC, 6) a true likeness

vine snake (Im, 575) a venomous Sri Lankan tree snake

wainscot chair (WS, 338, 347) a heavy wood chair decorated with carving

Washingtonia palm (POT, 34) a fan-type palm useful for shade and fencing

Watusi (CF, 96) Bantu speakers residing along Africa's Great Lakes

white-nigger (Kin, 160) a black person behaving privileged and educated; doctor-nigger; reading-nigger

white trash (Kin, 61) poor white uneducated Southerners

Windsor chair (Kin, 226) a sturdy wood chair with a curving back and projecting arms

wormholes (Govan interview) a link or shortcut between separate parts of space

xenogenesis (*Dawn,* 38) production of an organism that bears no resemblance to its parents

xenophobia (*Dawn,* 23; Sur, 19) fear of anything foreign or strange

Yoruban (*Dawn,* 77, POS, 230) a member of one of Africa's largest ethnic groups

yucca (POT, 34) a prickly shrub suited to arid landscapes

A Guide to Writing, Art, and Research Topics

1. Discuss the effectiveness of the following rhetorical and linguistic devices:

   - *euphemism* a pimp ... a livestock man specializing in lamb and chicken (*The Parable of the Talents*)
   - *action verbs* wept and cursed and stank (*Imago*)
   - *scriptural citation* from Genesis ("The Evening and the Morning, and the Night")
   - *fantasy* I'm learning to fly. (*The Parable of the Sower*)
   - *sarcasm* Shit, the devil himself is going to preach me a sermon! (*Mind of My Mind*)
   - *alliteration* For all of us, the living forest was full of light. (*Imago*)
   - *satire* Bread and circuses (Juvenal, 100 CE) (*The Parable of the Sower*)
   - *pun* Senn/sin; rites/rights (*Adulthood Rites*)
   - *direct address* Goddamn mongrel cub. (*Fledgling*)
   - *motif* "Womb" (*Dawn*)
   - *neologism* car family (*Clay's Ark*)
   - *contrast* We can grow or we can wither. (*The Parable of the Talents*)
   - *direct address* Girl, you come here not knowing how to do *nothing*. (*Kindred*)
   - *personification* flesh can only tell me what it is (*Wild Seed*)
   - *reflexive* He was himself. (*Adulthood Rites*)
   - *black dialect* This boy say he go for you ("Crossover")
   - *antitheses* desirable and dangerous, beautiful and lethal (*Imago*)
   - *assonance* enough to entire (*The Parable of the Talents*)
   - *folklore* Dracula (*Fledgling*)
   - *image* a piece of straw floating on a still pond (*Imago*)
   - *dramatic irony* I look like my father ("Near of Kin")
   - *cliché* the good old days (*The Parable of the Sower*)
   - *surmise* You must have been more lonely than I thought. ("A Necessary Being")
   - *blasphemy* symbolic cannibalism (*Wild Seed*)
   - *fragment* Take care other. ("Bloodchild")
   - *allusion* Hamlin/Pied Piper of Hamelin (*Fledgling*)

- *passive voice* Ceremony is needed. (*The Parable of the Talents*)
- *metaphor* just talk all over your mouth (*Kindred*)
- *consonance* I saw it die. I felt it die. (*The Parable of the Sower*)
- *tag question* It's difficult, isn't it? ("The Book of Martha")
- *slang* jailbait (*Fledgling*)
- *sophistry* to take root among the stars (*Earthseed*)
- *grotesque* patients gnawing at themselves among maggots, rats, cockroaches ("The Evening and the Morning, and the Night")
- *supplication* Jesus, Jesus, Jesus, *please!* (*The Parable of the Sower*)
- *commands* Aim just *there!* Relax. ("Positive Obsession")
- *dramatic foils* Eve and Barbara ("Childfinder")
- *humor* you're a girl, all right (*Fledgling*)
- *alliteration* prickly pride ("The Monophobic Response")
- *antithesis* I could have killed you; you could have killed me. ("A Necessary Being")
- *adapted grammar* pleasing itselves ("Amnesty")
- *oath* What the hell? (*The Parable of the Sower*)
- *simile* Like the grayness, like the giant on his throne ("The Book of Martha")
- *repetition* nowhere to go, nowhere to hide, nowhere to be free (*Dawn*)
- *parallelism* starving, 'bout naked, whipped, dragged, bit by dogs (*Kindred*)
- *aphorism* God is change (*The Parable of the Sower*)
- *imperative mood* rattle your bones at someone else (*Wild Seed*)
- *exaggeration* all the power was in male hands ("Why Is Science Fiction So White?")
- *spondee* the title ("Bloodchild")
- *pathetic fallacy* a dust storm (*Clay's Ark*)
- *expletive* an obvious "fuck you" smile (*The Parable of the Sower*)
- *rhetorical question* the title ("Why Is Science Fiction So White?")
- *backstory* Black Death (*The Parable of the Sower*)
- *irony* Victorville, California ("Amnesty")
- *hyperbole* I felt like hell all the time (*Mind of My Mind*)
- *taunt* "the all-important us" ("The Monophobic Response")
- *appositive* hurt by males—men (*Wild Seed*)
- *metaphor* that core where all the people came together (*Patternmaster*)
- *sense impression* traffic-light green eyes (*Mind of My Mind*)
- *rhetorical question* Was our Lord wrong? (*The Parable of the Talents*)
- *internal rhyme* If we go to them, woe to them. (Govan interview)
- *sibilance* the title ("Speech Sounds")
- *double entendre* astronauts, flying high on drugs (*The Parable of the Sower*)
- *cliché* your own kind (*Survivor*)
- *parallel construction* not quite bright enough, not quite quick enough ("Positive Obsession")
- *myth* title (*Lilith's Brood*)
- *vernacular* Swing both ways, do you? (*Fledgling*)

- *koan* We hear gunfire so much that we don't hear it. (*The Parable of the Sower*)
- *onomatopoeia* Tlic ("Bloodchild")

2. Account for the significance of two secondary characters and their impact on plot and theme, especially these:

Madison	Obsidian	Cougar
Isaac Jackson	Curt Loehr	Marcos Duran
Tahneh	Badger	Belen "Len" Ross
Joachim	Aaor	Asha Vere
Lady Darah	Kayce Alexander	Wright Hamlin
James Adio	Sarah	Rayal
Bernard Daly	Tate Rinaldi	

How do these characters influence significant action? feelings? memories? dialogue? Which secondary cast member would you omit? What role would you create for yourself as a secondary character on a Maryland plantation or in the Patternmaster or Xenogenesis series?

3. Contrast the settings and sources of melodrama, satire, or humor in two of these fictional situations:

- neutral colored cell in *Dawn*
- meeting a future mother-in-law in "The Evening and the Morning, and the Night"
- a talk with God in "The Book of Martha"
- accusing Neci of plotting child abuse in *Adulthood Rites*
- advertising and selling enslaved preschoolers in *Kindred*
- explosives in *Clay's Ark*
- reevaluating a family tree in "Near of Kin"
- branding slaves in *Wild Seed*
- imprisoning of a translator in "Amnesty"
- buying Marcus from Cougar in *The Parable of the Talents*
- stealing rabbits in *The Parable of the Sower*
- dismay at Lilith's garden in *Imago*
- comparing scars in *Fledgling*
- an axe battle in the jungle in *Dawn*
- teaching Dana in the cookhouse in *Kindred*

Which scenes provide visual effects for film, poster, or stage? Which would adapt to shadow puppets, cartoon, oral storytelling, radio, collage, anime, or pantomime?

4. Characterize the importance of motivation to the outcome of these scenes:

- Ina drinking symbiont blood
- a dwarf star stealing from a giant
- humans persecuting Noah in "Amnesty"
- extreme shyness in "Positive Obsession"
- considering self-sterilization
- shooting a dog

- leaving Romania
- revising in "Furor Scribendi"
- Valerie cautiously accepting a book
- setting a broken leg in *Kindred*
- Doro's origins in the 2030s BCE
- learning hominid sign language
- healing a tentacle
- loading starships for Mars

5. Compose an annotated map featuring these landmarks in Octavia's stories and novels:

Seattle	Baltimore	Pasadena
Sahara	Redhill School	seed villages
Los Angeles	Gobi	Washington
Robledo, California	Chesapeake Bay	Sacramento
Nubia	Niger River	Kush
Oregon	Mohave Desert	Cape Mendocino
Forsyth	Nigeria	upstate New York
Easton	San Jose	Amazon Basin

6. Account for the significance of three of the following terms to the action of Octavia's works:

dynasty	amnesty	ovipositor
quadruped	extraplanetary	nonbiodegradable
biosphere	psionic	neurosensory
cautionary tale	apocalypse	stoic
fascism	symbiont	sharer
Darwinian	psychokinetic	hyperempathetic
destiny	oracle	

7. Locate three examples of destinations as symbols of curiosity, ambition, escape, loyalty, love, or patriotism, particularly these:

Rina's duplex	Phoenix	L.A.
desert ruins	training room	Portland
Mojave bubble	gated community	Alaska
Philadelphia	Mars	Red Spruce
starship nursery	Christian America	Sudan
Dilg	camp	

8. Debate the wisdom of two of the following choices and explain the characters' perspective:

identifying a brother/ father	sex between diseased partners	burning women for nagging
publishing on the net	taking ten husbands	fleeing into the jungle
helping with a birth	avoiding truckers	meeting ooloi

| beating a rebel son bloody | accepting an uncle | fleeing drought |
| breeding rabbits | giving Valerie a book | avoiding a wino |

9. Discuss the role of history in two of Octavia's scenarios. Include background facts about these:

missile assaults in "Amnesty"	dying redwoods	burying orange peelings
formulation of insulin	military draft	proliferation of plastics
crash-landing in the desert	laws against teaching slaves to read	conservative demagoguery
nuclear war	success of the Royal Africa Company	persecuting gypsies

10. Discuss the pervasive motif of women's accomplishments in three of Octavia's works, especially these:

Kindred	*The Parable of the Sower*	"The Evening and the Morning and the Night"
"Speech Sounds"	*Dawn*	
Mind of My Mind	*Fledgling*	
Wild Seed		

Explain why the author values harmony and collaboration as well as independence or self-rescue in *Dawn* and *Wild Seed*.

11. Survey the rewards and recriminations of advanced age or declining health in two of Octavia's characters. Consider the actions of these:

Jules	Marcos Duran	Taylor Bankole
An-yanwu	Mrs. Sims	Theodora
Emma	Tate Rinaldi	Rayal
Naomi Chi	Tomás	Akin
Santos Ibarra Ruiz	Milo Silk	Tehreh
Keira Maslin	Lauren	Isaac
Nikanj	May	

How do elderly, addicted, or sickly characters make themselves indispensable?

12. Summarize two of the following quandaries as themes in Octavia's stories and novels:

unbridled jealousy	isolation	self-blinding
epidemic illness	orphaning	mother hunger
apocalypse	crossing rivers	standing guard
identity crisis	inherited disease	abduction from Africa
incestuous parents	migration	urban chaos

13. Contrast two romantic relationships from Octavia's writings. Choose from these examples:

| Jane/ex-con | Doro/An-yanwu | Valerie/Obsidian |
| Gan/T'Gatoi | Diut/Alanna Verrick | Keira/Stephen |

| Lilith Iyapo/Sam | Lauren/Bankole | Tomás/Jesusa |
| Alan/Lynn Mortimer | Shori/Wright Hamlin | Tahreh/Diut |

What attracts one person to another? Why are some liaisons foolish or risky?

14. Describe how Octavia presents two social issues in stories or novels, such as these:

urban chaos	tropical disease	partnership
colonialism	parental neglect	charity
bondage	street poor	arson
random shootings	pollution	false imprisonment
alcoholism	migration	cannibalism
medical research	zealotry	diaspora
capitalism	police corruption	

How well did she predict the future?

15. Arrange a literature seminar to introduce students to speculative fiction in Octavia's *The Parable of the Talents*. Explain the prominence of three of these common topics:

terra incognita	fostering	raids
extraterrestrials	dog collars	brainwashing
starship	resisters	infertility
cargo	sharers	guns
utopia	ritual	isolation

Conclude discussion of fantasy or sci-fi with proposals for cover art, a collection of journey lore or balladry, oral interpretation, chronologies, routes, costume or banquet sketches, or funerals.

16. Give the meaning and purpose for three of Octavia's story, speech, or novel titles:

Kindred	"Journeys"	"The Morning, the
"To the Victor"	"Childfinder"	Evening, and the
"Crossover"	"Devil Girl from Mars"	Night"
"Furor Scribendi"	*Dawn*	
Imago	*Fledgling*	

Analyze the verbal kenning in two of Octavia's unused titles: *Godshaper, Darkside,* "Worldmaking," "DiaPause," "Xenograft," "Sidelights," "Lifesong," "Breakthrough," and *Earthseed*.

17. What does Octavia's application of dreams, sex, reading, music, food, work, public service, martyrdom, travel, religion, friendship, and drugs have in common with antidotes to despair in one of these works:

H.G. Wells *The Time*	Michael Crichton's	Amy Tan's *The Kitchen*
Machine	*Jurassic Park*	*God's Wife*
Marion Zimmer	Leslie Marmon Silko's	Lois Lowry's *The Giver*
Bradley's *Firebrand*	*Ceremony*	Evgeny Zamyatin's *We*

Isaac Asimov's *I, Robot*	Lee Child's *The Enemy*	Richard Wright's
Thomas Keneally's	J.D. Robb's *Naked in*	"Between the World
Schindler's List	*Death*	and Me"
Kaye Gibbons' *Ellen*	Barbara Kingsolver's	
Foster	*Animal Dreams*	

Which of Octavia's protagonists embrace friendship as a refuge and outlet for alienation, pain, doom, or rage? How do ordered events in narrative or dialogue restore mental and spiritual release?

18. Summarize the wisdom of Earthseed as a religion. What attitudes toward contemporary worship does Octavia reveal in Lauren's baptism in *The Parable of the Sower*; healing by minister Eli Torrey and Rachel "Rae" Davidson in *Mind of My Mind*; Catholic parents in "The Evening and the Morning and the Night"; Christ icons in a museum in *Adulthood Rites*; An-yanwu's shrine in *Wild Seed*; publishing religious writings on the Internet in *The Parable of the Talents*; or missionaries in *Survivor*.

19. Characterize the motivation and style of daring in these dramatic situations:

- stopping a rapist at the door
- celebrating a plantation Christmas
- questioning God
- awakening survivors
- introducing Tino to Akin

- burning migrants alive
- resisting an underage flirt
- fleeing a riot on a bus
- rooming with DGD victims
- testifying to a hostile panel

- facing an axe murderer
- tasting plastic
- killing concentration camp guards
- escaping a Mojave bubble

20. Analyze the effects of jealousy, suspicion, or rivalry on two of these pairs from Octavia's novels and stories:

Diut/Natahk	the Reverend Olamina/	Kevin Franklin/Tom
Lauren Oya/Larkin	Keith	Weylin
Bankole	Liza/Dana Franklin	Tino/Wray Ordway
Shori/Katherine	Doro/An-yanwu	Barbara/Eve
Gabe/Tate	Asha Vere/Marcos	Thomas/An-yanwu
	Duran	

21. Summarize the significance of three of these details in Octavia's novels and stories:

obsidian	caste	bleeding tentacle
Christopher Columbus	inheritance	BB gun
climate change	male pregnancy	moonshine .
diaspora	ex-con	demagogue
enfolding	Kush	secret passage
Robinson Crusoe	beheading	truck
trickster	Phoenix	

22. Propose the choice of Octavia's *Kindred* or *Unexpected Stories* as a community read. Suggest an annotated news series or character web, historical backstory, taped readings, improvised dialogue, addition of a secondary character or characters, and new and untried ways of thwarting bondage. Make a dramatic timeline to express periods of exhilaration or change in the biographies of white heir Rufus Weylin and black writers Dana and Kevin Franklin.

23. Compare aloud the turmoil of political, religious, and socio-economic change in Octavia's *Kindred*, "Crossover," "A Necessary Being," *The Parable of the Sower*, "Speech Sounds," and *Adulthood Rites*. Include character responses to gang threats, suicide, child abuse, invasion, abandonment, lashing, abduction, alcoholism, or nuclear war. Why does gendered status endanger progress?

24. Account for two different types of encounters in Octavia's writing. Choose from these:

    - questioning family love in "Near of Kin"
    - debating changes with God in "The Book of Martha"
    - a street shooting in "Speech Sounds"
    - arranged marriage in *Mind of My Mind*
    - commandeering a housetruck in *The Parable of the Talents*
    - Tino's questions of his ooloi in *Adulthood Rites*
    - phoning an emergency number in "Bloodchild"
    - charging An-yanwu with witchcraft in *Wild Seed*
    - viewing a community fire in *Imago*
    - fighting Clayarks in *Patternmaster*
    - executing a racial purist in *Fledgling*
    - emptying the nursery in *Dawn*
    - religious fundamentalism in *The Parable of the Sower*
    - a special diet in "The Evening and the Morning and the Night."

25. Contrast types of resistance in three of Octavia's works. Include the following models:

    - against aliens in *Survivor* or *Dawn*
    - against cannibalism in "Bloodchild"
    - against rape in *Mind of My Mind*
    - against kidnappers in *Wild Seed*
    - against trickery in *Patternmaster*
    - against paints in *Parable of the Sower*
    - against outsiders in "A Necessary Being"
    - against humans in "Amnesty"
    - against mental fog at Dilg
    - against stalkers in "Childfinder"
    - against despair in "Crossover"
    - against prejudice in *Fledgling*
    - against patrollers in *Kindred*
    - against carjackers in *Clay's Ark*
    - against a bow and arrow in *Adulthood Rites*

26. Compare the maturation and risk-taking of three decisive women in *Dawn*, *Imago*, "Speech Sounds," "Amnesty," *Mind of My Mind*, *Clay's Ark*, *Fledgling*,

"Near of Kin," or *Kindred.* Specify the degree of threat in each situation, particularly to nature, family, and children.

27. List types of creativity in *The Parable of the Talents,* "Speech Sounds," "Furor Scribendi," "The Book of Martha," *Wild Seed, Dawn,* and "Childfinder." How do protagonists achieve great satisfaction from long-range plans? from the supernatural? from romance? from solitude? from survival crafts? from collaboration? from family? from persistence?

28. Summarize Octavia's views on choices in "The Evening and the Morning and the Night," "The Book of Martha," *Clay's Ark, Fledgling,* the Parable series, and "Amnesty." How do species, gender, age, religion, sexual orientation, incurable disease, or race affect character selections and outcomes? Why is An-yanwu's option more lethal than those of Tate Marah, Martha Bes, Shori Matthews, Keith Olamina, Rane Maslin, Lilith Iyapo, Marcos Duran, Belen Ross, Theodora Hardin, or Noah Cannon?

29. Outline sources of pride in Octavia's "Bloodchild." Why do training, risk, labor, community, parenting, altruism, surgery, and strength produce contentment in humans and aliens?

30. Account for humor in difficult times in Mary Chase's play *Harvey,* Gore Vidal's *A Visit to a Small Planet,* Avi's *Gold Rush Girl,* Eve Ensler's *The Vagina Monologues,* Richard Adams's *Watership Down,* Richard Peck's *A Long Way from Chicago,* or Karen Cushman's *Catherine Called Birdy.* Analyze situational satire in Octavia's picture of God eating a tuna fish sandwich and drinking sparkling cider with Martha Bes or Lauren Oya Olamina concealing her gender under men's clothes and hairstyle. How does the author illustrate ignorance? satire? naiveté? duplicity? trust?

31. Compare gendered obstacles to girls and women in Octavia's "A Necessary Being" and *Lilith's Brood* with similar expectations in one of these works:

Mary Stewart's *The Crystal Cave*	Margaret Atwood's *The Handmaid's Tale*	Malala Yousafzai's *I Am Malala*
Virginia Hamilton's *Zeely*	Robin McKinley's *Beauty*	Ursula LeGuin's "Sur"
Gary Paulsen's *Nightjohn*	Sandra Cisneros's *House on Mango Street*	Walter Dean Myers's *At Her Majesty's Request*

32. Describe forcible isolation and images of solitude in four of these characters:

Teray	Alanna	Shori
Martha Bes	Thomas	Akin
An-yanwu	Petra/Smoke	Jane
Karl Larkin	Lilith Iyapo	Carrie
Naomi Chi	Nikanj	Larkin Bankole

How do rituals and shared projects ease alienation?

33. Select four contrasting scenes from Octavia's stories and novels and describe their pictorial qualities, for example:

- safety on a Terran reservation
- rich white suburbanites at Olivar
- examining Joachim's motives
- packing handcarts with tools
- isolation in a spaceship cell or cave
- wearing a dreamask
- time travel to a Maryland plantation
- reading about Harriet Tubman
- alien bubbles in the Mojave Desert
- a fire that burns Amber's rifle and scope
- locating doorways hidden in stone walls
- obeying "the Founder"
- viewing a seaside slave camp
- a scent that elevates male libido
- visiting Dilg
- returning from prison

34. Discuss the sources of aggression in four of these pairs:

Jordan/stalkers   Doro/Mary Larkin   Jane/ex-con
Dana/Rufus   Lilith/raiders   Ina/Silks
Alanna/Thera Collier   Keith/paints   Zahra/polygamist
Natahk/Jules   Larkin/Kayce   Alexandra/raiders
Teray/Joachim   Cougar/Marcus   resister/Oankali
Curt/Joseph

In which relationships have emotions stabilized? What outside forces alter hostilities?

35. Contrast flaws and strengths in two of these secondary characters from Octavia's stories and novels:

Neila Verrick   Seth   the Reverend Olamina
Emma   Thomas   Neci
jerhuk   Naomi Chi   Belen Ross
James Adio   Bernard Daly Jhadya
Cheah   Paul Titus   Joe Shing

Which characters recognize their own weaknesses? talents? inescapable memories? needs for control, rest or medical treatment, sex, or camaraderie?

36. Write an extended definition of *conflict* using as an example the atmosphere of two of these examples:

- rescuing Bram in "Bloodchild"
- child endangerment by caging in *Clay's Ark*
- exiling Jodahs to the mothership/planet in *Imago*
- eating "dog biscuits" in "The Evening and the Morning and the Night"
- avoidance of light in *Fledgling*
- saving Nikanj's life in *Dawn*
- stopping multiple amputations in *Adulthood Rites*
- scolding Lauren Oya Olamina for a gun battle in *The Parable of the Talents*
- Karl Larkin's courtship of Mary in *Mind of My Mind*
- obeying God in "The Book of Martha"
- changing into a leopard in *Wild Seed*

- intervening in female abuse in "Speech Sounds"
- weaning the body from *meklah* in *Survivor*
- identifying Larkin's birthmark in *The Parable of the Talents*

Incorporate changes in characters from triumphs or failures, for example, Keira Maslin's pregnancy with a mutant after her father's death in *Clay's Ark* or Lilith Iyapo's reaction to bearing Joe's child following a conception engineered by Nikanj in *Dawn*.

37. List types of comfort in five of these scenes. Explain why the characters are in need of treatment or solace:

- loading handcarts in *Survivor*
- planting trees in *The Parable of the Talens*
- viewing torture through an open door in *Clay's Ark*
- healing Aaor's tumors in *Imago*
- sitting outdoors in "The Book of Martha"
- collecting rainwater in *The Parable of the Sower*
- fishing in *Dawn*
- being questioned in "Amnesty"
- boarding the *Silver Star* with An-yanwu and Okoye in *Wild Seed*
- harboring lost children in "Speech Sounds"
- killing deer in *Fledgling*
- hospitality to Tino the wanderer in *Adulthood Rites*
- shopping with the immortal Doro in *Mind of My Mind*

38. Write newspaper features about three characters who are killed, martyred, menaced, bereaved, or lost, especially these:

- Barbara in "Childfinder"
- Joseph Shing in *Dawn*
- Neci in *Adulthood Rites*
- Bram Lomas in "Bloodchild"
- Clayarks in *Patternmaster*
- Harry Balter in *The Parable of the Talents*
- Alice Greenwood in *Kindred*
- the astronaut in *The Parable of the Sower*
- police officer in "Speech Sounds"
- Tahreh's father in "A Necessary Being"

39. Cite occasions for computation in Octavia's works. Name the particulars of each situation, such as these:

- timing of a pregnancy in "Near of Kin," *Dawn,* or "Bloodchild"
- bus route in "Speech Sounds"
- age differences in *Fledgling*
- Teray's schooling at Redhill in *Patternmaster*
- distance from Robledo to the Oregon state line in *The Parable of the Sower*
- cost of a slave midwife or breeder in *Kindred*
- length of flight to Alpha Centauri in *The Parable of the Talents*
- the long pilgrimage of disciples to Cape

Mendocino in the Parable series
- distance from the ranch house to Barstow in *Clay's Ark*

- value of a Nigerian slave in *Wild Seed*
- the speed of crossing the desert on foot in two and a half days in "A Necessary Being"

- the distance Isaac travels from Easton, Maryland, to Mississippi in *Kindred*

Compare the level of mathematical and scientific skills demanded in other works, especially Lee Smith's *Mrs. Darcy and the Blue-Eyed Stranger*, Theodora Kroeber's *Ishi*, Arthur C. Clarke's *Childhood's End*, H.P. Lovecraft's "Rats in the Wall," Anne McCaffrey's *Dragonflight*, Robert A. Heinlein's *The Puppet Masters*, Madeleine L'Engle's *A Wrinkle in Time*, or Ray Bradbury's "There Will Come Soft Rains."

Bibliography

Primary Sources

Adulthood Rites. New York: Warner, 1988; in *Lilith's Brood*. New York: Warner, 2000, 249–517.

Bloodchild and Other Stories. New York: Four Walls, Eight Windows, 1995; New York: Seven Stories Press, 2005.

Clay's Ark. New York: St. Martin's Press, 1984.

Dawn. New York: Warner, 1987; in *Lilith's Brood*. New York: Warner, 2000, 1–248.

Fledgling. New York: Seven Stories Press, 2005; *Octavia E. Butler: Kindred, Fledgling, Collected Stories*. New York: Library of America, 2021.

Imago. New York: Warner, 1989; in *Lilith's Brood*. New York: Warner, 2000, 518–746.

Kindred (graphic novel), adapted by Damian Duffy and John Jennings. New York: Abrams Comicarts, 2017.

Kindred. New York: Doubleday, 1979; *Octavia E. Butler: Kindred, Fledgling, Collected Stories*. New York: Library of America, 2021.

Lilith's Brood. New York: Warner, 2000.

Mind of My Mind. New York: Doubleday, 1977.

The Parable of the Sower. New York: Four Walls, Eight Windows, 1993.

———. (graphic novel), adapted by Damian Duffy and John Jennings. New York: Abrams, 2021.

The Parable of the Talents. New York: Seven Stories Press, 1998.

Patternmaster. New York: Doubleday, 1976.

Seed to Harvest (omnibus). New York: Grand Central Publishing, 2007.

Survivor. New York: Doubleday, 1978.

Unexpected Stories. New York: Open Road Media, 2014.

Wild Seed. New York: Doubleday, 1980.

Xenogenesis. San Francisco, CA: Guild America Books, 1989.

Short Works and Oratory

Adams, Karen (pseud.). "To the Victor," Pasadena City College, 1965.

"Amnesty," www.syfy.com/scifi, 2003; *Callaloo* 27:3 (Summer, 2004): 597–616; *Bloodchild and Other Stories*. New York: Seven Stories Press, 2005, 147–186; *Octavia E. Butler: Kindred, Fledgling, Collected Stories*. New York: Library of America, 2021.

"As Ayla's World Turns," (review) *Washington Post* (3 September 1982): D4.

"Birth of a Writer," *Essence* 20 (May, 1989): 74. *See also* "Positive Obsession."

"Black Feminism: Searching the Past," (review) *Washington Post* (17 October 1983): B2.

"Bloodchild," *Asimov's Science Fiction Magazine* 8-6 (June, 1984): 34–54; *19185 Annual World's Best SF*. New York: DAW, 1985; *Best SF of the Year 14*. New York: Tor, 1985; *Nebula Awards 20*. New York: Harcourt Brace, 1985; *The Year's Best Science Fiction*. New York: St. Martin, 1985; *The Best of Isaac Asimov's Science Fiction Magazine*. New York: Ace, 1988; *Science Fiction: The Science Fiction Research Association Anthology*. New York: Harper & Row, 1988, 499–514; *Foundations of Fear*. New York. Doherty, 1992; *Invaders*. New York: Ace, 1993; *Visions of Fear*. New York: Tor, 1994; *Women of Wonder*. San Diego: Harcourt Brace, 1995; *Bloodchild and Other Stories*. New York: Four Walls Eight Windows, 1995, 1–32; *Short Stories for Students*. Detroit: Gale, 1999; *New Bones*. Upper Saddle River, NJ: Prentice Hall, 2001, 85–100; *Locus Awards*. New York: Eos, 2004; *Norton Anthology of African American Literature,* 2nd ed. New York: Norton, 2005, 2516–2529; *Prentice Hall Anthology of African American Literature*. New York: Prentice Hall, 2006, 306–313; *Octavia E. Butler: Kindred, Fledgling, Collected Stories*. New York: Library of America, 2021.

"The Book of Martha," *American Letters and Commentary* 16 (2004): 23–41; *Bloodchild and Other Stories*. New York: Seven Stories Press, 2005, 189–214; *Obsidian III* 6:2, 7:1 (Fall/Winter 2005-Spring/Summer 2006): 44–60; *Octavia E. Butler: Kindred, Fledgling, Collected Stories*. New York: Library of America, 2021.

"Brave New Worlds: A Few Rules for Predicting the Future," *Essence* 31:1 (1 May 2000): 164–166, 264.

"Childfinder," *Clarion Journal* (1971): 7, 9, 23–29, 31, 33, 52, 56, 178, 179; *Unexpected Stories*. New York: Open Road Media, 2014, 77–80; *Octavia E. Butler: Kindred, Fledgling, Collected Stories*. New York: Library of America, 2021.

"Crossover," *Clarion: An Anthology of Speculative*

Fiction and Criticism from the Clarion Writers' Workshop. New York: New American Library, 1971, 139–144; *Bloodchild and Other Stories.* New York: Seven Stories Press, 2005, 111–122; *Octavia E. Butler: Kindred, Fledgling, Collected Stories.* New York: Library of America, 2021.

Dawn, Part 1," *Analog Science Fiction/Science Fact* (27 April, 1981).

"Dawn, Part 2," *Analog Science Fiction/Science Fact* (25 May 1981).

"Dawn, Part 3," *Analog Science Fiction/Science Fact* (22 June 1981).

"Dawn, Part 4," *Analog Science Fiction/Science Fact* (20 July 1981).

"Discovery, Creation, and Craft," *Washington Post* 13:21 (22 May 1983): 1, 6.

"The Evening and the Morning and the Night," *Omni* 104 (May, 1987): 56–62, 108–120; *The Year's Best Science Fiction: Fifth Annual.* New York: St. Martin's, 1988; *The Evening and the Morning and the Night.* Eugene, OR: Pulphouse, 1991; *Ancestral House.* Boulder, CO: Westview, 1995; *Penguin Book of Modern Fantasy by Women,* London: Viking, 1995; *Dark Matter.* New York: Warner, 2000; *Making Callaloo: 25 Years of Black Literature, 1976–2000.* New York: St. Martin's 2002; *Bloodchild and Other Stories.* New York: Seven Stories Press, 2005, 33–70; *Daughters of the Earth.* Middletown, CT: Wesleyan University Press, 2006; *Lightspeed #73* (June 2016); *Octavia E. Butler: Kindred, Fledgling, Collected Stories.* New York: Library of America, 2021.

"Eye Witness: Butler's Aha! Moment," *O: The Oprah Magazine* 3:5 (May, 2002): 79–80.

"Flirting with a Fairy Tale: *Subject to Change,*" (review) *Washington Post* (17 July 1988): 7.

"Free Libraries: Are They Becoming Extinct?," *Omni* 15:10 (August, 1993): 4.

"Furor Scribendi," *L. Ron Hubbard Presents Writers of the Future IX.* Los Angeles, CA: Bridge Publications, 1993, 324–327; *Bloodchild and Other Stories.* New York: Seven Stories Press, 2005, 137–146; *Writers of the Future,* Vol. 23. Los Angeles, CA: Galaxy Press, 2007; *Octavia E. Butler: Kindred, Fledgling, Collected Stories.* New York: Library of America, 2021.

"Future Forum," *Starlog/Future Life* 17 (November, 1980): 55–56.

"Futurist Woman," *Essence* 9 (April, 1979): 12, 15.

"How I Built Novels Out of Writer's Blocks," *Writer's Digest* (June, 1999): 12–15.

"I shall be a bestselling writer...," www.huntington. org/sites/default/files/styles/photo_gallery/ public/photo-gallery/octavia-butler_4_0. jpg?itok=pqacPQbT, 1988.

"Imago" (excerpt) in *Postmodern American Fiction.* New York: Norton, 1989.

"The Lost Races of Science Fiction," *Transmission* (Summer, 1980): 16–18; "Why Is Science Fiction So White," *Garage* 15 (4 September 2018); *Octavia E. Butler: Kindred, Fledgling, Collected Stories.* New York: Library of America, 2021.

"The Monophobic Response," *Dark Matter: A*

Century of Speculative Fiction from the African Diaspora. New York: Aspect/Warner Books, 2000, 415–416; *Octavia E. Butler: Kindred, Fledgling, Collected Stories.* New York: Library of America, 2021.

"Near of Kin," *Chrysalis 4,* 1979, 163–175; *Bloodchild and Other Stories.* New York: Seven Stories Press, 2005, 73–85; *Octavia E. Butler: Kindred, Fledgling, Collected Stories.* New York: Library of America, 2021.

"A Necessary Being," *Unexpected Stories.* New York: Open Road Media, 2014, 11–76.

"Persistence," *Locus* 44:6 (June, 2000): 6.

"Speech Sounds," *Isaac Asimov's Science Fiction Magazine* 7:13 (mid–December, 1983); *The New Hugo Winners.* New York: Norton, 1989; *Norton Book of SF.* New York, Norton, 1993; *New Eves.* Stamford, CT: Longmeadow, 1994; *Bloodchild and Other Stories.* New York: Four Walls Eight Windows, 1995, 87–110; *Virtually Now.* New York: Persea, 1996; *A Woman's Liberation.* New York: Warner, 2001; *New Bones.* Upper Saddle River, NJ: Prentice Hall, 2001, 100–110; *Reload.* Cambridge, MA: MIT Press, 2002, 403–414; *Wastelands: Stories of the Apocalypse.* San Francisco, CA: Night Shade, 2008; *Octavia E. Butler: Kindred, Fledgling, Collected Stories.* New York: Library of America, 2021.

"Wild Seed" (excerpt), *Essence* 11 (January, 1981): 86–87.

"A World without Racism," *National Public Radio Weekend Edition* (8 January 2001).

Speeches and Interviews

"Black to the Future," (speech), 2004.

"Devil Girl from Mars: Why I Write Science Fiction," *Media in Transition,* MIT (19 February 1998); web.mit.edu/m-i-t/articles/butler–talk– index.html.

"Essay on Racism: A Science-Fiction Writer Shares Her View of Intolerance," *National Public Radio Weekend Edition* (1 September 2001).

"Fixing the World," (speech), 2005.

"The Influence of Libraries on My Life and My Writing," (speech), 2000.

"Journeys," *Journeys* 30 (October, 1995), speech at the Quill & Brush PEN/Faulkner Awards for Fiction in Rockville, Maryland. *See also* "The Monophobic Response."

"Octavia Butler Presents Her Novel *Kindred,*" (video). Rochester, NY: Nazareth College, March 3, 2003.

"Positive Obsession," (speech), *Bloodchild and Other Stories.* New York: Seven Stories Press, 2005, 123–136; *Octavia E. Butler: Kindred, Fledgling, Collected Stories.* New York: Library of America, 2021.

"Racing Toward the Millennium" (speech), Los Angeles: Los Angeles Public Library, 1996.

"Reading," College Park, MD: Vertigo Books, March 27, 2003.

"Science Fiction Writer Octavia Butler on Race,

Global Warming and Religion," (video), *Democracy Now,* www.democracynow.org/2005/11/11/science_fiction_writer_octavia_butler_on (11 November 2005).

"Self-Construction," (speech), 1982.

"Symbiosis," (speech), 1970–1990.

"Trickster, Teacher, Chaos, Clay" (speech), Newcomb College, New Orleans, Louisiana (2 November 1999).

Verse

"Erodus," poem, 1975.

"Hiroshima," poem, 1964.

"Parasite," poem, 1986.

"The Rain," poem, 1966.

Drafts and Manuscripts

"Adam," draft, 1962.

"Breaking the Riding Habit," draft, 1977.

"Cycle," draft, 1964.

"The End," draft, 1963.

"Evolution," draft, 1962.

"Factory Reject," draft, 1965.

"A Few Basic Facts of Planet Rainbow," ms., 2001.

"Final Right," draft, 1965.

"The Fire," draft, 1965.

"The Forgotten Years," draft, 1964.

"The Freak," draft, 1958.

"Good-by," draft, 1965.

"Grub," draft, 1985.

"I Come with the House," draft, n.d.

"In Days of Elderly," draft, 1967.

"Incident," draft, 1965.

"Interval," draft, 1967.

"The Kidnapping," draft, 1980.

"Let's Go," draft, 1958.

"Life," draft, 1962.

"Lineage," draft, 1965.

"The Master," draft, 1965.

Miriam, draft, n.d.

"My Reo My Cover," draft, 1958.

"Negroid," draft, 1965.

"The Night Before Christmas Gone Beat," draft, 1965.

"Night of Terror," draft, 1970.

"The Other Gift," draft, 1967.

"Platypus," draft, 1970–1990.

"The Price of Hate," draft, 1967.

"The Prison of One," draft, 1964.

"Quiet Love," draft, 1972.

"Red Dream," draft, 1965.

"Shepherds," draft, 1962.

"Soloist," draft, 1984.

"The Street," draft, 1968.

"They Walk among Us," draft, 1965.

"Those Wonderful Pills," ms., 1963.

"Time and Space," draft, 1970–1990.

"To Know God," draft, 1963.

"To the Victor," draft, 1965.

"Tory," draft, 1965.

"Tutor," draft, 1985.

"Verde," draft, 1965.

"The Whip," draft, 1960.

"White Cloud," draft, 1958.

"Worldmaking," draft, 1981.

Plays

"Bound Slave," fragment of a short story and screenplay, 1975.

"Dare," fragment of a screenplay for *On Being Black,* 1975.

"Darkside," fragment of a screenplay, 1975.

"One More Door," play, 1975.

"Revenge of the Leprechauns," play, 1960.

Essays

"Blacks and Christianity," essay, 1965.

"Cycles of Humiliation and Fear," an essay following the Rodney King beating, 1992.

"A Few Rules for Prediction the Future," essay, 1999.

"Finding Our Voices," essay, 1995.

"Just Three Months," essay, 1965.

"L.A. after O.J.," essay 1995.

"Loss," *Writer's Digest,* winner of fifth place (unpublished), 1967.

"The Militant Change in Civil Rights," essay, 1966.

"Novels Built by Writer's Blocks," essay, 1999.

"Retooling," essay, 1994.

"The Right Thing to Do," essay, 1962.

"SF Tourist," essay, 1983.

"Sidelights," essay, 1978.

"The Structure of No Longer at Ease," essay, 1973.

"Teachers," essay, 1990.

"Telling My Stories," essay, 1990.

"Transforming Moment," essay, 2003.

UN Racism Conference, essay, 2000.

Unfinished and Miscellaneous Works

"Above and Below," fragment, 1961.

"Accident," fragment, 1965.

"The Actor," fragment, 1964.

"Adaptability," fragment, 1963.

"Addict," fragment, 1970.

"Alanna," fragment, 1970.

"Alone," fragment, 1962.

"Amen," fragment, 1974.

"And the Heavens Claimed Their Own," fragment, 1964.

Asylum, sequel to *Fledgling,* also called *Flight,* 2001.

"Believers," fragment, 1972–1993.

Blindsight, proposed titles *Mindsight, Leavings,* and *The Eternal Flesh,* 1984.

"Blue," fragment, 1980.

"Breakthrough," fragment, 1967.

Canaan, fragment, 1975.

"The Dark Land," fragment, 1964.
Daughter of the Mourning, fragment, 1988.
"Death!," fragment, 1963.
"December 31," fragment, 1961.
"DiaPause," fragment, 2007.
"Dona Bartholomew," fragment, 1960–1980.
"Doro-Jesus Story," fragment, 1973.
Earthseed: The Books of the Living, proposed title *Earthseed: The First Book of the Living,* 1997.
"Ecstasy," fragment, 2006.
Eden, fragment, 2001.
"Elyano," fragment, 1970.
"The Encounter in Cajamarca," fragment, 1962.
Fire, Laughter, Emeralds, Rain: A Thesaurus of First Names, monograph, 2000.
"Flash," fragment, 1964.
The Flaying, fragment 1970–1990.
"Freedom," fragment, 1965.
"The Game," outline, 1964.
"Gerick," fragment, n.d.
"The Gift," fragment, 1968.
"Goat," fragment, 1970.
God of Clay, fragment, 1989.
"Green Night," fragment, 1965.
"He Made Things," fragment, n.d.
"Hechecera," fragment, 1975.
"Hope," story, 1960.
"How I Write," fragment, 1986.
"Human Resources," fragment, 2000.
"Hypnotic," essay, 1960–1975.
I Should Have Said... fragment, 1998.
"If This Goes On," essay, 1985.
"The Individual We," fragment, 1967.
"Into Infinity," fragment, 1962.
"Jodas/Thomas/Aaor," fragment, 1985.
"Juncture," fragment, 1985.
Leavings, fragment, 1984.
"Lifesong," fragment, 1970.
"Man's Best Friend," fragment, 1961.
"Mishaari," fragment, 1970.
Mortal Words, fragment, 2000.
"No God, No Heaven, Just a Hell," fragment, 1970.
"Only," fragment, 1965.
"Overseer," fragment, 1974.
Parable of the Trickster, fragment, proposed titles *Trickster* and *Teacher,* 2001.
Paraclete, fragment, proposed titles *O My Soul, Revelation,* and *Bodhisattva,* 2001.
"Pattern," fragment, 1967.
The Pride, fragment, 1975.
"Prison Planet," fragment, n.d.
"Pruning Hook," fragment, 2000.
"Revolution," fragment, 1964.
"Ruth," fragment, 1970.
"The Search," fragment, 1964.
"The Second Law of Thermodynamics," interview, 2001.
"Silver Star," fragment, 1963.
"Sky Level," fragment, 1964.
"The Slavers," fragment, 1961.
"Some Things That Are," notes, 1966.
Spiritus, fragment, 2001.
"Sunday Night," fragment, 1964.

"Supplanter," fragment, 1985.
"10 O'Clock Jesus," fragment, n.d.
"Trigon," outline, 1987.
"Vampire," fragment, 1970.
"Why Did I Write *Kindred?*," fragment, 1986.
"The Women," fragment, 1980.
"Xenograft," notes, 1997.

Secondary Sources

Assman, Jan. *Religion and Cultural Memory.* Stanford, CA: Stanford University Press, 2006.
Baccolini, Raffaella, and Rom Moylan, eds. *Dark Horizons: Science Fiction and the Dystopian Imagination.* London: Routledge, 2003.
Baldwin, James. *The Fire Next Time.* London: Michael Joseph, 1963.
Baraka, Amiri, and Amina Baraka, eds. *Confirmation: An Anthology of African American Women.* New York: Quill, 1983.
Barr, Marleen S. *Lost In Space: Probing Feminist Science Fiction and Beyond.* Chapel Hill: University of North Carolina Press, 1993.
Barrett, Michele. *Women's Oppression Today: The Marxist/Feminist Encounter.* London: Verso, 1988.
Bast, Florian. *Of Bodies, Communities, and Voices* (monograph). Heidelberg, Germany: Universitätsverlag, 2015.
Birringer, Johannes. *Kinetic Atmospheres: Performance and Immersion.* Abingdon, UK: Routledge, 2021.
Brown, Adrienne Maree. *Emergent Strategy: Shaping Change, Changing Worlds.* Chico, CA: AK Press, 2017.
———, and Walidah Marisha, eds. *Octavia's Brood: Science Fiction Stories from Social Justice Movements.* Oakland, CA: AK Press, 2015.
Brown, Jayna. *Black Utopias: Speculative Life and the Music of Other Worlds.* Durham, NC: Duke University Press, 2021.
Canavan, Gerry. *Octavia E. Butler.* Urbana: University of Illinois, 2016.
Castiglia, Christopher. *Bound and Determined: Captivity, Culture-Crossing, and White Womanhood from Mary Rowlandson to Patty Hearst.* Chicago: University of Chicago Press, 1996.
Collins, Patricia Hill. *Black Feminist Thought: Knowledge, Consciousness, and the Politics of Empowerment.* New York: Routledge, 2015.
Colmon, Jr., Clayton D. *On Becoming: Afrofuturism, Worldbuilding, and Embodied Imagination.* Newark: University of Delaware, 2020.
Cooper, Brittney C. *Beyond Respectability: The Intellectual Thought of Race Women.* Champaign: University of Illinois Press, 2017.
Cox-Palmer-White, Emily. *The Biopolitics of Gender in Science Fiction: Feminism and Female Machines.* New York: Routledge, 2021.
Davis-Secord, Jonathan. *Joinings: Compound Words in Old English Literature.* Toronto: University of Toronto Press, 2016.
Delany, Samuel R. *Occasional Views Volume 1.*

Middletown, CT: Wesleyan University Press, 2021.

Dery, Mark, ed. *Flame Wars: The Discourse of Cyberculture.* Durham, NC: Duke University Press, 1994.

Dickens, Risa, and Amy Torok. *Missing Witches: Recovering True Histories of Feminist Magic.* Berkeley, CA: North Atlantic Books, 2021.

Donawerth, Jane L. *Frankenstein's Daughters: Women Writing Science Fiction.* Syracuse: Syracuse University Press, 1997.

———, and Carol A. Wolmerten, eds. *Introduction to Utopian and Science Fiction by Women: Worlds of Difference.* Syracuse: Syracuse University Press, 1995.

Eisenberg, Ronald L. *Jewish Traditions.* Lincoln: University of Nebraska Press, 2020.

Fiskio, Janet. *Climate Change, Literature, and Environmental Justice: Poetics of Dissent and Repair.* Cambridge, UK: Cambridge University Press, 2021.

Francis, Consuela, ed. *Conversations with Octavia Butler.* Jackson: University Press of Mississippi, 2010.

Gates, Jr., Henry Louis. *The Slave's Narrative.* New York: Oxford University Press, 1985.

George, Lynell. *A Handful of Earth, a Handful of Sky.* Los Angeles, CA: Angel City Press, 2020.

Goodwin, Matthew David. *The Latinx Files: Race, Migration, and Space Aliens.* New Brunswick, NJ: Rutgers University Press, 2021.

Granja, David Jacobo Viveros, María Catalina Caro Torres, and María Alejandra Velasco Velandia. *Living British Literature: From the Anglo-Saxon World to the Early Renaissance.* Bogota, Colombia: Universidad Pedagógica Nacional, 2021.

Hall, Alice, ed. *The Routledge Companion to Literature and Disability.* London: Routledge, 2020.

Hampson, Daphne. *After Christianity.* London: SCM Press, 2012.

Hampton, Gregory Jerome. *Changing Bodies in the Fiction of Octavia Butler: Slaves, Aliens, and Vampires.* Lanham, MD: Lexington Books, 2014.

Hanganu-Bresch, Cristina, and Kelleen Flaherty. *Effective Scientific Communication: The Other Half of Science.* New York: Oxford University Press, 2020.

Haraway, Donna. *Primate Visions: Gender, Race, and Nature in the World of Modern Science.* New York: Routledge, 1989.

Henighan, Tim, ed. *Brave New Universe: Testing the Values of Science in Society.* Ottawa: Tecumseh Press, 1980.

Hobson, Janell. *When God Lost Her Tongue.* London: Routledge, 2022.

Holden, Rebecca J., and Nisi Shawl, eds. *Strange Matings: Science Fiction, Feminism, African American Voices, and Octavia E. Butler.* Seattle, WA: Aqueduct, 2013.

Ibrahim, Habiba. *Black Age: Oceanic Lifespans and the Time of Black Life.* Albany: New York University Press, 2021.

Iheka, Cajetan. *African Ecomedia: Network Forms,* *Planetary Politics.* Durham, NC: Duke University Press, 2021.

Imarisha, Walidah, et al., eds. *Octavia's Brood: Science Fiction Stories from Social Justice Movements.* Oakland, CA: AK Press, 2015.

Jackson, Michael. *Coincidences: Synchronicity, Verisimilitude, and Storytelling.* Berkeley: University of California Press, 2021.

Japtok, Martin, and Jerry Rafiki Jenkins, eds. *Human Contradictions in Octavia E. Butler's Work.* Cham, Switzerland: Palgrave, Macmillan, 2020.

Jenkins, Jerry Rafiki. *The Paradox of Blackness in African American Vampire Fiction.* Columbus: Ohio State University Press, 2019.

Johnson, Clifton Zeno. *Race in the Galactic Age: Sankofa, Afrofuturism, Whiteness and Whitley Strieber.* Albany: State University of New York, 2019.

Jones, Gwyneth. *Imagination/Space: Essays and Talks on Fiction, Feminism, Technology, and Politics.* Seattle, WA: Aqueduct, 2009.

Kord, Susanne. *12 Monkeys.* Bedfordshire, UK: Auteur Press, 2019.

Kuhad, Urvashi. *Science Fiction and Indian Women Writers: Exploring Radical Potentials.* London: Routledge India, 2021.

Lennard, John. *Reading Octavia E. Butler: Xenogenesis/Lilith's Blood.* Penrith, CA: Humanities-Ebooks, 2012.

Leonard, Elisabeth Anne, eds *Into Darkness Peering: Race and Color in the Fantastic.* Westport, CT: Greenwood, 1997.

Lewis, Sophie. *Full Surrogacy Now: Feminism against Family.* London: Verso, 2021.

Lillvis, Kristen. *Posthuman Blackness and the Black Female Imagination.* Athens: University of Georgia Press, 2017.

Mao, Douglas. *Inventions of Nemesis.* Princeton, NJ: Princeton University Press, 2020.

Mbembe, Achille. *Critique of Black Reason.* Durham, NC: Duke University Press, 2017.

McCaffrey, Larry, ed. *Across the Wounded Galaxies.* Urbana: University of Illinois Press, 1990.

Melzer, Patricia. *Alien Constructions: Science Fiction and Feminist Thought.* Austin: University of Texas Press, 2021.

Menely, Tobias. *Climate and the Making of Worlds.* Chicago: University of Chicago Press, 2021.

Michel, Frann. *The Female Face of Shame.* Indianapolis: Indiana University Press, 2013.

Miller, Joshua, ed. *The Cambridge Companion to Twenty-First Century American Fiction.* Cambridge, UK: Cambridge University Press, 2021.

Montgomery, Maxine Lavon. *The Postapocalyptic Black Female Imagination.* London: Bloomsbury, 2021.

Morris, David. *Public Religions in the Future World: Postsecularism and Utopia.* Athens: University of Georgia Press, 2021.

Nanda, Aparajita, and Shelby Crosby, eds. *God Is Change: Religious Practices and Ideologies in the Works of Octavia Butler.* Philadelphia: Temple University Press, 2021.

O'Neall, John Belton. *The Negro Law of South Carolina*. Columbia, SC: J.G. Bowman, 1848.

Parker, Kendra R. *Black Female Vampires in African American Women's Novels, 1977–2011*. Lanham, MD: Lexington Books, 2018.

_____. *Gale Researcher Guide: Octavia Butler and Afrofuturism*. Boston: Cengage Learning, 2018.

Pickens, Theri Alyce. *Black Madness: Mad Blackness*. Durham, NC: Duke University Press, 2019.

Pisters, Patricia. *New Blood in Contemporary Cinema: Women Directors and the Poetics of Horror*. Edinburgh, UK: Edinburgh University Press, 2020.

Pitts, Michael. *Alternative Masculinities in Feminist Speculative Fiction: A New Man*. Lanham, MD: Lexington Books, 2021.

Plumwood, Val. *Feminism and the Mastery of Nature*. London: Routledge, 1993.

Potts, Stephen W. "We Keep on Playing the Same Record," *Science Fiction Studies* 23 (November, 1996): 331–338.

Pratt, Mary Louise. *Os Olhos do Império: Relatos de Viagem e Transculturaçao*. London: Routledge, 1992.

Pryse, Marjorie, and Hortense J. Spillers, eds. *Conjuring: Black Women, Fiction, and Literary Traditions*. Bloomington: Indiana University Press, 1985.

Qadeer, Haris, and P.K. Yasser Arafath, eds. *Sultana's Sisters: Genre, Gender, and Genealogy in South Asian Muslim Women's Fiction*. London: Routledge, 2021.

Rajan, Arshad Ahammad, and Nada Rajan, eds. *Literature, Theory and the History of Ideas*. Newcastle upon Tyne, UK: Cambridge Scholars, 2021.

Reed, Thomas Vernon. *The Bloomsbury Introduction to Postmodern Realist Fiction: Resisting Master Narratives*. New York: Bloomsbury, 2021.

Reyes, Patrick B. *The Purpose Gap: Empowering Communities of Color to Find Meaning and Thrive*. Louisville, KY: Westminster John Knox Press, 2021.

Rieder, John. *Colonialism and the Emergence of Science Fiction*. Middletown, CT: Wesleyan University Press, 2008.

Rodrigues, Sara, and Ela Przybylo, eds. *On the Politics of Ugliness*. Cham, Switzerland: Palgrave Macmilllan, 2018.

Rouillard, Linda Marie. *Medieval Considerations of Incest, Marriage, and Penance*. Cham, Switzerland: Springer Nature, 2020.

Sargent, Pamela. *Women of Wonder*. New York: Penguin, 1974.

Setka, Stella. *Empathy and the Phantasmic in Ethnic American Trauma Narratives*. Lanham, MD: Lexington Books, 2020.

Steinbock, Eliza, and Marianna Szczygielska, eds. *Tranimacies: Intimate Links Between Animal and Trans* Studies*. London: Routledge, 2021.

Suvin, Darko. *Metamorphosis of Science Fiction*. Bern, Switzerland: Peter Lang, 2016.

Tate, Claudia, ed. *Black Women Writers at Work*. New York: Continuum, 1983.

Thomas, Sheree R., ed. *Dark Matter: A Century of Speculative Fiction from the African Diaspora*. New York: Warner Aspect, 2000.

Toliver, S. R. *Recovering Black Storytelling in Qualitative Research: Endarkened Storywork*. London: Routledge, 2021.

Torgovnick, Marianna. *Primitive Passions: Men, Women, and the Quest for Ecstasy*. Chicago: University of Chicago Press, 1998.

Trafford, James, and Pete Wolfendale, eds. *Alien Vectors: Accelerationism, Xenofeminism, Inhumanism*. Abingdon, UK: Routledge, 2020.

Tüzün, Hatice Övgü. Dystopias and Utopias on Earth and Beyond. London: Routledge, 2021.

Vakoch, Douglas A. *Dystopias and Utopias on Earth and Beyond*. New York: Routledge, 2021.

Ventura, Patricia, and Edward K. Chan, eds. *Race and Utopian Desire in American Literature and Society*. Cham, Switzerland: Palgrave Macmillan, 2019.

Vint, Sherryl. *Bodies of Tomorrow: Technology, Subjectivity, Science Fiction*. Toronto: University of Toronto Press, 2007.

Williams, Algie Vincent, III. *Patterns in the Parables: Black Female Agency and Octavia Butler's Construction of Black Womanhood*. Ann Arbor: University of Michigan, 2011.

Womack, Ytasha. *Afrofuturism: The World of Black Sci-Fi and Fantasy Culture*. Chicago: Lawrence Hill Books, 2013.

Articles, Interviews, Essays

Abbott, Carl. "Pasadena on Her Mind: Exploring Roots of Octavia E. Butler's Fiction," *Western Historical Quarterly* 49:3 (2018): 325–334.

Afful, Adwoa. "Wild Seed: Africa and Its Many Diasporas," *Critical Arts* 30:4 (August, 2016): 93–104.

Al-Nuaimi, Sami Abdullah, Zainor Izat Zainal, Mohammad Ewan Awang, and Noritah Omar. "Afrofuturism and Transhumanism: New Insights into the African American Identity in Octavia Butler's *Dawn*," *Pertanika Journal* 29:2 (2021): 977–992.

Alderman, Naomi. "Dystopian Dreams: How Feminist Science Fiction Predicted the Future," London *Guardian* (25 March 2017): 2.

Alessio, Carolyn. "Review: *The Parable of the Talents*," *Chicago Tribune* (20 December 1998): F3.

_____. "Talking with Octavia E. Butler," *Philadelphia Inquirer* (10 January 1999): Q2.

Allen, Marlene D. "Octavia Butler's Parable Novels and the Boomerang of African American History," *Callaloo* 32:4 (Fall, 2009): 1353–1363, 1387.

Allison, Dorothy. "The Future of Female," *Village Voice* (19 December 1989): 67–68.

"Alternative Universe," *Los Angeles Times* (18 October 1985).

Anandrao, Navle Balaji. "Female Characters in Science Fiction: Archetypal Messengers of Social Equity & Equality," *International Multilingual*

Journal for Arts and Humanities 1:6 (August, 2021): 106–118.

_____. "Futuristic Vision of a Millennial World: Science Fiction of Octavia Butler," *Literary Cognizance* II-2 (September, 2021): 3–10.

Anderson, Crystal S. "'The Girls Isn't White': New Racial Dimensions in Octavia Butler's *Survivor*," *Extrapolation* 47:1 (Spring, 2006): 35–50, 53.

Andreolle, Donna Spalding. "Utopias of Old, Solutions for the New Millennium," *Utopian Studies* 12:2 (2001): 114–123.

Banfield, Bever-leigh. "Octavia Butler: A Wild Seed," *Hip* 5:9 (1981): 48–50, 72, 74, 77.

Barnes, Stephen. "Interview," *American Vision* 15:5 (October-November, 2000): 24–28.

Bates, Karen Grigsby. "Interview," *NPR Morning Edition* (10 July 2017).

Batiste, Stephanie L., Mary Anne Boelcskevy, and Shireen K. Lewis. "Interview," *Journal of Black Studies and Research* 48:4 (6 November 2018).

Baudou, Jacques. "Octavia Butler," *Le Monde* (2 March 2006): 29.

Beal, Frances. "Interview," *Black Scholar* 17:2 (March/April, 1986): 14–18.

Behrent, Megan. "The Personal Is Historical: Slavery, Black Power, and Resistance in Octavia Butler's *Kindred*," *College Literature* 46:4 (2019): 795–828.

Berger, Michele. "Review: *Parable of the Sower*," *Black Scholar* 24:4 (Fall, 1994): 52–53.

Berry, Michael. "A Frighteningly Real Parable," *San Francisco Chronicle* (17 April1994): 3.

Best, Stephen. "Interview" (video). University of California, Berkeley, 2004.

Boccara, Ella. "Female Identity and Race in Contemporary Afrofuturist Narratives: *Wild Seed* by Octavia Butler" (dissertation). University of Montreal, December 16, 2020.

Bogstad, Janice. "Interview," *Janus* 14:4 (Winter, 1978–1979): 28–32.

Bonner, Frances. "Difference and Desire, Slavery and Seduction: Octavia Butler's Xenogenesis," *Foundation* 48 (Spring, 1990): 50–61.

Botting, Eileen Hunt. "Predicting the Patriarchal Politics of Pandemics from Mary Shelley to Covid-19," *Frontiers in Sociology* 6 (24 March 2021): 1–8.

Boulter, Amanda. "Polymorphous Futures: Octavia E. Butler's Xenogenesis Trilogy" in *American Bodies: Cultural Histories of the Physique*. Washington Square: New York University Press, 1996, 170–185.

Boyd, Valerie. "Gauging the Price of Being Human," *Atlanta Journal-Constitution* (5 November 1995): L8.

Bradley, Adam. "Revenge of the Blerds," *New York Times Magazine* (28 March 2021): 66–70.

Brisman, Avi. "The Fable of 'The Three Little Pigs': Climate Change and Green Cultural Criminology," *International Journal for Crime, Justice and Social Democracy* 8:1 (2019): 46–69.

Brown, Charles N. "Interview," *Locus* 21:10 (October, 1988).

Burt, Stephanie. "Octavia Butler Wanted to Write a 'Yes' Book," *National Republic* (27 May 2021).

Calvin, Ritch. "An Octavia E. Butler Bibliography (1976–2008)," *Utopian Studies* 19:3 (2008): 485–516.

Canavan, Gerry. "Bred to Be Superhuman: Comic Books and Afrofuturism in Octavia Butler's Patternist Series," *Paradoxa* 25 (2013): 253–287.

_____. "Recovering Octavia E. Butler's Lost Parables," *Los Angeles Review of Books* (9 June 2014).

_____. "Science Fiction and Utopia in the Anthropocene," *American Literature* 93:2 (2021): 255–282.

Carr, Elston. "Jump-Start the Time Machine," *LA Weekly* (19 March 1992): 36–37.

Cellini, Lisa A. "Invasion of the Writers," *Lansing State Journal* (13 July 1989): C1.

Charles, Ron. "Love at First Bite," *Washington Post* (30 October 2005).

Colley, Linda. "Perceiving Low Literature: The Captivity Narrative," *Essays in Criticism* 53:3 (2003): 199–218.

Crisp, Marty. "Interview," (Lancaster, PA) *Sunday News* (11 February 1996): H3.

Curtis, Claire P. "Theorizing Fear: Octavia Butler and the Realist Utopia," *Utopian Studies* 19:3 (2008): 411–431.

Davidson, Carolyn S. "The Science Fiction of Octavia Butler," *Sagala* (Summer, 1981) 2:1: 35.

Davis, Marcia. "Obituary," *Washington Post* (28 February 2006).

Doerksen, Teri Ann. "Octavia E. Butler: Parables of Race and Difference" in *Into Darkness Peering*. Westport, CT: Greenwood, 1997, 21–34.

Donawerth, Jane L., and Kate Scally. "'You've Found No Records': Slavery in Maryland and the Writing of Octavia Butler's *Kindred*," *Extrapolation* 58:1 (2017): 1–6.

Due, Tananarive. "Interview," *Essence* 50:4 (4 October 2019): 72–75.

Dundas, Deborah. "The Brilliance of Black Storytellers," *Toronto Star* (17 February 2018): E12.

Dunkley, Kitty. "Becoming Posthuman: The Sexualized, Racialized, and Naturalized Others of Octavia E. Butler's *Lilith's Brood*" in *The Bloomsbury Handbook to Octavia E. Butler*. New York: Bloomsbury, 2020, 95–116.

Elliot, Jeffrey. "Interview," *Thrust* 12 (Summer, 1979): 19–22.

"Exhibitions Open at SAAG," *Lethbridge* (Alberta) *Herald* (26 September 2020): A4.

Flood, Alison. "Perseverance Martian Landing Point Named after Octavia E. Butler," London *Guardian* (10 March 2021).

Flyn, Cal. "The Best Books about the Post-Human Earth," London *Guardian* (16 August 2021): 26.

Foster, Frances Smith. "Octavia Butler's Black Female Future Fiction," *Extrapolation* 23:1 (Spring, 1982): 37–49.

Fox, Margalit. "Obituary," *New York Times* (3 March 2006): C16.

Friedman, Gabriella. "Unsentimental Historicizing: The Neo-Slave Narrative Tradition and the

Refusal of Feeling," *American Literature* 93:1 (2021): 115–143.

Fry, Joan. "Interview," *Poets & Writers* 25:2 (March/April, 1997): 58–69.

Gale, Nikita. "After Words: On Octavia Butler's 'Speech Sounds,'" *Resonance* 1:4 (2020): 462–466.

George, Lynell. "Black Writers Crossing the Final Frontier," *Los Angeles Times* (22 June 2004).

Glave, Dianne. "Interview," *Callaloo* 26:1 (2003): 146–159.

Govan, Sandra Y. "Connections, Links, and Extended Networks," *Black American Literature Forum* 18:2 (Spring, 1984): 82–87.

_____. "Homage to Tradition: Octavia Butler Renovates the Historical Novel," *MELUS* 13:1–2 (Spring/Summer, 1986): 79–96.

_____. "Interview," *Obsidian III* 6:2/7:1 (2005–2006): 14–39.

Gowler, David B. "Selfish and Proud: The Good Samaritan, Octavia Butler, and Wearing a Mask" in *A Chorus of Voices: The Reception History of the Parables*. Oxford, UK: Newstex, 3 July 2020.

Grant, Glenn. "Black Woman Author Is Rarity in SF," (Montreal) *Gazette* (26 March 1994): I3.

_____. "Review: *The Parable of the Sower*," (Montreal) *Gazette* (4 March 1995): H4.

Grecca, Gabriela Bruschini. "'A Racist Challenge Might Force Us Apart': Divergence, Reliance, and Empathy in *Parable of the Sower* by Octavia Butler," *Ilha do Desterro* 74:1 (January-April 2021): 347–362.

Grewe-Volpp, Christa. "Octavia Butler and the Nature/Culture Divide" in *Restoring the Connection to the Natural World*. Hamburg, Germany: LIT, 2003.

Grinberg, Emanuella. "Celebrating Octavia Butler: A Visionary among Futurists," *CNN* (10 March 2016).

Guerrero, Paula Barba. "Post-Apocalyptic Memory Sites: Damaged Space, Nostalgia, and Refuge in Octavia Butler's *Parable of the Sower*," *Science Fiction Studies* 48:1 (2021): 29–45.

Hampton, Gregory. "In Memoriam: Octavia E. Butler (1947–2006)," *Callaloo* 29:2 (Spring, 2006): 245–248.

Harris, Mark. "This 2000 Nebula Nominees Range from Spacey Parable to Full-Blooded Heroic Fantasy," *Vancouver Sun* (13 May 2000): H10.

Harrison, Rosalie. "Interview," *Equal Opportunity Forum* 8 (November, 1980): 30–34.

Hartman, Saidiya, Farah Jasmine Griffin, Shelly Eversley, and Jennifer L. Morgan. "Whatcha Gonna Do?," *Women's Studies Quarterly* 35:1–2 (2007): 299–309.

Heideman, Eric M. "Review: *Mind of My Mind*," (Minneapolis, MN) *Star Tribune* (26 March 1995): 73.

Hinton, Anna. "Making Do with What You Don't Have: Disabled Black Motherhood in Octavia E. Butler's *Parable of the Sower* and *Parable of the Talents*," *Journal of Literary & Cultural Disability Studies* 12:4 (2018): 441–457.

Holden, Rebecca J. "The High Costs of Cyborg Survival," *Foundation* 72 (Spring, 1998): 49–56.

Howard, Mimi. "New Sun: A Feminist Literary Festival," *London Art Monthly* 445 (April, 2021): 37.

Hunt, Samantha. "What Is a Teenage Girl?," *International New York Times* (27 January 2021).

Jackson, H. Jerome. "Sci-Fi Tales from Octavia E. Butler," *Crisis* 101:3 (April, 1994): 4.

Johnson, Ikea M. "On Compassion and the Sublime Black Body: Octavia E. Butler's *Parable of the Sower*," *Journal of Comparative Literature and Aesthetics* 43:2 (Summer, 2020): 95–101.

Jonas, Gerald. "Review: *Clay's Ark*," *New York Times* (29 December 1996): 16.

Jones, Esther L. "More Than Just Escapism: Science Fiction Builds Mental Resiliency," *Hispanic Outlook in Higher Education* 30:9 (June/July, 2020): 18–19.

Kaplan, Tugba Akman. "Identity and Language Formation within an Afrofuturistic Scope in Octavia Butler's Kindred," *Biruni University 1st International Congress* (12 June 2021): 43–51.

_____. "The Importance of Surrounding Communities in Identity Formation within Afrofuturistic Context," *Year 2021* 9 (21 August 2021): 261–275.

Kaplan-Levenson, Laine. "Sci-Fi Writer Octavia Butler Offered Warnings and Hope in Her Work," *Morning Edition*. Washington, D.C.: NPR (24 February 2021).

Kearse, Stephen. "The Essential Octavia Butler," *New York Times* (15 January 2021): 12–13.

Keil, Roger. "Global Urbanization Created the Conditions for Current Coronavirus Pandemic," (Toronto) *Canadian Press* (19 June 2020).

Kelly, Deirdre. "The Brave New World of Female Science Fiction," (Toronto) *Globe and Mail* (25 February 2013): A17.

Kelly, Tasha, and Jan Berrien Berends. "Octavia E. Butler Mouths Off!," *Terra Incognita* (Winter, 1996).

Kenan, Randall. "Interview," *Callaloo* 14:2 (Spring, 1991): 495–504.

Keyes, Allison, "Octavia Butler's *Kindred* Turns 25," *Tavis Smiley Show, National Public Radio* (4 March 2004).

Kilgore, De Witt Douglas, and Ranu Samantrai. "A Memorial to Octavia E. Butler," *Science Fiction Studies* 37:3 (November, 2010): 353–361.

Kiran, Ayesha. "Human Identity and Technophobic Posthumanism in Octavia Butler's *Dawn*," *Indiana Journal of Arts & Literature* 2:8 (2021): 1–15.

Lange, Emily. "Creativity and Sacrifice in Two Short Stories from Octavia Butler and Maurice Broaddus," *Femspec* 20:2 (2020): 26–45.

Lee, Judith. "'We Are All Kin': Relatedness, Mortality, and the Paradox of Human Immortality" in *Immortal Engines: Life Extension and Immortality in Science Fiction and Fantasy*. Athens, GA: University of Georgia Press 1996, 170–182.

Lievens, Laura. "The Only Lasting Truth Is Change: An Analysis of Earthseed Spirituality" (master's thesis), Université Catholique de Louvain, Belgium, 2020.

Lilvis, Kristen. "Mama's Baby, Papa's Slavery? The Problem and Promise of Mothering in Octavia E. Butler's 'Bloodchild,'" *MELUS* 39:4 (Winter, 2014): 7–22, 220.

Littleton, Therese. "'Black to the Future': Fest Is Mothership for African Americans in Science Fiction," *Seattle Times* (6 June 2004): K1.

Livingstone, Josephine. "Old English," *New York Times Magazine* (6 January 2019): 24–25.

Loos, Martijn, Johanna Kaszti, and Rick van der Waarden. "The Body as Heterotopia," *Junctions: Graduate Journal of the Humanities* 5:2 (2021): 18–32.

Lucas, Julian. "Stranger Communities," *New Yorker* 97:4 (15 March 2021): 73–76.

Mabe, Chauncey. "Sci-fi Pioneer Took the Road Less Traveled," (Fort Lauderdale) *South Florida Sun Sentinel* (28 February 1999): D1, D5.

Mackenthun, Gesa. "Sustainable Stories: Managing Climate Change with Literature," *Sustainability* 13:7 (2021): 4049.

Magedanz, Stacy. "The Captivity Narrative in Octavia E. Butler's *Adulthood Rites*," *Extrapolation* 53:1 (2012): 47–59.

Matthews, Aisha. "Give Me Liberty or Give Me (Double) Consciousness," *Third Stone* 2:1 (2021): 1–21.

McGee, Robyn. "Octavia Butler: Soul Sister of Science Fiction," *Fireweed* 73 (Fall, 2001): 60.

McGonigal, Mike. "Interview," *Index* (1998).

McHenry, Susan. "Otherworldly Vision: Octavia Butler," *Essence* 29:10 (February, 1989): 80.

McKoy, Sheila Smith. "Yemonja/Yemoja/Yemaya Rising," *Recovering the African Feminine Divine in Literature, the Arts, and Practice: Yemonja Awakening.* Lanham, MD: Lexington Books, 2020, 55–68.

Mehaffy, Marilyn, and AnaLouise Keating. "Radio Imagination: Octavia Butler on the Poetics of Narrative Embodiment," *MELUS* 26:1 (2001): 45–76.

Miller, Jim. "Post-Apocalyptic Hoping," *Science Fiction Studies* 25:2 (July, 1998): 336–360.

Miller, Kristie. "What Time-Travel Teaches Us about Future-Bias," *Philosophies* 6:2 (2021): 38.

Minister, Meredith. "How to Live at the End of the World" in *Who Knows What We'd Make of It, If We Ever Got Our Hands on It?* Piscataway, NJ: Gorgias Press, 2020: 285–306.

Mixon, Veronica. "Future Woman: Octavia Butler," *Essence* 9 (April, 1979): 12, 15.

Mizota, Sharon. "She Blazed Sci-Fi Trails," *Los Angeles Times* (31 October 2016): E4.

Morgan, Glyn. "New Ways: The Pandemics of Science Fiction," *Interface Focus* 11:5 (12 October 2021).

Morrison, Monique. "Octavia Butler Speaks," *FEMSPEC* 4:2 (September, 2004): 305–306.

Mulligan, Rikk. "Renewing the Sense of an Ending," *Extrapolation* 59:2 (2018): 205–209.

Nagl, Dominik. "The Governmentality of Slavery in Colonial Boston, 1690–1760," *Amerikastudien/American Studies* 58:1 (2013): 5–26.

Nanda, Aparajita "A Palimpsestuous Reading of Octavia Butler's *Lilith's Brood*" in *Palimpsests in Ethnic and Postcolonial Literature and Culture.* Cham, Switzerland: Palgrave Macmillan, 2021.

Nayar, Pramod K. "Vampirism and Posthumanism in Octavia Butler's *Fledgling*," *Notes on Contemporary Literature* 41:2 (2011): 6–10.

Norwood, Chico. "Science Fiction Writer Comes of Age," *Los Angeles Sentinel* (16 April 1981): A15.

"Octavia E. Butler at African American Museum Tonight," *Los Angeles Sentinel* (24 March 1999): A9.

Okorafor-Mbachu, Nnedi. "Octavia's Healing Power" in *Afro-Future Females.* Columbus: Ohio State University Press, 2008, 241–243.

Olusegun, Elijah Adeoluwa. "Breaking Mythical Barriers Through a Feminist Engagement with Magical Realism" in *African Women Writing Diaspora.* Lanham, MD: Lexington Books, 2021, 103–137.

O'Neill, Caitlin. "Towards an Afrofuturist Feminist Manifesto" in *Critical Black Futures.* Singapore: Palgrave Macmillan, 2021, 61–92.

Palwick, Susan. "Interview," *ISLE* 6:2 (Summer, 1999): 149–158.

Park, Ed. "Parable of the Butler," *Harper's Magazine* 342:2049 (February, 2021): 93–97.

Peck, Claudia. "Interview," *Skewed* (n.d.): 18–27.

Phillips, Julie. "L.A.'s Burning," *Village Voice* (15 February 1994): 91.

Pickens, Theri. "'You're Supposed to Be a Tall, Handsome, Fully Grown White Man': Theorizing Race, Gender, and Disability in Octavia Butler's *Fledgling*," *Journal of Literary & Cultural Disability Studies* 8:1 (2014): 33–48, 126.

Pirani, Fiza. "Who Is Octavia Butler?," *Atlanta Journal-Constitution* (22 June 2018).

Piziks, Steven. "Interview," *Marion Zimmer Bradley's Fantasy Magazine* 37 (Fall, 1997).

"The Pop Culture That Got Us Through 2020," *Minneapolis World* (radio) (29 December 2020).

Porter, Yvette. "Interview," *Essence* 35:6 (October, 2005): 96.

Potts, Stephen W. "We Keep Playing the Same Record," *Science Fiction Studies* 23:3 (1996): 331–338.

Pough, Gwendolyn D., and Yolanda Hood. "Speculative Black Women: Magic, Fantasy, and the Supernatural," *Femspec* 6:1 (June, 2005): ix.

Prakash, M., and K. Lavanya. "Transformation of the Human Race in Octavia E. Butler's *Clay's Ark*," *European Journal of Molecular & Clinical Medicine* 7:11 (2020): 1729–1731.

Radel, Felecia Wellington. "Timely 'Parable' Gets a Bit Graphic," *USA Today* (9 February 2020): C2.

Ransom, Amy. "Octavia's Legacy," *Extrapolation* 57:1/2 (2016): 235–239.

"Review: *Clay's Ark*," *Kirkus Review* (15 February 1984).

Reynolds, Susan Salter. "An Appreciation," *Los Angeles Times* (3 March 2006): E1.

Robinson, Dena. "Imagining a More Just Supreme Court," *Ms.* (9 October 2018).

Rowell, Charles H. "Interview," *Callaloo* 20:1 (Spring, 1997): 47–66.

Royal, Derek Parker. "Introduction: Coloring America: Multi-Ethnic Engagements with Graphic Narrative," *MELUS* 23:3 (2007): 7–22.

Salvaggio, Ruth. "Octavia Butler and the Black Science-Fiction Heroine," *Black American Literature Forum* 18:2 (Summer, 1984): 78–81.

Sanders, Joshunda. "Interview," *Motion Magazine* (14 March 2004).

Sargent, Lyman Tower. "African Americans and Utopia: Visions of a Better Life," *Utopian Studies* 31:1 (2020): 25–96.

Schalk, Sami. "Experience, Research, and Writing" in *Palimpsests in Ethnic and Postcolonial Literature and Culture*. Cham, Switzerland: Palgrave Macmillan, 2021, 153–177.

Schweitzer, Darrell. "Interview" in *Speaking of the Fantastic II*. Rockville, MD: Wildside, 2004, 21–36.

———. "Watching the Story Happen," *Interzone* 186 (February, 2003): 21.

"Sci-Fi Author Saw Endless Possibilities," (Don Mills, Ont.) *National Post* (4 March 2006): WP10.

"Science Fiction Writer Octavia E. Butler to Be Honored at Leimert Park Village Book Fair," *Los Angeles Sentinel* (15 May 2008): A8.

See, Lisa. "Interview," *Publishers Weekly* 240 (13 December 1993): 50–51.

Shawl, Nisi. "Daughter of Necessity," *Poets and Writers* (March/April, 1997); *Callaloo* 20:1 (Winter, 1997).

Smith, Alex. "Novelist 'Did a Great Job' Seeing Our Future," *Minneapolis Star Tribune* (25 April 2019): E1, E3.

Smith, Shirlee. "Octavia Butler: Writing Is Finding Out That You Can," *Pasadena Star-News* (13 February 1994): A14.

Smythe, S.A. "Black Life, Trans Study: On Black Nonbinary Method, European Trans Studies, and the Will to Institutionalization," *Transgender Studies Quarterly* 8:2 (2021): 158–171.

Sonune, Pravin. "Feminism, Women, and Science Fiction of Octavia Butler," *Epitome Journals* 7:4 (April, 2021): 54–67.

Spector, Nicole Audrey. "John Jennings and Damian Duffy Are Disturbing the Peace," *Publishers Weekly* 266:44 (4 November 2019): 33–34.

Stamberg, Susan. "Interview," *National Public Radio Weekend Edition* (29 December 2001).

Steinem, Gloria. "Octavia Butler's *Parable of the Sower*" in *Parable of the Sower & Parable of the Talents Boxed Set*. New York: Seven Stories Press, 2019.

Stewart, Jocelyn Y. "Obituary," *Los Angeles Times* (28 February 2006): B10.

Taylor-Guthrie, Danille. "Writing Because She Must," *Chicago Tribune* (31 March 1996): 5.

Thomas, Rochell D. "Tracing Octavia Butler's Footsteps," *Los Angeles Review of Books* (2 December 2016).

Timberg, Scott. "A Timely, Timeless Appeal," *Los Angeles Times* (18 April 2010): E8.

Tribble, Jon. "Review: *Parable of the Talents*," *Chicago Tribune* (27 December 1998): 14–4.

Troy, Maria Holmgren. "Negotiating Genre and Captivity: Octavia Butler's *Survivor*," *Callaloo* 33:4 (Fall, 2010): 1116–1131.

Tucker, Jeffrey. "'The Human Contradiction': Identity and/as Essence in Octavia E. Butler's 'Xenogenesis' Trilogy," *Yearbook of English Studies* 27:2 (2007): 164–181.

Turner, Jenny. "Ready to Go Off," *London Review of Books* 43:4 (18 February 2021).

"University of California Riverside: Afrofuturist Comics and Writing 'in a Time of Great Calamity.'" Washington, D.C.: Targeted News (20 June 2020).

Vado, Karina. "On Genomics and Identity," *Extrapolation* 60:2 (2019): 210–215.

Wanzo, Rebecca. "The Unspeakable Speculative, Spoken," *American Literary History* 31:3 (Fall, 2019): 564–574.

Warga, Wayne. "Corn Chips Yield Grist for Her Mill," *Los Angeles Times* (30 January 1981): 5–15.

Warner, John. "Worried about Climate Change? 2 Octavia Butler Books Written in the 1990s Seem Prescient Today," *Chicago Tribune* (21 October 2018): 10.

Weeks, Linton, and John Schwartz. "The Past Is Back as the Future Is Present," *Vancouver Sun* (23 May 2000): A9.

Weixlmann, Joe. "An Octavia E. Butler Bibliography," *Black American Literature Forum* 18:2 (Spring, 1984): 88–89.

Wellington, Elizabeth. "A Mix of History, Magic," *Philadelphia Inquirer* (26 February 2020): C1-C2.

West, Amy. "Our Guests of Honor," *Readercon 14* (12–13 July 2002): 1–8.

Weston, Kevin. "Interview," (San Francisco) *Chronicle* (13 February, 2004).

Whatcott, Jess. "Crip Collectivity Beyond Neoliberalism in Octavia Butler's *Parable of the Sower*," *Lateral* 10:1 (Spring, 2021).

White, Ted. "Love with the Proper Stranger," *Washington Post* (25 June 1989): 8.

Whiteside, Briana. "Blogging about Octavia Butler," *CLA Journal* 59:3 (March, 2016): 242–250.

Williams, Sherley Anne. "On Octavia E. Butler," *Ms.* 14:9 (March, 1986): 70–73.

Yancy, George. "Black Woman Pioneers Science Fiction Writing," *Philadelphia Tribune* (16 January 1996): E13.

Yazell, Bryan. "A Sociology of Failure: Migration and Narrative Method in U.S. Climate Fiction," *Configurations* 28:2 (Spring, 2020).

Yerman, Forrest Gray. "Finding the Superhero in Damian Duffy's and John Jennings Graphic Novel Adaptation of Octavia Butler's *Kindred*," *Bloomsbury Handbook to Octavia E. Butler*. London: Bloomsbury, 2020, 259–273.

Young, Earni. "Return of Kindred Spirits," *Black Issues Book Review* 6:1 (January-February 2004): 30–33.

Zaki, Hoda M. "Utopia, Dystopia, and Ideology in the Science Fiction of Octavia Butler," *Science Fiction Studies* 17 (1990): 239–251.

Zimmer, Marion. "Interview," *Marion Zimmer Bradley's Fantasy Magazine* (July, 2005).

Electronic

Agranoff, David. "Interview," https://podcasts.apple.com/gb/podcast/pfdw-20-octavia-butlers-parable-sower-interview-damian/id1524359471?i=1000495542300.

Aldama, Frederick Luis. "Anatomy of a Panel: John Jennings, Damian Duffy, and *Parable of the Sower*," http://www.comicosity.com/anatomy-of-a-panel-john-jennings-damian-duffy-and-parable-of-the-sower/.

Baska, Ariel. "Review," *Comics Bookcase,* www.comicsbookcase.com/reviews-archive/kindred-graphic-novel-adaptation (10 November 2020).

Bochert, Andrea. "A Talk with Comic Creator Damian Duffy," https://www.lapl.org/collections-resources/blogs/lapl/talk-comic-creator-damian-duffy (15 June 2021).

Campbell, James. "Variable Otherness in Octavia Butler's Xenogenesis," www.diva-portal.org/smash/get/diva2:1436640/FULLTEXT01.pdf (Spring, 2020).

Carby, Hazal. "Knowing Yourself, Historically" www.invisibleculturejournal.com/pub/knowing-yourself-historically/release/1 (15 November 2020).

Dee, Nat. "Octavia E. Butler and Inclusivity in Science Fiction," acriticofeverything.wordpress.com/2020/08/11/octavia-e-butler-and-inclusivity-in-science-fiction/ (11 August 2020).

Devney, Bob. "Orbita Dicta" in *The Devniad Book 82,* www.devniad.com (July, 2002).

Fowler, Karen Joy. "Remembering Octavia Butler," *Salon,* www.salon.com/2006/03/17/butler_3/ (17 March 2006).

Gilson, Kimberly. "Coercion in Octavia E. Butler's Xenogenesis," https://dalspace.library.dal.ca/handle/10222/77973 (March, 2020).

Ha, Vi. "On Persistence: Octavia E. Butler & Central Library," www.lapl.org/collections-resources/blogs/lapl/persistence-octavia-e-butler-central-library (11 June 2019).

Hall, John. "Parable of the Sower: A Positive Afrofuturist Obsession," https://sites.middlebury.edu/bltnmag/2021/05/28/4749/ (28 May 2021).

Hammie, Jessica. "Learn or Die," https://www.smilepolitely.com/arts/learn_or_die_a_review_of_parable_of_the_sower/ (23 April 2020).

Harper, Steven. "Interview," curiousfictions.com/stories/2159-steven-harper-an-interview-with-octavia-e-butler (27 May 2019).

Lackey, Tyler. "Afrofuturism and Spirituality," https://ssrn.com/abstract-3906952 (12 August 2021).

Mendoza, Barnabe Sebastian. "Mythic Fertility, Impurity, and Creolization in the Works of Octavia E. Butler," (doctoral thesis), https://rucore.libraries.rutgers.edu/ers-lib/64065/, 2020.

Moore, Carl R. "Review: *Clay's Ark*" in *Deep Dark Night,* https://carlrmoore.com/2020/09/21/573/.

"Octavia Butler," *Voices from the Gap,* http://voices.cal.umn.edu/ (23 April 2003).

"Octavia Butler Genealogy," www.wikitree.com/wiki/Guy-1059.

Pomeranz, John. "Interview," www.youtube.com/watch?v=KG68v0RGHsY (April, 2000).

"Review: *Dawn*," *Fantasy Book Reviews,* www.fantasybookreview.co.uk/Octavia-Butler/Dawn.html.

Rose, Charlie. "Interview" //charlierose.com/videos/28978 (1 June 2000).

Sanders, Joshunda. "Interview," https://joshunda.medium.com/an-interview-with-octavia-butler-2004-8933300df98a (2004).

Timmons, Greg. "How Slavery Became the Economic Engine of the South," www.history.com/news/slavery-profitable-southern-economy (2 September 2020).

Whiteside, Brianna. "Review: *Clay's Ark*," *Cultural Front,* www.culturalfront.org/2013/03/octavia-butlers-clays-ark.html.

Index